D1478160

Last Works

ALSO BY MARK C. TAYLOR

Last Works

Lessons in Leaving

Mark C. Taylor

Yale

UNIVERSITY PRESS

New Haven & London

Yale University Press books may be purchased in quantity for educational, business,
or promotional use. For information, please e-mail sales.press@yale.edu (U.S. office)
or sales@yaleup.co.uk (U.K. office).

Set in Bulmer type by Westchester Publishing Services.
Printed in the United States of America.

Library of Congress Control Number: 2017940587

ISBN 978-0-300-22439-9 (hardcover : alk. paper)

A catalogue record for this book is available from the British Library.

This paper meets the requirements of ANSI/NISO Z39.48-1992 (Permanence of Paper).

10   9   8   7   6   5   4   3   2   1

For
Jackson Noel
Taylor Virginia
Selma Linnea
Elsa Ingrid

The great thing is to last and get your work done and see and hear and learn and understand; and write when there is something that you know; and not before; and not too damned much after. Let those who want to save the world if you can get to see it clear as a whole. Then any part you make will represent the whole if it is made truly.

—Ernest Hemingway, *Death in the Afternoon*

Contents

Acknowledgments

AS THE YEARS PASS AND THE BOOKS accumulate, the debts grow. Words are never merely one's own, but are also borrowed from others known and unknown, named and unnamed. Books are messages sent in bottles that sometimes land on distant shores and return to surprise the author. Every writer needs thoughtful readers who are honest enough to tell him what to keep and what to cut. For this and much else, I am indebted to Jack Miles, John Chandler, George Rupp, Gil Anidjar, Jeffrey Kosky, Thomas Carlson, Sophie Cabot Black, Debra Winter, Paul Lieberman, Michael LeWitt, and Esa Saarinen. I would also like to express my appreciation to Don Fehr, for his commitment to ideas more than sales; Jennifer Banks, the rare editor who is truly a gifted writer; Andrew Stark, for his thoughtful comments; and Margaret Weyers, for keeping track of what I am constantly losing. Though I have been teaching for half a century, the classroom remains as mysterious as the day I started. I usually know after the first day whether a class will work or not work. When it "clicks," it is magical and both teacher and students know something special is happening. In the spring of 2015, my seminar "Last Works" at Columbia University was such a magical trip, and I remain eternally grateful to everyone who made it happen. Had that been my last class, and perhaps it should have been, I would have ended satisfied. Nothing I have written over the years would have been possible without the gift of patient support from my family: Dinny, Aaron, Kirsten, Frida, Jonathan, and Beryl. Such a debt can never be repaid. Finally, endings can sometimes also be beginnings—if not for oneself, then for others. *Last Works* is, among other things, a letter to my grandchildren—Jackson Noel, Taylor Virginia, Selma Linnea, and Elsa Ingrid. My hope is that some of what I have learned along the way might be helpful to them as they attempt to negotiate the perilous future we are leaving them.

Summer Solstice, 2016
Stone Hill

Errant Reflections

I DO NOT KNOW IF THIS WILL BE my last book. You never know when, where, or how the end arrives. Every work might be the last work, every class the last class, every game the last game, every day the last day. Even when anticipated, the end arrives unexpectedly—like a thief in the night. Having once "died without dying," I thought I had taught my last class and written my last book. But I was granted a reprieve, a temporary reprieve that grows shorter every day. Such an experience, if it was an experience, shifts the axis of the world even if ever so slightly. Things no longer line up as they once did; shadows are darker, and light is brighter. Your sense of time changes profoundly because you begin to realize that you never have time because time always has you. Time is not ours to take, give, spend, save, share, or waste; rather, it is a gift that is not at your disposal, and the gift of time is inseparable from "the gift of death."

Ending and leaving are not the same. It is possible to end without leaving, and to leave without ending. Leaving, like ending, is a matter of time, or, more precisely, of timing. When to leave? How to leave? Some leavings are chosen, others are not; some leavings bring relief, even joy, others bring pain, even suffering. To ask what it means to leave is also to ask what it means to stay—to stay too long, or not long enough. There is a right time and a wrong time to leave. Though his end was traumatic, Ernest Hemingway offered sage advice about leaving. "The great thing is to last and get your work done and see and hear and learn and understand; and write when there is something that you know; and not before; and not too damned much after."[1] In matters of life and death, timing is everything.

1

Far too many people today have forgotten how to leave, and so stay on, and on, and on until they become a burden to others. Though leaving can occur at any time, it is most consequential near the end—the end of a relationship, a career, a life. There are many reasons people linger—some are financial, some are social, most are psychological. In my experience, people refuse to leave because they fear what might or might not come next. To retire is to withdraw from the life one has lived so that one has time to explore lives that might have been or might yet be. But today, retirement and the leisure it is supposed to bring have become quaint memories of a slower world where life was less frenzied. Puritanism runs deep in the American grain even for those who deny it. When worth and identity are bound to job or career, to retire is to become nobody. All too often people cling to work not because they enjoy what they are doing but because they fear doing nothing. Perhaps, however, there is no better way to end than by pondering nothing.

We live during an age when many people are convinced that technology can solve every problem—even human mortality. When the will to power becomes the will to mastery, death becomes little more than an engineering problem. "Live long enough to live forever" becomes the motto for the generation that dwells in the cloud.[2] As for the ancient Gnostics, the body appears to be nothing but meat whose weight is a burden to be shed. When the code is cracked and escape velocity reached, you can go on forever. Such techno-fantasies are both disingenuous and dangerous for both humanity and the planet. To be human is to know and accept that everything and everyone ends. "Human," after all, derives from the "humus"—the organic material decomposing and composing the ground, soil, earth from which everything comes and to which everyone returns. *Last Works: Lessons in Leaving* is an effort to bring thought back down to earth by exploring the final limit that constitutes our being and nonbeing. The art of living is learning to leave gracefully.

In search of lessons in leaving, I have concentrated on the last works authors wrote. Some knew they were writing their last work, others did not. It is not always easy to decide which work is the last. Some writers left unfinished manuscripts for others to complete, others composed texts so unlike their previous work that they seem to have been written by a different author. It is, of course, as impossible to understand any last work apart from both earlier works and the life of the author as it is to understand the earlier works and the life of the author apart from his or her last work. Did they write too little or too much? Did the end come too soon or too late? If they stopped writing, why did they end? If they could not stop writing, what prevented them from ending?

As I approach the end, or, rather, the end approaches me, I pause to return to the ghosts with whom I have lived, and who have lived on through me for half a century. My selection has been guided by writers who have guided me as I have wrestled with the questions of life and death. Though I have known these writers well most of my life, at this late date I have been surprised by how much I did not know or had forgotten about their works and especially their lives. So many died so young yet accomplished so much, and so many of their lives were so frightfully difficult. Hegel once wrote that the happy eras are the blank pages of history. The works of the writers considered in the following pages suggest that contented lives remain unwritten and troubled lives cultivate great literature.

I have tried to create a dialogue among my ghosts even when they knew nothing about one another. Are there common threads about ending and leaving that run through their writings? How do they face or avoid ending and leaving? Have they shared similar experiences, or is each life so different from others that no one has anything in common? I write not as a historian or literary critic but as one who is what once was called a philosopher, who believes that the works of writers who matter harbor enduring lessons in leaving that teach us how to live for the brief time that remains.

Completion

Søren Kierkegaard (1813–1855): *The Moment*

The unwise are accustomed to speak as if some were not sick; but methinks the
difference between men in respect to health is not great enough to lay much
stress upon. Some are reputed sick and some are not. It often happens that the
sicker man is the nurse to the sounder.

—Henry David Thoreau, *A Week on the Concord and Merrimack Rivers*

Memento Mori

As I look back over more than four decades of reading, teaching, and writing, it is beginning to become clear that this book began, like so much else,
with Søren Kierkegaard. In August 1984, I had been invited to give a talk
at a Hegel conference in Helsinki. I decided to take our son, Aaron, who
was eleven at the time, with me to visit friends in Denmark. We had lived
in Copenhagen five years earlier, where Aaron had attended kindergarten
and had become fluent in Danish. I thought a few days back in Denmark
might refresh his Danish. The friends with whom he stayed spoke to him
in Danish and their kids took him to school with them. As always, Aaron
rose to the challenge and remembered more Danish than I expected he
would.

The last thing we did before leaving Denmark was to go to the Assistents Cemetery to pay homage to Kierkegaard. Having long imagined
doing grave rubbings of writers I fondly called my ghosts, I brought with
me a piece of pellon (a thin, translucent material) and a large black crayon.

4

Søren Kierkegaard's grave

With Aaron standing guard and freaking out whenever a police siren sounded, I climbed over the fence surrounding the family plot, taped the pellon to the gravestone, and began rubbing.

After listing the names and dates of the deceased, the inscription on the gravestone reads:

> In a little while,
> I shall have won,
> The entire battle
> Will at once be done.

Then I may rest
In halls of roses
And unceasingly,
And increasingly
Speak with my Jesus.

The words are not Kierkegaard's but are from a hymn, "Halleluja, jeg har min Jesum funden," composed by Hans Adolph Brorson. On May 14, 1847, Kierkegaard wrote in his journal, "I wish that on my grave might be put 'The Individual,'" but his fate was what his late follower Jacques Derrida had feared—his last wish was not honored by those who survived him.[1] Before leaving the cemetery, for reasons I would not understand for a long time, I collected some dirt from Kierkegaard's grave, and smuggled it into the United States.

A few years later, I received a package from a former student who was studying in Germany. When I opened it, I found a rubbing of Hegel's gravestone. Two graves, two writers, either/or, both/and. Kierkegaard and Hegel: the two poles between which both my intellectual life and my soul are suspended. Alfred North Whitehead famously declared that all people are born either a Platonist or Aristotelian; I believe all people are born either a Hegelian or a Kierkegaardian. Their writings present not merely competing philosophical positions, but alternative ways of being-in-the-world. The challenge of life, I believe, is to find a way to live betwixt and between these two. These rubbings were the first in a collection that now includes more of my ghosts: Karl Marx, Edgar Allan Poe, Herman Melville, Emily Dickinson, Jean-Paul Sartre, and Wallace Stevens. They hang in the living rooms of my Williamstown home and New York City apartment. When I eventually visited Dorotheenstadt Cemetery in Berlin in 1990, I pulled out a clump of the ivy covering Hegel's grave, and once again smuggled it to the States.

It is still growing in my home, and, on occasion, I give a friend or special student a clipping to plant. These cemetery trips were followed by others, and led to a book—*Grave Matters* (co-authored with my former student Christian Lammerts, 2002), and an exhibition at the Massachusetts

G. W. F. Hegel's grave

Museum of Contemporary Art (2002). At each grave we visited, we collected dirt and put it in film canisters. For the Mass MOCA exhibition, I
created a sculpture with this dirt that hangs in the barn where I work.

When I visited Melville's grave in Woodlawn Cemetery in the Bronx,
I found the ivy I wished covered Kierkegaard's grave. I cut a piece of the
ivy, grew roots, planted it, and started a new ivy chain. There is a certain
symbolic logic to this madness. Since I found no ivy on Kierkegaard's grave,
Melville had to serve as a substitute. When modern European philosophy
crossed the Atlantic, Hegelianism was translated into the Transcendentalism of Emerson and Thoreau, and Kierkegaardism became the dark Romanticism of Poe, Hawthorne, and Melville. In my endless effort to mediate
Hegel and Kierkegaard, I grafted the Melville ivy onto the Hegel ivy, and
the hybrid is thriving in a ceramic pot on the desk where I am writing.

The structure of *Last Works* repeats the course I have been following since I first read Kierkegaard and Hegel in college in 1967–68. My first
book, *Kierkegaard's Pseudonymous Authorship: A Study of Time and the Self*
(1975), was followed by *Journeys to Selfhood: Hegel and Kierkegaard* (1980),

which began with Kierkegaard and ended with Hegel. Several years later in *Altarity* (1987), I rewrote this book by reversing the order, beginning with Hegel and ending with Kierkegaard, and in between suspended a series of writers influenced by their works, who, in turn, have influenced me. One of the questions that remains after all these years is who will have the last word. *Last Works* begins with Kierkegaard and ends with Thoreau, who stands in for Hegel, who is conspicuously missing. Thoreau brings philosophical abstractions down to earth, where it becomes possible to find the infinite in the finite, and in this way enables one to go on even when hope is faint. Finally, a less obvious, though no less important reason that Thoreau gets the last word—the love of his work is where my mother, a literature teacher, and my father, a science teacher, met, and, thus, where my life truly began.

Secrets

He was young when he died. So young, like many others whose work changed more than philosophy, theology, art, and literature. Kierkegaard, 42; Schiller, 45; Novalis, 28; Thoreau, 44; Poe, 39; Kafka, 40; Shelley, 29; Keats, 25; Byron, 36; Mozart, 35; Schubert, 31; van Gogh, 37; Camus, 46; Plath, 30; Wallace, 46. So young, so creative, so productive, and so much left unfinished. It is as if lives intensify when they are compressed. Would they have continued to burn brightly had they lived longer, or would their flame have faded and left them and us in darkness and silence, like Nietzsche staring blankly into the void, Poe lying on a Baltimore street in a drunken stupor, or Melville laboring anonymously in a New York customs house? What guidance can the works of writers who die so young offer to those who live long enough to struggle with the infirmity and fragility of old age?

Kierkegaard's work was compressed even more than his life. Everything he published was written in fourteen short years, between 1841 and 1855. In addition to the astute philosophical works for which he is best known, he also wrote edifying and religious discourses, countless articles in the popular press, and a weighty twenty-volume journal, which he was confident would be published after his death. All of this with no secretary, no staff, no interlibrary loan, no typewriter, no computer, no Google. Just the solitary Søren standing alone at his desk, with pen and paper, scribbling in handwriting that often is illegible. It helped, of course, that he had no family, and never had to hold down a job because he was able to live on the modest inheritance his father left him. The range and volume of his work are remarkable. Only a person possessed could do so much in such a little time. But what possessed Kierkegaard? Did he know? Is it possible for us to know?

Kierkegaard harbored secrets he never betrayed to others and, perhaps, even to himself. Deliberately teasing future readers, he wrote in his journal, "After my death no one will find in my papers the slightest information (this my consolation) about what really has filled my life; no one will find the inscription in my innermost being that interprets everything and that often turns into events of prodigious importance to me that which the world would call bagatelles and which I regard as insignificant if I remove the secret note that interprets them."[2] As the years passed and the pages of the journal continued to grow, it became clear that Kierkegaard was not sure how to interpret his own life. Like the navel of Freud's dreams, the "secret note" that holds the key to decoding the story of his life turns out to be the point of contact with the unknowable. This inaccessible interiority limns all speech with silence, and renders all discourse indirect. Recalling the crown of the crucified Christ, he refers to these secrets cryptically as "the thorn in the flesh." Even when published in his own name, his writings are pseudonymous. Intentionally and unintentionally, he leaves hints—hints about the guilt of the father and absence of the mother, which haunt all his works.

Michael Pederson Kierkegaard was a man whose life was repeatedly interrupted by death—the death of two wives and the deaths of five of his seven children. The demands of his highly successful textile business prevented him from marrying until he was in his late thirties. In 1794, Michael married Kirstine Røyen, the sister of his business partner, Mads Røyen. Two years later she died, leaving Michael childless. On April 27, 1797, before the year of mourning had expired, Michael married Ane Sørensdatter Lund, who had been Kirstine's maid, and less than five months after the marriage, the couple's first child, Maren Kirstine, was born. To say that

Michael was ambivalent about the marriage would be an understatement. His marriage contract included the following clause: "should the unexpected happen, that the temperaments cannot be united, it must be permitted us to live separate from table and bed, in which case my future wife will take her body linens and clothes, in addition to which I will give her once and for all 300 *rigsdaler* yearly as long as she lives."[3] In spite of such uncertainty, the marriage survived. In the years that followed, Ane bore six more children, the youngest of whom, Søren Aabye, was born on May 5, 1813, when Ane was forty-five and Michael was fifty-six. Having buried three of her seven children, Ane died on July 31, 1834.

Michael's relation to Søren was no less ambivalent than his relation to Ane. On February 2, 1797, less than three months after his fortieth birthday, Michael signed over his flourishing business to M. A. Kierkegaard and Christian Agerskov, and completely withdrew from the world of business and commerce to devote himself to theological reading and religious reflection. The date is critically important. Michael and Ane, I have noted, married on April 27, 1797, and Maren Kirstine was born in September 1797. Maren must have been conceived in December 1796. It is probable that Michael learned of the likelihood of Ane's pregnancy late in January 1797. Within a matter of weeks or even days he gave up his business and turned away from public life.

The theology that preoccupied Michael reflected the Protestant pietism that was then sweeping Denmark. One of the chief tenets of this religious outlook is the thoroughgoing sinfulness of human nature, which is inextricably bound up with sensuality in general and sexuality in particular. Michael became obsessed with his guilt and need for redemption. As the years passed, he came to see in his youngest son the possibility for the salvation he so ardently desired for himself. Though he never put it in these terms, Søren was Michael's Isaac—the son sacrificed in the name of the Father. Toward that end, Michael subjected Søren to an extraordinarily rigorous religious upbringing, which left an indelible impression on his son. Looking back on his youth, Søren remarks, "It's terrible when I think, even for a single moment, over the dark background that from the earliest time was part of my life. The dread with which my father filled my soul, his own awful melancholy, the many things in this respect I can't write down."[4] Secrets, always secrets within secrets. What can't Kierkegaard write about his father?

Though always passionately devoted to Michael, Søren became increasingly anxious about the inheritance of guilt his father had left him. This anxiety eventually led to a conflict between father and son. In 1838, several months before the death of the father (August 8, 1838), Søren records in his journal what he describes as "the great earthquake":

> Then it was that the great earthquake occurred, the frightful upheaval that suddenly drove me to a new and infallible principle for interpreting all the phenomena. Then I surmised that my father's old-age was not a divine blessing, but rather a curse, that our family's exceptional intellectual capacities were only for mutually harrowing one another; then I felt the stillness of death deepen around me, when I saw in my father an unhappy man who would survive us all, a memorial cross on the grave of all his personal hopes. A guilt must rest on the entire family, a punishment of God must be upon it: it was supposed to disappear, obliterated by the mighty hand of God, erased like a mistake, and only at times did I find a little relief in the thought that my father had been given the heavy duty of reassuring us all with the consolation of religion, telling us that a better world stands open for us even if we lost this one, even if the punishment the Jews always called down on their enemies should strike us: that remembrance of us would be completely obliterated, that there would be no trace of us.[5]

Kierkegaard never explained what precipitated this "earthquake." This strange event seems to be "the secret note" he claimed to have removed from all his writings.

Or *almost* removed. Seven years after the earthquake, Kierkegaard offered a possible clue in the most "autobiographical" of his pseudonymous writings, " 'Guilty?'/'Not Guilty?': A Passion Narrative, A Psychological

Experiment by *Frater Taciturnus,*" published on April 30, 1845, as the third part of *Stages on Life's Way.* This diary, purportedly written by a certain Quidam, recounts the painful process by which a young man breaks his engagement because of what he believes to be his religious obligation. The story is repeatedly interrupted by entries dated midnight on the fifth of every month that have nothing to do with the events Quidam records.[6] Though not immediately apparent, these entries are allegorical accounts of Kierkegaard's personal life. In the present context, the most important allegory is entitled "Solomon's Dream." In this *aparté,* Quidam or Frater Taciturnus, whose name, like that of Johannes de Silentio, suggests that his words harbor silence, or Kierkegaard, or an Other (it remains unclear who the author is). The tale of Solomon, Nathan, and David tells the story of Kierkegaard's father:

> Thus Solomon lived happily with the prophet Nathan. The father's strength and the father's achievement did not inspire him to deeds of valor, for in fact no occasion was left for that, but it inspired him to admiration, and admiration made him a poet. But if the poet was almost jealous of his hero, the son was blissful in his devotion to the father.
>
> Then one day the son visited his royal father. In the night he awoke at hearing movement where the father slept. Terror seizes him, he fears it is a villain who would murder David. He steals nearer—he beholds David with a crushed and contrite heart, he hears a scream of despair from the repentant soul.

Faint, powerless, impotent at the sight, he returns to his couch, he falls asleep, but he does not rest, he dreams that David is an ungodly man, rejected by God, that the royal majesty is the sign of God's wrath upon him, that he must wear the purple as a punishment, that he is condemned to rule, condemned to hear the people's benediction, whereas the Lord's righteousness secretly and hiddenly pronounces judgment upon the guilty one; and the dream suggests the suspicion that God is the God not of the pious but of the ungodly, and that one must be an ungodly man to be God's elect—and the terror of the dream is this contra-diction.[7] The secret of the father fragments, divides, splits the son; with self set against self, Kierkegaard became what Hegel had described as "unhappy consciousness."

Michael is David, Ane is Bathsheba, Søren is Solomon. The story of Solomon is the story of the violation of the mother by the father. Because the son (Søren) identifies with the father (Michael), the son bears the guilt of the father's sin. The guilt of the father visited upon the son is complex, for Michael's sin involves multiple violations. On the most obvious level, Michael violates Ane by seducing her out of wedlock; his bastard child, Maren Kirstine, testifies to this violation. It is also clear that this deed is a breach of religious duty and ethical obligation. There are, however, less obvious dimensions of Michael's guilt. Ane, I have noted, had been the maid in the household of Michael and his first wife. His violation of Ane is, there-fore, at the same time a violation of Kirstine, whom he always considered to be his real wife.

It seems that Michael and Ane had no maid. Michael apparently thought there was no need for a maid because Ane was already his domes-tic. What role did Ane play in the economy of the Kierkegaard household? What secrets did she harbor? Since none of her children left any direct testi-mony, it is impossible to be sure, but suspicions are unavoidable. As Hegel famously observed, "no man is a hero to his valet"—or to his maid. Since Ane was both mother and maid, it seems unlikely she was as domesticated as Michael presumed. Never completely at home in the house of the father, Ane always remained *uhyggelig, unheimlich*—uncanny. Provoking both fascination and dread, the uncanny is, in Kierkegaard's words, "a *sympa-thetic antipathy* and *an antipathetic sympathy*."[8] Is the secret of secrets that Kierkegaard cannot stop writing about the guilt of the father or the absence of the mother?

Kierkegaard could never bring himself to write his mother's name. Ane Sørensdatter Lund's name does not appear anywhere in either his published writings or journal—not once! Though she remains unnamed, there is, however, a fragment about the mother in his journal dated 1836: "Children who remember their mother."[9] Was Søren such a son? Does he write about her by not writing about her? Do his texts express love for an Other, who is missing or lacking? Is "mother" the name of the unnameable his works guard? When used as a common noun rather than a proper name, *kirkegaard* means cemetery (*kirke,* church + *gaard,* yard, which is where cemeteries are located in Danish churches). Within the complex topography of Kierkegaard's anthropology, secrets become crypts that bar opening. The sign of the barred subject is, as Lacan suggested, $. Derrida's commentary of Karl Abraham and Maria Torok's *The Wolfman's Magic Word* exposes the void at the heart of the Kierkegaardian subject. "The self," Derrida argues, is "a cemetery guard. The crypt is enclosed within the self, but as a strange, foreign place, prohibited, excluded. The self is not the proprietor of what he guards. He makes the rounds like a proprietor, but only the rounds. He turns around and around, and in particular he uses all his knowledge of the grounds to turn visitors away. 'He stands there firmly, keeping an eye on the comings and goings of the nearest of kin who claim—under various titles—to have the right to approach the tomb. If he agrees to let in the curious, the injured parties, the detectives, it will only be to serve them with false traces and fake tombs.'"[10] An outside that is inside turns everything inside out, and outside in. Like Poe's Dupin, readers of Kierkegaard become detectives who try to crack the case by following traces designed to mislead.

Existential Pedagogy

Kierkegaard's complex psychological inheritance weighed heavily on him throughout his life. During his university years, he lacked direction and was uncertain what he should study. The two most likely career paths would prepare him to be a priest or a professor, but neither alternative was attractive. Representatives of the Danish state church were preaching a comfortable version of Christianity that Kierkegaard believed was the opposite of true Christian faith, and his professors were promoting a speculative version of Hegel's cultural Protestantism that provided the justification for the priests' false gospel. His confusion and uncertainty reached a crisis point in the summer of 1835.

Recognizing his son's deepening problems, the usually parsimonious Michael financed a two-month trip for Kierkegaard during June and July of 1835 to the small fishing village of Gilleleje in northern Zealand. Deeply troubled and professionally confused, Kierkegaard desperately needed to get away from Copenhagen to try to find a direction for his life. During the early weeks of his retreat, his journal records a leisurely pace of life with quiet walks in fields, through woods, and along the seashore. As the end of his stay draws near, the tone changes abruptly. On August 1, 1835, Kierkegaard wrote an entry entitled "To Find the Idea for Which I Am Willing to Live and Die." The experience he reported has all the marks of a classical religious conversion, or, what Erik Erikson, in a more contemporary idiom labeled an identity crisis. "What I really lack is to be clear in my mind *what I am to do,* not what I am to know, except in so far as a certain understanding must precede every action. The thing is to understand myself, to see what God really wishes *me* to do; the thing is to find a truth which is true *for me,* to find *the idea for which I can live and die.*"[11] While Kierkegaard's existential crisis was not resolved for several years, he returned from Gilleleje refreshed and was able to continue his studies. During this critical period, he fell under the spell of Georg Hamann, whose writings about the way religious faith answers questions philosophy raises played an important role in Kierkegaard's reassessment of Christianity. His intellectual dilemma was, as always, inseparable from his personal problems. Reconciliation with the heavenly Father could not occur until he resolved the conflict with his earthly father. On August 8, 1838, Michael Pedersen Kierkegaard died at the age of eighty-two. Three days later, Søren, who was twenty-five, wrote in his diary, "My father died on Wednesday, the 8th, at 2 o'clock in the morning. I had so deeply wished that he might live a couple of years longer, and I view his death as the final sacrifice his love made for me. Because he has not died *from* me, but died *for* me, in order that I might still amount to something, if that is possible."[12]

This is a particularly telling comment because Kierkegaard appropriates Luther's theological formulation to describe the death of his father. Turning from the objective machinations of Catholicism's church universal to the subjective experience of the individual believer, Luther insisted that Christ died "for us" (*pro nobis*). The death of the father frees the son to return to the faith he had doubted and to fulfill the religious obligation Michael had laid on him. Kierkegaard now had a mission that he came to describe as "the reintroduction of Christianity into Christendom."[13] The fulfillment of this mission, however, came at a high cost—he had to sacrifice his relation to the only woman he ever loved, Regina Olsen. Five years later, in *Fear and Trembling,* which was the best work Kierkegaard wrote, he indirectly explained the reasons for his decision not to marry Regina through the story of Abraham's sacrifice of Isaac. In this retelling of the biblical narrative, the son displaces the father. As Michael (Abraham) had sacrificed his son (Søren) to save himself, so Søren (Abraham) sacrifices Regina (Isaac) to save others.

The direction of Kierkegaard's religious mission grew out of his diagnosis of the illness he believed infected modern society. Beneath the façade of bourgeois complacency and respectability lurks a hidden melancholy he describes as the "hysteria of spirit," which can be cured only through "the essentiality of the religious in the single individual."[14] Christianity— true Christianity—is a "radical cure" that promises to lead individuals from inauthentic to authentic selfhood. The problem Kierkegaard faces is that "what the sick man most desires is just what feeds the disease."[15] He must, therefore, develop an educational strategy that will make it possible for individuals first to recognize their actual condition, and then to cure themselves by making responsible decisions.

Kierkegaard's existential pedagogy rests on a sophisticated understanding of modernity that anticipates many of the ills plaguing today's information and media culture. He was the first critic of what he regarded as the dehumanizing effects of mass media. His focus was the newspaper industry in nineteenth-century Europe. Ever the champion of the individual, Kierkegaard was convinced that modern mass media repressed individual thinking and acting by transforming people into unknowing vehicles for the opinions and interests of others he labeled "the crowd." In his brief 1845 book *The Present Age,* which was the first influential work in media criticism, he writes, "And eventually human speech will become just like the public: pure abstraction—there will no longer be someone who speaks, but an objective reflection will gradually deposit a kind of atmosphere, an abstract noise that will render human speech superfluous, just as machines make workers superfluous. In Germany there are even handbooks for lovers; so it probably will end with lovers being able to sit and speak anonymously to each other. There are handbooks on everything, and generally speaking education soon will consist of knowing letter-perfect a larger or smaller compendium of observations from such handbooks, and one will excel in proportion to his skill in pulling out the particular one, just as the typesetter picks out letters."[16] *Politics for Dummies, Love for Dummies, Art for Dummies, Ethics for Dummies, Faith for Dummies.* The correlative dangers of depersonalization and homogenization that Kierkegaard identified so early become even more evident with the spread of mass media throughout the twentieth century. The noise Kierkegaard hears reverberates everywhere today and eventually drove one of the most sensitive and insightful interpreters of contemporary media culture, David Foster Wallace, mad.

Kierkegaard was convinced that the abstraction endemic to modern media was reinforced by the speculative version of Christianity taught in university classrooms and preached from pulpits in the state church. By appropriating Hegel's dialectical mediation of opposites, Danish writers and theologians like Johan Ludvig Heiberg and Frederik Christian Sibbern erased the "infinite qualitative difference" between god and man by collapsing transcendence into immanence, dissolved the uniqueness of the singular individual in the anonymity of universal humanity, and, most perniciously, socialized religion by reconciling church and state. In nineteenth-century Denmark, everyone was a member of the Lutheran state church by birth. In contrast to the early days of Christianity, when people suffered and died for their faith, in modern Denmark, membership in the church is a prerequisite for worldly success. Priests were little more than civil functionaries paid to perform the ceremonies and keep records of birth, baptism, marriage, and death. Kierkegaard labeled this condition "Christendom" and argued that it was the betrayal, rather than the fulfillment, of the Christian message. Instead of reassuring people that Christianity required nothing more than being a good bourgeois citizen with a job and a family, Kierkegaard, following Luther, insisted that every individual must work out his or her salvation in "fear and trembling."

To help people overcome the illusion that everyone is a Christian and make them realize the eternal significance of every decision, Kierkegaard developed a pedagogical strategy that would meet individuals where they were and led them through what he described as the "stages on life's way." His model was Socrates, who pleaded ignorance in an effort to lead people to truth. "My task," Kierkegaard explains, "was to cast Christianity into reflection, not poetically to idealize it (for the essentially Christian, after all, is itself the ideal), but with poetic fervor to present the total ideality at its most ideal—always ending with: I am not that, but I strive."[17] Unlike the know-it-all speculative philosopher and self-satisfied priest, the Socratic educator neither offers results nor provides solutions. Question marks, not periods, punctuate his dialogue. His goal is to disturb, disrupt, dispel illusion—in short, he strives not to make life easier, but to make it more difficult, though no harder than it really is. Kierkegaard is persuaded that if "it is an illusion that all are Christians, and if there is anything to be done about it, it must be done indirectly, not by one who vociferously proclaims himself an extraordinary Christian, but by one who, better instructed, is ready to declare that he is not a Christian at all. That is, one must approach from behind the person who is under an illusion. Instead of wishing to have an advantage of being oneself that rare thing, a Christian, one must let the prospective captive enjoy the advantage of being the Christian, and for one's own part have resignation enough to be the one who is far behind—otherwise one will certainly not get the man out of his illusion, a thing that is difficult in any case."[18]

Kierkegaard's method of indirect communication is both writerly and performative. Between 1843 and 1849, he published a series of remarkable pseudonymous writings, in addition to numerous other works under his own name. The epigram to *Stages on Life's Way,* edited by Hilarius Bookbinder, could serve as a summary of his entire pseudonymous authorship: "Such works are mirrors, when an ape looks in, no apostle can look out."[19] Instead of identifying with and offering direct guidance to the reader, Kierkegaard maintains, the author must withdraw from the dialogic relationship and leave the reader alone with the imagined possibilities presented in the work. "When in reflection upon the communication the receiver is reflected upon, then we have ethical communication. The maieutic. The communicator disappears, as it were, makes himself serve only to help the other to become."[20] Retiring behind the curtain of his pseudonyms, Kierkegaard directs the reader away from the writer and toward his or her own existential dilemmas and possibilities.

During the years he was working most intensely on his pseudonymous writings, Kierkegaard carefully crafted a public persona designed to conceal his identity as their author. He always enjoyed walking on the streets of Copenhagen and carrying on conversations with people he met. Between 1843 and 1846, he deliberately struck the pose of a ne'er-do-well *flâneur* who was interested in nothing other than aesthetic pleasures. All the while, he was working late into the night in one of the most astonishing outbursts of creativity in the history of philosophy. Initially, Kierkegaard intended to end the pseudonymous authorship with *Concluding Unscientific Postscript.* In a postscript to the *Postscript,* dated February 1846, he admitted for the first time that he was the author of the pseudonymous writings. His "First and Last Declaration" makes his intentions clear. "For I am impersonal, or am personal in the second person, a *souffleur,* who has poetically produced the *authors,* whose preface in turn is their own production, as are even their own names. So in the pseudonymous works there is not a single word that is mine, I have no opinion about these works except as third person, no knowledge of their meaning except as a reader, not the remotest private relation to them, since such a thing is impossible in the case of a doubly reflected communication. One single word of mine uttered personally in my own name would be an instance of presumptuous self-forgetfulness, and dialectically viewed it would incur with one word the guilt of annihilating the pseudonyms."[21] He published two additional pseudonymous works, *The Sickness unto Death* (1849) and *Training* or *Practice in Christianity* (1850), both written by Anti-Climacus, who is the counterpart to Johannes Climacus, the author of *Philosophical Fragments* and *Concluding Unscientific Postscript. The Sickness unto Death* lays bare the structural interpretation of selfhood that underlies all of

Kierkegaard's work, and *Practice in Christianity,* which Kierkegaard later admitted should not have been pseudonymous, begins what will soon become his attack on Christendom.

The pseudonymous authorship presents an alternative existential dialectic to the one Hegel elaborated in *Phenomenology of Spirit.* While Hegel charts the development from isolated individuality to membership in an integrated socio-natural whole, Kierkegaard traces a gradual differentiation from the natural and social totality to solitary selfhood. He identifies three stages on life's way—the aesthetic, characterized by either sensuous desire or endless reflection; the ethical, in which people make decisions guided by purportedly universal moral standards; and the religious, in which singular individuals define themselves through radically free, self-conscious decisions. Only Christianity discloses the severe demands of authentic selfhood. In Kierkegaard's interpretation of human existence, everything can change in the blink of an eye—*Øjeblikket*—the instant or the moment.

Although Kierkegaard's understanding of the moment is a cornerstone of his entire philosophical position, he develops his most explicit and complete analysis of the nature of *Øjeblikket* in the "Interlude" in *Philosophical Fragments.* Between the discussion of "the contemporary disciple" of the God-Man and the latter-day believer, described as "the disciple at second hand," he addresses the question: "Is the past more necessary than the future? Or, when the possible becomes actual, is it thereby made more necessary than it was?"[22] These questions provide the occasion for a consideration of the dynamics of becoming. Kierkegaard begins by asserting that all genuine becoming entails a change that amounts to a transition from not existing to existing, or from possibility to actuality. He emphatically rejects any suggestion that the actualization of possibility is effected by means of a necessary transition. In contrast to Hegel, who, looking back, thinks he can discern the necessary unfolding of personal and historical development, Kierkegaard resolutely faces forward by confronting an open future toward which individuals move through their free decisions. The paradigmatic moment of decision, which reveals the eternal significance of every decision for existing individuals, is the response to the Christian Incarnation.

Since Kierkegaard regards God as radically transcendent and "infinitely and qualitatively different" from humankind, the claim that God freely became embodied in a particular person constitutes an "Absolute Paradox" that cannot be rationally comprehended. The Absolute Paradox forces an "absolute decision"—*either* believe *or* be offended. There is no middle ground, no mean between these extremes. Christianity demands decision, an "eternal decision in time," which "is the most intensive intensity, the most intensive leap."[23] The necessity for a decisive response is a function of the absurdity of the God-Man. The Incarnation confronts human reason with its limitations, establishes its boundaries, and irrevocably separates the rational from the actual. Faith and reason, religious belief and philosophical knowledge, are not implicitly one, as Hegel and his followers insisted, but are antithetical. The individual must believe "against reason," for the object of faith is an "offense" to reason, the "shipwreck" of reason, the "crucifixion" of understanding.

In a manner analogous to Kierkegaard's indirect existential maieutic, the God-Man poses an unavoidable choice: "When one says, 'I am God; the Father and I are one,' that is a direct communication. But when he who says it is an individual man, quite like other men, then this communication is not just perfectly direct; for it is not just perfectly clear and direct that an individual man should be God—although what he says is perfectly direct. By reason of the communicator, the communication contains a contradiction, it becomes indirect communication, it puts to you a choice, whether you will believe him or not."[24] The response to this either-or is decisive for an individual's eternal identity. Through the decisions that constitute personal history, the self defines itself, and assumes a concrete and unique identity by which he or she differentiates himself or herself from all other selves. Faith is a radical venture, an unmediated leap in which the self transforms itself. In the moment of decision, the individual, singled out from all others and standing before the wholly other God, is completely responsible for the self he or she freely becomes. This transformative resolution happens at a depth of inwardness that is incommensurable with outward expression.

The moments of Incarnation and faith are mirror images of each other. The eternal God becomes temporal in the moment of Incarnation, and the temporal individual becomes eternal in the moment of faith.

Authentic selfhood is a coincidence of opposites in which contraries are brought together in the passion of free resolution. All of life is a leap of faith in which individuals must make decisions without certain knowledge or secure ethical norms. In Kierkegaard's existential pedagogy, radically free individuals must choose the rules by which they choose. This is what Kierkegaard describes as "the madness of decision." The awareness of abyssal freedom and uncertainty in the face of the eternal stakes of decisions create dread and anxiety, which leave the individual in a state of fear and trembling. Kierkegaard's sojourner is a solitary pilgrim who settles in no earthly city and is at home in no worldly kingdom. Obedient to his transcendent Lord, the wayfarer wanders through a confusing world in ceaseless search of the self he can never truly become. "This is how Christianity presents it," Kierkegaard writes. "Before you lies an eternity—your fate is decided in this life, by how you use it. You have perhaps thirty years left, perhaps ten, perhaps five, perhaps one, perhaps only one month, one day: frightful earnestness."[25]

Mission Accomplished

Kierkegaard's last work was a series of nine pamphlets entitled *Øjeblikket,* published under his own name from May 24, 1855, to September 24, 1855. The last issue was written on September 1, 1855, but was not published until 1881. Throughout September of his final fall, he was suffering multiple ills, and at the end of the month collapsed on a Copenhagen street. When his condition continued to deteriorate, he was taken to Frederick's Hospital, where he died forty-one days later.[26] Michael's ghost continued to haunt Kierkegaard until the end of his life, creating a conflict between his religious mission and his hesitation to speak in his own name for fear of dishonoring his father by offending his priest.

Jakob Peter Mynster was the Bishop of Zealand and, more important, Michael's trusted pastor. From Kierkegaard's point of view, however, Mynster was something of a confidence-man who "issued counterfeit notes." Shortly after the publication of *Concluding Unscientific Postscript,* he visited the Bishop to express disagreement with his interpretation of Christianity.

Kierkegaard did not, however, criticize him publicly until one month before his own death. Mynster's funeral turned into a grand event for Copenhagen society. In his memorial sermon, Hans Lassen Martensen, Kierkegaard's erstwhile theology professor and Mynster's successor, praised the beloved Bishop. "From this man, whose precious memory fills our hearts, our thoughts are led back to the whole series of witnesses to the truth, stretching across the ages, from the days of the Apostles up to our times. . . . Our departed teacher also served as a link to this holy chain of witnesses to the truth, to the honor of God Our Father."[27] These words were so incendiary for Kierkegaard that a few weeks later, he unleashed his "attack on Christendom," which continued until his death. The first dozen articles appeared in *Fædrelandet,* and when Kierkegaard became self-conscious about publishing in the popular press he had so vehemently criticized, he issued the final ten articles at his own expense in *The Moment.* The first salvo of the campaign, entitled "Was Bishop Mynster a 'Witness to the Truth'? One of 'The Authentic Witnesses to the Truth?' Is *This the Truth?*," reveals the dark vision of Christianity that informed the last years of Kierkegaard's life. I quote Kierkegaard's criticism of Mynster at length because it both summarizes the main points in his attack on the church and expresses the increasingly bitter tone of the last chapter of his life. "A witness to the truth, one of the authentic witnesses to the truth, is a person who is flogged, mistreated, dragged from one prison to another. And then finally—the last advancement, by which he is admitted to the first class in the *Christian* order of precedence among the authentic witnesses to the truth—then finally, for this is indeed one of the authentic witnesses to the truth Prof. Martensen talks about, then finally is crucified or beheaded or burned or broiled on a grill, his lifeless body thrown away by the assistant executioner into a remote place, unburied—this is how a witness to the truth is buried!—or burned to ashes and cast to the winds so that every trace of this 'refuse,' as the apostle says he has become, might be obliterated."[28] Mynster betrayed Kierkegaard's view of true Christianity and, by extension, of authentic selfhood by preaching an illusory version of the gospel reassuring people that faith was a birthright that made no serious demands on their lives.

Confronted with this lie, Kierkegaard called for what Nietzsche several decades later would label a "transvaluation of values." Since God is radically transcendent rather than immanent in nature and history, as Hegel, Schleiermacher, and their many followers claimed, time and eternity, self and God, and the profane and the sacred can never be mediated or reconciled. In the first issue of *The Moment,* Kierkegaard explains the meaning of the pamphlet's title. "I call it: The Moment. Yet what I want is not something ephemeral . . . ; no, it was and is something eternal: by means of the ideals, against illusions. . . . I do not urge anyone to subscribe; I rather ask everyone at least to think twice before he does. Eternally he will not regret heeding my words, but it is quite possible that he could regret it temporally. He himself is then to consider whether it is the eternal he wants or the temporal. I, who am called Either/Or, cannot serve anyone with both-and."[29] The moment, then, is the instant of decision, which passes as quickly as the blink (*blikket*) of the eye (*Øje*): either God or world, time or eternity, death or life. The history of modernity in which the religious and the secular are gradually reconciled, Kierkegaard argues, has been one long misunderstanding. The original Christianity of the New Testament has nothing to do with life in this world; rather, it is a lifelong training in militancy against it.

As the end approaches, Kierkegaard's vision of Christianity becomes more severe, and his life more tortured. He develops a dialectical theology that is diametrically opposed to Hegel's philosophy. Instead of reconciling opposites by disclosing their implicit identity, Kierkegaard insists that opposites can never be reconciled, and, therefore, "the essentially Christian is the positive that is recognizable by the negative."[30] The Christ of Christendom is the negation of the Jesus of the New Testament. "No, New Testament Christianity (it is the Christianity of Jesus Christ, for the apostle has already altered it somewhat) is pervaded with the thought: there is a life and death battle between God and man; God hates man just as man hates God. Consequently if you want to be loved by God and to love God (and this is what it is to be a Christian), you must come to be despised, cursed, etc."[31]

As Kierkegaard's view of life in this world darkens and suffering becomes the sign of a faithful relation to God, many of his outbursts seem designed to provoke the hostility and hatred he believes to be the mark of the success of his mission. Commenting on Rousseau in his last seminar, to which we will return, Derrida illuminates the pathology to which Kierkegaard finally succumbed. "I also speak of exacerbation and exasperation because here we are dealing with the isolation of a persecuted man in the middle of the city. . . . Being alone in this way, [Rousseau] claims to be unique in the sense that he pushes a certain perversity in favoring the perversion of the others, the persecutors, to the point of voluntarily cooperating with them and choosing to isolate himself in the solitude his persecutors want to impose on him. As for them, they are sadistic, but as for him, he is masochistic."[32]

In contrast to Mynster's gospel of accommodation, Kierkegaard preached a gospel of martyrdom, which calls upon believers to imitate Christ by following him along the *Via Dolorosa*. The true disciple becomes what, following Hegel's description of "unhappy consciousness," he describes in the first volume of *Either/Or* as "the Unhappiest Man." "But if you do have the courage to want to have the courage that fears most to be in error, then you can also get to know the truth about becoming a Christian. The truth is: to become a Christian is to become, humanly speaking, unhappy for this life; the proportion is: the more you involve yourself with God and the more he loves you, the more you will become, humanly speaking, unhappy for this life, the more you will come to suffer in this life."[33] The darker this life becomes, the brighter the next life appears. Rather than an end, death becomes a deliverance from the travails of earthly existence.

"It is finished!" After sucking sour wine from a sponge, Jesus, according to the Gospel of Luke, let out a cry and then uttered his last words, "Father, into thy hands I commit my spirit" (Luke 23:46). The Gospel of John amends these words, "Having received the wine, he said, 'It is finished!' He bowed his head and gave up his spirit" (John 19:30). In a highly Kierkegaardian book, *You Must Change Your Mind,* Peter Sloterdijk points out that the Greek *tetelestai* is rendered in Latin as *consummatum est,* which usually is translated, "It is finished." Sloterdijk suggests a more assertive, perhaps even militant, translation, "mission accomplished."[34] The more vehemently his critics attacked Kierkegaard, the more confident he became that the mission he had first imagined in Gilleleje twenty years earlier had been accomplished. Through his pseudonymous writings and attack on the Danish state church he had, in fact, reintroduced Christianity to Christendom. In his last journal entry, written only ten days after he completed the final number of *The Moment,* he expressed weariness and readiness for the eternal life he was confident was coming. "The destiny of this life is to be brought to the extremity of life-weariness. . . . I came into existence against God's will. The guilt, which in one sense is not mine even though it makes me an offender in God's eyes, is to give life. The punishment corresponds to the guilt: to be deprived of all zest for life, to be led into the most extreme life-weariness. . . . What pleases [God] even more than the praise of angels is a human being who in the last lap of life, when God seemingly changes into sheer cruelty and with the most cruelly devised cruelty does everything to deprive him of all zest for life, nevertheless continues to believe that God is love, that God does it all out of love. Such a human being becomes an angel. In heaven it is easy to praise God, but the period of learning, the time of schooling is the most strenuous."[35]

During the final weeks of his life, Kierkegaard's friend Emil Boesen regularly visited him in the hospital, and ten years later recorded the memory of their conversations. Knowing that the end was near, Boesen asked Kierkegaard if he would like to receive communion, but he declined, saying he could not accept the ritual administered by "civil servants of the Crown," who "have nothing to do with Christianity."[36] These were the last words Kierkegaard spoke to Boesen. During the final week of his life, Kierkegaard was conscious, but paralyzed, and could not speak. On November 11, 1855, Søren Aabye Kierkegaard died at the age of forty-three.

His funeral turned into a boisterous, controversial affair. Though Kierkegaard had been alienated from his brother, Peter Christian Kierkegaard, and had refused to allow him to visit while in the hospital, Peter was responsible for making the funeral arrangements. While not agreeing with the attack on Christendom, Peter understood that for his brother it was an expression of his belief in, rather than rejection of Christianity. Thus, he decided that the funeral should be held in Copenhagen's central cathedral, where Mynster and Martensen had preached. After the service, he would be buried in the family plot in Assistents Cemetery, not far from the Bishop's grave. On November 18, people packed the cathedral and lined the street leading to the *kierkegaard*. Peter delivered the eulogy without notes and only recorded his recollection of his remarks years later. By the time the hearse carrying Kierkegaard's body arrived, the cemetery was overrun by curious bystanders. As the casket was lowered into the grave, a fifteen-year-old distant cousin, Troels Frederik Lund, stepped forward to protest that this Christian burial betrayed the religious mission to which Kierkegaard had devoted his life.

Kierkegaard, like Poe, was buried in a grave that remained unmarked for almost twenty years. In 1865, H. P. Barford, the first editor of Kierkegaard's posthumous papers, discovered instructions for the burial site that Kierkegaard had written in 1846. After rearranging the stones marking his parents' graves, Kierkegaard requested, "The entire grave site is then to be leveled and sown with a fine species of low grass, but the four corners will each have a little spot of exposed earth, and in each such corner there should be planted a little bush of Turkish roses, as I believe they are called, some very tiny, dark red ones. On the tablet (the one on which is to be written what had been written on the large flat stone, specifically the names of my late sister and brother) there will be plenty of room, so my name can be placed there:

Søren Aabye, born May 5, 1813, died—

and then there will also be room for a little poem, which can be set in small letters."[37]

Turkish roses—not ivy. The words of this poem are inscribed on the gravestone whose rubbing Aaron and I did so many years ago. And the earth Kierkegaard requested remain exposed is in a small black film canister sitting on the desk where I am writing these words.

Dust to Dust
Ashes to Ashes
Earth to Earth

Immanence

Friedrich Nietzsche (1844–1900): *Ecce Homo, Will to Power*

The True is thus the Bacchanalian revel in which no member is sober;
yet because each member collapses as soon as he drops out, the revel is just
as much transparent and simple repose.
—G. W. F. Hegel, *Phenomenology*

Living Death

It is the stare that arrests. The vacant—no, more than vacant—stare. As if
staring into the void and seeing nothing. But how does one see nothing?
After years, almost a decade, of ranting, raving, screaming, silence. Total
silence . . . absolute silence for two years. What was he seeing? What was
he hearing? What was he thinking? Eleven years, eleven long years
without a single comprehensible word. Alive but not alive, dead but not
dead—living death. A few weeks before falling silent, Nietzsche wrote, "one
has to die several times while still alive."[1] What does it mean to live death?
Is living death the continuation of life or its end? Do I survive when the
"I" does not? Nietzsche might know, but he's not talking.

Everything ends or almost ends with an embrace, an embrace not of a beloved but of a wounded horse. Hemingway might have been thinking about
Nietzsche's collapse when he wrote in *Death in the Afternoon*, "I cannot
see a horse down in the street without having it make me feel a necessity
for helping the horse."[2] On January 3, 1889, a few days after arriving in

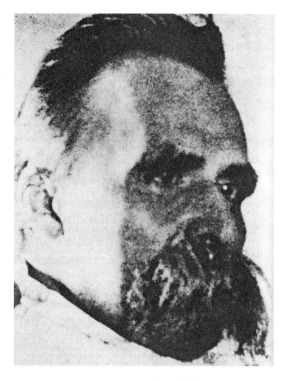

Nietzsche's stare

Turin from Nice, Nietzsche left the rooming house on Piazzo Carlo Alberto across from the opera house, and saw a cab driver beating a horse.[3] Without a moment's hesitation, he flung his arms around the horse's neck and fell to the street unconscious. When he awoke, he was mad and never spoke another sane word until he died on August 25, 1900. The story of Nietzsche's collapse is well known; less well known is what led up to it and what happened after it occurred.

Nietzsche's slip into madness was the culmination of his lifelong struggle with physical and psychological ills. He was born in Rocken, Germany, where his father, Karl Ludwig, was the last in a long line of Lutheran pastors dating back to the seventeenth century. When he was only four, his father, who had suffered epileptic seizures, severe headaches, depression, and mental instability, died at age thirty-six from what was diagnosed as "softening of the brain." During the last sane year of his life, Nietzsche recalled the lasting impact of his father's death. "When I awoke that morning I heard weeping and sobbing all around me. My dear mother entered in tears and wailed: 'Oh God! My dear Ludwig is dead!' Although I was still very young and inexperienced I had an idea of what death was: the thought that I was forever parted from my beloved father seized hold on me and I wept bitterly. The days that followed were filled with tears and with preparations for the funeral. Oh God! I had become a fatherless orphan, my dear mother had become a widow!"[4]

A year after his father's death, Nietzsche's infant brother Joseph died unexpectedly. Forced to vacate the parsonage, his mother, Franziska, moved with her son and daughter, Elisabeth, first to Naumberg, and later to Weingarten, where they lived with their grandmother and aunt. At age fourteen, Nietzsche left home to attend boarding school, and returned thirty-one years later so his mother could care for him until her death. His father's illness and early death left a profound mark on Nietzsche. Though he devoted his life to destroying the Lutheran religion of his forbearers, he came to regard the inheritance of his father's physical and psychological illnesses as an unexpected advantage for his life's mission. In one of his last works, *Ecce Homo,* he wrote, "my father's *wicked* heritage came to my aid—at bottom, predestined to an early death. Sickness *detached me slowly:* it spared me any break, any violent and offensive step. I did not lose any good will and actually gained not a little. My sickness also gave me the right to change all my habits completely; it permitted, it *commanded* me to forget; it bestowed on me the necessity of lying still, of leisure, of waiting and being patient.—But that means, of thinking" (287).

From a very young age, Nietzsche, like his father, suffered poor eyesight and severe headaches, which sometimes incapacitated him for weeks. More troubling than these physical maladies, however, were mood disorders, delusions, and depression. At the time of the attack in Turin, he was diagnosed with progressive paralysis caused by syphilis. Most critics ever since have attributed Nietzsche's mental illness to syphilis, which he supposedly contracted during a visit to a Cologne brothel in 1865. In 2008, however, D. Hemelsoet, K. Hemelsoet, and D. Devreese published an exhaustive study, "The Neurological Illness of Friedrich Nietzsche," in the Belgian journal *Acta Neurologica Belgica* in which they dispute this diagnosis. After surveying all available evidence, they conclude that "Nietzsche suffered from cerebral autosomal dominant arteriopathy with subcortical infarcts and leukoencephalophy or CADASIL, an inherited, generalized small-artery disease caused by mutations . . . of the small arteries penetrating the cerebral white matter. Clinically, CADASIL is mainly characterized by association of migraine, in mood disorders, ischaemic strokes and dementia. It starts in early adulthood and on average leads to death in 10 or 20 years."[5] If this diagnosis is correct, Nietzsche would be the first well-documented historical case of this condition.

Whatever its physiological or neurological cause, the months leading up to Nietzsche's collapse were unusually difficult. From the time he resigned his professorship at the University of Basel in 1879, he had lived an itinerant life, wandering from city to city, living in hotels and rooming houses. He eventually fell into a pattern of spending winter in Nice, spring in Turin, summer in Sils-Maria, and fall back in Turin. Nietzsche's writings received absolutely no attention until the Danish critic Georg Brandes discovered his work shortly before his collapse. Nietzsche always traveled anonymously and, like Kierkegaard, enjoyed walking city streets "incognito." In a letter to music critic Carl Fuchs in the spring of 1888, he recorded his sense of discouragement, if not depression. "How everything slips away! How everything scatters! How silent life is becoming! No human being in sight who knows me."[6] Shortly after his arrival in Turin, his mood changed completely, and he described a moment of ecstasy and expressed the expectation of an impending transformation.

> If one had the slightest residue of superstition left in one's system one could hardly reject altogether the idea that one is merely incarnation, merely mouthpiece, merely a medium of overpowering forces. . . . One hears, one does not seek; one accepts, one does not ask who gives; like lightning, a thought flashes up, with necessity, without hesitation regarding its form—I never had any choice. A rapture whose tremendous tension

occasionally discharges itself in a flood of tears—now the pace quickens involuntarily, now it becomes slow; one is altogether beside oneself, with the distinct consciousness of subtle shudders and of one's skin creeping down to one's toes; a depth of happiness in which even what is most painful and gloomy does not seem something opposite but rather conditioned, provoked, a *necessary* color in such a superabundance of light. (300–301)

This transformation came at a critical time in Nietzsche's career. In 1884, he began writing material for what he expected to be his magnum opus. The first time he mentions *The Will to Power: Attempt at a Transvaluation of All Values* publicly is in *The Genealogy of Morals* (1887). But, like David Foster Wallace struggling to bring order to the chaos of notes and drafts he could never assemble into a last work, Nietzsche gave up the idea of a big book and decided to write four shorter works published under the subtitle of his abandoned project. R. J. Hollingdale observes, "As the projected masterwork grew smaller Nietzsche's claims for it grew greater and reached their climax at just the time he had, it seems, decided to suppress it altogether: this was to lose touch with reality, and madness, open and undisguised followed."[7]

Before interminable darkness and silence descended, Nietzsche enjoyed a brief creative period unlike any other than Kierkegaard's outburst before he died and Melville's brief creative period before he fell silent. It is as if the premonition of the end of his sane life released an energy he could not contain. In the last year of his fragile mental stability, he completed six works, four during the last five months before his collapse.

> *The Wagner Case* (May 1888)
> *The Twilight of the Idols* (August–September 1888)
> *The Anti-Christ* (August–September 1888)
> *Nietzsche contra Wagner* (foreword dated Christmas, 1888)
> *Dionysus-Dithyrambs* (dedication dated January 1, 1889)
> *Ecce Homo* (November–December 1888)

He began his autobiographical *Ecce Homo* on October 14, which was his forty-fourth birthday, and, astonishingly, reported to his friend and Protestant theologian Franz Overbeck on November 13 that he had delivered the manuscript to the publisher. In the midst of this frenzy, Nietzsche expressed an "autumnal" calm that reflected a sense that his work had reached maturity and was ripe for harvesting. "Yesterday, with your letter in hand, I took my usual afternoon walk outside Turin. Everywhere the purest October light. A splendid tree-lined path that led me for about an hour right along the Po; the trees were scarcely touched yet by autumn. I am now the most grateful man in the world—*attuned to autumn* in every good sense of the words: it is now my magnificent *harvest time.* Everything has become easy for me, everything is turning out well for me, although it is hardly possible that anyone has ever had such tremendous things as objects of their labor. . . . My plan is to hold out here until November 20 (it is a somewhat *frosty* plan, since winter is coming early!)."[8] Though Nietzsche could not have known it at the time, the winter that was fast approaching would last for the rest of his life.

Nietzsche's productivity during the autumn of 1888 is all the more remarkable when these works are read from the perspective of the calamitous events that followed. Over the years, many commentators scoured his works for hints of the madness that soon would consume him. It cannot be denied that his final writings give evidence of a mind becoming unhinged. The title, *Ecce Homo,* is borrowed from the Gospel of John. " 'Behold the Man!' said Pilate. The chief priests and their henchman saw him and shouted, 'Crucify! Crucify!' 'Take him and crucify him yourselves,' said Pilate; 'for my part I find no case against him' " (John 19:4–6). As we will see, Nietzsche's identification with Jesus recalls Kierkegaard's *imitatio Christi,* but the message Nietzsche delivers is the opposite of the gospel according to Søren. The titles of the sections of *Ecce Homo* reinforce the megalomania of the title.

Why I am so Wise
Why I am so Clever
Why I Write Such Good Books
Why I am a Destiny

These excesses should not, however, overshadow the importance of this brief work. In a few pages, Nietzsche provides details about his personal life, surveys his writings, and summarizes major themes and issues that pre-occupied him throughout his career. But it is the subtitle more than anything else that reveals the significance of his last work: *How One Becomes What One Is.* For a person as troubled as Nietzsche, this is the daunting challenge of a lifetime. *Ecce Homo* is, in my judgment, the most courageous work in the history of philosophy.

In the weeks after his collapse, Nietzsche's behavior became extremely erratic. The proprietor of the rooming house reported bouts of howling and endless piano playing. On some occasions, he was observed dancing around his room enacting what appeared to be Diony-sian rites.[9] In early January, letters he wrote and signed "The Crucified" and "Dionysus" alarmed his friends. To Cosima Wagner: "Ariane, I love you. Dionysus."[10] To Peter Gast, who considered himself Nietzsche's only disciple:

Turin, January 4, 1889

To my maestro Pietro.

Sing me a new song: the world is transfigured and all the heavens are full of joy.

The Crucified

And to his friend since his university days, Overbeck, his last words:

January 6, 1889

To friend Overbeck and his wife. Although you so far demon-strated little faith in my ability to pay, I yet hope to demonstrate that I am somebody who pays his debts—for example, to you. I am just having all anti-Semites shot.

Dionysus[11]

As the letters became more deranged, Overbeck and Gast became more alarmed. They journeyed to Turin, where they consulted with a local physician and decided to transfer Nietzsche to Basel, where doctors diagnosed "Paralysis progressiva." Though he seemed to have suffered a complete mental breakdown, there were intermittent periods of clarity and rationality. When his mother arrived in Turin on January 14, Nietzsche recognized her. Franziska insisted that her son return home, where she could care for him. His Basel physician and Overbeck disagreed, so they compromised by sending him to the clinic of Otto Binswanger in Jena. His condition did not improve, and Franziska finally got her wish—Nietzsche returned to the home he left thirty-one years earlier. Hemelsoet and his colleagues summarized Nietzsche's worsening condition. "In March 1890, Nietzsche's mother decided to take care of her son and he left the asylum in Jena. In 1891, severe memory problems evolved, together with apathy, irritability, behavioral disorders, lack of insight, aggression, change of character and personality, loss of self-control, regression (with childish interest and thoughts), increasing delusions and prosopagnosia. His mental disorder at that time fulfilled the diagnostic criteria for dementia, with severe memory problems, involvement of other higher cortical functions and his activities in daily life and on his professional activities."[12]

Friends and associates continued to visit him, though Nietzsche did not recognize them. His longtime friend and German classical scholar Erwin Rohde reported after a visit in 1894, "I saw the unhappy man himself: he is totally apathetic, recognizes no one but his mother and sister, speaks hardly a single sentence for a month at a time; his body has become shriveled up and weak, although his face has a healthy color. . . . But he clearly feels nothing more, neither happiness nor unhappiness." A few months later, Gast wrote to Overbeck, "Nietzsche lies upstairs all day dressed in a flannel gown. He does not look bad, has grown very quiet and gazes ahead with a dreamy and very questioning expression. . . . He hardly recognized me anymore."[13]

As Nietzsche was drifting into a catatonic state, his colleagues and his sister, Elisabeth Förster-Nietzsche, were engaged in a struggle over his literary estate and, by extension, his legacy. When Overbeck and Gast left Turin, they took responsibility for his papers. They published what Nietzsche had completed and began to catalogue his vast collection of unfinished work. At the time of Nietzsche's breakdown, Elisabeth was in Paraguay, where she and her husband, Bernhard Förster, had gone to establish a pure Aryan community named Nueva Germania. When the experiment failed, Bernhard committed suicide, and in 1892, Elisabeth returned to Germany to pursue her political agenda by appropriating her brother's writings to advance the National Socialist cause. In 1894, she moved the Nietzsche Archive to Weimar, home of Goethe, Schiller, and Wagner. On the first floor, Elisabeth created a museum dedicated to Nietzsche filled with photographs and memorabilia, while on the second floor, he sat in silent solitude. When Franziska died in 1897, Elisabeth assumed total control over her incapacitated brother. Though Nietzsche had always been critical of German society and culture, and had railed against the Reich, Elisabeth mythologized her brother as the prophet of the coming New Age. Unschooled in philosophy, she enlisted Rudolf Steiner, eventual founder of Anthroposophy, to help her understand her brother's writings. His description of activities at the archive in Weimar shows that Steiner was all too willing to lend his considerable talents to promoting the Nietzsche myth. "While we were busy downstairs arranging his manuscript treasures for the world—he sat enthroned on the veranda above in solemn awfulness, unconcerned with us, like a god of Epicurus. Whoever saw Nietzsche at this time, as he reclined in his white, pleated robe, with the glance of a Brahman in his wide-deep-set eyes beneath busy eye-brows, with the nobility of his enigmatic, questioning face and the lionine, majestic carriage of his thinker's head—had the feeling that this man could not die, but that his eye would rest for all eternity upon mankind and the whole world of appearance in this unfathomable exultation."[14] Such adulation represented the final misunderstanding. Ever prescient, in the concluding section of *Ecce Homo,* Nietzsche wrote, "I have the terrible fear that one day I will be pronounced *holy*" (326).

More important than these farcical charades was the control Elisabeth exercised over Nietzsche's writings. After returning from Paraguay, she swindled Franziska and took responsibility for Nietzsche's literary corpus. Elisabeth quickly ousted Overbeck and Gast and began assembling material for what eventually became *The Will to Power.* She decided which selections should be published and determined the organization of the book using editorial criteria shaped more by her political ambitions than her brother's philosophical commitments. While many of Nietzsche's opinions are controversial and easily misinterpreted, Elisabeth, who had no understanding of the subtlety and complexity of her brother's work, distorted his ideas to support a political vision he would have abhorred. In a fragment, which Lesley Chamberlin reports was not discovered until 1969, Nietzsche expressed the depth of his lifelong difficulties with Elisabeth as well as his mother. "When I look for the deepest contrast to myself, the inexhaustible meanness of instinct, I find over and over my mother and my sister—to believe myself related to such *canaille* would be to blaspheme against my divine nature. The treatment I experience from my mother and sister's side, to this very moment, inspires me with a terror beyond words: at work here is a perfect machine of Hell, with infallible certainty as to the moment when I can be bloodily wounded—in my highest moments . . . for that's the time when all strength needed to defend oneself against poisonous worms is lacking."[15]

Though Nietzsche completed *Ecce Homo* in 1888, it was not published until 1908. When the work appeared, it had been edited by Elisabeth, who disingenuously blamed her mother for censoring passages the family felt were offensive. Attempting to explain the reason for her deletions from Nietzsche's manuscript, she wrote, "His nearest and dearest have become enemies, who have torn him to pieces. These three sheets, which were addressed to my husband in Paraguay, and to our mother, contain attacks upon Wagner, Schopenhauer, Bismarck, the Emperor, Professor Overbeck, Peter Gast, Frau Cosima Wagner, my husband, my mother, and myself. He signed all his letters at the time 'Dionysus' or 'The Crucified One.' Even these notes contain passages of arresting beauty, but on the whole they are clearly the work of a fevered brain. In the first years after my brother's stroke, when we all cherished the vain hope he might recover, these papers were all destroyed by my mother."[16] Dionysus, once the figure of "gay wisdom," becomes the guise of madness.

Swallowing the Sea

What is madness and what does it mean to be mad? There is, undoubtedly, a neurological, even chemical basis for many mental disorders. But not all madness is physiological; madness can also be a matter of perspective. The Bible, for example, suggests that worldly wisdom is folly, and the folly of faith is the wisdom that saves. Nietzsche joined the cast of tricksters and holy fools by deliberately assuming the persona of a madman to deliver his most enduring message.

> *The madman.* Have you not heard of that madman who lit a lantern in the bright morning hours, ran to the market place, and cried incessantly: "I seek God! I seek God!"—As many of those who did not believe in God were standing around just then, he provoked much laughter. Has he got lost? asked one. Did he lose his way like a child? asked another. Or is he hiding? Is he afraid of us? Has he gone on a voyage? Emigrated?—Thus they yelled and laughed.
>
> The madman jumped into their midst and pierced them with his eyes. "Whither is God?" he cried; "I will tell you. *We have killed him*—you and I. All of us are his murderers. But how did we do this? How could we drink up the sea? Who gave us the sponge to wipe away the horizon? What were we doing when we unchained the earth from the sun? Whither is it moving now? Are we not plunging continually? Backward, sideward, forward, in all directions? Is there still any up or down? Are we not straying as through an infinite nothing? Do we not feel the breath of empty space? Has it not become colder? Is not night continually closing in on us? Do we not need to light the lanterns in the morning? Do we hear nothing yet of the noise of the gravediggers who are burying God? Do we smell nothing as yet of the divine decomposition? Gods, too, decompose. God is dead. God remains dead. And we have killed him."[17]

The madman's prophetic announcement dramatically captures the sense of confusion, uncertainty, and disorientation that has characterized life for many people since the turn of the twentieth century. In nineteenth-century Europe, however, Nietzsche's words were calculated to be inflammatory and strike at the very heart of bourgeois society, which he found so utterly offensive. When his critique of Christianity is read back-to-back with Kierkegaard's attack on Christendom, they appear to be both astonishingly similar and surprisingly different. Both argued that many of the problems of modernity grow out of a cultural Protestantism that can be traced to Luther. Struggling to free himself of the burden of generations of Lutheran pastors, Nietzsche declared, "Luther, this calamity of a monk, restored the church and, what is a thousand times worse, Christianity, at the very moment *when it was vanquished.—*Christianity, this denial of the will to life become religion!—Luther, an impossible monk who, on account of his own 'impossibility,' attacked the church and restored it" (320). But Luther was a complicated figure, and his heritage is not quite as simple as Nietzsche suggests. The phrase "God himself is dead" was first used in the Lutheran Good Friday Hymn, written by Johann von Rist (1607–67), and its next occurrence was in Hegel's *Phenomenology of Spirit* (1807). Though he never acknowledged it, Nietzsche's transvaluation of values is, in effect, a poetic rendering of Hegel's abstruse philosophical system, which, Hegel always insisted, was actually inspired by Luther's Protestantism. Hegel and Kierkegaard meet in Nietzsche, and the mediator of this "holy" trinity is Martin Luther.[18]

While Nietzsche is famous or infamous for his declaration of the death of God, it is rarely noted that he did not completely reject religion. Like Kierkegaard and many others, he distinguished the religion *of* Jesus from contemporary Christianity. As we will see in more detail below, nineteenth-century Protestantism was for Nietzsche the negation of the religion Jesus preached. In *The Antichrist* he argues, "I go back, I tell the *genuine* history of Christianity. The very word 'Christianity' is a misunderstanding: in truth, there was only *one* Christian, and he died on the cross. The 'evangel' *died* on the cross. What has been called 'evangel' from that moment was actually the opposite of that which *he* had lived: '*ill* tidings, a *dysangel.'*"[19] Just as Kierkegaard devoted his life to the reintroduction of Christianity into Christendom, so Nietzsche was committed to crushing contemporary Christianity by restoring the original religion of Jesus. Both accomplished their mission in a remarkably short time before dying or going mad at a very young age. As their criticism of religion and society grew more heated and provoked hostile responses, Kierkegaard and Nietzsche identified with the suffering Jesus. Kierkegaard regarded himself as a "martyr for the truth," and Nietzsche signed his final correspondence "The Crucified," "The Antichrist," and "Dionysus." They agree that the only way to restore true religion is to negate Christianity's negation of the original religion of Jesus.

In spite of these striking similarities, their diagnoses of the ills plaguing modern society and their prescriptions for their cure are diametrically opposed. For Kierkegaard, the death of the transcendent God leads to the immanence of the divine, which identifies opposites that should be kept apart—self/other, God/world, divinity/humanity, infinitude/finitude. The return of the radically transcendent God poses a radical choice for the solitary self: *either* time *or* eternity. For Nietzsche, by contrast, Kierkegaard's version of Christianity is a distortion of the religion of Jesus that was introduced by Paul and inevitably leads to nihilism. The death of the transcendent God issues in the immanence of the infinite in the finite that reconciles the opposites tearing selves asunder, and thereby makes life in this world bearable. Jesus preached the gospel of "Gay Science" in which worldly existence is infinitely valuable.

Though commentators often point to the way the metaphors Nietzsche chose to evoke the far-reaching implications of the death of God anticipate the anxieties unleashed by the disasters of the era that was dawning, one extremely important image is consistently overlooked: "How could we drink up the sea? Who gave us the sponge to wipe away the horizon?" Here the sea—age-old image of creation, destruction, disorder, and unfathomability—does not simply disappear but is internalized, rendering the self as mysterious as vast oceans once had been. For Nietzsche and Kierkegaard, the process of interiorization that creates labyrinthian subjectivity begins with Luther's turn to the subject. The cornerstone of Luther's reformation was his rejection of the Catholic Church's insistence that a person's relation to God is indirect and must be mediated by the ecclesiastical hierarchy of pope, bishops, and priests. Each individual, Luther insisted, has a direct personal and private relation to God that is sealed in inwardness. Kierkegaard's declaration that "truth is subjectivity" makes explicit the implications of Luther's notion of faith. "When subjectivity is the truth," he writes in *Concluding Unscientific Postscript,* "the conceptual determination of the truth must include an expression for the antithesis to objectivity, a memento of the fork in the road where the way swings off; this expression will at the same time serve as an indication of the tension of the subjective inwardness. Here is such a definition of truth: *An objective uncertainty held fast in an appropriation-process of the most passionate inwardness is the truth,* the highest truth attainable for an *existing* individual."[20] Though the target of Kierkegaard's criticism was Hegelian philosophy rather than the Catholic Church, his insistence on the subjective appropriation rather than the objective mediation of religious commitment transforms the structure of subjectivity. This new configuration of inwardness does not, however, erase altarity—the outer world, other selves, and the radically other God remain, but now reflect the impenetrability of the self's own inwardness.

Nietzsche radicalized Kierkegaard's account of the subjectivity of truth by developing a perspectivism in which truth is thoroughly relative because it is constituted relationally. In one of the fragments included in *The Will to Power,* he argues,

> Against positivism, which halts at phenomena—"there are only *facts*"—I would say: No, facts is precisely what there is not, only interpretations. We cannot establish any fact "in itself": perhaps it is folly to want to do such a thing.
>
> "Everything is subjective," you say; but even this is interpretation. The "subject" is not something given, it is something added and invented and projected behind what there is.—Finally, is it necessary to posit an interpreter behind the interpretation? Even this is an invention, hypothesis.

In so far as the word "knowledge" has any meaning, the
world is knowable; but it is *interpretable* otherwise, it has no
meaning behind it, but countless meanings.—"Perspectivism."[21]

For Nietzsche, as for Hegel, being is relational because identity is differential. The specific identity of any thing or person is constituted by
interrelations with other things and persons. "The 'thing-in-itself' [is]
nonsensical," he argues. "If I remove all relationships, all the 'properties,'
all the 'activities' of a thing, the thing does not remain over; because thing-
ness has only been invented by us owing to the requirements of logic, thus
with the aim of defining communication (to bind together the multiplicity
of relationships, properties, activities)."[22] When extended from persons
and things to perspectives and worldviews, this relational ontology leads
to a relativistic epistemology. Each perspective emerges through the ongoing interplay with other perspectives; nothing is fixed and every perspective
must adapt or perish. There is no underlying unity to this process, and no
single perspective should be absolutized. There are countless perspectives and, therefore, endless meanings. The existential dilemma is not,
as many of Nietzsche's critics claim, meaningless, but, to the contrary, the
infinite proliferation of meanings.

In a manner reminiscent of Heraclitus, in Nietzsche's world, everything is constantly in flux. Incessant change creates the sense of uncertainty
and disorientation. In a vain effort to control this flux, people project stable notions of self, world, thing, and God behind the play of appearances.

"Ends and means"	as interpretations (not as facts)
"Cause and effect"	and to what extent perhaps
"Subject and object"	*necessary* interpretations? (as
"Acting and suffering"	required for "preservation")—all
"Thing-in-itself and	in the sense of a will to power.[23]
appearance"	

This gesture creates a bifurcation between the "real" world and the "apparent" world. Christianity and its philosophical transcriptions perpetu-

ate the lie that truth and the Real are never here-and-now but are always elsewhere—above or below, in the past or the future. From this perspective, the only way to affirm otherworldly truth and reality is to negate the world of appearances. From the time Nietzsche resigned his professorship at the University of Basel to his last sane day, his primary purpose was to bring truth back down to earth by dispelling the illusion of a transcendent reality above, beyond, behind, or beneath the only world we can ever know. *Ecce Homo* is the last chapter in this long endeavor. Nietzsche's crusade has a negative and a positive moment: he must first overcome nihilism, which encourages self-denial, and, then, show people the way to self-affirmation, which allows them to become who they are.

Unhappy Consciousness

As I have noted, Nietzsche abandoned his plan to publish *The Will to Power*. While Elisabeth's editorial criteria are often questionable, her selection of the opening aphorism effectively captures the primary target of Nietzsche's criticism during the last months he wrote. "Nihilism stands at the door: whence comes this uncanniest of all guests? Point of departure: it is an error to consider 'social distress' or 'physiological degeneration' or, worse, corruption as the cause of *nihilism*. . . . Rather: it is in one particular interpretation, the Christian-moral one, that nihilism is rooted." Whereas most critics claim that nihilism results from the loss of religious faith and the decline of moral standards, Nietzsche insists that Christianity and morality actually cause nihilism. Nihilism, he proceeds to explain, is *"That the highest values devalue themselves."*[24] The transvaluation of values reverses nihilism by overturning "the Christian-moral" interpretation of life. The key to this revolution is, as Hegel had realized, the death of God. The death of God, however, is not a single event, but a complex process that takes many years. Nietzsche calls for the death of the transcendent God Kierkegaard had worshipped, and proclaims the birth of an immanent divine whose progressive self-realization Hegel traced.

What Nietzsche labels nihilism, Hegel describes as "unhappy consciousness." Hegel's entire philosophical system is an extended pedagogy for people oppressed by the burden of unhappy consciousness. His difficult prose should not obscure the importance of his psycho-historical analysis. Unhappy consciousness, he maintains, is a symptom of the uncertainty, insecurity, and anxiety caused by the death of God. With the disappearance of God, there seems to be no stable reality grounding thought and guiding action. In the *Phenomenology of Spirit,* he writes, unhappy consciousness is "the tragic fate of the certainty of self that aims to be absolute. It is the consciousness of the loss of all *essential* being in this *certainty of itself,* and of the loss even of this knowledge about itself—the loss of substance as well as of the self, it is the grief that expresses itself in the hard saying that 'God is dead.' "[25] So understood, unhappy consciousness represents the culmination of the inward turn of consciousness that begins with Luther's inward faith and ends with Kierkegaard's subjectivization of truth and its extension in Nietzsche's perspectivism. The price of such self-certainty is the loss of the objective world as well as what had been believed to be transcendent reality. Though this process reconciles both the divine and the human, and the infinite and the finite, the resulting coincidence of opposites is initially experienced as inward fragmentation. Self-consciousness becomes divided and "self-contradictory." On the one hand, it is "self-liberating, unchangeable, and self-identical," and, on the other hand, it is "self-entangling and self-perverting," and it is the awareness of this "self-contradictory nature of itself."[26]

Suspended between opposites that cannot be reconciled, the tensions of the split subject reach the breaking point. In an effort to relieve these tensions, individuals confess their inner division and project the seemingly unchangeable part of themselves into a transcendent realm for which they long. While this beyond is represented in different ways—the transcendent God, the Platonic realm of forms, and abstract moral ideals—its affirmation inevitably entails negation: the other-worldly God is worshipped by denying this world, essential forms are known by seeing through appearances, and moral ideals are affirmed by repressing sensuous desires.

For Nietzsche, this "Nay-Saying" grows out of "the Christian-moral" view of the world and is thoroughly nihilistic. Defiantly declaring himself to be "the first immoralist," he declared on the last page of his last book,

"The concept of 'God' invented as a counter concept to life—everything harmful, poisonous, slanderous, the whole hostility unto death against life synthesized in this concept in a gruesome unity! The concept of the 'beyond,' the 'true world' invented in order to devalue the only world that is— in order to retain no goal, no reason, no task for our earthly reality! The concept of the 'soul,' the 'spirit,' finally even *'immortal* soul,' invented in order to despise the body, to make it sick, 'holy'; to oppose with a ghastly levity everything that deserves to be taken seriously in life, the questions of nourishment, abode, spiritual diet, treatment of the sick, cleanliness and the weather" (334). During the last months of his writing life, Nietzsche's attack on Christianity became militantly aggressive. It was as if he knew time were running out and he had to deliver his message as forcefully as possible. Reversing the religion of Jesus, Paul "invented a god who 'ruins the wisdom of the world.' "[27] Nietzsche recalls Marx's famous criticism by arguing that Christianity is an "opiate" for the weak, who are unable to embrace the world in all its beauty, ambiguity, and, yes, horror. Pastors and priests secure their own power and influence by preaching a gospel that encourages resentment and rewards passivity. Rather than cultivating what William James described as "healthy-mindedness," Christianity, Nietzsche maintains, "persuades men to *nothingness!*" This religion of the sick thrives best when people are unhappy. " 'Consequently, man must be made unhappy'—this was the logic of the priest in every age."[28] When this world becomes little more than a "vale of tears" or the "valley of the shadow of death," the aim of life becomes death. But just when death seems to have become the end of life, it disappears—people no longer die, they pass—pass beyond this world plagued by sorrow and suffering to a better life. "The 'beyond'—why a beyond, if not as a means for *besmirching* this world?"[29] And then, the final words of *Ecce Homo:* "Have I been understood?— *Dionysus versus the Crucified*" (335). Who is this Dionysus?

Bacchanalian Revel

Dionysus is the Greek god of the grape harvest and wine, who is worshipped in festivals of madness, fertility, and religious ecstasy. He is also known as

Bacchus, whose *thyrsus* (wand) is covered with ivy and drips with honey. Perhaps that is why Hegel's grave is covered with ivy, and it is definitely why ivy from his grave grows in the barn where I am writing these words. In the most poetic lines from a very unpoetic work, Hegel writes, "The evanescent itself must . . . be regarded as essential, not as something fixed, cut off from the True, and left lying who knows where outside it, any more than the True is to be regarded as something on the other side, positive and dead. Appearance is the arising and passing away that does not itself arise and pass away, but is 'in itself,' and constitutes the actuality and movement of the life of truth. The True is the Bacchanalian revel in which no member is sober; yet because each member collapses as soon as he drops out, the revel is just as much transparent and simple repose." The death of God empties transcendence into immanence, and thereby transforms unhappy consciousness into a joyful affirmation of the world as it is. From this perspective, the eternal is not the opposite of the temporal, but is the eternal return of appearances arising and passing away. This play of appearances is the *via crucis* in which crucifixion and resurrection coincide *in this world.* Hegel summarizes the theological position that informs his philosophical vision: "But the life of Spirit is not the life that shrinks from death and keeps itself untouched by devastation, but rather the life that endures it and maintains itself in it. It wins its truth only when, in utter dismemberment, it finds itself. It is this power, not as something positive, which closes its eyes to the negative, as when we say of something that it is nothing or is false, and then, having done with it, turn away and pass on to something else; on the contrary, Spirit is this power only by looking the negative in the face, and tarrying with it. This tarrying with the negative is the magical power that converts it into being."[30]

From his first work to his last signature, Nietzsche was obsessed with Dionysus. Though his views of this figure changed subtly over the years, the Greek god always represented the principle of affirmation that informs all of Nietzsche's writings. His first work, *The Birth of Tragedy* (1872), is structured around the dialectical relationship between Apollo, who expresses reason and the *principium individuationis,* and Dionysus, who embodies excess and the shattering of the principle of individuation. The world as we know it emerges through the creative-destructive interplay of order or structure and disorder or anti-structure. No longer a transcendent creator, God becomes "the supreme artist, amoral, recklessly creating and destroying, realizing himself by his acts of the embarrassment of his riches and the strain of his internal contradictions." The world, in turn, is a work of art, and individuals, insofar as they are actively productive, are incarnations of the divine principle of creativity. As if describing Hegel's notion of Spirit, Nietzsche writes, "to the extent that the subject is an artist he is already delivered from individual will and has become a medium through which the True Subject celebrates His redemption in illusion."[31] As we will see below, the redemption of the True Subject through the world is at the same time the redemption of the world through the True Subject because the two are ultimately one. Nietzsche underscores this point with his idiosyncratic interpretation of the Dionysian ritual. "Now the gospel of universal harmony is sounded, each individual becomes not only reconciled to his fellow but actually at one with him—as though the veil of Maya had been torn apart and there remained only shreds floating before the vision of mystical Oneness. Man now expresses himself through song and dance as the member of a community; he has forgotten how to walk, how to speak, and is on the brink of taking wing as he dances. Each of his gestures betokens enchantment; through him sounds a supernatural power. . . . He feels himself to be godlike and strides with the same elation and ecstasy as the gods he has seen in his dreams. No longer the *artist,* he has himself become a *work of art:* the productive power of the whole universe is now manifest in his transport, to the glorious satisfaction of the primordial One."[32]

By the time Nietzsche wrote *Ecce Homo* and the fragments eventually included in *The Will to Power,* he had developed reservations about terms like "True Subject," "mystical Oneness," and "the primordial One." He realized that such notions were really "shadows" of the "One God" he was so intent on murdering, and the "true world" whose reality he vehemently denied. The death of the Christian God marks the end of the belief in a true world above or beyond the apparent world. Once again referring to the wisdom of pre-Socratic philosophers, Nietzsche writes, "Heraclitus will remain eternally right with his assertion that being is an empty fiction.

The 'apparent' world is the only one: the 'true' world is merely added by a lie."[33] The denial of the other world is the "redemption of this world." For the immoralist, the real is not elsewhere but is here-and-now in the personal, social, cultural, and natural processes of the creative-destructive whole.

With this critical turn, the contrast between Apollo and Dionysus becomes the opposition between the Christian Christ and Dionysus. Nietzsche gives his most concise summary of the two modes of being-in-the-world represented by these two figures in a fragment included in *The Will to Power*.

> Dionysus versus the "Crucified": there you have the antithesis. It is *not* a difference in regard to their martyrdom—it is a difference in the meaning of it. Life itself, its eternal fruitfulness and recurrence, creates torment, destruction, the will to annihilation. In the other case, suffering—the "Crucified as the innocent one"—counts as an objection to this life, as a formula for its condemnation.—One will see that the problem is that of the meaning of suffering: whether a Christian meaning or a tragic meaning. In the former case, it is supposed to be the path to a holy existence; in the latter case, being is counted as *holy enough* to justify even a monstrous amount of suffering. The tragic man affirms even the harshest suffering: he is sufficiently strong, rich, and capable of deifying to do so. The Christian denies even the happiest lot on earth: he is sufficiently weak, poor, disinherited to suffer from life in whatever form he meets it. The god on the cross is a curse on life, a signpost to seek redemption from life; Dionysus cut to pieces is a *promise* of life: it will be eternally reborn and return again from destruction.[34]

As we have seen, according to Nietzsche, Paul invented Christianity through a transvaluation of the values Jesus had preached. In contrast to Christians, who deny themselves and this world for the sake of the afterlife, Jesus was a "free spirit" whose knowledge was, from the perspective of true believers, "pure foolishness." "Such a spirit who has *become free*," Nietzsche explains, "stands amid the cosmos with a joyous and trusting fatalism, in the *faith* that all is redeemed and affirmed in the whole—*he does not negate any more*. Such a faith, however, is the highest of all possible faiths: I have baptized it with the name of *Dionysus*."[35] Far from fleeing the world in pursuit of a transcendent realm of perfection, Jesus affirms this world with all its joys and sorrows.

Though Nietzsche insists that the free spirit "does not negate any more," Jesus's vision can, paradoxically, only be affirmed through negation. If Christianity is the negation of Jesus, then his way of life must be affirmed by negating the Christ of the church. The Antichrist, therefore, is the true follower of Jesus. Once again, Hegel anticipates Nietzsche's insight; in Hegel's dialectical vision, true affirmation requires the negation of a negation.

> *But that is the concept of Dionysus himself.* . . . The psychological problem in the type of Zarathustra is how he says No and *does* No to an unheard-of degree, to everything to which one has so far said Yes, can nevertheless be the opposite of a No-saying spirit; how the spirit who bears the heaviest fate, a fatality of a task, can nevertheless be the lightest and most transcendent—Zarathustra is a dancer—how he that has the hardest, most terrible insight into reality, that has the "most abysmal idea," nevertheless does not consider it an objection to existence, not even to its eternal recurrence—but rather one reason more for being himself the eternal Yes to all things, "the tremendous, unbounded saying Yes and Amen."—"Into all abysses I still carry the blessings of my saying Yes."—*But this is the concept of Dionysus once again.* (306)

Here as elsewhere Nietzsche expresses his final vision in surprisingly religious language. "Jesus," he declares, "abolished the very concept of 'guilt'— he had denied any cleavage between God and man; he *lived* this unity of

God and man as his 'glad tidings.'" Instead of transcendent and other-worldly, the divine is immanent in the world, or, in different terms, finitude is the self-realization of the infinite. In Nietzsche's realized eschatology, the kingdom of God is earthly, perhaps even earthy. "The 'kingdom of heaven' is a state of the heart—not something to come 'above the earth' or 'after death.' . . . The 'hour of death' is *no* Christian concept—an 'hour' time, physical life and its crises do not even exist for the teacher of 'glad tidings.' The 'kingdom of God' is nothing that one expects; it has no yesterday and no day after tomorrow, it will not come in 'a thousand years'—it is an experience of the heart; it is everywhere, it is nowhere."[36] There is neither life after death nor any other world than this one. The challenge, then, is not to live a life of denial that supposedly prepares one for the next world, but to live the fullest life possible in the only world there is. Morality and most forms of religion require people to negate or repress what they are and become what they are not by fulfilling morally ideal laws or following authoritative divine dictates. Nietzsche's challenge is not to "wish oneself to be different" but to become what he or she is. *Ecce Homo: How One Becomes What One Is.* This is what he means by "amor fati"—love of fate. "My formula for greatness in a human being is *amor fati:* that one wants nothing to be different, not forward, not backward, not in all eternity. Not merely bear what is necessary, still less conceal it—all idealism is mendaciousness in the face of what is necessary—but *love* it" (258).

My claim that *Ecce Homo* is the most courageous work in the history of philosophy might have seemed hyperbolic, but I do not think it is. To appreciate the force of Nietzsche's extraordinary last work, it is neces-sary to recall not only the way he suffered physically and psychologically throughout his life, but also the extraordinary difficulties he faced while he was writing his last works. Rather than the cheap words of an armchair scholar who teaches and writes for a living, they are the passionate words of a thinker whom life has crucified, and yet has the courage to say "Amen!—So be it!" In this moment, he finds "bliss not as something promised," but as there because he lived and acted "in such and such a way."[37]

D

After the end of prose, poetry—*Dionysus-Dithyrambs.* Nietzsche began this collection in 1880, and in mid-November, before his breakdown, he gathered the fragments under the title *Zarathustra's Songs.* There were other poems scattered throughout his writings, but Nietzsche, like Melville, ended with poetry after his last work. The themes are similar to those he probed during his final autumn, though his meaning is not always as clear as in those fall days. The final stanzas in the penultimate section, "Ariadne's Lament," are the most telling.

> Sign of necessity!
> Supreme star of being!—
> That no desire attains,
> That no No desecrates
> Eternal Yes of being
> Eternally I am your Yes:
> For I love you, O eternity!—[38]

Intrigued by the excerpt of these late poems, I went to the library to find a copy of the *Dionysus-Dithyrambs,* but it was not in the collection. I finally tracked down the text online and was surprised to discover that it included Nietzsche's signature, "Dionysus," in his handwritten script.

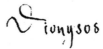

Nietzsche's signature Dionysus

Mark C. Taylor, homage to Nietzsche

I have always been fascinated by the question of why a person is drawn to one writer or work instead of another, or to one writer or work at one time and not another. More often than not, it seems that the attraction is affective rather than merely cognitive. This attraction is difficult to understand and impossible to explain. The longer I have pondered this experience, the more convinced I have become that there are some things that can be apprehended but not comprehended. To develop this insight, I have begun exploring ways of writing without words.

I was intrigued by the elegance of Nietzsche's D, and decided to enlarge its image, and then make a steel sculpture of it. For the past several years, I had been creating land art as well as steel, stone, and bone sculptures in the Berkshire Mountains where I live.[39] After much planning and long hours of working with local metal craftsmen, we completed the work I designed.

The sculpture is fifteen feet tall and weighs approximately 1,200 pounds. As I tried to understand what I was doing, I realized that I was reversing Hegel's translation of artistic images and religious representations

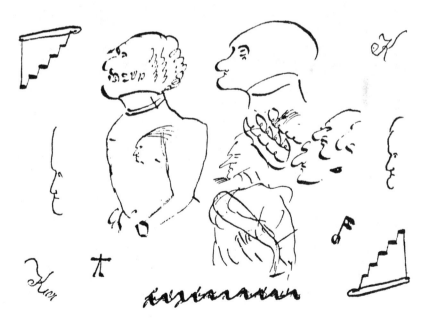

Kierkegaard's signature

Mark C. Taylor, homage to Kierkegaard

into philosophical concepts by translating philosophical concepts into artistic forms. The next work I did is an homage to Kierkegaard, which I designed from the K of his signature. It is sixteen feet tall and sixteen feet long, and weighs more than a ton.

The final work, at least for now, is an homage to Hegel, designed from the H of his signature. It is fifteen feet tall and eighteen feet wide, and weighs about one and a half tons.

Hegel, Kierkegaard, Nietzsche—the "holy" trinity that has shaped everything I have written over the years. In developing my work on Stone Hill, I extended my vision from Europe to America by constantly keeping in mind two other artists who lived along the same highway where I am writing—Melville and Thoreau. The placement of the three sculptures is deliberate: Nietzsche's $\mathcal{D}$ stands between Kierkegaard's $\mathcal{K}$ and Hegel's $\mathcal{H}$. In this $\mathcal{D}$, I hope others will see the wisdom of the words of Nietzsche's Dionysus/Zarathustra, which are my favorite in all philosophy.

> Did you ever say "Yes" to one joy? Oh my friends, then you also said "Yes" to *all* pain. All things are entwined, enmeshed, enamored—
>
> —did you ever want Once to be Twice, did you ever say "I love you, bliss—instant—flash—" then you wanted *everything* back.

Hegel's signature

Mark C. Taylor, homage to Hegel

—Everything anew, everything forever, everything en-
twined, enmeshed, enamored—oh, thus you love the world—
—you everlasting ones, thus you love it forever and for all
time; even to pain you say: Refrain but
—come again! *For joy accepts everlasting flow!*[40]

This vision of "Dionysus, the Antichrist" is a profound lesson in leaving
to which I will return as the end of *Last Works* approaches.

Ecce Homo. First prose, then poetry, and finally silence. Darkness fell,
and all that remained was the empty stare.

Waiting

Maurice Blanchot (1907–2003): "The Instant of My Death," *Awaiting Oblivion*

> For the listener, who listens in the snow,
> And, nothing himself, beholds
> Nothing that is not there and the nothing that is.
> —Wallace Stevens, "The Snow Man"

Secrets

Is it possible to write a biography about an invisible man? The endlessly obscure Maurice Blanchot offers a hint in an essay entitled "Parler, ce n'est pas voir" (Speaking is not seeing): "Perhaps there is an invisibility that is still a manner of something letting itself be seen, and then another that turns itself away [*se détourne*] from everything visible and everything invisible." What would it mean for the invisible to become visible, and the visible to become invisible? Is it possible to reveal by concealing, and to conceal by revealing? Does withdrawal attract? How might this play of hide-and-seek be written? "How can we discover the obscure?; how can it be brought out into the open? What would this experience of the obscure be, whereby the obscure would give itself in its obscurity?" (IC, 33, 44).[1]

Maurice Blanchot's enigmatic first novel, or, more precisely, *récit*, *Thomas the Obscure*, published during the German occupation of Paris (1941), begins with a person sitting on the shore of the sea.[2] Casting his gaze toward the mist, "his eye found nothing to cling to, and it seemed to him

that he was staring into the void with the intention of finding help there."
When nothing appears, Thomas, if that is his name, slowly slides into the
water.

> As he swam, he pursued a sort of reverie in which he confused
> himself with the sea. The intoxication of leaving himself, of
> slipping into the void, of dispersing himself in the thought of
> water, made him forget every discomfort. And even when this
> ideal sea with which he was becoming ever more intimate had
> in turn become the real sea, in which he was virtually drowned,
> he was not moved as he should have been: of course, there was
> something intolerable about swimming this way, aimlessly,
> with a body which was of no use to him beyond thinking that
> he was swimming, but he also experienced that sense of relief
> as if he had finally discovered the key to the situation, and, as
> far as he was concerned, it all came down to continuing his
> endless journey, with an absence of organism in an absence
> of sea. (TO, 8)

Thomas is as obscure as the elusive author who created him—he has no
personal history, no job, no friends, and no identifiable location; even his
name is doubtful. Haunted by Melville and his confidence-man, Blanchot's
title underscores his irrepressible doubt by alluding to the Apocrypha.
Thomas in Aramaic and Hebrew is not only a proper name but also an
epithet meaning twin or a double. In the apocryphal "Acts of Thomas,"
Thomas appears as the twin brother of Jesus. Thomas is, of course, also
the name of the disciple whose doubt drove him to stick his finger in the
holes riddling the body of the crucified Lord. As the author's double, this
doubting Thomas indirectly reveals Blanchot's duplicitous identity by concealing it.

Throughout his life, Blanchot consistently sought obscurity. Though
he lived well into the age of viral media and celebrity culture, he never spoke
on radio or in public, never appeared on television, and avoided photog-
raphers. During the last four decades of his life, there are almost no photo-

graphs of him. Beyond his influential, though not widely known, literary corpus, few facts are known about Blanchot's life, and these are not particularly revealing. He was born September 22, 1907, in the village Devrouze, Saône-et-Loire, and died February 20, 2003, in Mesnil-Saint-Denis. He attended the University of Strasbourg, where he studied German philosophy, giving special attention to Hegel and Heidegger. This period marked the beginning of his lifelong friendship with Emmanuel Levinas. After completing his education, Blanchot became a journalist and, during the 1930s, wrote for many right-wing publications like *Journal des Débats* and *Combat*. Though critics charged him with anti-Semitism, he also edited the anti-Nazi publication *Le Rempart,* and contributed to *Aux Écoutes,* which Paul Lévy founded to alert people to the dangers created by Hitler's rise to power.[3] During the occupation, Blanchot remained in Paris and turned his attention to writing critical essays and fiction. His contributions to *Nouvelle Revue Française* in the 1950s and 1960s proved to be very influential for other writers.

In his ongoing effort to avoid publicity, Blanchot spent most of his life outside of Paris. In 1947, he left Paris for the village of Eze in southern France, but returned briefly in 1968 to join the protests staged by university students. During these demonstrations, he met Derrida, with whom he remained in contact until the end of his life. This was the last time anyone knowingly saw Blanchot in public. After *les manifestations,* he withdrew to Mesnil-Saint-Denis, where he lived and worked until his death. Not even his closest friends saw him for the final thirty-five years of his life. During this time, his writing became less frequent and more elusive. After *L'Entretien Infini* (*The Infinite Conversation,* 1969), he published nothing for five years, when his final book-length work, *Le pas au-delà* (The step/not beyond), appeared. Blanchot's three-and-a-half-page last work, "The Instant of My Death," appeared in 1994. In his eulogy, delivered on the occasion of Blanchot's cremation (February 24, 2003), Derrida stressed the importance of his friend's withdrawal.

> I became used to hearing . . . [his] name differently from the
> way I would hear the name of that other person, the incompa-

rable author who is quoted and inspires us: I heard it differently
from the way I heard the great name of a man whom I admire
both for his power of exposition, in thought and in life, *and* for
his power of withdrawal, his exemplary modesty, a discretion
unique in this age, one that always kept him far away, as far
away as possible, deliberately, by ethical and political principle,
from all the rumors and all the images, from all the temptations
and all the appetites of culture, from all that urges and hurries us
toward the immediacy of the media, of the press, of photography, of the screen.[4]

During an age obsessed with publicity, Blanchot's obscurity created an obsessive fascination with his work among many leading French intellectuals. The modesty of his life is reflected in the reticence of his writing.

In the early 1980s, I was considering editing a volume entitled *The
French Kierkegaard,* which would include essays by prominent philosophers and writers. I had read a brief review of Kierkegaard's *Journals* that
Blanchot had written in the 1940s, and suspected his debt to Kierkegaard
ran deep. What intrigued me about Blanchot's review was his discussion
of the way Kierkegaard's notion of the secret informed his pseudonymous
strategy and influenced his assumption of an incognito to disguise his writerly intentions. "To a certain extent," Blanchot writes, "without ceasing
to speak of himself and to reflect on the events of his existence, Kierkegaard is determined not to say anything important about it and bases his
greatness on the safeguarding of the secret. He explains himself and he veils
himself. He exposes himself and he protects himself. He uncovers himself
but only (luring our minds by a veritable seduction) in order to put us in
contact with the substance of his shadows and to refuse us that which would
explain everything to us."[5] In discussing Kierkegaard, Blanchot indirectly
illuminates his own life and work. As we have seen, Kierkegaard struggles
to fathom his own subjectivity to discover truths he poses for others to ponder. The question of secrecy that preoccupies him is not merely personal,
but is also structural—there is a depth of selfhood, which, like the navel of
Freud's dream, is a point of contact with the unknowable. Thus, all com-

munication is, in some sense, indirect. Commenting on Kierkegaard, Blanchot underscores one of the most important presuppositions of his own writings, "There is no communication unless what is said appears like the sign of what must be hidden. The revelation is wholly in the impossibility of revelation. . . . Everything is dialectics with Kierkegaard because the only way to say the truth without unveiling it is to pursue it as if it could not be attained, in an effort that does not allow either completion or rest."[6] When revelation is, paradoxically, concealment, and concealment is revelation, something is always hiding.

Two aspects of Kierkegaard's secret are especially important for Blanchot. First, the secret renders the work of art interminable, and the writer forever restless. If the secret were ever disclosed, the work would be finished. "To write," Blanchot explains in *The Space of Literature*, "is to make oneself the echo of what cannot cease speaking—and since it cannot, in order to become its echo I have, in a way, to silence it. I can bring to this incessant speech the decisiveness, the authority of my own silence. I make *perceptible*, by my silent meditation, the uninterrupted affirmation, the giant murmuring upon which language opens and thus becomes image, becomes imaginary, becomes a speaking depth, an indistinct plenitude that is empty. This silence has its source in the effacement toward which the writer is drawn."[7] The writer, like Thomas the Obscure, disappears into words that conceal rather than reveal what he struggles to say. Second, the secret isolates the person who guards it, and communication threatens "the treasure of solitude."[8] Secrecy creates a distance between couples who seem to be close. In an essay suggestively entitled "The Essential Solitude," Blanchot considers the importance of solitude for the writer. "The writer's solitude, that condition which is the risk he runs, seems to come from his belonging, in the work, to what always precedes the work." In this way, writing involves an inevitable passivity—the writer is written as much as he writes. Solitude creates the space for the writer to become open to a strange otherness that writes through him. "The writer seems to be the master of his pen; he can become capable of great mastery over words and over what he wants to make them express. But his mastery only succeeds in putting him, keeping him in contact with the fundamental passivity where the word, no longer anything but its appearance—the shadow of a word—never can be mastered or even grasped. It remains the ungraspable that is also unreleasable: the indecisive moment of fascination" (SL, 24, 25). It was the search for this essential solitude that led Blanchot to withdraw from the world and spend the last thirty-five years of his life alone.

I decided to invite Blanchot to contribute an essay for the volume I had planned. In the days before the Internet, I had no idea how to contact him, so wrote to him in care of his publisher, Gallimard. I did not really expect a reply, but, much to my surprise, a few weeks later a short letter dated November 29, 1984, arrived from Blanchot. It was a very generous letter in which he admitted that he rarely responds to inquiries. He expressed his abiding interest in Kierkegaard and said that he remained intrigued by Levinas's resistance to Hegel. He suggested that perhaps Levinas thought Kierkegaard had not adequately questioned the notion of the subject. It was written on a small piece of notepaper in a very fine hand. Though not surprised, I was nonetheless disappointed that Blanchot would not contribute to the book, and eventually gave up the project. A few months later, I was planning a trip to Paris. In the relatively small circle of Blanchot's colleagues and associates, his insistence on solitude was legendary. Derrida never saw him after 1968, and Edmond Jabès, whom Blanchot regarded as one of his closest friends, never met him. I once asked Jabès about his relationship with Blanchot, and he told me that his "closeness was marked by distance." Jabès and Blanchot never met face to face, and communicated regularly through brief handwritten letters and notes just like the one I had received. Such reclusiveness is rare but not unknown in an age when most writers and artists seem to have an insatiable desire for publicity. One thinks of Salinger and Pynchon hiding in plain sight. Whether calculated or not, aversion to publicity sometimes creates more interest in the author and his works than the endless chatter agents promoting books generate. Of course, I knew that Blanchot had deliberately chosen the life of solitude, but, having established contact, I decided to write to him to ask if we might meet to discuss the importance of Kierkegaard for his work.

This was not the first time that Kierkegaard had drawn me into conversation with a major writer. While still an undergraduate at Wesleyan

University, I published my first article on the importance of Kierkegaard and the Swiss theologian Karl Barth, who was deeply influenced by Kierkegaard, in John Updike's fiction. While researching my essay, I had the audacity to write to Updike to ask him if I might interview him. In a letter dated January 31, 1967, he declined my request, indicating that he does not give interviews because he believed works should be considered on their own and not in relation to the life of the author. Unlike Blanchot, Updike did not withdraw from society. He acknowledged his profound debt to Kierkegaard and Barth and went so far as to say that they had made it possible for him to survive and be creative. Updike knew Blanchot's work and thought highly of it. In a review of his early endlessly enigmatic work, Updike wrote, "Blanchot's tortuous, glimmering style in *Death Sentence* is a kind of posthumous one, traced with many hesitations and denials by the ghostly hand of narrative. It conceals as it tells."[9] I will return to the question of style in the next section. For the moment, it is important to note that while "death sentence" is not an incorrect translation of Blanchot's *L'arrêt de mort,* it does not capture the multiple nuances of the title. A better translation would be *The Arrest of Death.* In this rendering, "of" is a double genitive, and, thus, the title suggests both that death is arrested and that death arrests. Such duplicity and ambiguity are crucial for Blanchot and make translating his work almost impossible.

My letter to Blanchot asking to meet with him was a deliberate provocation. Once again, he generously responded (June 29, 1985) with characteristically paradoxical words suggesting the reason he had chosen a life of solitude. He said that he always confided in the written more than the oral, and explained that he lived apart to remain close to those who were close to him. He then encouraged me to see Claude Lanzmann's film *The Shoah* while I was in Paris. The brevity of the letter and the duplicity of the language could have been written by no one other than Maurice Blanchot. Writing/speech, absence/presence, closeness/distance, proximity/remoteness, separation/connection, presence/absence, belatedness, deprivation, remembrance, *l'écart, l'entretien.* Virtually all the themes that preoccupy Blanchot are expressed in a few seemingly simple words. As I have pondered the letters of Updike, Blanchot, and, as we will see, Derrida over the years, they have raised more questions than they have answered about gifts and much else. I count them among my most cherished possessions.

Life After Death

Death obsesses Blanchot; it is not clear, however, whether he pursues death or death pursues, persecutes, chases, hunts, haunts him. Life, he insists, is always life *after* death. In other words, life is lived, on the one hand, in the wake of the death of others as well as the perpetual dying necessary for living, and, on the other hand, life moves toward death, which is always approaching in its perpetual withdrawal. The ambiguity of "after"—subsequent to, and in pursuit of—captures the temporal tension of finite human existence. Always *in medias res,* living transpires betwixt and between an origin that is always already past and a future that is forever *à-venir,* and thus never arrives. Insofar as Blanchot is always after death, he is what Nietzsche described as a "posthumous man." In *Twilight of the Idols,* which, we have seen, was one of his last works, Nietzsche wrote, "Posthumous men—I, for example—are understood worse than timely ones, but *heard* better. More precisely: we are never understood—*hence* our authority."[10] Blanchot, more than Nietzsche, has rarely been understood; indeed, his writing borders on the unreadable because his style—if it is a style—is insistently enigmatic, paradoxical, and strange. It is no exaggeration to say that Blanchot's writings are more mysterious than any I have ever read.

Blanchot's debt to Nietzsche runs deep, but his Nietzsche is not the Nietzsche I presented in the previous chapter. Rather than arguing that unhappy consciousness is overcome through the disappearance of transcendence in immanence, Blanchot's Nietzsche traces the boundary between unhappiness and happiness, which is always imminent but never present. The difference between these two readings of Nietzsche, which might be something like difference "itself," turns on alternative understandings of the eternal return. I have read the eternal return as a radical affirmation that the world, as it is, is what it ought to be; Blanchot, by contrast, argues that the eternal return "hollows out" affirmation in "the affirmation of non-coincidence." In an essay entitled "On a Change of Epoch: The Exigency of Return," Blanchot argues that deferral staged through the eternal return "does not mark the waiting for an opportune moment that would be historically right; it marks the untimeliness of every moment since the return is already detour—or better: since we can only affirm the return as detour that hollows out the affirmation and, in this hollowing out, makes it return from the extreme of itself back to the extreme of itself, not in order to coincide with it, but rather to render it again more affirmative at a mobile point of extreme non-coincidence" (IC, 278). Rather than the full realization of immanence, Blanchot's return inscribes the eternal return of the imminence of all presence and every present. The question of the return will return at the end of this chapter. At this point, it is important to understand that the time of this detour is "the space of writing."

"The Instant of My Death" was not, strictly speaking, Blanchot's last work. In retrospect, however, it is clear that this three-and-a-half-page text and the purported experience it recounts are the *futur antérieur* of everything he wrote. Half a century transpired between the "event," 1944, when Blanchot was thirty-seven, and the work, 1994, when he was eighty-seven. Four years after its initial publication, "The Instant" was reissued with a concluding unscientific postscript, running ninety-three pages, written by Derrida, entitled "Demeure: Fiction and Testimony." The longer I study Blanchot and Derrida, the less certain I am where One ends and the Other begins. Their dialogue becomes what Blanchot describes as "l'entretien infini," the infinite conversation. The margin traced by the *entre* of this *entretien* (*entre*, between + *tenir*, to hold, keep) opens the possibility of writing.

Blanchot's brief story begins with a first-person account of an event that did not take place. Near the end of World War II, the narrator writes, "I remember a young man—a man prevented from dying by death itself—and perhaps the error of injustice." As the tale is spun, the narrator becomes the central character. Though Blanchot remains circumspect, there are hints that the story is autobiographical. At the time of its publication, critics questioned his motives. As I have noted, in his early political writings, Blanchot staked out a right-wing position that led some people to charge him with anti-Semitism. By publishing the work so late in life, Derrida suggests, "One might insinuate that he is exploiting a certain irresponsi-bility of literary fiction in order to pass off, like contraband, an allegedly real testimony, this time not fictional, coming to justify or exculpate in a historical reality the political behavior of an author it is easy to identify with both the narrator and central character. In this space, one can put forward the hy-pothesis that Blanchot intends finally to mark, by means of a fiction so obvi-ously testimonial and autobiographical in appearance (auto-thanatographical in truth), that he is someone the Germans wanted to shoot in a situation where he would visibly have been on the side of the Resistance fighters" (D, 55). While the question of why Blanchot wrote and published "The In-stant" when he did remains unanswerable, its implications for his writing are far-reaching.

At one level, the narrative Blanchot recounts is straightforward; at other levels, it is not. With the Allies gaining ground and the end of the war imminent, the Germans became even more ferocious than they had been. A nameless young man and his family were holed up in a large cha-teau, when there was a knock at the door. Opening the door, the young man heard a Nazi lieutenant scream, "Everyone outside—*Tous dehors*." The young man asked the officer to allow his family to remain inside, and, when the officer agreed, the young man was left to face what seemed to be a cer-tain death alone. The lieutenant ordered his men to line up to form a firing squad. Then, just when they were about to execute the young man, noise from a nearby battle erupted and the soldiers were ordered to rush to the aid of their comrades. With the execution interrupted, one of the soldiers turned to the young man and said, "'We're not Germans, Russians,' and, with a sort of laugh, 'Vlassov army,' and made a sign for him to disappear." Whether this was a cruel joke or a genuine stay of execution, which deferred the inevitable instant of death, the young man felt he had actually "died with-out dying." The closing lines of the story record the lifelong effect of this non-experience of death. "There remained, however, at the moment when the shooting was no longer but to come, the feeling of lightness that I would not know how to translate: freed from life? the infinite opening up? Neither happiness, nor unhappiness. Nor the absence of fear and perhaps already the step/not beyond [*le pas au-delà*]. I know, I imagine that this unanalyzable feeling changed what there remained for him of existence. As if the death outside of him could only henceforth collide with the death in him. 'I am alive. No, you are dead'" (3–9).

Is this story autobiographical? Is it fact or fiction? Truth or a lie? If it is fictive, can it be true? What if the only way to tell what really happened were through fiction? What if truth-sayers are confidence-men who can only tell the truth by lying? Whether autobiographical or not, *après coup*, Blanchot was alive as dead.

Blanchot inserts a seemingly inconsequential "fact" in the midst of his fiction that illuminates the story by unsettling it. "On the façade [of the chateau] was inscribed a date, like an indestructible reminder, the date 1807. Was he cultivated enough to know this was the famous year of Jena, when Napoleon, on his small gray horse, passed under the windows of Hegel, who recognized in him the 'spirit of the world,' as he wrote to a friend? Lie and truth: for as Hegel wrote to another friend, the French pillaged and ransacked his home. But Hegel knew how to distinguish the empirical and the essential" (I, 7). The alleged event to which the date 1807 testifies took place while Hegel was completing his most important work, *Phenomenology of Spirit*, which was published that year. Few works have directly and indirectly influenced so many writers, theologians, philosophers, artists, economists, and politicians. Derrida spoke for several generations of French writers and intellectuals when he wrote in a book tellingly entitled *Positions*, "We will never be finished with the reading or rereading of Hegel, and, in a certain way, I do nothing other than attempt to explain myself on this point."[11] Though not always visible, Hegel's ghost haunts Blanchot. While profoundly indebted to him, his entire oeuvre is designed to resist the closure of Hegel's speculative system. The single passage around which recent French, and, by extension, American literary and critical debates raged is from the preface to the *Phenomenology of Spirit*, which, we have seen, is important for understanding both Kierkegaard's and Nietzsche's work.

But the life of Spirit is not the life that shrinks from death
and keeps itself untouched by devastation, but rather the life

that endures it and maintains itself in it. It wins its truth
only when, in utter dismemberment, it finds itself. It is this
power, not as something positive, which closes its eyes to
the negative, as when we say of something that it is nothing
or is false, and then, having done with it, turn away and pass
on to something else; on the contrary, Spirit is this power only
by looking the negative in the face, and tarrying with it. This
tarrying with the negative is the magical power that converts
it into being.[12]

As I suggested in the previous chapter and we will see in more detail in later
chapters, Hegel's system is a sustained effort to translate Christian religious
images and representations into philosophical concepts. Within this
scheme, personal experience and history *as a whole* become a salvation narrative in which every failure leads to a greater good, and every loss is redeemed. In the introduction to the *Phenomenology,* he describes the path
from the most rudimentary to the most complete form of knowledge as following "the stations of the cross." Just as Jesus's death overcomes death,
so every negation in Hegel's speculative story is negated in and through the
self-realization of Spirit. Crucifixion always leads to resurrection, and,
therefore, the negated is not dead and gone, but lives on as the necessary
condition of what comes after it. In this dialectical process, truth is not confined to a transcendent eternal realm but emerges in space (nature) and
time (history).

In an essay entitled "The Absence of the Book," Blanchot labels
this theological narrative "The Book." In contrast to the work or text, the
Book *presents* a continuous and coherent narrative with a clear beginning,
middle, and end. In every such story, nothing is left out, excluded, or obscure; there is no excess, surplus, or remainder. Commenting on Hegel's
version of the story, Blanchot writes,

. . . with increasing refinement and truth these forms all
assume that the book contains knowledge as the presence of
something virtually present and always immediately accessible;

if only with the help of mediations and relays. Something is there that the book presents in presenting itself and which reading animates, which reading reestablishes—through its animation—in the life of a presence. Something that is, on the lowest level, the presence of a content or a signified thing; then, on a higher level, the presence of a form, of a signifying thing or of an operation; and, on a higher level still, the development of a system of relations that is always already there, if only as a future possibility. The book rolls up time, unrolls time, and contains this unrolling as the continuity of a presence in which present, past, and future become actual. (G, 146)

Blanchot is convinced that the impact of the Book extends far beyond the pages of theological and philosophical works. His entire effort as a writer is to subvert what he regards as the totalizing ideology of the Book. This is why he notes the date 1807 and mentions Hegel by name in his last work, which, in a paradoxically Hegelian way, returns to the beginning of his own oeuvre. Derrida unravels some of the threads that intersect in the tangled lines of Blanchot's *récit*.

The women who leave know, as does the young man, as does the last man and his shadow, witness to a witness, that death has already arrived, because it is inescapable. One is not re-suscitated from this experience of inescapable death, even if one survives it. One can only survive without surviving it. If one wanted to speak here of resurrection through the experi-ence of a Christlike passion (the Germans would be the Ro-mans this time), there would be no Christology, no speculative Good Friday, no truth of religion in the absolute knowledge of Hegel, whose spectral shadow will not be long in passing. But all of this—the Passion, the Resurrection, absolute Knowl-edge—is mimicked, repeated, and displaced. Already in life without life of this *survivance*, henceforth, as it were fictional, all knowledge will tremble, and with it all testimonial statement

in the form of knowledge: "I know—do I know it—," without
question marks. (D, 62–63)

Speculative or Spectral? Two versions of a ghost story—one holy, one
not. The difference between the two—always *l'entre-deux*—is death, the
experience or non-experience of "inescapable death." Surviving without
surviving, life without life, death without death. How is this "without"
(*sans*) to be read? How can it be written? And what provokes this fear and
trembling? Might it be "the gift of death"?

Posthumous Writing

The work of a posthumous man must be posthumous writing. Blanchot,
like Kierkegaard, realized that to be effective, criticism must be indirect;
rather than asserting direct opposition, he exposes inherent faults others
attempt to cover by turning their arguments against them. In crafting his
work, Blanchot always chooses his words very carefully. The title "The Absence of the Book," for example, like everything else he wrote, must be
read in at least two ways. "Of" is a double genitive: first and most obviously,
the absence of the book means that the book is missing, has yet to be found,
or, perhaps, has not yet been written; second, the absence *of* the book is
the absence the book harbors as an inescapable remainder it is constructed
to erase. It is this latter absence that haunts Blanchot and his work.

Blanchot uses different words to suggest an alternative to the
book: work, text, literature, fragment, speech or word (*la parole*), and,
like Derrida, writing. The common characteristic of all these terms is
the suggestion of the incompletion, openness, inadequacy, even failure
of language. Writing, in the strict sense of the term, enacts, stages, or performs its own failure to re-present reality in a coherent narrative. Instead
of presenting his position directly, Blanchot elaborates his interpretation
of writing by exposing the "internal" disruption of the *Phenomenology*'s
purportedly continuous and complete narrative. The argument turns
on the representational capacity of language. While Hegel would not deny
Blanchot's provocative claim that "the word is the death of the thing," he

would interpret it differently. In "Literature and the Right to Death," Blanchot delineates his argument by contrasting it with Hegel's position.

> A word may give me its meaning, but first it suppresses it. For me to be able to say, "This woman," I must somehow take her flesh and blood reality away from her, cause her to be absent, annihilate her. The word gives me the being, but it gives it to me deprived of being. The word is the absence of that being, its nothingness, what is left of it when it has lost being—the very fact that it does not exist. Considered in this light, speaking is a curious right. In a text dating from before *The Phenomenology*, Hegel, here the friend and kindred spirit of Hölderlin, writes, "Adam's first act, which made him master of the animals, was to give them names, that is, he annihilated them in their existence (as existing creatures)." Hegel means that from that moment on the cat ceased to be a uniquely real cat and became an idea as well. The meaning of the word, then, requires that before any word is spoken there must be a sort of immense hecatomb, a preliminary flood plunging all of creation into a total sea. God had created living things, but man had to annihilate them. Not until then did they take on meaning for him, and he in turn created them out of the death into which they had disappeared. (G, 42)

By the time he had developed his speculative system, Hegel believed that the Logos always overcomes death by sublating every absence first in opaque representational images, and then in transparent philosophical concepts. Blanchot, by contrast, insists that death is insurmountable and, therefore, absence is latent in all presence. "When I speak," Blanchot writes, "death speaks in me. My word is a warning that at this very moment death is loose in the world, that it has suddenly appeared between me, as I speak, and the being I address: it is there between us as the distance that separates us, but this distance is also what prevents us from being separated, because it contains the condition for all understanding. Death alone allows me to grasp what I want to attain; it exists in words as the only way they can have meaning. Without death, everything would sink into absurdity and nothingness" (G, 43).

Contrary to expectation, the seeds of Blanchot's (and Derrida's) interpretation of writing can be found at the beginning of the Book of books. Hegel's enormously complex book actually presents a familiar three-part narrative, which is implicit in many of the writers considered in these pages: union—division/fragmentation—re/union; identity—difference/opposition—identity/identity—in difference. Hegel begins the long progression toward Absolute Knowledge with the most rudimentary form of knowledge—sense certainty. In the condition of immediacy, self and world as well as subject and object remain undifferentiated; there is a total immersion in the here-and-now. This original moment can be interpreted theologically as union with God, philosophically as the identity of subject and object as well as accident and substance, and psychologically as union of self and mother. While Hegel realizes that this simplicity, oneness, union, and identity cannot be experienced or comprehended as such, he does not think it is unrepresentable. To explain how what seems to be incomprehensible can nonetheless be comprehended, he proposes a thought experiment.

> It is, then, sense-certainty itself that must be asked: "What is the *This?*" If we take the "This" in the twofold shape of its being as "Now" and as "Here," the dialectic it has in it will receive a form as intelligible as the "This" itself is. To the question: "What is Now?," let us answer, e.g., "Now is Night." In order to test the truth of this sense-certainty a simple experiment will suffice. We write down this truth; a truth cannot lose anything by being written down, any more than it can lose anything through preserving it. If now, this noon, we look again at the written truth we shall have to say that it has become stale.

The Now is never present as such, or in Blanchot's terms, the moment, the instant is only present as absent; it can only be recognized as past. Though intended to present thing in word, writing actually negates the presence of the thing created by the absence of the word. This absence, Hegel proceeds to argue, is overcome because what is negated is preserved in what displaces it. The example he uses to make this point is even more suggestive than he could have realized.

> The Now that is Night is *preserved,* i.e. it is treated as what it professes to be, something that *is;* but it proves itself to be, on the contrary, something that is *not.* The Now does indeed preserve itself, but as something that is *not* Night; equally, it preserves itself in the face of the Day that now is, as something that also is not Day, in other words, as a *negative* in general. This self-preserving Now is, therefore, not immediate but mediated; for it is determined as a permanent and self-preserving Now *through* the fact that something else, viz., Day and Night, is *not.*[13]

But what if, as Nietzsche insists, Midnight is not Midday? What if there is another night, a night that is, paradoxically, within as well as beyond what we ordinarily know as day and night? In this night, Blanchot avers, "absolute darkness is also absolute clarity" (F, 156). Far from familiar, such a night would be forever strange; never reassuring, it would be endlessly fascinating. If day re-marks the beginning in which light dawns ever anew, the night beyond night would be the origin from which day and night, as well as all the differences and oppositions that structure the world, would emerge and to which they would return. Neither light nor dark but something in between, this other night would be the realm of shades that wander and drift but never settle. The darkness of this netherworld could never be dispersed. The light of reason might try to clarify the obscure, but it would always fail to grasp the other night with strict oppositions and precise combinations: either this or that . . . both this and that. Shades always slip away because light inevitably creates shadows. Shades of difference haunt the world, leaving nothing clear or precise—absolutely nothing. If this placeless place and timeless time that always appear by disappearing had a logic, it would be fuzzy. The night beyond yet within night is the space/spacing that simultaneously opens and closes the possibility and impossibility of Blanchot's writing. How can that which cannot be represented be written? Not with words that are proper and sentences that are precise, but, perhaps, with words that are obscure and sentences that are irreducibly ambiguous.

Sometimes the least conspicuous words are the most revealing. Not a noun, not a verb, but a preposition that marks and remarks the pre-position of every word. What does it mean to be a preposition? To be pre-positional? What is placed before? Who is placed before? Does "before" imply a certain after? Does "after" imply a certain before? Might "after" always be "before" what never arrives? Might "before" always be before what is never present? After life. Afterlife. Life without death? Or death without life? Without—*Sans*—With Out. What does it mean to be without? What does it mean to be with out? With a certain outside (*dehors*) that is not precisely outside, but is inside without being appropriated, internalized, incorporated? No word is more important for Blanchot than "without." Derrida correctly argues that this signature trait of Blanchot's style can be traced to the "experience" of dying without dying that the narrator, who presumably is Blanchot himself, recounts in "The Instant of My Death."

> He lives, but he is no longer living. Because he is already dead, it is a life without life. All of the phrases that Blanchot tirelessly forms from the model "X without X" ("to live without living," "to die without dying," "death without death," "name without name," "unhappiness without unhappiness," "being without being," etc.) have their possibility . . . in what happened there, that day, at that actual instant, that is, that henceforth, starting from that stigmatic point, from the *stigma* of a verdict that condemned him to death without death being what ensued, there will be for him, for the young man, for his witness and for the author, a death without death and thus a life without life. Life itself freed from life; one might just as well say that life has been relieved of life. . . . A life without life, an experience of lightness, an instance of "without," a logic without logic of the "X

without X," or of the "not" or of the "except," of the "being without being," etc. (D 88–89)

Blanchot's "without" falls *between* the alternatives of Hegel's dialectic in which opposites are synthesized, and Kierkegaard's dialectic in which opposites paradoxically coincide. *Neither* both/and *nor* either/or, "without" is a repetitious play of give-and-take that recalls the *fort/da* tracing the absent presence and present absence of the mother in Freud's account of the death instinct in *Beyond the Pleasure Principle.* In Blanchot's translation of Freud's insight, the lost origin and the final end are present as absent, and, therefore, every present is "hollowed out" from "within" in such a way that the void that is at once the womb and tomb of human life can never be a-voided. As we will see in the next chapter, Freud argues that the perfect union of Eros and Thanatos marks the inaccessible origin and impossible end of life. Life is a matter of differences that is lived *between* Eros and Thanatos. Since there can be no life without death, life is always lived in the shadow or shade of death. "If we are to speak, we must see death, we must see it behind us. When we speak, we are leaning on a tomb, and the void of the tomb is what makes language true, but at the same time void is reality, and death becomes being. There is being—that is to say, a logical and expressible truth—and there is a world, because we can destroy things and suspend existence. This is why we can say that there is being because there is nothingness: death is man's possibility, his chance, it is through death that the future of a finished world is still there for us; death is man's greatest hope, his only hope of being man" (G, 55).

Every sentence is a death sentence. "When I first begin," Blanchot writes, "I do not speak in order to say something, rather a nothing demands to speak, nothing speaks, nothing finds its being in the word and the being of the word is nothing. This formulation explains why literature's ideal has been the following: to say nothing, to speak to say nothing" (G, 43). For Blanchot, unlike Hegel, there is no recovery from the originary loss. The lack "of" language is not sublated in a "higher" union, but remains as the present absence and absent present of every instant. This insight distinguishes Blanchot's "Instant" from Kierkegaard's "Instant," Nietzsche's

"Midnight/Midday," Melville's "Whiteness," Poe's "Abyss," Woolf's "Moments of Being," and Hemingway's "Now." Never totally present, "*l'instant* is always also *en instance*"—out(-)standing, pending, looming. So understood, the instant is the horizon of life, which, unlike Nietzsche's horizon, can never be swallowed up, though it swallows every One.

The unrecoverable here-and-now, which appears by disappearing, marks and remarks the point of difference. This difference, like Derrida's *différance,* is "the outside's reserve; the outside is the exposition of difference; difference and outside designate the originary disjunction—the origin that is the very disjunction, always disjoined from itself. Disjunction, where time and space would rejoin by their mutual disjoining, coincides with that which does not coincide, the non-coinciding that in advance turns away from all unity" (IC, 161). While Blanchot's language is deliberately obscure, his point is clear. Each instant presupposes a disjunction that differentiates it from every other instant. This disjunction opens an interval or gap that is a spacing, and this spacing implies a strange timing. That is to say, as soon as the instant is here-and-now, it is always also there-and-gone. Forever elusive, what is always missing, lacking, and in default approaches every present by withdrawing from it. The writer is always after this inaccessible before; if his style had a name, it would be "fragmentary."

The Book, we have seen, binds and rebinds past, present, and future in a continuous narrative that tends to be circular.[14] The final aim of the Book is the refusal of death. When every negation is negated, whatever had been lost is re-collected, re-membered in a present that is redemptive. Fragmentary writing, by contrast, is a response to "the exigency of discontinuity." In *The Writing of the Disaster,* Blanchot explains, "Fragmentation, the mark of a coherence all the firmer in that it has to come undone in order to be reached, and reached not through a dispersed system, or through dispersion as a system, for fragmentation is the pulling to pieces (the tearing) of that which never has preexisted (really or ideally) as a whole, nor can it ever be reassembled in any future presence whatever. Fragmentation is the spacing, the separation effected by a temporalization that can only be understood—fallaciously—as the absence of time" (WD, 60). The fragment, then, is not a piece or splinter of a prior whole or totality; whatever is present here-and-now is constituted in its specificity by a differential spacing that inscribes a temporal delay rendering every fragment incomplete. The incessant failure to complete the narrative of history or story of life leads to repeated disappointment for anyone who longs for solutions rather than dissolution. For Blanchot, this failure is the success of writing. Though his understanding of "the work of art" (*l'oeuvre d'art*) differs from his predecessors', Blanchot's fragments recall both Kierkegaard's unphilosophical fragments and Nietzsche's associative aphorisms—they are brief, discontinuous (even when thematically repetitive), and deliberately spaced. The interplay of black words and white space accentuates intervals that language cannot articulate in transparent prose, but without which language remains inarticulate. The task of the posthumous writer is to fashion a style that "does not exclude, but seeks to include the moment of discontinuity: it moves from one term to its opposite, for example, from Being to Nothingness. But what is *between* the two opposites? A nothingness more essential than Nothingness itself—the void of a between, an interval [*Un néant plus essentiel que le Néant même, le vide de l'entre-deux, un intervalle*] that continually hollows itself out and in hollowing itself out becomes distended: the nothing as work [*oeuvre*] and movement" (IC, 7–8). This Nothingness is the refusal *of* death.

Living Death

There is another refusal *of* death—a refusal that does not attempt to master death by resurrecting the dead, but that responds to death's refusal by living death. The question that remains after all is said and done is: How can death be lived day in and day out, in sickness and in health, without succumbing to its terrifying allure? In Blanchot's own words, "The most profound question is this experience of turning away [*détournement*] in the mode of questioning that is foreign, anterior, or posterior to any question. Man is turned toward that which turns away and turns itself away [*est tourne vers cela qui détourne—et se détourne*]" (IC, 24). As always, the issue is time. The time of death is the time of waiting—delay, deferral, detour; the time of life is the interval without arrival, erring without direction (*sens*), expectation without hope. The question of living death turns on the strange logic of "without."

It is time to return to "The Instant of My Death." As we have seen, this *récit* recounts an event that did not take place in which an anonymous young man named only "*il*" "dies without dying." Nothing happened and this nothing completely transformed his life by creating a sense of the unbearable lightness of non-being. It is worth repeating the last words of the narrative. "There remained, however, at the moment when the shooting was no longer but to come, the feeling of lightness that I would not know how to translate: freed from life? the infinite opening up? Neither happiness, nor unhappiness. Nor the absence of fear and perhaps already the step/not beyond [*le pas au-delà*]. I know, I imagine that this unanalyzable feeling changed what there remained for him of existence. As if the death outside of him could only henceforth collide with the death in him. 'I am alive. No, you are dead' " (I, 7–9). Does this fear, which is never absent, provoke a trembling that responds to the exigency of death? And where does *le pas au-delà* take one?

On the first page of *Le pas au-delà* (The step/not beyond), Blanchot answers this question by describing a "time without present." "Time, time: the step not beyond that is not accomplished in time would lead outside of time, without this outside being intemporal, but there where time would fall, fragile fall, according to this 'outside of time in time' towards which writing would attract us, were we allowed, having disappeared from ourselves, to write within the secret of the ancient fear" (PA, 1). This "outside of time in time" is not the interruption of the eternal in the temporal, as in Kierkegaard's *Øjeblikket*, but is the trace of an absolute past that eternally withdraws to release every present instant. This past, which Blanchot describes elsewhere as "terrifyingly ancient," disrupts temporal continuity through a reversal in which it returns as the always out-standing future. To rephrase this important but difficult point: the past that was never present eternally returns as the future that never arrives to disrupt the present that never is. This is why the instant is never the origin or even the beginning, but is always (a) second.

The future of life is undeniably death; but death, Blanchot insists, is impossible or, in terms he borrows from Heidegger, is "the possibility of impossibility" (WD, 70). Rather than providing reassurance of the immortality of the soul, the impossibility of death confirms the inescapable mortality of the individual. At one level, Blanchot's claim seems trivial. I can never die because when death is present, I am not, and when I am present, death is not. At another level, however, his point is infinitely profound. Life is always a matter of survival; that is to say, we are constantly living (*vivre*) on (*sur*) the verge of death. So understood, death is the "limit-experience" that defines life. In *Le pas au-delà,* Blanchot offers a confession that illuminates all of his writing. "In a certain way, and forever, we have known that death was only a metaphor to help us crudely represent the idea of a limit to ourselves, while the limit excludes any representation, any 'idea' of the limit" (PA, 52). To suggest that death is a metaphor is not, of course, to deny its reality. Though death is endlessly deferred, it nonetheless lies *within* life as the condition of life's own possibility. The passing of the present releases the time in which I live and on which the thoughtful "I" dwells. "The very instant of death, which is never present," Blanchot writes, "is the celebration of the absolute future, the instant at which one might say that, in a time without present, what has been will be" (SL, 114). The absolute future is always yet to come (*à-venir*), and thus is absolutely imminent—it approaches without ever arriving and, therefore, must be forever awaited.

Blanchot's most extensive meditation on awaiting (*l'attente,* which means both awaiting and expecting, and suggests *latent* [*latent,* hidden, concealed, secret]) is *Awaiting Oblivion* (*L'Attente l'oubli*). This brief work takes the form of a dialogue between what most interpreters understand to be an anonymous man (*il*) and a nameless woman or women (*elle*[*s*]), which takes place in a typically empty hotel (*hôtel*) room.[15] This work is, however, better read as a monologue of an anonymous man (*il*) and his unavoidable double—death (*LA mort, elle*). Blanchot mixes genders and genres, confuses narrators, and scrambles tenses to create a work that tries to think the unthinkable by thinking death—not thinking about *death,* but thinking death itself. Death speaks through the posthumous writer (and who is

not a posthumous writer?), in a way that makes "what is ungraspable inescapable" (SL, 31). *Elle parle* fragmentarily:

> Waiting waits. Through waiting, he who waits dies waiting. He
> maintains waiting in death and seems to make of death the wait-
> ing for that which is still awaited when one dies.
>
> Death, considered as an event that one awaits, is incapa-
> ble of putting an end to waiting. Waiting transforms the fact of
> dying into something that one does not merely have to attain
> in order to cease waiting. Waiting is what allows us to know that
> death cannot be awaited.
>
> He who lives in a state of waiting sees life come to him as
> the emptiness of waiting and waiting as the emptiness of the
> beyond of life. The unstable indeterminateness of these two
> movements is henceforth the space of waiting. At every step
> [*pas*] one is here, and yet beyond. But as this beyond is reached
> without being reached through death, it is awaited and is not
> reached; without knowing that its essential characteristic is to
> be able to be reached only in waiting.
>
> When there is waiting, nothing is awaited. (O, 27)

To live death is to await nothing unknowingly by remembering the infinite
forgetting of oblivion. The forgetting of oblivion involves both my forgetting death, and death forgetting me. After the death of God, and in the absence of immortality, oblivion, which is absolute forgetting without any
possibility of remembering, awaits everyone. To face death is to confess I
will be absolutely forgotten. Such waiting requires patience, which always
involves suffering. Death and dying expose the radical passivity of all finite human beings. To live is to suffer dying; the most profound suffering is
undergone not only in times of distress, illness, or when the end of life draws
near, but occurs in every passing moment, in every fleeting instant of life.
For Blanchot, this suffering is not redemptive—in the passion of the instant,
resurrection does not follow crucifixion. Life is always after death because
there is no after life.

Even when anticipated, death arrives unexpectedly, like a thief in the night. Patience awaits what can and cannot be controlled; impatience attempts to take control of life by mastering death. The most radical act of impatience is suicide. "By committing suicide I want to kill myself at a determined moment. I link death to now: yes, now, now. But nothing better indicates the illusion, the madness of this 'I want,' for death is never present. There is in suicide a remarkable intention to abolish the future as the mystery of death: one wants in a sense to kill oneself so that the future might hold no secrets, but might become clear and readable, no longer the obscure reserve of indecipherable death. Suicide in this respect does not welcome death; rather, it wishes to eliminate death as future, to relieve death of that portion of the yet-to-come which is, so to speak, its essence, and to make it superficial, without substance and without danger" (SL, 104). Paradoxically, suicide is the denial rather than the affirmation of death.

Always suffered and never mastered, death is (a) given; it cannot be sought but must be awaited patiently. The secret of secrets, which Blanchot repeatedly tells by not telling, is that death is a gift that cannot be returned. In one of the fragments near the end of *Awaiting Oblivion*, Blanchot offers what is, in effect, a comment on "The Instant of My Death." This important passage, like so many in his work, is virtually untranslatable. I will, therefore, cite it first in French and then in English. It is important to recall that I understand this text as a monologue between a man and the death that dwells within him. Rather than read the pronoun "*elle*" as "she," I will read "*elle*" as "it," which refers to *la mort*.

> *Qu'elle attendît l'événement de l'historie même ou elle aurait volu, par la vérité des mots choisis par lui, accéder à une fin dont il fût si responsable qu'elle eût représenté le don de sa mort à lui, c'est ce qu'il apprenait par l'attente, essayant de l'en détourner par l'oubli, par l'attente.*[16]

That it [*elle*] waited for the event of the story itself, where it [*elle*] would have liked, through the truth of the words chosen by him, to arrive at an end for which he would have been so responsible that it would have represented the gift of his death [*le*

don de sa mort], is what he learned through waiting, trying to
turn it [*elle*] away from this end through waiting, through forgetting. (O, 83–84)

In this remarkable fragment, Blanchot transforms death from the dreaded
end of life into a gift whose perpetual non-arrival keeps the future open.
Death not only takes, but also gives life. Contrary to expectation, dying
without dying frees one *for* as well as *from* life. Struggling to explain Blanchot's tortured words, Derrida anticipates his own "gift of death," which
he offered at my urging three years later.

> This "neither immortal nor eternal" might resemble the rever-
> sal of the earlier, sentenceless ellipsis: "dead—immortal." But
> this is not the case at all. The "dead—immortal" did not in the
> least signify eternity. The immortality of death is anything save
> the eternity of the present. The abidance that we will discuss
> does not *remain* like the permanence of an eternity. It is time
> itself. This non-philosophical and non-religious experience of
> immortality *as death* gives without rupturing solitude, in the
> ecstasy itself: it gives compassion for all mortals, for all humans
> who suffer; and the happiness, this time, of not being immor-
> tal—or eternal. At this instant there can be elation, the lightness
> in the immortality of death, happiness in compassion, a shar-
> ing of finitude, a friendship with finite beings, in the happiness
> of not being immortal or eternal. (D, 69)

Unhappy consciousness is not overcome by the temporal becoming eternal
in *Øjeblikket,* but is transformed into the restless happiness that comes with
the final acceptance of the inescapability of human finitude and mortality.

Ghosts

Sigmund Freud (1856–1939): *Moses and Monotheism,*
Beyond the Pleasure Principle

> But having a place nowhere, having no stable place, no *topos* outside the
> survivors, the image or memory of the dead one become ubiquitous, he or she
> invades the whole space and the whole time, which are purely interiorized
> (in the form of an absolutely pure and not empirically determined sensibility).
> The dead one is both everywhere and nowhere, nowhere because everywhere,
> out of the world and everywhere in the world and in us.
>
> —Jacques Derrida, *The Beast and the Sovereign,* II

To Stay or to Leave?

Freud's Last Session is a play by Mark St. Germain staged as dialogue on the
question of God between Christian apologist C. S. Lewis and apparent non-
believer Freud. The exchange takes place on September 3, 1939. Having finally fled Vienna for London a year earlier, Freud is eighty-three, and in
twenty days will be dead; Lewis, a veteran of World War I, is visiting from
Oxford. The play opens with a BBC announcer reporting Prime Minister
Neville Chamberlain's ultimatum that all German troops must be immediately withdrawn from Poland. Sounding more like a U.S. president than a
British prime minister, Chamberlain concludes his remarks, "Now may
God bless you all. May He defend the right. It is the evil things that we
shall be fighting against—brute force, bad faith, injustice, oppression and
persecution—and against them I am certain that the right will prevail."
Freud responds,

FREUD. I thank your God who "blesses" me with cancer I won't be here to see another. (*The phone rings.*) Excuse me. (*Picks it up.*) Yes? I heard . . . No; give your lecture, your students will need you . . . Doctor Schur will be here in half an hour . . . Who could rest now? Good. We'll talk then. (*Freud hangs up.*) My daughter Anna. I underestimated Hitler. I thought he would be satisfied after brutalizing Austria.

LEWIS. How long ago did you leave?

FREUD. A year and four months. The brownshirts broke down our door to arrest me; take me in for questioning. Anna insisted I was too sick, that she would go in my place. I refused, but they took her anyway. Twelve hours she was gone. Twelve hours I was certain I had lost her. When she was released I bribed everyone necessary to leave the country immediately. But it took near tragedy for me to see Hitler for the monster he is.[1]

The question is not why Freud stayed in Vienna so long, but why he finally left. Why didn't he stay longer and suffer martyrdom at the hands of the Nazis? That surely would have secured his legacy, which was his primary concern during the last years, months, weeks, and days of his life. He was old, very old, and sick, very sick. More than thirty operations for cancer of the mouth and still counting. The Nazis had been harassing the father of the "Jewish science" of psychoanalysis, even going so far as to publicly burn his books. When brownshirts had wanted to take him in for questioning, and who knows what else, Anna would not hear of it, and insisted on going in his place. A very Freudian story of substitution, but with an important twist—the daughter, not the son, takes the father's place, thereby transforming the story of Oedipus into the story of Antigone. Anna and Antigone will return at the end of the story.

What kind of a father lets his daughter go in his place to what might well have been a brutal death? Perhaps a father who was so obsessed with his legacy that he could not stop writing even as cancer ravaged his body and war raged throughout the world. Was leaving Vienna at the last moment a strategic mistake? Might his legacy have been better served by an act of martyrdom? But how would such a death be understood? Would it be a generous act of self-sacrifice, or a calculated act of self-interest? What if the death of the father is not murder but suicide? Might the story of Freud's life be better understood as a Christian rather than a Jewish story?

In his last work, *Moses and Monotheism,* Freud retells the story of Moses through the paradigmatic Christian story—the death and resurrection of Jesus. His concern is less about the past of the foundational religions of the West than about the future of his personal reputation and the psychoanalytic movement he founded. In Freud's version of the Christian story, the death of the father leads not to the redemption of murderous sons, but to the survival of a father who becomes more powerful in death than he had been in life.[2]

In 1900, the year Nietzsche died, Freud purchased his collected works but confessed thirty-one years later, "I have rejected the study of Nietzsche although—no, because—it was plain that I would find insights in him very similar to psychoanalytic ones."[3] Freud and Nietzsche's lives intersected indirectly at several points. In addition to their mutual involvement with the enigmatic Lou Andreas-Salomé, in 1882, Freud referred his famous patient Anna O to the Swiss psychiatrist Robert Binswanger, who worked at the Bellevue Sanatorium, where Otto Binswanger would treat Nietzsche seven years later.[4] Freud obviously realized that he and Nietzsche were preoccupied with many of the same issues. Though Freud's bourgeois family life seemed more settled than Nietzsche's itinerant solitary life, they shared a sense of deep inward division and persistent outward conflict that fueled their work. In the midst of a global cataclysm and with death fast approaching, Freud was compelled to ask a final question: If God is dead and the soul is not immortal, is there any prospect for life after death? *Moses and Monotheism* represents his attempt to answer this question.

Freud wrote his last work in the midst of traumatic political and personal circumstances. He was born in the Pribor in what is now the Czech Republic on May 6, 1859, and died in London on September 13, 1939, twelve days after Hitler invaded Poland, launching World War II. Freud's father, Jacob, was a wool merchant, and his mother, Amalia, was Jacob's third wife and twenty years his younger. Jacob had two sons from his first marriage, and he and Amalia had five daughters and two sons other than Sigmund, or Sigismund Schlomo, as he was formally named. The complex dynamics of this extended family with such significant age differences provided ample material for Freud's later investigations. Members of Jacob's family were Hassidic Jews, but he did not raise his children in a religious household. Nevertheless, he insisted that his son should know biblical history and become familiar with Jewish customs. On Freud's thirty-fifth birthday, Jacob gave his son his own bible with the inscription, "It was the seventh year of your age that the spirit of God began to move you to learning."

Financial difficulties forced the family to move first to Leipzig, and then to Vienna in 1869. Freud always had ambivalent feelings about Vienna, which he described at various times throughout his life as "disgusting," "abominable," and "oppressive." And yet, it was very difficult for him to leave the city even when the political situation became impossibly difficult. Looking back from his place of exile at the end of his life, he confessed, "one had still very much loved the prison from which one has been released."[5] The prison bars that held Freud captive were both personal and political. From his earliest days, his life and work were haunted by death. His brother Julius, who was only seventeen months younger than Freud, died in infancy. In later years, his interpretation of the rage he had felt at his brother's death and guilt he experienced when he died became one of the cornerstones of his psychoanalytic theory. Many other deaths followed: parents, siblings, aunts, uncles, nieces, nephews, and Sophie—above all, his beloved daughter, Sophie. Some of these deaths were natural, some were suffered in Nazi concentration camps, and some were suicides. The constant and often unexpected presence of death in life eventually forced Freud to think beyond the pleasure principle.

When Freud entered the University of Vienna at the age of seventeen, he intended to study law rather than science, though he was always interested in philosophy and especially literature. He was drawn to the writings of Friedrich Schiller, and even went so far as to suggest that his mature theory of the drives could be traced to Schiller's analysis of "hunger and love." At the university, Freud studied with the influential German philosopher Franz Brentano, and carefully read the work of the post-Hegelian philosopher Ludwig Feuerbach, whose books *The Essence of Christianity* and *The Essence of Religion* anticipated many of Freud's arguments about religion. While Freud eventually became committed to the principle of scientific empiricism, his lifelong interest in literature, art, and philosophy deeply influenced his work. He admitted to Wilhelm Fleiss, "I knew no longing other than that for philosophical insight, and I am now in the process of fulfilling it, as I steer from medicine over to psychology."[6] It is not a surprise that in 1930, Freud was awarded the prestigious Goethe Prize for literature.

After completing university, Freud began research on aphasia and cocaine at the Vienna General Hospital, but when it became clear that anti-Semitism made a university career impossible, he decided to start a private practice. The same year, he married Martha Bernays, with whom he had five children—three sons and two daughters. It was a typical bourgeois family for the time, with Martha attending to domestic matters and protecting her husband from responsibilities that would distract him from his work. Their relation was cordial but not particularly intimate; indeed, after the birth of their last child, Anna (1895), they ceased sexual relations. By the time of Freud's death, Anna, the favored daughter after Sophie's death (1920), had replaced Martha as the woman at the center of his life.

Austria had a long history of anti-Semitism, which became much worse during Freud's lifetime. Political problems were compounded by financial uncertainties. Stock market crashes in 1873 and 1929 not only created enormous economic challenges, but also unleashed outbreaks of virulent anti-Semitism. In a refrain that is painfully familiar, conspiracy theorists blamed a cabal of Jewish bankers for the global financial woes. When the Austrian kroner lost 19/20 of its value, bread and meat disappeared from shops, and everyone suffered, but none more than Jews. Economic hardship and religious and cultural repression, however, were not the whole story. As Carl Schorske explains in his seminal *Fin-de-Siècle Vienna,* the end of the nineteenth and beginning of the twentieth century was also a time of enormous artistic and cultural creativity. The Sessions, Oskar Kokoschka, Otto Wagner, George Stefan, Robert Musil, Adolf Loos, Hugo von Hofmannsthal, Gustav Mahler, and Gustav Klimt all lived and worked in Vienna during this period. Vienna appeared to be an extraordinarily vital modern cosmopolitan city, and this is precisely what made the impending cataclysm so incomprehensible.

With Fascism on the rise and Hitler pressuring Austria to join the Reich, Freud's position in Vienna became increasingly tenuous. Yet even when he became more pessimistic about the political situation, he resisted leaving the city where he had lived and worked for most of his life. As late as 1937, he was still not convinced that Austria would capitulate. "I do not believe that Austria left to itself would degenerate into Nazism. That is the difference over against Germany that, as a rule, is neglected."[7] For a while, Chancellor Kurt von Schuschnigg attempted to avoid the inevitable by following a policy of accommodation. Even more surprising, the Catholic Church, which in earlier days Freud had criticized for its anti-Semitic tendencies, offered effective resistance before reverting to old prejudices. In the end, Freud's assessment of his homeland proved tragically mistaken. On March 11, Schuschnigg was forced to resign and was replaced by Arthur Seyss-Inquart, who was a member of the Austrian Nazi party. The next day, Hitler invaded Austria and met no resistance; indeed, Austrians proved to be at least as violently anti-Semitic as the Germans. "Incidents in the streets of Austrian cities and villages right after the German invasion," Peter Gay explains, "were more outrageous than those Hitler's Reich had yet witnessed. The obscene anti-Semitic slanders of such Nazi journals as the *Stürmer,* the regulations restricting Germany's Jews in their practice of professions, the Nuremberg racial laws of late 1935, the villages proudly advertising that they were 'clean of Jews'—*Judenrein*—were giving Germany's Jews a foretaste of hell. But they had suffered comparatively little of the kind of wholesale random violence that spread across Austria after the Anschluss: Austria in March 1938 was a dress rehearsal for the German pogroms of November."[8] The situation became so bad that during the spring of 1938 more than five hundred Jews committed suicide. When Anna proposed suicide as an alternative to suffering at the hands of the Nazis, Freud defiantly rejected it. Later that year, his colleague Otto Binswanger sent a coded message to Freud encouraging him to immigrate to Switzerland. The pressure on Freud was building, but, once again, he delayed leaving. He did, however, start to make plans for his departure by illegally transferring funds to foreign banks.

Reichsführer Heinrich Himmler urged the arrest of Freud and his followers but was dissuaded by Hermann Göring. Nevertheless, the Gestapo invaded Freud's office and home, held his son, Martin, for a day, and searched Freud's personal files as well as the editorial office for the International Psychoanalytic Association. A week later, the brownshirts returned to arrest and question Anna. After what Freud described as the worst day of his life, Anna was released through what seems to have been back-channel negotiations. Freud had had enough and decided it was time to leave Austria.

While the world was collapsing around him, Freud's health was rapidly deteriorating. He always worried about illness, old age, and death. Though he lived to be eighty-three, Freud was always convinced he would die at the age of sixty-two. When he was thirty-eight, he confessed to Fleiss that he was possessed by "my death deliria." His erstwhile student Karl Abraham visited him in 1907 and reported "unfortunately, old-age seems to obsess him." What the Danes call "round birthdays" especially unsettled him. At fifty, he was preoccupied with "dark thoughts of decrepitude," even though he was in good health, and at sixty, he announced he was entering dotage.[9] By the time he actually was old, dread of the ills age brings transformed his fear into a longing for death. On his eightieth birthday, he wrote to Austrian novelist Stefan Zweig, "I cannot reconcile myself to the wretchedness and helplessness of being old, and look forward to the transition into nonbeing with a kind of longing."[10] We will see in the next section that Freud eventually concluded that the attraction of dying he felt during his final years is one of two basic drives in life. Strangely, the fixation on his own decline and death did not deter Freud from smoking, or move him to seek timely medical care for life-threatening illness. Like any true addict, Freud placed more importance on cigars than on life itself. He periodically attempted to quit, but continued smoking until he was eighty-one. During some periods of his life, Freud smoked as many as twenty cigars a day, and, when doctors had to wire together his diseased bones, he went so far as to pry open his jaws with a clothespin so he could squeeze a cigar into his mouth. In an exercise of typical Freudian ambivalence, he constantly courted the very death he desperately wanted to avoid.

While his strategies of avoidance were endless, they were, of course, futile. In February 1923, Freud began a struggle with cancer that would take his life sixteen years later. When he had detected a growth on his palate six years earlier, he chose to ignore it. When the growth flared up again, Freud was convinced it was cancerous, but kept his condition secret because he feared doctors would make him give up cigars. "Smoking," he nonetheless confessed, "is accursed as the etiology of this tissue rebellion." His physician, Felix Deutsch, eventually discovered the growth and, like Freud, diagnosed it as malignant epithelioma. Concerned about upsetting his famous patient, Deutsch told Freud that the growth was a leukoplakia, which was benign. Rather than seeking the advice of a specialist, Freud turned to a rhinologist named Marcus Hajek about whom he had previously expressed reservations. Peter Gay explains, "His choice—the mistake—was, as his daughter Anna said years later, Freud's alone. In the end, Hajek fully justified Freud's doubts. He knew the procedure he was recommending was merely cosmetic and really pointless, and casually performed the surgery in the outpatient department of his own clinic. Only Felix Deutsch accompanied Freud, and he did not stay through the operation; it was as though by treating the matter as a bagatelle he could wish away Freud's cancer."[11] Wishes to the contrary notwithstanding, Freud's condition remained so extremely serious that Hajek's incompetence almost cost Freud his life. In the weeks following the surgery, Freud continued to deceive himself and lie to others, but he knew the truth. His depression deepened when his favorite grandson, Heinele, contracted tuberculosis and died. After his colleague Binswanger lost his son, Freud wrote to him, "since Heinele's death, I no longer care for my grandchildren, but also take no pleasure in life. This is also the secret of the indifference—people have called it bravery—toward the danger to my own life."[12]

When more traces of cancer were found and additional operations were necessary, Freud could no longer deny the undeniable. So much tissue had to be removed from his mouth and jaw that he had to be fitted with an oral prosthesis, which he wore for the rest of his life. Though the cancer did not return until 1936, Freud had to undergo more than thirty minor operations for precancerous lesions. Continuing medical problems and constant pain did not prevent him from maintaining a busy schedule of seeing patients and writing. However, physical frailty and the rapidly deteriorating political situation soon drove Freud to the breaking point. On June 4, 1938, he and his family departed Vienna for London by way of Paris.

Freud remained ambivalent about leaving Austria up to the end. Even though he insisted on bringing eighteen adults and six children with him, he was forced to leave behind four sisters to face an uncertain fate. Freud's escape involved political intrigue reaching to the highest levels of the French and United States governments. William Bullitt, with whom Freud had co-authored an essay on Woodrow Wilson, was the American ambassador to France at the time. Bullitt had been monitoring Freud's situation for months, and when it reached the crisis point, he persuaded President Roosevelt to intervene with German authorities on Freud's behalf. With the President's backing, the U.S. State Department pressured Germany to release Freud, insisting that to force a person of his stature to die in captivity and make him a martyr would cause widespread outrage that would create political problems. In spite of such extraordinary diplomatic efforts, Freud continued to resist leaving as late as March 1939. Ernest Jones reports that Freud insisted "he could not leave his native land; it would be like a soldier deserting his post."[13] But when the Gestapo detained Anna, Freud finally gave in and left Vienna "to die in freedom." Even after this decision, Freud would not have been able to escape certain death without the support of his former patient Princess Marie Bonaparte, the great-granddaughter of Napoleon, who went on to write *The Life and Works of Edgar Allan Poe: A Psycho-analytic Interpretation*. When the Gestapo tried to block Freud's release, she met the Nazis' financial demands, thereby removing the last obstacle for the departure of Freud and his family.

In London, Freud was received as the celebrity he always secretly longed to be. People sent him letters from all over England, and autograph seekers even sought him out. After moving to Maresfield Gardens, he received visitors, the most noteworthy of whom were Leonard and Virginia

Woolf. The Woolfs' Hogarth Press had published English translations of Freud's works for years. Leonard, who was Jewish, surely appreciated the difficulties Freud and his family had faced. Indeed, when he and Virginia feared a Nazi takeover of England, they had developed a detailed plan to commit suicide together. Leonard recognized the strength Freud's perseverance required, and, after their visit, commented, "He was extraordinarily courteous in a formal, old-fashioned way—for instance, almost ceremoniously he presented Virginia with a flower. There was something about him as of a half-extinct volcano, something sober, suppressed, reserved. He gave me the feeling which only a very few people whom I have met gave me, a feeling of great gentleness, but behind the gentleness, great strength."[14] Virginia was less generous in her response to Freud.

> *Sunday 29 January*
> Dr Freud gave me a narcissus. Was sitting in a great library with little statues at a large scrupulously tidy shiny table. We like patients on chairs. A screwed up shrunk very old man: with a monkey's light eyes, paralyzed spasmodic movements, inarticulate: but alert. On Hitler. Generation before the poison will be worked out. About his books. Fame? I was infamous rather than famous. Didn't make £ 50 by his first book. Difficult talk. An interview. Daughter & Martin helped. Immense potential, I mean an old fire now flickering. When we left he took up the stand What are *you* going to do? The English—war.[15]

By the time the Woolfs visited Freud, he was in the final stage of his struggle with cancer. A few months earlier, his surgeon had come from Vienna to operate on Freud yet again. When his physician Hans Pichler recommended another radium and X-ray regimen, Freud doubted it was worth it. "I don't deceive myself about the chances of the final result at my age. I feel tired and exhausted by all that they do to me. As a way to the unavoidable end it is as good as any other although I would not have chosen it myself."[16] By early September 1939, England was under attack. The air raid

sirens that are the background for Woolf's *Between the Acts* continually interrupted daily life at Maresfield Gardens. In 1929 during his first appointment with his physician Max Schur, Freud asked him, "Promise me
also: when the time comes, you won't let them torment me unnecessarily."[17]
On September 21, 1939, the time had come. Freud asked Schur to fulfill
his promise, and after consulting with Anna, who initially resisted, they
agreed to his request. When Schur injected Freud with an overdose of morphine, Freud lapsed into a coma from which he never awoke. Two days
later, the father of psychoanalysis died; the unrecorded cause of death—
suicide.

Death as Love as Death

The twentieth century began with the publication of Freud's *The Interpretation of Dreams* on November 4, 1899, and Nietzsche's death on August 25, 1900. While dreams had been the subject of speculation since
ancient times, Freud's innovation was to claim to have developed a scientific method for their interpretation. The cornerstone of his argument is the
principle of wish fulfillment. Our deepest wishes, he argues, are our most
ancient desires, which are hidden deep in our personal and collective unconscious. For Freud, as for Kierkegaard, Nietzsche, and Melville, the self
is inwardly divided; there is an "other" within that can only speak indirectly. Every person wears a mask that reveals his or her most inward desires by concealing them. These desires, which cannot be expressed
directly, must be disguised through a process Freud labels dream-work.
This analysis presupposes a distinction between the latent and the manifest
content of the dream. The latent content constitutes dream thoughts, which
are a person's true desires, and the manifest content represents disguised
wishes. To explain how dreams are formed, Freud uses the analogy of linguistic translation.

> The dream-thoughts and the dream-content are presented to
> us like two versions of the same subject-matter in two different
> languages. Or, more properly, the dream-content seems like a

transcript of the dream-thoughts into another mode of expression, whose characters and syntactic laws it is our business to discover by comparing the original and the translation. The dream-thoughts are immediately comprehensible, as soon as we have learnt them. The dream-content, on the other hand, is expressed as it were in a pictographic script, the characters of which have to be transposed individually into the language of the dream-thoughts. If we attempted to read these characters according to their pictorial value instead of according to their symbolic relation, we should clearly be led into error.

While dream-work translates unconscious dream-thoughts into conscious dream-content, dream interpretation reverses this process by retranslating the manifest into the latent content. However, even if one knows the "syntactic laws" of dream-work, interpretation always remains incomplete and, thus, is endlessly revisable because, Freud admits, "There is at least one spot in every dream at which it is unplumbable—a navel, as it were, that is its point of contact with the unknown."[18]

    This account of *how* dreams are formed does not explain *why* they are formed. In his constant effort to secure the scientific status of his argument, Freud borrows the principle of equilibrium from physics. The personality, he argues, is, in effect, a negative feedback system that operates through the redistribution of energy known as libido. Since our most primitive desires are at odds with the social reality in which people live, satisfaction must be indirect and can only be partial; in different terms, full satisfaction is endlessly deferred. Dreams function as a release valve or tension-reduction mechanism that restores a semblance of balance to the personality for a brief time. The deferral of complete satisfaction inevitably leads to the further accumulation of tension, which must be repeatedly released. Pleasure, according to Freud, is a negative rather than a positive experience; in the simplest terms possible, pleasure results from the reduction of tension in the personality, and displeasure results from the increase in tension. "In the theory of psychoanalysis," Freud explains, "we have no hesitation in assuming that the course taken by mental events is automatically regulated by the pleasure principle. We believe, that is to say, that the course of those events is invariably set in motion by an unpleasurable tension, and that it takes a direction such that its final outcome coincides with the lowering of that tension—that is, with the avoidance of unpleasure or the production of pleasure."[19] At the time Freud wrote *The Interpretation of Dreams,* he thought not only dreams but all of life could be explained in terms of the pursuit of pleasure and the avoidance of displeasure. Then death intervened in his personal life and analytic practice as well as world politics, and everything changed.

Freud's death delirium was exacerbated by personal suffering, family deaths, and two world wars. During and after World War I, some of his patients recounted dreams in which they relived traumatic experiences from their past. This seemed to contradict the interpretation of dreams as fulfillment of wishes that are the expression of the pleasure principle. Fearing his entire theory was wrong, Freud fell into a deep depression, but, after further reflection, he revised his analysis to incorporate the new data. In 1920, he published the results in *Beyond the Pleasure Principle.* "It is clear that the greater part of what is re-experienced under the compulsion to repeat must cause the ego unpleasure, since it brings to light activities of repressed instinctual impulses. That, however, is unpleasure of a kind we have already considered and does not contradict the pleasure principle: unpleasure for one system and simultaneously satisfaction for the other. But we come now to a new and remarkable fact, namely that the compulsion to repeat also recalls from the past experiences which include no possibility of pleasure, and which can never, even long ago, have brought satisfaction even to instinctual impulses which have since been repressed." Rather than producing pleasure by reducing tension, dreams that repeat traumatic experiences actually increase tensions. "These dreams," Freud explains, "are endeavoring to master the stimulus retrospectively, by developing the anxiety whose omission was the cause of the traumatic neurosis. They thus afford us a view of the function of the mental apparatus which, though it does not contradict the pleasure principle, is nevertheless independent of it and seems to be more primitive than the purpose of gaining pleasure and avoiding unpleasure." And then he adds two crucial sentences that changed the entire course of psychoanalysis. "This would seem to be the place, then, at which to admit for the first time an exception to the proposition that dreams are fulfillments of wishes. . . . If there is a 'beyond the pleasure principle,' it is only consistent to grant that there was also a time before the purpose of dreams was the fulfillment of wishes."[20] Since Freud always associated the primitive with the foundational, the admission that there is something more original than the pleasure principle required a rethinking of the entire operation of the psychic apparatus.

As I have noted, Freud was very concerned to establish the legitimacy of psychoanalysis. But his lifelong fascination with philosophy, religion, and literature often led him to elaborate his "scientific" findings in mythological, philosophical, and even theological speculations. His most interesting works are his most speculative: *Totem and Taboo, Civilization and Its Discontents, Beyond the Pleasure Principle,* and *Moses and Monotheism.* At the crucial moment when he thought his theoretical edifice was crumbling, he turned to philosophers for guidance—Schopenhauer, Schiller, and above all, Plato. In the final pages of *Beyond the Pleasure Principle,* Freud suggests that his revised theory is, in effect, a reinterpretation of Plato's myth of origins. This passage is important for Freud's argument, and illuminates other writers I am considering in this book. Commenting on Plato's account of the origin of the sexual instinct in the *Symposium,* he writes, "Shall we follow the hint given us by the poet-philosopher, and venture upon the hypothesis that living substance at the time of its coming to life was torn apart into small particles, which have ever since endeavored to reunite through the sexual instincts? That these instincts, in which the chemical affinity of inanimate matter persisted, gradually succeeded, as they developed through the kingdom of the protista, in overcoming the difficulties put in the way of that endeavor by an environment charged with dangerous stimuli—stimuli which compelled them to form a cortical layer? that these splintered fragments of living substance in this way attained a multicellular condition and finally transferred the instinct for reuniting, in the most highly concentrated form, to the germ-cells?—But here, I think the moment has come for breaking off."[21]

Freud's psychoanalytic theory reinscribes the most ancient myth in the Western philosophical and theological tradition. This narrative has three parts: primal unity or identity, division or fragmentation, and reunion or recovery. Originally self/world and subject/object are one; the world as we know it emerges through a process of differentiation that eventually leads to opposition and conflict. The goal of life is to recover unity or one-ness by overcoming the tensions created by unreconciled differences and oppositions. This process ends with the return of organic life to inorganic matter. Though this story has many versions, the plot is always the same: Unity—Division—Unity; One—Many—One; Identity—Difference—Identity.

Until he encountered the repetition compulsion associated with traumatic experience, Freud's analysis had been governed by two closely related binaries—conscious/unconscious and pleasure principle/reality principle. He now adds a third, which complicates the other two—Eros/Thanatos. In Freud's rendering of the Platonic myth of origins, the Greek gods reappear as instincts, which, he explains, are "the representatives of all the forces originating in the interior of the body and transmitted to the mental apparatus." Instincts are essentially conservative or, in Freud's words, "an instinct is an urge to restore an earlier state of things." Organic development is not regulated simply by internal mechanisms, but also by the function of external influences. This leads to a regressive rather than a progressive view of human and historical development. "Those instincts are therefore bound to give a deceptive appearance of being forces tending towards change and progress, whilst the fact that they are merely seeking to reach an ancient goal by paths alike old and new. . . . It must be an *old* state of things, an initial state from which the living entity has at one time or another departed and to which it is striving to return by the circuitous paths along which no development leads. If we are to take it as a truth that knows no exception that everything dies for *internal* reasons—becomes inorganic once again—then we shall be compelled to say that *'the aim of all life is death'* and, looking backwards, that *'inanimate things existed before living ones.'*"

Freud was acutely aware of the possible criticisms of his theory. He was especially concerned that his interpretation of the death instinct seems at odds with Darwin's account of the survival of the fittest. In an effort to reconcile apparently opposite positions, he argues, "The hypothesis of self-preservative instincts, such as we attribute to all living beings, stands in marked opposition to the idea that instinctual life as a whole serves to bring about death. Seen in this light, the theoretical importance of the instincts of self-preservation, of self-assertion and of mastery greatly diminishes. They are component instincts whose function is to assure that the organism shall follow its own path to death, and to ward off any possible ways of return to inorganic existence other than those which are immanent in the organism itself. . . . What we are left with is the fact that the organism wishes to die in its own fashion. Thus, these guardians of life, too, were originally the myrmidons of death." It was precisely the wish to die in his own fashion that led Freud to ask Schur to promise to aid in his suicide when the time came.

As soon as Freud advances this argument, he seems to withdraw it. "But let us pause for a moment and reflect. It cannot be so. The sexual instincts, to which the theory of neuroses gives a quite special place, appear under a very different aspect." The sexual instincts, he concludes, are "the true life instincts. They operate against the purpose of the other instincts, which leads by reason of their function, to death. . . . It is as though the life of the organism moved with a vacillating rhythm. One group of instincts rushes forward so as to reach the final aim of life as swiftly as possible; but when a particular stage in the advance has been reached, the other group jerks back to a certain point to make a fresh start and so prolong the journey." With this additional revision, the internal oppositions dividing the self are compounded. In contrast to his erstwhile student Carl Jung, who espoused a "monistic" instinct theory, Freud proposes a "dualistic" instinct theory. Not only is there an opposition between consciousness and unconsciousness, but the unconscious itself is divided by two instincts that are constantly at war with each other.

Freud still was not satisfied with this solution. "We started out from the great opposition between the life and death instincts. Now object-love itself presents us with a second example of a similar polarity—that between love (or affection) and hate (or aggressiveness). If only we could succeed in deriving one from the other!"[22] It is important to understand that he is not proposing a reversion to instinctual monism, but is moving toward what can best be described as a dialectical relationship of opposites. At the furthest extreme, opposites are inverted and each becomes its own other. In other words, Thanatos becomes Eros and Eros becomes Thanatos. In quest of one's own death, Thanatos is temporally deferred by being deflected outward in the form of aggression. Hostility toward the other, however, is at the same time identification with the other. When mutual aggression culminates in what Hegel describes as "the struggle to death," two become one. At this point, manifest hate is revealed as latent love. In a similar manner, the self-preservation of Eros presupposes the loss of individuality in the union represented in the child. Hegel once again anticipates Freud. "What in the first instance is most the individual's own is united into the whole in the lovers' touch and contact; consciousness of a separate self disappears, and all distinction between the lovers is annulled. The mortal element, the body, has lost the character of separability, and a living child, the seed of immortality, of the eternally self-developing and self-generating [race], has come into existence. What has been united [in the child] is not divided again."[23] When Eros and Thanatos become one, the circle of life closes. For Freud, however, such closure can only be approached asymptotically; life is lived *between* an original and a final unity. Since unity, harmony, and wholeness are always elsewhere, the Freudian subject is what Hegel describes as unhappy consciousness, and Nietzsche labels nihilistic.

Surviving God

Freud was obsessed with religion. Though he was a confirmed atheist, psychoanalysis can be read as a secularized theology developed to ensure survival after the death of God. The culmination of his theological speculations is *Moses and Monotheism,* whose original title was *Moses the Man and the Monotheistic Religion.* Uncertain of the historical accuracy and scientific validity of his argument, Freud considered giving his last work the subtitle "A Historical Novel." During the final six years of his life, he admitted this book "haunted me like an unlaid ghost."[24] It is important to recall the extraordinarily difficult personal and political circumstances in which Freud wrote *Moses and Monotheism.* With his health failing and the

Nazis closing in, Freud continued to write with a perseverance that is nothing less than amazing. Gay notes, "In early May 1935, [Freud] reported to Arnold Zweig that he was neither smoking nor writing, but that 'Moses' will not let my imagination go.' The project, he confessed, to [Max] Eitingon a few days later, 'has become a fixation with me.' He added, 'I cannot get away from him and further with him.' "[25] In his final months, he was still a man possessed even though he could never be sure what possessed him.

Freud realized that some people would consider his argument about Moses an attack on religion or even anti-Semitic. Many colleagues and critics urged him to withhold publication, but Freud persisted. He begins the book by acknowledging these concerns: "To deny a people the man whom it praises as the greatest of its sons is not a deed to be undertaken lightheartedly—especially by one belonging to that people." But he continues, "No consideration, however, will move me to set aside truth in favor of supposed national interests" (3). The political situation in Europe during the 1930s further complicated the decision of whether or not to publish the book. Quite unexpectedly, the Catholic Church emerged for a brief period as a protective shield against Germany's "reversion to barbarism." "We are living here in a Catholic country under the protection of that Church, uncertain how long the protection will last. So long as it does last I naturally hesitate to do anything that is bound to awaken the hostility of that Church. It is not cowardice, but caution; the new enemy [i.e., National Socialism]—and I shall guard against anything that would serve his interests—is more dangerous than the old one, with whom we have learned to live in peace" (67–68). After Germany invaded Austria, however, the Catholic Church flipped and started persecuting rather than protecting Jews. When Freud finally fled Austria for London, he was at last free to complete the book he knew would provoke a hostile response.

With his health failing and death approaching, Freud became even more concerned about his legacy and the future of the psychoanalytic movement. There can be little doubt that one of the reasons for his obsession with Moses was that he saw his own fate reflected in the life and death of the father of the Jewish religion. Just as Moses was killed by followers who were unable to accept the rigors of the new religion he sought to impose, so Freud worried about suffering rejection at the hands of rebellious sons whose discipline he created. For all his concern about authoritarianism in politics, he was much less worried about his own authoritarianism in the psychoanalytic movement. At one point, he went so far as to claim that any textual deviation from the words of the master are tantamount to murder. "In its implications the distortion of a text resembles a murder: the difficulty is not in perpetrating the deed, but in getting rid of its traces."[26]

Freud begins his analysis of Moses by posing the question of the role of "The Great Man" in history. "How is it possible," he asks, "that one single man can develop such extraordinary effectiveness, that he can create out of indifferent individuals and families *one* people, can stamp this people with its definite character and determine its fate for millennia to come?" (136). He frames this issue in terms of the work of one of his former students. "In 1909 Otto Rank, then still under my influence, published at my suggestion a book entitled: *Der Mythus von der Geburt des Helden* [The myth of the birth of the hero]. It deals with the fact 'that almost all important civilized peoples have early woven myths around and glorified in poetry their heroes, mythical kings and princes, founders of religions, of dynasties, empires and cities—in short, their national heroes. Especially the history of their birth and of their early years is furnished with fantastic traits; the amazing similarity, nay, literal identity, of those tales, even if they refer to different, completely independent peoples, sometimes geographically far removed from one another, is well known and has struck many an investigator" (7). The most important characteristic of the typical hero turns out to be not his birth, but his relation to his father. Drawing on Rank, Freud claims, "A hero is a man who stands up manfully against his father and in the end victoriously overcomes him" (9). I will return to the substance of this claim below; for the moment, it is important to underscore how this argument relates to two aspects of Freud's personal life. First, as the founder of psychoanalysis, Freud was the son who rebelled against his fathers in the scientific establishment by appropriating their methods to establish a science they did not deem legitimate. The second point is suggested by a seemingly inconsequential aside, which is crucial for the entire argument that follows. In citing Rank's work, Freud notes that at the time he wrote his book on the hero myth, Rank was "still under my influence." Though Freud does not say so directly, he implies that Rank, as well as other former students, is no longer under his influence. Freud, therefore, is both the rebellious son and the father slain by the textural rather than sexual transgressions of his own rebellious sons. To maintain his authority and ensure his legacy, Freud reinterprets the story of Moses through the sacrifice of Christ, thereby effectively Christianizing Jewish history.[27]

Freud traces the origin of monotheism to Egypt's eighteenth dynasty. One of his most insightful and provocative claims is that monotheism and imperialism are inseparably related. An empire with imperialist ambitions, he argues, needs a universal God rather than competing tribal deities. Then, as now, one empire under one god. In an effort to secure his authority and forge a unified political community out of multiple tribes worshipping competing Gods, Amenhotep IV, who later changed his name to Ikhnaton, invented monotheism. His new God, Aton, was radically transcendent, completely abstract, and totally intolerant of other gods. Needless to say, the priests of the displaced deities resisted the new religion, and eventually rebelled by killing the founding father. Freud speculates that one of the followers of Ikhnaton ruled an area encompassing a Semitic tribe that had immigrated several generations earlier. This leader attempted to revive monotheism by imposing it on the Jews, who proved to be as recalcitrant as the Egyptians, and the leader once again suffered death at the hands of his followers. When conflict inevitably broke out, Moses, who was a member of the tribe, reimposed monotheism with the same result. The Jews, unwilling to comply with the rigorous mandates of the transcendent God, murdered Moses, and monotheism entered what Freud describes as a period of "latency." "Yet the religion of Moses did not disappear without leaving any trace; a kind of memory of it had survived, a tradition perhaps obscured and distorted. It was this tradition of a great past that continued to work in the background, until it slowly gained more and more power over the mind of the people and at last succeeded in transforming the God Jahve into the Mosaic God and in waking to a new life the religion which Moses had instituted centuries before and which had later been forsaken" (87).

Freud acknowledged that in developing his interpretation of Moses, he returned to the analysis he developed a quarter of a century earlier in *Totem and Taboo.* In that work he presents his own myth of origin by appropriating Darwin's notion of a cannibalistic primal horde ruled by an all-powerful father, who alone had sexual relations with the females he controlled. Frustrated sons rebel by killing and eating the father, but their effort to free themselves from his domination fails. Consumed by guilt for their deed, the sons express remorse by offering "deferred obedience" to the father. In this way, the dead father returns more powerful than ever. Initially it appears that Freud is doing little more than using his account of the Oedipal complex to explain the origin of religion. His argument, however, is more nuanced. In an effort to substantiate his analysis, Freud turns to Christianity, which informs his original interpretation of the primal horde. This reconstructed narrative unexpectedly turns out to be a ghost story in which Freud becomes the leading character.

Through a comparison of Christianity with Mithraism, Freud noted that in the emergence of Christianity, a religion of the son displaces a religion of the father. "We may perhaps infer from the sculptures of Mithras slaying a bull that he represented a son who was alone in sacrificing his father and thus redeemed his brothers from their burden of complicity in the deed. There was an alternative method of allaying their guilt and this was first adopted by Christ. He sacrificed his own life and so redeemed the company of brothers from original sin."[28] Freud credits Paul with being the first to trace Jewish guilt back to the original sin of killing the father. According to the ancient code of justice, the only adequate compensation for a death is another death. In this scheme, guilty sons can only be redeemed by the death of an innocent son. But Freud realizes that the situation is considerably more complex than a simple case of retributive justice. Anticipating his later theory of the instincts, he suggests that Jesus's self-sacrifice is actually an act of aggression. In a crucial passage that is even richer than Freud realized, he argues,

The very deed in which the son offered the greatest possible atonement to the father brought him at the same time to the at-

tainment of his wishes *against* the father. He himself became
God, beside, or, more correctly, in place of, the father. A
son-religion displaced the father-religion. As a sign of this
substitution the ancient totem meal was revived in the form
of communion, in which the company of brothers consumed
the flesh and blood of the son—no longer the father—obtained
sanctity thereby and identified themselves with him. Thus we
can trace through the ages the identity of the totem meal with
animal sacrifice, with the theanthropic human sacrifice and
with the Christian Eucharist, and we can recognize in all these
rituals the effect of the crime by which men were so deeply
weighted down but of which they must nonetheless feel so
proud. The Christian communion, however, is essentially a
fresh elimination of the father, a repetition of the guilty deed.[29]

The interpretation of Christianity is crucial for understanding Freud's preoccupation with Moses in his last work.

   Freud's interpretation of Christianity as a religion of the son displac-
ing a religion of the father is misleading. Unlike the exclusive monotheism
of Judaism, the Christian God is triune—Father, Son, and Holy Spirit or
Holy Ghost. According to orthodox Christology, Jesus is "fully God and
fully man." Rather than becoming the Father through what appears to be
an act of self-sacrifice, the Son is always already the Father, and the Father
is always already the Son. As we will see, believers are united with God in
the person of the Holy Ghost through the Eucharistic ritual. At this point,
it is important to understand that since the Son is the Father and the
Father is the Son, the death of the Son is at the same time the death of the
Father, and vice versa. Furthermore, inasmuch as Jesus freely chooses his
death, he actually commits suicide. This implies an important point that
Freud overlooks: since the willing self-sacrifice of the Son is also the willing
self-sacrifice of the Father, what Freud interprets as deicide is simultaneously God's suicide through which God dies and is reborn in the interior
lives of believers. As Jack Miles argues in *Christ: A Crisis in the Life of God,*
"The self-martyrdom of God Incarnate was an inspiration for Christian

martyrs during the first three centuries of church history. Imperfectly distinguished from martyrdom, suicide did not become a theoretical problem for Christianity until martyrdom itself became a practical problem for the church. This happened when the Roman empire became Christian and dissident Christians began using martyrdom against the now established church as effectively as their forebears had used it against the empire. It was only then that a sharp distinction between glorious martyrdom and shameful suicide began to be actively propagated."[30] Did Freud, like Kierkegaard, understand himself to be a martyr who had to die to ensure the survival of his legacy? The answer to this question is not clear, but unbeknownst to Freud, there are clues in the third person of the trinity.

In traditional Christian theology, the Son, who is also the Father, must die so that the Holy Spirit can come to earth to unite believers with God. The more closely one studies *Totem and Taboo,* the less clear it becomes whether Freud interprets the Eucharist through his account of the totem meal, or whether he bases his understanding of the totem meal on his interpretation of the Eucharist.[31] In either case, the ritual does not merely commemorate what took place *in illo tempore,* but is the reactualization of the originary event. Just as Jesus's self-sacrifice is an expression of both devotion to and aggression toward the Father, so participation in the Eucharist is simultaneously an expression of devotion to and aggression toward the incarnate God. Like the cannibalistic brothers of the primitive horde, Christian believers eat the body and drink the blood of the Father-Son. By so doing, God and believers become one. The etymological association between "host," which is the name of the communion wafer, and "ghost" suggests the process by which the dead Father is consumed by his followers. By eating the host, believers internalize the Holy Ghost. This apparent reconciliation with the Father comes at a high price; instead of overcoming inward and outward division, this union further fragments individual believers. The consumption of God divides the self—the dead Father is reborn as the Holy Ghost, who now haunts every person. So understood, this ritual repeats the ancient pattern in which the dead father proves to be more powerful than the living father. This twist in the story explains why God might commit suicide. Far from selfless, the Father's self-sacrifice is calculated to maintain His authority over rebellious sons even after his death.

With these insights, we can return to *Moses and Monotheism* and reconsider the reasons for Freud's obsessive preoccupation with this work while he was extremely ill and on the verge of dying. In an astonishing passage, he identifies Moses and Christ. "It is an attractive suggestion that the guilt attached to the murder of Moses may have been the stimulus for the wish-fantasy of the Messiah, who was to return to give his people salvation and the promised sovereignty over the world. If Moses was this first Messiah, Christ became his substitute and successor. Then Paul could with a certain right say to the peoples: 'See, the Messiah has truly come. He was indeed murdered before your eyes.' Then also there is some historical truth in the rebirth of Christ, for he was the resurrected Moses and the returned primeval father of the primitive horde as well—only transfigured, and as a Son in place of his Father" (114). This passage reveals Freud's strategy throughout *Moses and Monotheism*—he actually interprets Moses through Christ. In his provocative essay "Jesus and Monotheism," Gil Anidjar explains the implications of this argument. "Freud's return, that is, the return of Freud, has always meant a return to Jesus and to Christianity—our 'Christian unconscious,' as Paul Vitz has it. Or so it should have meant. *Moses and Monotheism* is one version (or two?) of other textual renderings. Moses *translates* Oedipus and the primal father rather than simply repeating either of them. And then there is Jesus—that pervasive if little acknowledged translation. Or is it the original? Back to Freud, at any rate, and back to Jesus, back to murder and its future. For, if *Moses* clearly constitutes a rewriting of *Totem and Taboo,* and if Jesus retrospectively replaces Moses (and indeed Oedipus), there is little doubt that this substitution, this translation (the latency of Christianity), plausible as it is, is not sufficient to provide an exhaustive reading of *Moses and Monotheism*."[32] To complete this line of analysis, it is necessary to add a final displacement, which is also an identification.

Ikhnaton ↔ Oedipus ↔ Moses ↔ Christ ↔ Freud

To understand the reason Freud stresses these displacements/identifica-tions, it is necessary to pose an unasked question that underlies *Moses and Monotheism:* If, as Nietzsche declared and Freud confirmed, God is dead and there is no immortal soul, how is life after death possible?

In the last years and months of his life, Freud was quietly preoccu-pied with the question of immortality. In the opening pages of *Moses and Monotheism,* he underscores an important difference between early Egyp-tian beliefs and Moses's version of monotheism. "There is another differ-ence between the two religions that the explanations I have attempted do not touch. No other people of antiquity has done so much to deny death, has made such careful provision for an afterlife; in accordance with this the death-god Osiris, the ruler of that other world, was the most popular and indisputable of all Egyptian gods. The early Jewish religion, on the other hand, had entirely relinquished immortality; the possibility of an existence after death was never mentioned in any place. And this is all the more re-markable since later experience has shown that the belief in a life beyond can very well be reconciled with a monotheistic religion" (20). Freud attri-butes the denial of life after death to Ikhnaton's religion of Aton. As the tombs of pharaohs amply demonstrate, ancient Egypt was obsessed with the afterlife. All of this changed, Freud argues, when Ikhnaton imposed radical monotheism on his people. To secure the future belief in Aton, he had to erase every trace of all other gods, especially the popular Osiris, who ruled the realm of the living dead. When Moses appropriated Egyptian monotheism, he accepted the denial of the afterlife. Freud maintains that this important point of agreement is proof of Moses's Egyptian identity. "We were astonished—and rightly so—that the Jewish religion did not speak of anything beyond the grave, for such a doctrine is reconcilable with the strict-est monotheism. This astonishment disappears if we go back from the Jewish religion to the Aton religion and surmise that this feature was taken over from the latter, since for Ikhnaton it was a necessity in fighting the popular reli-gion, where the death-god Osiris played perhaps a greater part than any god of the upper regions. The agreement of the Jewish religion with that of Aton in this important point is the first strong argument in favor of our thesis" (28–29). Staring death in the face, Freud could not accept the complete denial of the afterlife. To affirm the possibility of immortality after the death of God, Freud returns to a proposal advanced in *Totem and Taboo*—the collective unconscious.

"An event such as the elimination of the primal father by the company of his sons must invariably have left ineradicable traces in the history of humanity; and the less it itself was recollected, the more numerous must have been the substitutes to which it gave rise." The only way to account for this psychic inheritance is by the postulation of a collective unconscious. "Without the assumption of a collective mind, which makes it possible to neglect the interruptions of mental acts caused by the extinction of the individual, social psychology in general cannot exist. Unless psychological processes were continued from one generation to another, if each generation were obliged to acquire its attitude to life anew, there would be no progress in this field and next to no development."[33]

In Freud's collective "Christian unconscious," everyone is a sinner by virtue of shared guilt for the murder of the father. Since what is repressed does not disappear but remains in the collective unconscious, we are all haunted by ghosts of the past. The dead live and speak through the living even, indeed, perhaps especially, when they are denied. Freud's psychoanalytic theory reinscribes Hegel's dialectic in which overt negation is covert affirmation. By denying the doctrine of the father, sons reaffirm his abiding significance. With this turn of his argument, Freud could die confident that his legacy would live on in and through its denial by rebellious sons.

There is, however, a final bitter irony of Freud's last days. In the end, his legacy depended less on his rebellious sons than on his devoted daughter. Two days before his death, Freud said to his doctor, "Fate has been good to me, that it should still have granted me the relationship with such a woman—I mean Anna, of course." Then he turned to Schur and said, "'you remember our "contract" not to leave me in the lurch when the time had come. Now it is nothing but torture and makes no sense.'" Gay reports what followed: "Then, after a slight hesitation, he added, 'Talk it over with Anna, and if she thinks it's right, then make an end of it.' As she had been for years, so at this juncture, Freud's Antigone was first in his thoughts. Anna Freud wanted to postpone the fatal moment, but Schur insisted that to keep Freud going was pointless, and she submitted to the inevitable, as had her father. The time had come; he knew and acted."[34] The faithful daughter did not feel compelled to kill her father to ensure, albeit indirectly, that his legacy would survive his death. To the contrary, his work would live on in hers. What other immortality is possible after the death of God?

Trembling

Jacques Derrida (1930–2004): *The Beast and the Sovereign,* II; "Comment ne pas trembler?"

You don't have to think very hard to realize that our dread . . . of being trapped inside a self (a psychic self, not just a physical self), has to do with angst about death, the recognition that I'm going to die, and die very much alone, and the rest of the world is going to go merrily on without me. I'm not sure I could give you a steeple-fingered theoretical justification, but I strongly suspect a big part of real art fiction's job is to aggravate this sense of entrapment and loneliness and death in people, to move people to countenance it, since any possible human redemption requires us first to face what's dreadful, what we want to deny.

—David Foster Wallace

Gifts

This began with two gifts separated by nine years—an "original" lithograph signed not once but twice, and a book that is not a book, which is both by and "about" the writers who haunt these pages. Once again the issue is *This*—the here-and-now. If *This* is no longer Hegel's here-and-now, might it be either Kierkegaard's Moment or Blanchot's Instant? While this, here-and-now, might be a gift, it cannot be (a) present. Who gives a gift that is not a present? What gives a present that is not (a) present? Who or what comes before the gift/present? What is the gift/present after?

Not one but two, two gifts. A double origin that forever remains duplicitous. In their wake, questions linger. What is a gift? Is a gift possible or does it remain (the) impossible? How is a gift given? How can a gift be received? What gives in all giving?

A gift must be given freely and without any expectation of return. Gifts are, therefore, "aneconomic"—they fall outside every circuit of exchange and interrupt all symmetry. In *Given Time: I. Counterfeit Money,* Derrida offers a concise definition of a gift.

> A gift could be possible, there could be a gift only at the instant an effraction in the circle will have taken place, at the instant all circulation will have been interrupted and *on the condition* of this instant. What is more, this instant of effraction (of the temporal circle) must no longer be part of time. That is why we said "on the condition of this instant." This condition concerns time but does not *belong* to it, does not pertain to it without being, for all that, more logical than chronological. There would be a gift only at the instant when the *paradoxical* instant (in the sense in which Kierkegaard says of the paradoxical instant of decision that it is madness) tears time apart. In this sense one would never have the time of a gift. In any case, time, the "present" of the gift, is no longer thinkable as a now, that is, as a present bound up in the temporal synthesis. (GT, 9)[1]

Since the present is always a present, time is always given and as such remains a gift. However, if the gift of time as well as every other gift interrupts the circuit of exchange, then how can it be acknowledged? To acknowledge a gift is to incur a debt (*Schuld*), which inevitably entails a certain guilt (*Schuld*). The debt of the recipient, paradoxically, cancels the gift by giving the donor a return on his investment, even if that return is nothing more than the other's confession of *Schuld*. This is why Derrida suggests that perhaps "the very figure of the gift is the impossible" (GT, 7). In this strange aneconomy, the true gift would not be recognized as such, or would be forgotten—absolutely forgotten as if nothing had occurred—absolutely nothing. "This *forgetting of the gift,*" Derrida explains, "cannot be a simple non-experience, a simple non-appearance, a self-effacement that is carried off with what it effaces. For there to be a gift event (we say event and not act), something must come about or happen, in an instant, in an instant that no doubt does not belong to the economy of time, in a time without time, in such a way that the forgetting forgets, that it forgets *itself,* but also in such a way that this forgetting, without being something present, presentable, determinable, sensible or meaningful, is not nothing. What this forgetting and this forgetting of forgetting would therefore give us to think is something other than a philosophical, psychological, or psychoanalytic category" (GT, 17).

Though I had corresponded with Derrida, I did not meet him until April 1983. I had hoped to spend the academic year in Paris writing what became *Erring: A Postmodern A/Theology,* but was not able to secure funding, so I went to the National Humanities Center in North Carolina. After completing the book, I traveled to Paris to begin my next project. I spent two months studying Derrida's notoriously difficult and astonishingly creative *Glas* (1974), which is a hypertext *avant la lettre. Glas,* which means the tolling of church bells when the funeral procession passes, is Derrida's most extensive engagement with Hegel. The argument revolves around the tension between Hegel's analysis of the family and holy family, on the one hand, and, on the other, his own family and illegitimate son, Ludwig, whom he shunned and sent off to war, from which he never returned. In a comparison as unlikely as it is revealing, Derrida contrasts Hegel's life and writings with the life and work of the writer, political activist, and criminal Jean Genet. Invoking a distinction *Glas* subverts, the form or style of this work is even more revolutionary than its substance. Written in two columns that are incised, interrupted, and displaced, Derrida creates a polyphonic work that fragments all narrative continuity. The focus of my analysis that spring was Derrida's use of the figure of the bastard (*bâtard*) as trope for writing. My work eventually led to an essay entitled "Rewriting," which is the penultimate chapter in *Altarity* (1987). I intended *Altarity* to be a rewriting of *Journeys to Selfhood: Hegel and Kierkegaard* (1980), which began with Kierkegaard and ends with Hegel. *Altarity,* by contrast, begins with Hegel and ends with Kierkegaard, and in between suspends a series of writers influenced by their work. By using Derrida as an introduction to Kierkegaard, I attempted to suggest an alternative genealogy of deconstruction, post-structuralism, and postmodernism.

Kierkegaard played an unexpected role in the events of that spring. I transformed the aborted French Kierkegaard volume into a series of books entitled "Kierkegaard and Postmodernism." While working on this series, I stumbled on an intriguing book by Sylviane Agacinski, *Aparté: Conceptions et Morts de Søren Kierkegaard,* and decided to have it translated for the series.[2] In the course of negotiating the translation, Sylviane and I exchanged quite a few letters, and, when I told her I was coming to Paris, she encouraged me to get in touch with her. We first met at a café and had a delightful conversation. She assumed I knew Derrida personally, and upon learning we had never met, she promised to get us together. A few weeks later, the three of us had dinner in her right-bank apartment. Derrida picked me up, stopped to get some ice cream to take to Sylviane, and we drove together across the city trying to arrive before the ice cream melted. It quickly became apparent that Derrida knew his way around Sylviane's apartment. We had a delightful evening, and Sylviane and I met several other times during my stay. A few years later, I learned that she and Derrida had a long and sometimes tumultuous relationship, and together had a son named Daniel. Sylviane is a distinguished philosopher who went on to marry Lionel Jospin, the prime minister of France, who ran against Jacques Chirac for the presidency of the country.

Though Sylviane is never mentioned by name, the correspondence recorded in the first section of *The Post Card: From Socrates to Freud and Beyond,* "Envois," appears to be an account (whether fictional or not remains unclear) of the affair. In the first entry, dated June 3, 1977, Derrida writes:

> Yes, you were right, henceforth, today, now, at every moment [NB], on this point [NB] of the *carte,* we are but a minuscule residue "left unclaimed": a residue of what we have said to one another, of what, do not forget, we have made of one another, of what we have written one another. Yes, this "correspondence,"

you're right, immediately got beyond us, which is why it all
should have been burned, all of it, including the cinders of the
unconscious—and "they" will never know anything about it.
(*Post Card,* 7)

Eventually, Derrida did burn the letters and to his dying day regretted the
decision to do so. In an exchange with his younger colleagues Jean-Luc
Nancy and Philippe Lacoue-Labarthe at a conference in Strasbourg just
four months before his death, he confessed, "I once destroyed a correspondence. With a fierce determination: I tried to reduce it to shreds—it didn't
work; I burnt it—that didn't work. . . . I destroyed a correspondence I
should not have destroyed and I will regret it for the rest of my life. As for
the rest—and here we are speaking of the problem of the archive—I've never
lost or destroyed anything" (S, 27). Burnt letters. Reducing words to ashes,
Derrida incinerated, cremated the illegitimate trace of a corpus he wanted
to keep secret.

Though our paths eventually parted, I have burnt neither Derrida's
nor Sylviane's letters. Her generous introduction began what became a long
conversation with Derrida; over the years, we met frequently and corresponded often. His letters were always handwritten in a script that is almost indecipherable. These letters, like those from Blanchot, Updike, and
others, will be part of my legacy to my son and daughter.

A couple of weeks before I was scheduled to leave Paris, Derrida told
me he had a small gift he wanted to give me. It was an "original" lithograph
by one of his favorite artists, Valerio Adami. To call a lithograph original
is, of course, an oxymoron because it is always already a copy of a copy.
Half of what made this work so special was Adami's signature written in
pencil along the bottom border of the work. Adami had become intrigued
by *Glas* and did a series of drawings and paintings interpreting the work.
Derrida responded to Adami's work in an essay entitled "Derrière le
mirror," which was later translated and published as "+R (Into the Bar-
gain)" in *The Truth in Painting.*

The lithograph is a remarkable work that shows an extraordinarily
sophisticated understanding of Derrida's argument. Like *Glas,* the work

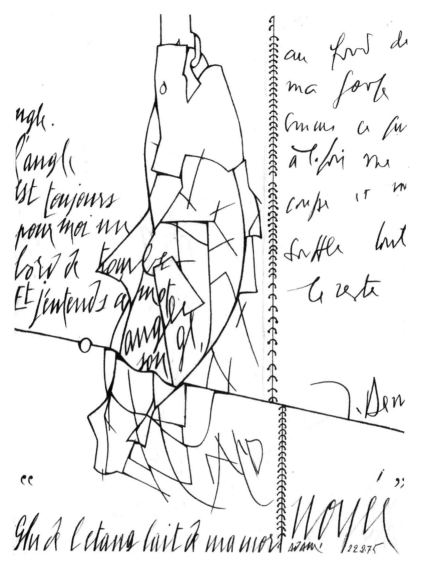

Valerio Adami, study for a drawing after *Glas*

is divided into two columns joined and separated by the spiral of a note-book. Superimposed on bright colors (red, orange, yellow, and aqua), in black letters there are fragments from *Glas* transcribed in Adami's handwriting on the left-hand column and Derrida's handwriting on the right-hand column. The lines have been chosen very carefully to include key words in Derrida's argument, and each line is strategically cut off. The central feature of the work is a large hooked fish that has been lifted out of the water. Beneath the tail of the fish, under the aqua blue of the sea, Adami has written: "glu de l'étang lait de ma mor-noyée," which might be translated "glue of the pool milk of my drowned dea-." The last syllable of the most important word in this phrase has been cut off—*mor-*, which suggests *lait de ma mort* (milk of my death), as well as *lait de ma mere* (milk of my mother). *Mere* (mother) echoes *mer* (sea).

At the bottom of the right column just above *noyée* (drowned), Adami has replicated Derrida's signature but once again has cut off the final syllable: J. Der. Above the fragmented name there is a single word: *le reste:* rest, remainder, remains, residue, trace, vestige. The other half of what makes this gift so valuable to me is Derrida's signature directly below his abbreviated name.

> *Pour Marc Taylor*
> *Paris le 15 juin 1983*
>   *J. Derrida/.*

As always with Derrida, every detail is important: the proper name, the place (here), the date (now), followed by "/". How is this final token to be read? Is "/" the trace of the spacing and timing of *différance?* Why does he end with "."? Is this a period or a point? If a point, what is the point? Whose point is this? Is it Freud's unplumable "point of contact with the unknown"? Or is it his friend Edmond Jabès's "point of no return," which he associates with the Kabbalah's *Zim Zum?*

> "God refused image and language in order to be
> Himself the point. He is image in the absence of
> images, language in the absence of language, point in
> the absence of points," he said.[3]

Is this the *punctum* of Roland Barthes's photograph that signals "he is going to die"? "I read at the same time: This will be and this has been; I observe with horror an anterior future of which death is the stake. By giving me the absolute past of the pose (aorist), the photograph tells me death in the future."[4] Or is the point nothing?

How can such an enigmatic work be understood? How can one respond to such a remarkable gift? Derrida's signature creates a lure that sets a trap I suspect he knew I could not avoid. He realized that it would be impossible for me not to respond, and he also knew that by responding I would cancel the gift by acknowledging my profound debt to him. Far from a gift freely offered with no expectation of return, the lithograph was an investment, which, following Freud, is calculated to ensure his legacy. By making this bet Derrida won—everything I have written since that April spring is directly or indirectly indebted to him.

But who or what is this responsive indebted *I*? In *Derrière le miroir*, Derrida "baptizes" Adami's "drawing" *Ich*.

> . . . in the fish drawing which I shall baptize *Ich:* without the author's authorization, in order to take it from him in turn and hold it at the end of my line, with an apparently simple line, without a reel, without the interposed machine turning and fishing all by itself under the wheels of the train, in *La meccanica dell'avventura* (which dates from a month later).
>
> *Ich,* snatched fish body, foreign body of a word to involve *another language* (Adami often does it) in the play of signatures and the agonistic outbidding speculating on the *I.* Truncated body or overcharged matrix (there are so many in Adami), bait for the Christic phallus (*Ichthys*), track, graph or trace (*Ichnos*) of a voiceless bit. (TP, 157)

These three letters I C H suggest endless associations that further complicate both *Glas* and the lithograph.

As Blanchot has argued, the Book is a theological invention that is most fully realized in Hegel's speculative philosophy. By "rolling up and unrolling time," the Book tells the story of the progression of the *Ich* from sense certainty to Absolute Knowledge. In Hegel's comprehensive system, this philosophical knowledge completely unfolds the truth first revealed by

Christ. Derrida unwrites the Hegelian Book in a text woven from two inter-
laced columns that form a CHIasmus. A chiasmus is a rhetorical inversion of
the second of two parallel structures. As the inversion of the ICH, the CHI
of chiasmus enacts the trope it designates. Explaining a further nuance of
ICH, Derrida writes, "Everything passes through this chiasmus, all writing
is caught in it—frequents it" (TP, 166).[5] The CHI of chiasmus is written as a
cross that is a double-cross—X. The two arms of the cross appear to be two
intersecting incomplete Mobius strips, or an open-ended double infinity.
The site or non-site of intersection is the empty center around which
everything revolves without coming full circle. This center that decenters
self-consciousness is a pit that sinks into the underworld.[6]

　　　There is a further aspect of the *Ich* that is important for Derrida's reading of Adami's painting. We have seen that the *point* of departure for
Hegel's narrative of self-consciousness, the *Ich* (subject), is the correlate of
the *This* (object). Just as the here-and-now of the *This* vanishes in the effort to grasp it, so the *Ich* appears by disappearing. By signing his gift to
me, Derrida's dated signature enacts the disappearance of the here (Paris)
and the now (15 Juni 1983) in writing. To underline this point, he ends with
"." What is not immediately evident is that this writing, like all writing, is
a death sentence—the gift, as Derrida stresses elsewhere, is always poison
(German, *Gift*).

　　　Derrida's personal signature actually repeats a disappearance that has
already (*déjà*) occurred.[7] As I have noted, when Adami transcribes Derrida's name, he cuts off the -*rida*. Derrida underscores the importance of this
gesture.

　　　　My signature—who will attest to its authenticity in this repro-
　　　　duction of a reproduction? and what if Adami had imitated it,
　　　　like my writing? and what if I had forged his on the left?—my
　　　　signature is also cut off, before the *da*. What is detached—falls
　　　　overboard—is also a piece of the other's [i.e., Adami's] name
　　　　(*da*) and one of the most obsessive motifs in *Glas*.
　　　　　　The *da* is not there, *hic et nunc,* but it is not lacking. Like
　　　　color? We'll have to see later: what [*ce qui*] makes itself strong

[*fort*] from the monumental fall—falls [*tombe,* also tomb] over-board. (TP, 158–59)

When *da* is translated from French to German, its significance becomes apparent. In German, *da* means "there." Derrida's missing *da* is written in the margins of Heidegger's *Da-sein* and Freud's *fort-da.* The *da* of *sein* is missing—it is, in other words, gone (*fort*). Adami's drawing, Derrida's text, and their chiasmus-like intertwining create an endless play of *fort-da,* which Freud has taught us is a symptom of the death instinct.

> déjà, already. Death has already taken place, before everything. How is one to decipher this strange anteriority of a déjà that is always already shouldering you with a cadaver? And if, as I have demonstrated elsewhere . . . *I am* and *I am dead* are two statements indistinguishable in their sense, then the already [*déjà*] that I am [*je suis,* which can also be translated as 'I follow' or 'I go after'] sounds its own proper *glas,* signs itself its own death sentence [*arrêt de mort*], regards you in advance, sees you advance without any comprehension of what you will have loved, following, in a column, the funeral march of an erection everyone will intend to have available from now on.
>
> A more or less argot translation of the *cogito:* "I am therefore dead." This can only be written. (G, 92)

Hoc est corpus meum. Corpus as corpse to be consumed by sons, who are indebted to the ghost of the father. Since every sentence is a death sentence, every gift is the gift of death. To accept this death, which can be neither accepted nor denied, is to be consumed by death.

A second gift—a text that is not a book. In the fall of 2002, Derrida and I attended a conference at Le Mans devoted to the question "Comment penser l'argent?" The evening before I left to return to the States, we had dinner together in Paris. In the course of our conversation, I asked him what problem he planned to explore in his seminar that year. When he said he would once again analyze the secret, I replied, "You know, you have been avoiding Kierkegaard far too long. You should do the seminar on Kierkegaard." Whether or not my suggestion influenced him, he devoted his seminar that year to *Fear and Trembling.* Three years later, I published the work that came out of that seminar in my Religion and Postmodernism series with the title, borrowed from Blanchot, *The Gift of Death.* Echoing Blanchot, Derrida explains, "*the gift is not a present,* the gift of something that remains inaccessible, unpresentable, and as a consequence secret. The event of this gift would link the essence without essence to the gift of secrecy. For one might say that a gift that could be recognized as such in the light of day, a gift destined for recognition, would immediately annul itself. The gift is the secret itself, if the secret *itself* can be told. Secrecy is the last word of the gift which is the last word of the secret" (GD, 29–30).

As I have stressed, the gift imposes the impossible responsibility of responding without responding. This issue, Derrida insists, is not only psychological, but also theological. Commenting on the God of Abraham by way of Kierkegaard's rendering of the story of Isaac, Derrida writes, "The crypto- or mysto-genealogy of responsibility is woven with the double and inextricably intertwined thread of the gift and of death: in short, of the *gift of death.* The gift made to me by God as he holds me in his gaze and in his hand while remaining inaccessible to me, the terribly dissymmetrical gift of the *mysterium tremendum* only allows me to respond and only rouses me to the responsibility it gives me by making a gift of death [*en me donnant la mort*], giving the secret of death, a new experience of death'" (GD, 33). "The secret of death," "a new experience of death," is nothing other than "dying without dying."

In the fall of 2006, I assigned *The Gift of Death* as the last work in my course Religion and the Modern World. Three days before the class on this text, I had a biopsy for cancer and developed a serious infection. I should not have traveled from Williamstown to New York City but felt obligated to teach Derrida's work because it brought together so many of the themes I had been developing throughout the course. The class ended at noon; two hours later my fever spiked, and at 7:00 p.m., my blood pressure dropped to 50/20, and my liver and kidneys shut down. I had developed a severe case of septic shock, and for two days the doctors gave me very little chance of surviving. After five days in the intensive care unit, five more days in the hospital, and a month on intravenous antibiotics, my condition stabilized. Five months later I had to undergo surgery for cancer. This experience was as close as I can imagine to what Blanchot describes as dying without dying. In the months between the septic shock and surgery for cancer, I realized that I might have taught my last class and written my last work. *After God* was finished but not edited. I asked my close friend Jack Miles to see the book through to publication if I did not survive the cancer surgery.

That experience or non-experience transformed everything. Reflecting on those dark days, I have written, "You never come back from elsewhere because elsewhere always comes back with you."[8] Once you "experience" death, it shadows you like an uncanny double you cannot escape. The past decade has, in effect, been life *after* death for me. Contrary to expectation, the experience of dying without dying has been extraordinarily liberating. Living (with) death has allowed me to let go of the past and the future and to dwell in the present differently. As I have attempted to understand what happened and what didn't happen, I have turned to the ghosts with whom I have lived for many years. As Heidegger has taught us, to think (*denken*) is to thank (*danken*). There is more to tell, always more to tell, but for the moment, I pause to thank Blanchot and Derrida for "the gift of death," which is helping me to think about the event that has not yet occurred. I realize, of course, that this thanks cancels the gift that made it possible.

Parting Words

Time: Wednesday 5:00–7:00 Ten to twelve times a year for fifty-three years.

Place: Sorbonne (1960–1964), Ecole normale supérieure (1964–1984), Ecole des hautes études en sciences sociales (1984–2003).

The last seminar: *The Beast and the Sovereign,* II, December 11, 2002–March 26, 2003. The first session begins, "I am alone"; the last session begins: "What does it mean to bear [*porter, tragen*]?" There is an overwhelming poignancy to Derrida's words throughout his last seminar. Everyone knew this was his last class, if not his last public appearance. And yet, he proceeds as if he were going to return in the fall for another seminar. Derrida notes passages that need more detailed analysis, suggests readings for the "vacation," and, with time running out, sighs, "Ah, life will have been so short!" and then adds, "As I have to conclude as quickly as possible, I will not be able to take with the required precision and proximity the work of reading and interpretation of the semantic, syntactic and lexical network of *Walten,* at least in *Introduction to Metaphysics,* in which this network is peculiarly rich and plentiful. I am sure that if you want to, you can do it without me" (B, 273, 285). He is not improvising; as always, he was reading from a written manuscript. Finally, begging his audience for one more minute, he explains what he has been after from the beginning—the beginning not just of his last seminar, but the beginning of his entire corpus. "I would like to end, if you'll give me one more second, on a single final question from Heidegger that could be given many readings and that I leave you to appropriate as you wish as you watch the war on television, in Iraq, but also closer to us. Heidegger writes this, which seems to mark the limit of *Gewalt* or of *Gewalt-tagigkeit.* It's about what will basically have been besieging this seminar, behind the cohort of cremators and inhumers of every order, and other guardians of the mourning to come: death itself, if there be any, our theme" (B, 290). Then, as always, quoting Heidegger a final time, he adds, "Das ist der Tod [it is death]." The death as well as the mourning was, of course, Derrida's "own." Four months after he spoke these words, he was dead.

Derrida not only knew that he was dying, but was also surrounded by death. Delivering eulogy after eulogy, he repeatedly assumed the role of survivor for the generation of 1968: Roland Barthes (1980), Paul de Man (1983), Michel Foucault (1984), Louis Althusser (1990), Edmond Jabès (1991), Louis Marin (1992), Sarah Kofman (1994), Gilles Deleuze (1995); Emmanuel Levinas (1995), Jean-François Lyotard (1998).[9] There were others. On February 20, 2003, six days before the seventh seminar, Maurice Blanchot died, and Derrida gave the eulogy on the occasion of his cremation. Nor was the specter of death merely personal. Six days before the final session of the last seminar, the war with Iraq, which Derrida had publicly opposed, broke out.

When he was diagnosed with pancreatic cancer in May 2003, Derrida knew he would not recover and did not have long to live. Nevertheless, he was determined to delay the end as long as possible. He began a regime of chemotherapy at the Institut Curie that left him weak and sometimes hallucinatory. In spite of his deteriorating condition, he continued to teach and write, and kept up a grueling travel schedule that took him to Santa Barbara, Portugal, Israel, London, Avignon, and Strasbourg. He even attended a conference on his work in Rio De Janeiro, where, on August 16, 2004, he presented a three-hour opening address entitled "Pardon, Reconciliation, Truth: What Genre?" By September, he was too weak to write or travel. A month later, he slipped into a coma, and on October 9, 2004, he died at the age of seventy-four. Before entering the hospital for the last time, he left instructions for the disposition of his bodily remains. He chose burial rather than cremation, and wanted to be buried in Ris-Orangis, where he had lived most of his life. He asked to be buried outside the Jewish section of the cemetery so his wife, Marguerite Aucouturie, could join him. Though many people traveled great distances to pay their final respects, Derrida had left instructions that there should be no official ceremony. Family and close friends accompanied the hearse to the cemetery, and at the graveside, his son, Pierre, read words Derrida had composed.

Jacques desired neither ritual nor prayer. He knows by experience what a trial it is for the friend who performs them. He asks me to thank you for coming, and to bless you, he begs you not to be sad, and to think just of the many happy times that you gave him the chance to share with him.

Smile at me, he says, as I will have smiled at you until the end.

Always prefer life and never stop affirming survival.

I love you and I am smiling at you from wherever I am.[10]

Derrida was as controversial in death as he was in life. Two days after his death, a vitriolic obituary by Jonathan Kandell appeared on the front page of the *New York Times*.[11] The following day, I received a call from David Shipley, who was then the editor of the op-ed page of the *Times*. David had studied with me when Derrida's influence was at its height, and asked me to write an essay to counterbalance Kandell's irresponsible portrayal of Derrida. After attempting the impossible task of summarizing Derrida's extraordinarily complex writings in less than one thousand words, I concluded,

> But small things are the measure of the man. In 1986, my family and I were in Paris and Mr. Derrida invited us to dinner at his house in the suburbs 20 miles away. He insisted on picking us up at our hotel, and when we arrived at his home he presented our children with carnival masks. At 2 a.m., he drove us back to the city. In later years, when my son and daughter were writing college papers on his work he sent them letters and postcards of encouragement as well as signed copies of several of his books. Jacques Derrida wrote eloquently about the gift of friendship but in these quiet gestures—gestures that served to forge connections among individuals across their differences—we see deconstruction in action.[12]

Corpse and Corpus

Seminar on a seminar, text on a text. *Logos spermatikos*.[13] Seminars (*semen*, seed; *seminarium*, seed plot) spread seeds (of the father) with the hope that some will impregnate, take root, *bear* fruit, and thereby leave a legacy. According to Heidegger, the *logos spermatikos* is the logos of what he describes as the Western onto-theological tradition. But there is another *logos*—the *logos apophantikos*, which does not spread its excess but withdraws perhaps into a point.[14] This is the *logos* of what Heidegger calls "godless thinking," which so-called negative theologians have long talked about by not talking about. Derrida explains that for Heidegger, "thought with-

out God [*das gott-lose Denken*], and thus atheistic or a-theological thinking under the regime of onto-theology, and thus the thinking of those
who, as philosophers, declare themselves to be atheists (and this is indeed
the case of Heidegger, among others)—well, that they, that their thinking
without God is perhaps closer to the divine God, to the divinity of God,
more open to it than the thinking of a theism, or of a philosophical belief
in the God of the philosophers and of onto-theology" (B, 214). Is it possible that death is the gift of this godless God?

Derrida might well have said of Heidegger what he said of Hegel: "We
will never be finished with the reading and rereading of Heidegger, and,
in a certain way, I do nothing other than attempt to explain myself on this
point." For Derrida, Heidegger is to philosophy what Blanchot is to literature. He devotes his last seminar to Heidegger's 1929–1930 seminar, *The
Fundamental Concepts of Metaphysics: World, Finitude, Solitude*. Two additional texts by Heidegger also play an important role in Derrida's final
argument—*Identity and Difference,* and "What Is Metaphysics?" In an unexpected gesture, Derrida also considers Daniel Defoe's *Robinson Crusoe,*
which helps him explore the island on which he finds himself stranded.

With death fast approaching, Derrida remained true to the method
he had always followed. He looks for the overlooked, through which he so-
licits the return of the repressed. "As you see," he tells his listeners, "late
in my life of reading Heidegger, I have just discovered a word that seems
to oblige me to put everything in a new perspective. And that is what happens and ought to be meditated on endlessly. If I had not conjoined in one
problematic the beast *and* the sovereign, I wager that the force and organ-
izing power of this German word that is so difficult to translate, but that
informs, give form to the whole Heideggerian text, would never have appeared to me as such" (B, 279). That word is, of course, *Walten,* and this
is the last word of the last seminar. "The question, that was the question of
the seminar, remains entire: namely that of knowing who can die. To whom
is this power given or denied? Who is capable of death, and, through death,
of imposing failure on the super- or hyper-sovereignty of *Walten?*" (B, 290).

World, Finitude, Solitude. Given the timing of the last session of the
last seminar, it is not surprising that Derrida begins at the end—solitude.

"I am alone." What does it mean to be alone—absolutely alone? "Our seminar," he continues to explain, "will have as its horizon not only the questions
of solitude, loneliness, insularity, isolation and therefore exception, including the sovereign exception. It will have as its horizon the questions of what
'inhabit,' 'cohabit,' 'inhabit the world' mean—and therefore the question
of what *world* means" (B, 11). Solitude, finitude, and world intersect in
the experience or non-experience of death. Heidegger argues that only
in being-toward-death does a person become aware of his or her absolute
uniqueness, which Derrida, following Kierkegaard, labels "singularity."
Like the radical particularity of the here-and-now indicated by the proper
name and date, singularity cannot be grasped in concepts or expressed
linguistically—it is utterly idiomatic. As Kant teaches in the First Critique,
self and world are codependent—there is no self without world, and no
world without self.[15] The two seminars on the beast and the sovereign extend the exploration of the question of the animal that preoccupied Derrida during the last years of his life. Heidegger argued that animals, like
stones, have no world and, therefore, cannot properly die; they expire but
do not die *sensu strictissima*. The examination of the problem of the world
is at the same time an exploration of the enigma of death, and, by extension, the meaning of finitude, or, in David Foster Wallace's memorable
words, "what it is to be a fucking human being."

    Derrida cites and recites a single line from a poem by Paul Celan
whose rhythmic repetition sets the pace for *The Beast and the Sovereign:*
"*Die Welt ist fort, ich muss dich tragen*—The world is gone, I must bear
you." He had previously written on Celan and nowhere more movingly than
his meditation entitled *Cinders*.[16] Cinders, ashes haunt Derrida's final
thoughts. *Die Welt ist fort:* in being-toward-death, *da-sein* becomes itself
by facing an absence (*fort*) that is the impossibility of its presence, and,
therefore, the impossibility of its very being. This play of *fort/da* reenacts
Freud's death instinct in which life and death are not opposites but are
folded into each other in living death. "I am alone." No one can die in my
place. In this sense, though there are others, each individual is irreplaceable. But what does it really mean to be alone? Derrida continues in his first
paragraph, "I know a sentence that is still more terrifying, more terribly

ambiguous than 'I am alone,' and it is, isolated from any other determining context, the sentence that would say to the other: 'I am alone with you.' Meditate on the abyss of such a sentence: I am alone with you, with you I am alone, alone in all the world" (B, 1). Is this an echo of Blanchot's essential solitude, which creates an "unavowable community," or Jean-Luc Nancy's "inoperative community [*communauté désoeuvrée*]"?[17] When all is said and done, solitude is what everyone has in common. Essential solitude emerges not only when we are alone, but also when we are with others who sometimes are very close to us. What characterizes all such experiences is the awareness that they cannot be shared. Solitude, therefore, involves a profound paradox: we are most apart when we are most together, and most together when we are most apart.

In an interminable sentence that Derrida seems either unable or unwilling to end, he joins solitude, world, and death. It is as if by continuing to write and to speak he can delay or defer the end he knows is inescapable. Illness, war, death; solitude, isolation, loneliness—this constitutes the finitude that makes us human. Everyone is stranded on an island with no (speculative good) Friday to save him or her.

The world can disappear in at least two ways: I can withdraw from the world, or the world can withdraw from me. The end of the world is not only the loss of the present, but is also the loss of the future. In the absence of resurrection, what will remain of my remains (*le reste*), both bodily and literary? *Die Welt est fort, ich muss dich tragen.* Who is speaking in this *ich,* and what does it mean to bear (*tragen*)? *Ich,* we have discovered, is sometimes fishy, and it is not clear what fish can bear, even if they are whales.

One of the primary themes throughout the last seminar is the choice between cremation and burial or, in Derrida's terms, the "cremators" and the "inhumers." Noting that his generation is the first for which there is a widespread choice of whether to be buried or cremated, he goes so far as to claim that this decision actually defines modernity.[18] Even when a live option, cremation is often avoided. For an Algerian Jew, cremation is even more fraught because it is a political as well as a personal issue. At one level, Derrida's approach to the choice between burial and cremation is abstract and analytic—he considers the pros and cons of each alternative. Inhumation, he argues, "promises to give me time and space, some time and some space. Apparently more humane, less inhumane than cremation, this humane in-humation seems to assure me that I will not be instantaneously annihilated without remainder. In any case, my remains will be more substantial than ashes and my disappearance will require or will take time" (B, 160). In addition to this, the grave marks a site to which friends and loved ones can return to mourn their loss. The downside of burial is the possibility of being buried alive, and the prospect of bodily decay. Cremation, by contrast, seems to be cleaner, more efficient, and more cost effective. Whereas burial is "the non-disappearance of my corpse after my own disappearance," "cremation makes my body disappear" (B, 161). The disappearance of the corpse leaves no place for mourning. "But having a place nowhere, having no stable place, no *topos* outside the survivors, the image or memory of the dead one becomes ubiquitous, he or she invades the whole space and the whole time, which are purely interiorized. . . . The dead one is both everywhere and nowhere, nowhere because everywhere, out of the world and everywhere in the world and in us. Pure interiorization, pure idealization of the dead one, his or her absolute idealization, his or her dematerialization in the mournful survivor who can only let himself be invaded by a dead one who has no longer any place of his or her own outside—this is both the greatest fidelity and the utmost betrayal, the best way of keeping the other while getting rid of her or him" (B, 169).

Though not immediately apparent, Derrida brings together Hegel and Freud in a surprising way. We have seen that both Hegel's speculative philosophy and Freud's myth of origin can be understood as ghost stories. While Hegel's "spectral" spirituality issues in a salvation narrative in which the dead are redeemed by what comes after them, in Freud's tale the dead father returns more powerful than ever to haunt sons who want to replace him. To underscore this point, Derrida returns to the pivotal sentence in the *Phenomenology of Spirit,* which we have already considered.

> Spirit attains to its truth only when it finds itself again in this absolute tearing [*in der absoluten Zerrissenheit*], it is torn between the life that it is and the death that it is also, since it bears that death within it like mourning. This spirit (but when one

says *Geist,* in German, one indeed says Spirit, but also, spirit defined as a specter or a revenant, a ghost . . .), this spirit that has the strength to *bear death,* this spirit is a power [*Macht*], but the power not to turn away from the negative, and therefore the courage, at bottom, not only to look it in the face, but to take the time to look it in the face, to make this gaze last, not to be content with a quick glance, not to look death in the face for a moment and then look away from it the next moment. That's what *bear* means: it is also to bear looking death in the face in an enduring, durable way, taking the time, giving oneself the time that one thus gives to death. (B, 153)

After the death of God, how is it possible for isolated individuals to bear death? If death is a gift, perhaps redemption is achieved through works. In the instant of death, nature and spirit become corpse and corpus—the question of survival becomes a "matter" of literary remains.

Derrida's obsession with his corpse is a symptom of his concern about his corpus. To face death, as if what is never present could ever be faced, is to confront the loss of control. Derrida decides to be buried rather than cremated, but worries that his survivors will not honor his wish. "What will one do," he wonders, "what will the *other,* the other *alone,* do with me as living dead, given that I can only *think* my dead body, or rather *imagine* my corpse, if anything else is to happen to it, as living dead in the hands of the other? The other alone" (B, 117). And then in one of the most revealing passages in his entire corpus, he adds,

> The other appears to me as the other as such, *qua* he, she, or they who might survive me, survive my decease and then proceed as they wish sovereignly, and sovereignly have at their disposal the future of my remains, if there are any.
> *That's what is meant, has always been meant by "other."*
> But having my remains at their disposal can also take place before I am absolutely, clearly and distinctly dead, meaning that the other, the others, is what also might not wait for me to be dead to do it, to dispose of my remains: the other might

bury me alive, eat me or swallow me alive, burn me alive, etc.
He or she can put me to a living death, and exercise thus his or
her sovereignty. (B, 127, emphasis added)

The other is the one who disposes of my remains after (or even before) I am dead. At the end of the day, it all comes down to legacy—a question of survival or its impossibility. After the death of God, can there be a "secular resurrection"?

Derrida was always concerned with his legacy. In his final interview, he admits, "the trace I leave signifies to me at once my death, either to come or already come upon me, and the hope that this trace survives me. This is not a striving for immortality; it's something structural. I leave a piece of paper behind, I go away, I die: it is impossible to escape this structure, it is the unchanging form of my life. Each time I let something go, each time some trace leaves me, 'proceeds' from me, unable to be reappropriated, I live my death in writing. It's the ultimate test: one expropriates oneself without knowing exactly what's left behind. Who is going to inherit, and how? Will there be any heirs?" (LF, 32–33). Like Freud near the end of his life, Derrida was concerned that his work would live on after him. His discussion of "Freud's Legacy" in *The Post Card* anticipates what would become his own concern. Extending the *fort/da* of the death instinct to Freud's life, Derrida identifies "a very singular concern: . . . that of producing the institutions of his desire, of grafting his own genealogy onto it, of making the tribunal and the juridical tradition of his inheritance, his delegation as a 'movement,' his legacy, his *own*" (PC, 299). As we have seen, in his attempt to secure his legacy, Freud sought to reel back both what and whom he had sent out into the world. Derrida, of course, always resisted calling deconstruction a movement and was reluctant to claim a legacy. Nonetheless, he wanted followers, and, through his endless travels and countless nights in hotels as anonymous as Nietzsche's guesthouses and Blanchot's rooms, he sought to spread the word about deconstruction with missionary zeal.

I personally experienced this preoccupation with legacy. As I noted, Derrida was extremely generous to me and my family. By the end of the 1980s, however, I realized that developments in the intellectual climate as well as the larger world required changes in my thinking. With mounting global social, economic, and environmental problems, it was no longer sufficient to claim that all systems and structures exclude differences and repress otherness through processes of homogenization and totalization. As networking technologies accelerated the process of globalization, it became necessary to find a new way to think holistically. The task I set for myself was to imagine a non-totalizing structure that still could act as a whole. In search of such a novel structure, I took the lessons Derrida had taught me and turned to theories of emerging complex adaptive systems, which were being developed in the social and natural sciences. Unfortunately, the preeminent philosopher of difference did not tolerate differences very well. Though we never had a formal break, our years-long correspondence ended, and I was left to wonder if his many gifts were really gifts, or were long-term investments in his future legacy.

Derrida's lifelong interest in the archive is testimony to his concern with his legacy.[19] Friends who knew him better than I report that he kept everything in an archive that eventually became unmanageable. He died in the midst of a contentious disagreement over the archive he had donated to the University of California, Irvine, in 1990. In response to a dispute between the university and one of his former students, Derrida threatened to restrict authorization for people to use the materials. After his death, there were suits and countersuits between his heirs and the university, which were not settled until 2007. The lingering question from all of these episodes is: When is a gift not a gift?

Derrida always insisted that the archive is more about the future than the past. As that which is destined to return, the archive is the specter or ghost (*revenant*) that keeps the future open. He re-collects his past in his archive in anticipation of a future he will never see and cannot control. A few weeks before his death, Derrida admitted, "in my anticipation of death, in my relation to death to come, which I know will annihilate me, obliterate me completely, there is, beneath the surface, a testamentary desire, that is, the desire that *something* survive, be left behind, transmitted" (S, 23). While his concern with his legacy intensified with the proximity of death, he confessed that death had always haunted him and the question of

survival preoccupied him. But this question is, to say the least, complicated. How does one live on? Through what or in whom does one live on?
The most obvious answer for a writer is that one lives on through his or
her works. The work, however, is always unfinished, incomplete, and,
thus, open. Appearances to the contrary notwithstanding, an author's
work is never merely his or her own because it is always the occasion for
the work of others, which changes what had seemed to be "my own."
Hegel's work, for example, is different because of Marx, and Kierkegaard's
work is different because of Derrida. Just as with death, the corpse is
handed over to the other, so the moment an author sends his corpus into the
world, he loses control over it. This is Derrida's point when he argues that
the work "is a *quasi*-technical or prosthetic apparatus" that is in some sense
autobiographical. "Every written confession through which the author
calls and names himself, that it presents itself through this linguistic and
prosthetic apparatus—a book—or a piece of writing or trace in general . . .
which speaks of him without him, according to a trick that constructs and
leaves in the world an artifact that speaks all alone and all alone calls the
author by his name, renames him in his renown [*le renomme en sa renom-
mée*] without the author himself needing to do anything else, not even to
be alive" (B, 86–87).

When consumed, appropriated, assimilated, the work returns (*revi-
ens*) to the sender as strange. What appears to be survival of the author in
the work actually results in Poe's greatest fear, premature burial, because
Derrida is convinced that "the book is living dead, buried alive and swallowed up alive" (B, 130). Sons who were supposed to preserve the father's
legacy cannibalize his work by turning it to their own ends. "Like every
trace, a book, the survivance of a book, from its first moment on, is a living-
dead machine, sur-viving, the body of a thing buried in a library, a bookstore,
in cellars, urns, drowned in the worldwide waves of the living web, etc., but a
dead thing that resuscitates each time a breath of living reading, each time the
breath of the other or the other breath, each time an intentionality intends it
and makes it live again by animating it" (B, 131).

With the deadly survival of the work, we return to the loss of the world
and the question of *tragen*—to bear, carry, convey, transport. *Die Welt ist
fort, ich muss dich tragen.* What does it mean to bear another? Does bear-

ing give birth? Inflict suffering? Entomb? Or, perhaps, involve all of this and more?" "*Ich muss dich tragen,*" Derrida maintains, can mean only one of two things.

1. Either carry the other out of the world, where we share at least this much knowledge without phantasm that there is no longer a world, a common world: I carry you into the void . . .

2. Or else, second hypothesis, that where there is no world, where the world is not here or there, but *fort,* infinitely distant over there, that what I must do, with you and carrying you, is make it that there be precisely a world, just a world, if not a just world, or do things so to speak as if there were a world . . . the only thing that can make it possible that I can live and have or let you live, and leaving a trace in the world, that belongs to the world, without a trace left or retained in the world that is going away, that will go away . . . leaving no trace, a world that has forever been going to leave and has just left, going away with no trace, the trace becoming trace only by being able to erase itself. (B, 268)

Whether *tragen* carries into the void, bears the void within it, or temporarily delays the end of the world in traces that inevitably erase themselves, the strangeness (*Unheimlichkeit*) of spectral (*revenant*) works that return to their sender reveals the nothingness that haunts human finitude. At this point (NB), we are left to ask with Heidegger, "How is it with the Nothing?"

Fear and Trembling

In April 2004, Derrida reluctantly agreed to an interview for *Le Monde* conducted by Jean Birnbaum, who was the nonfiction editor. Derrida was suspicious of *Le Monde* because he did not think they had treated his work fairly in the past. The interview remained unpublished until August, when, with Marguerite's encouragement and support, he completed the final editing. Birnbaum reports that Derrida, doubtlessly recognizing that these might well be his last words to the general public, devoted scrupulous attention to the text. The interview was published August 19, 2004, with the title "Learning to Live Finally." After reading the article, Derrida sighed, "It's an obituary."[20] Birnbaum listened to the tapes again after the interview appeared, and reported his response, "The voice of a *ghost* that is already contemplating the irreparable. Cheerful and gentle, it is the voice of a *spectral child* who does not yet know anything about life, and who is just beginning to learn—finally. 'I see myself dead cut off from you in your memories that I love and weep like my own children at the edge of my grave'" (LF, 17).

"Learning to Live Finally" is, perhaps, Derrida's clearest and most straightforward statement of the personal and philosophical questions that had preoccupied him throughout his lifetime. Sensitive to the moment of the interview, Birnbaum turns his attention to ghosts and asks Derrida, "Here at the outset of our interview, then, let's return to *Specters of Marx*. A crucial book, a defining work devoted entirely to the question of a justice to come, and which begins with this enigmatic exordium: 'Someone, you or me, comes forward and says: *I would like to learn to live finally.*' More than ten years later, where are you today with regard to this desire to 'know how to live'?" (LF, 22). Derrida's response is extremely revealing.

> I never *learned-to-live*. In fact not at all! Learning to live should mean learning to die, learning to take into account, so as to accept absolute mortality (that is without salvation, resurrection, or redemption—neither for oneself nor for the other). . . . I have never learned to accept it, to accept death, that is. . . . I remain uneducable when it comes to any kind of wisdom about knowing-how-to-die or, if you prefer, knowing-how-to-live. I still have not learned or picked up anything on this subject. The time of the reprieve is rapidly running out. (LF, 24–25)

Life after death—always *after* death. Once more the duplicity of "after." In the absence of "salvation, resurrection, or redemption," what prospect is there for life after death? Derrida's mood, or, in Heidegger's term, *Stimmung*, is not simply the result of approaching death, but has characterized his life from the beginning because he has always been convinced that all life is forever after death. Like Blanchot, Derrida was always living death, and, as a result, even his happiest moments were tinged with melancholy. The most profound melancholy, which Kierkegaard called his "secret mistress," is invisible to the eyes of others. The melancholic spirit travels incognito—while seeming to be absorbed in the moment, he floats above the world, watching from without, knowing the moment will pass, and uncertain it will ever arrive again. In melancholy, the present is never fully present but is always past even before it arrives. The trace of this impending past is most haunting in precisely those moments that are supposed to be complete.

"Given time." But who gives? What gives? The answer, or non-answer, Derrida concludes, lies in the long-overlooked words *Walten,* which means to rule, govern, hold sway, have complete control over, and authority, and *Gewalt,* which means power, authority, dominion, and control. *Walten* and *Gewalt* suggest a certain violence that is not always manifested as such. Heidegger identifies what he describes as the "superhuman violence of *Walten.*" "The sense of sovereign and superhuman violence of *Walten,* of the all-powerful reign of *physis,*" Derrida explains, "appears most clearly in Heidegger's elucidation when he makes clear that humans themselves are dominated, crushed, under the law of this sovereign violence. Man is not its master, he is traversed by it, 'gripped [*transi*],' says the French translation for *durchwalten,* man is dominated, seized, penetrated through and through by the sovereign violence of the *Walten* that he does not master, over which he has neither power nor hold" (B, 41). Derrida admits that it is impossible to respond to such sovereign power—*Walten* must be suffered passively. By labeling *Walten/Gewalt* "superhuman," Heidegger, and Derrida following him, suggest that it is something like "le pas au-delà"—the step as well as the not beyond, which exceeds and simultaneously constitutes human finitude. In his interpretation of *Walten/Gewalt,* Derrida echoes the words Freud borrows from Goethe to end *Totem and Taboo,* "In the beginning is the deed." So understood, *Walten/Gewalt* is the originary violence that is the "origin" of the world, which is both the gift of life and the gift of death.

Commenting on Heidegger's *Introduction to Metaphysics,* Derrida explains that *Walten/Gewalt* is "the exercise of an archi-originary force, of a

power, a violence, before any physical, psychic, theological, political determination, in a moment I shall even say before any ontic or ontological
determination" (B, 104). That which is "before" beings (ontic) and Being
(ontological) is nothing—nothing other than the "ontological difference,"
which is, in the final analysis (and this *is* the final analysis), virtually indistinguishable from *différance*.

> Whatever the translation here, we must clearly see that Hei-
> degger intends to mark the fact that if Being and beings as such
> *are* [*wesen:* comment: active, quasi-transitive, and announcing
> *walten*] as different, they are [*wesen*] different only as the same,
> remaining the same, and in the internal splitting of the same of
> the *Unter-Scheid,* where the hyphen thus inscribes this union
> of the same in difference. Whence the insistence, immediately
> afterward, on the *between,* the *Zwischen,* which slips itself into
> the same without in a sense dissociating it from itself, without
> making of it two things or two different beings, where however
> a certain unique difference, a certain heterogeneity, a certain al-
> terity has precisely been what arrives and supervenes, what
> happens between the supervening of Being and the arrival of
> beings as such. (B, 254)

As the condition of the possibility of all opposites and every opposition,
this "between" is neither one nor the other, but is a different difference,
which is, in words borrowed from Kierkegaard, "infinitely and qualitatively
different." In a manner reminiscent of the *logos apophatantikos,* this margin of difference (*die Zwischen* inscribed as "/"), which approaches by disappearing, clears the space and opens the time (*aletheia*) where all beings
dwell. The original donation of beings as well as Being cannot be grasped
(*greifen*) in concepts (*Begriffe*) but must be apprehended in moods that are
anterior to thinking. Derrida attempts to explain this point by quoting Heidegger's *Fundamental Concepts of Metaphysics.* "The fundamental concern of philosophizing [*Das Grundbemuhen des Philosophierens*] pertains
to being gripped [*Ergriffenheit*], to awakening [*Werkung*] and planting it

[to its cultivation, *Pflanzung*]. All such being gripped [*Ergriffenheit*], however, comes from and remains in an *attunement* [*Stimmung*]. To the extent that conceptual comprehending [*das Begreifen*] and philosophizing is not some arbitrary enterprise alongside others, but happens in the *ground* of human Dasein [*im* Grunde—emphasized—*des menschlichen Daseins*], the attunements out of which our being gripped [*Ergriffenheit*] philosophically and our philosophical comprehension [*Begrifflichkeit*] arise are always necessarily fundamental attunements [*Grundstimmungen*] of Dasein" (B, 111). While Aristotle maintains that philosophy begins in wonder, Heidegger claims that philosophizing begins with gripping moods, the most important of which is, in this context, anxiety.

In contrast to fear, which always has a determinate object, anxiety, as Kierkegaard argued in *The Concept of Anxiety* (1844), is the apprehension of nothing. This nothing, Heidegger explains, "makes itself known with beings and in beings expressly as a slipping away of the whole." This slipping away marks the instant when *Die Welt ist fort*. The nothingness of this instant, which is neither present nor absent, haunts everything and everyone, rendering them uncanny (*unheimlich*). So understood, nothing "is not some fortuitous incident. Rather, as the repelling gesture toward the retreating whole of beings, it discloses these beings in their full but heretofore concealed strangeness [*Unheimlichkeit*] as what is radically other—with respect to the nothing."[21] If beings (*Dasein*) are "radically other" than *Das Nichts,* then nothing is radically other than beings, and, it is necessary to add, nothing other than Being itself (*Sein*). In this undialectical reversal, Derrida unexpectedly discerns the secret name of what once was called God.

After the last seminar, after the last interview, there was yet another conference and another "presentation"—"Comment ne pas trembler?" Derrida notes at the outset of his remarks that this title echoes an address he had given twenty years earlier in Jerusalem—"Comment ne pas parler?" In August 2004, after his last round of chemotherapy, Derrida and Marguerite traveled to Meina on the shore of Lake Maggiore to visit their longtime friend Valerio Adami at his drawing academy. It was here that Derrida celebrated his seventy-fourth and final birthday. The influential Caribbean writer and critic Edouard Glissant had organized a conference in honor of Adami on the theme "How Not to Tremble."[22] With a gesture to his friend and collaborator Adami as well as himself, Derrida explains, "The artist is someone who becomes an artist only when his hand trembles, in other words when he basically does not know what is going to happen to him, when what is going to happen to him is dictated by the other."[23] Though his remarks were brief, they are remarkable for their disclosure of Derrida's preoccupations during the last weeks of his life. He honors Adami by returning to Kierkegaard's *Fear and Trembling*, which, we have seen, he had probed in *The Gift of Death*.

Derrida begins by noting the two times when he had trembled—the first was political, in 1942–43 during bombing raids in Algeria; the second was personal, during the recent chemotherapy treatment for his cancer. His question is not only how to avoid trembling, but also what makes one tremble? He approaches these questions by reconsidering the issue of the secret around which *The Gift of Death* is organized. "The secret," he writes, "always makes one tremble." Since what occasions trembling remains a secret, "the thought of trembling is a singular experience of non-knowledge [*non-savoir*]," which "is always the experience of a passivity, absolutely exposed, absolutely vulnerable, passive before an irreversible past as well as before an unforeseeable future." To elucidate this trembling, Derrida turns to Paul by way of Kierkegaard. "If Paul says 'farewell' [*a-Dieu*] and takes his leave while asking [his addressees] to obey, while commanding [them] to obey (for one does not ask for obedience, one commands or orders it), it is because God himself is absent, concealed and silent, apart, hidden—the very moment one must obey him." Borrowing a term form Rudolph Otto's important but overlooked book, *The Idea of the Holy,* Derrida labels this secret the "*mysterium tremendum.*" "God," Derrida explains, "is the cause of the *mysterium tremendum,* and given death [*la mort donnée*] is always what makes one tremble and also what makes one weep." He draws this final insight in his homage to Adami from Kierkegaard. "What makes one tremble in the *mysterium tremendum?* It is the gift of infinite love, the dissymmetry between the divine gaze, which sees me and my own, which does not see the same one who sees me, it is the given death [*la mort donnée*] and bears the irreplaceable, that is the disproportion between the infinite gift and my finitude, the responsibility as culpability, sin, salvation, repentance, and sacrifice. Like the title of Kierkegaard's, *Fear and Trembling*, the *mysterium tremendum* carries a reference at least indirectly to Saint Paul."

While never here-and-now, the God who makes one tremble is the non-original origin of all presence and every present. Commenting on this God in *The Gift of Death*, Derrida writes, "God is the name of the absolute other and as unique (the God of Abraham defined as the one and unique)" (GD, 68). In the moment, in the instant of my death, I am gripped by fear and trembling because I am delivered over to an other that has at its disposal "the future of my remains, if there are any. That's what is meant, has always been meant, by 'other'" (B, 127). With time quickly running out, Derrida's final lesson in leaving is that time is always given—it is never ours to keep, waste, spend, or save. To live is to survive in a present that is never present but is always already past and, thus, forever yet to come. In the absence of "salvation, resurrection, or redemption," the gift of life is the gift of death, and the gift of death is the gift of life.

SIX

Delirium

Edgar Allan Poe (1809–1849): *Eureka,* "Annabel Lee"

No, but I wish to go under; to visit the profound depths; once in a while
to exercise my prerogative not always to act, but to explore; to hear vague,
ancestral sounds of boughs creaking, of mammoths; to indulge impossible desires
to embrace the whole world with the arms of understanding—impossible to those
who act. Am I not, as I walk, trembling with strange oscillations and vibrations
of sympathy, which, unmoored as I am from a private being. . . .
But I am aware of our ephemeral passage.

—Virginia Woolf, *The Waves*

Orphan

The neighborhood where I live in New York City is haunted by Poe. A
few blocks south near the corner of Broadway and 84th Street is the site
of the farmhouse where Poe lived when he wrote "The Raven." This
poem, which was published in the *New York Evening Mirror* on January 29, 1845, made Poe an overnight celebrity.[1] The raven's "Nevermore"
in response to the narrator's repeated inquiries about his deceased
lover might well serve as a refrain for all of Poe's writings. The room
described in the poem was on the second floor of the house where, hard
though it is to believe today, Poe could look out the open window through
which the raven flew and see lakes and a forest stretching to the Hudson
River. He liked to walk in the area and, during the summers of 1843 and
1844, he would often stop to sit atop nearby Mount Tom in what is now

Riverside Park, to gaze at the river while letting his imagination roam freely.

When the farmhouse was scheduled for demolition in the late nineteenth century, William Hemstreet bought the fireplace and mantle Poe alludes to in the poem for $5.

> Ah, distinctly I remember it was in the bleak December;
> And each separate dying ember wrought its ghost upon the
> floor.[2] (81)

In recognition of the centenary of Poe's birth (1909), Hemstreet presented the fireplace and mantle to Columbia University, where I now teach. Rather than displaying the memento prominently as then-president Nicholas Murray Butler had promised, the Raven Mantle disappeared for over a hundred years. In 2012, two journalists with the tenacity and investigative savvy of one of Poe's detectives tracked it down and embarrassed Columbia into putting it on display. It now sits enclosed in glass in the rare book room of the library that bears President Butler's name.[3]

Two blocks east of my apartment there is a subway station for the train that runs between Manhattan and the Bronx. A short ride takes you to Fordham, where Poe, his wife Virginia, and her mother and his aunt, Maria Clemm, moved in 1846. Like the Upper West Side of Manhattan, Fordham was largely rural at the time; farmhouses and small dwellings lined Kingsbridge Highway. Poe rented a cottage near St. Johns, which is now Fordham University. This is where Poe spent the last years of his life (1846–49), and wrote his last poem, "Annabel Lee." The cottage has been moved a few blocks from its original site and has been restored as closely as possible to the condition in which Poe left it.

The ceilings are low and the rooms are small and sparsely furnished. On the first floor there is the desk where Poe wrote, and on the second floor there is the rope bed where Virginia died on January 30, 1847. In 1863, Mary Gove, who was reputed to be a mesmerist, Swedenborgian, phrenologist, and homeopath, recalled the cottage more fondly than appears justified

Edgar Allan Poe's Raven Mantle

today. "The cottage had an air of taste and gentility that must have been lent to it by the presence of its intimates. So neat, so poor, so unfurnished, and yet so charming a dwelling I never saw."[4]

Mrs. Gove was not the only one to idealize the house. In the last short story he wrote, "Landor Cottage," Poe describes what appears to be the cottage and its setting in Edenic terms that reflect one of his most basic aesthetic principles of "variety in unity."

On this peninsula stood a dwelling-house and when I say that this house, like the infernal terrace seen by Vathek, *"était d'une architecture inconnue dans les annals de la terre,"* I mean, merely that its *toute ensemble* struck me with the keenest sense of combined novelty and propriety—in a word poetry . . . and

Poe Cottage, Fordham, New York

> I do *not* mean that the merely *outré* was perceptible in any
> respect.
>
> In fact nothing could be more simple—more utterly un-
> pretending than this cottage. Its marvelous *effect* lay altogether
> in its artistic arrangement *as a picture.* I could have fancied,
> while I looked at it, that some eminent landscape-painter had
> built it with his brush. (892–93)

One of the reasons Poe was so drawn to the cottage was that it represented
the possibility of stability in a life that had been uprooted from birth. His
parents were actors who led an itinerant life roaming from Richmond to
Philadelphia to New York before settling in Boston. His mother, Elizabeth
Arnold, immigrated to Boston from England in 1796, and had her stage de-
but at the age of nine. When she was only fifteen, she married Charles Hopkins, who died two years later. Within six months, she married again, this
time to a ne'er-do-well member of the troupe, David Poe, from Baltimore.

She had two sons, William Henry Leonard (1807) and Edgar (1809), and a daughter, Rosaline (1810). David was an alcoholic and deserted the family shortly after moving them to New York City and just before Rosaline was born. Poe never saw his father again.

Once-widowed and abandoned with three young children, Elizabeth was dirt poor and struggled to support her family by continuing to travel with the troupe. But in 1811, while performing in Richmond, she began to spit blood, and a few months later died of tuberculosis, leaving Poe an orphan at the age of two. Much of his life and work can be understood as an effort to recover the mother he never knew. The three children were split up, and Poe went to live with a prosperous Richmond merchant, John Allan. Though Allan never adopted Poe, he supported him until their relationship broke down over Poe's drinking and gambling debts during his first year at the University of Virginia. Unable to support himself, Poe lied about his age and enlisted in the army, which, predictably, proved to be a disaster. After orchestrating his dismissal by telling the truth about his age, he tried the military once again by enrolling in West Point. Military discipline proved unbearable for such an undisciplined person. Poe provoked his own court martial and expulsion from the academy. During this tumultuous period, he was writing poetry, and by the time he left West Point in 1831, he had published three volumes of poems.

More important than his aborted military career and early publications was his marriage to his thirteen-year-old first cousin, Virginia Clemm. Poe was twenty-seven at the time. Though criticized and sometimes ostracized for the marriage, Poe and Virginia's love for each other seems to have been genuine, though the precise nature of their relationship continues to be the subject of speculation. Some biographers and critics insist that the marriage was troubled and never consummated. Virginia was frail, and Poe, who suffered periods of serious mental instability like his father and brother, was an alcoholic. To make matters worse, chronic poverty prevented Poe from providing adequately for Virginia and her mother, who lived with the couple. When Virginia also developed tuberculosis in 1842, Poe sank into deep depression and began drinking more than ever. He was acutely aware of his tenuous condition and wrote to a friend, "Each time I felt all the agonies of her death—and at each accession of the disorder I loved her more dearly and clung to her life with more desperate pertinacity. But I am constitutionally sensitive— nervous in a very unusual degree. I became insane, with long intervals of horrible sanity."[5]

Professional and financial difficulties forced Poe and his family to move several times, which had an adverse effect on Virginia's condition. The decision to move to the Fordham cottage was largely prompted by his hope that the rural environment would be therapeutic for Virginia. As her illness progressed, Poe's expressions of affection grew more desperate. On July 12, 1846, he wrote to his failing wife, "You are my *greatest* and *only* stimulus now, to battle with this uncongenial, unsatisfactory, and ungrateful life."[6] With Virginia's condition rapidly getting worse, the winter of 1846 proved to be unbearably difficult. Too ill to write, Poe was unable to generate any income, and was driven to the extreme measure of taking out newspaper ads soliciting financial support. Mary Gove's recollection once again is instructive.

> The autumn came, and Mrs. Poe sank rapidly in consumption, and I saw her in her bed chamber. Everything here was so neat, so purely clean, so scant and poverty-stricken, that I saw the sufferer with such a heartache as the poor feel for the poor. There was no clothing on the bed, which was only straw, but a snow white spread and sheets. The weather was cold, and the sick lady had the dreadful chills that accompany the hectic fever of consumption. She lay on the straw bed, wrapped in her husband's great-coat, with a large tortoise-shell cat on her bosom. The wonderful cat seemed conscious of her great usefulness. The coat and the cat were the sufferer's only means of warmth, except as her husband held her hands, and her mother her feet.[7]

On January 20, 1845, Virginia died and was buried in a nearby plot. Her body was later moved to Baltimore, where she is buried next to Poe and her mother.

In the months before Virginia's death, Poe's depression often left him unable to write. After an initial collapse when she died, he became manic; with Virginia gone, the demons that had pursued him throughout his life ran wild. His ambition for writing returned and he revived his lifelong dream of founding and editing a literary journal, which he named *The Stylus.* In pursuit of funding, he traveled from Richmond to New York City by way of Baltimore and Philadelphia. In the midst of all this turmoil, he somehow had periods of extraordinary creativity and astonishing productivity. In 1848, he published the 40,000-word *Eureka: Prose Poem,* which was his last work and remains one of the most sophisticated philosophical poems in the history of American literature.

The most bizarre aspect of Poe's behavior during the last years of his life was his series of desperate relationships with women. As his life with Virginia and her mother made clear, Poe had serious issues with sexuality. It often seems as if he was in love with womanhood or women in general rather than with real individual women. George Rex Graham, who was an editor and publisher with whom Poe worked on his proposed literary journal, wrote of Poe's relation to Virginia, "His love for his wife was a sort of rapturous worship of the spirit of beauty."[8] Poe actually suggests the pertinence of Graham's observation when he writes in "Landon's Romance": " '*Romance*' provided my readers fully comprehend what I would here imply by the word—'romance' and 'womanliness' seem to me to be convertible terms:—and, after all, what man truly *loves* in woman is, simply, her *womanhood*" (896). Women, then, are always the faint trace of "Woman," who, in the final analysis, is the figure of the lost mother. In rapid succession, Poe had relationships with a Providence widow named Sarah Helen Whitman; Annie Richmond, to whom he turned when his proposed marriage to Sarah unraveled; and even Sarah Elmira Royster, who had been his first love when he was a boy in Richmond.

His relationship with Maria Clemm was, however, the most revealing of all. In the absence of his own mother as well as Virginia, Poe started calling his aunt "Mother." Though he traveled frequently after Virginia's death, he and his mother-in-law continued to share the Fordham cottage. In 1837, he had headed north with the hope of finding support for his literary ambitions among the elites in northeastern literary society. A decade later, growing tensions between the North and the South led him to conclude that his chances for his magazine were better in the South, so he planned to return to Richmond. Suffering from anxiety, paranoia, and serious delusions, Poe was returning to Richmond from New York when he stopped in Philadelphia, where there was a cholera epidemic. On July 7, 1848, he wrote to his mother-in-law:

> My *dear, dear* Mother,—I have been *so* ill—have had the cholera, or spasms quite as bad, and can now hardly hold the pen.
>
> The very instant you get this, *come* to me. The joy of seeing you will almost compensate for our sorrows. We can but die together. It is no use to reason with *me* now; I must die. I have no desire to live since I have done "Eureka." I could accomplish nothing more. For your sake it would be sweet to live, but we must die together. You have been all in all to me, darling, ever beloved mother, and dearest friend.

Five days later, his condition stabilized and he continued his journey. As he approached Richmond, he wrote to Maria again. "The weather is awfully hot, and, besides all this, *I am so homesick I don't know what to do* [emphasis added]. I never wanted to see any one half so bad as I want to see my own darling mother. It seems to me that I would make any sacrifice to hold you by the hand once more, and get you to cheer me up, for I am terribly depressed. I do not think that any circumstances will ever tempt me to leave you again. When I am with you I can bear anything, but when I am away from you I am too miserable to live."[9] Though he never explicitly acknowledged it, Poe realized time was running out.

Poe's death is as shrouded in mystery as one of his uncanny tales. In the weeks prior to his death, he was traveling and lecturing to raise money for *The Stylus*. That summer he had joined the Sons of Temperance and claimed to be sober, but nothing is clear about his last days. According to the best estimates, Poe left Richmond for New York on September 27. After this trip, he planned to return to Richmond and apparently marry Sarah

Elmira Royster. Friends reported that he was in good spirits before he left. Six days later, his friend J. E. Snodgrass received an unexpected message.

> Baltimore City, Oct. 3, 1849
>
> Dear Sir,—
>
> There is a gentleman, rather the worse for wear, at Ryan's 4th ward polls, who goes under the cognomen of Edgar A. Poe, and who appears in great distress, & he says he is acquainted with you, and I assure you, he is in need of immediate assistance.
>
> Yours, in haste,
> Jos. W. Walker[10]

It remains unclear where Poe had been during the last week of his life. When Snodgrass found him, he was delirious and dressed in someone else's tattered clothes. He took him to the Washington College Hospital, where, Arthur Quinn reports, "he remained unconscious until three o'clock the next morning, but even on regaining partial consciousness, he was unable to tell Dr. Moran, the attending physician, how he had come to the condition in which he was found. From this state of utter despair and self-reproach he passed into a violent delirium, which lasted until Saturday evening."[11] The next day, October 7, 1849, Edgar Allan Poe died; two days later, he was buried near the Presbyterian Cemetery, where he remained until 1875, when his remains were moved and reburied beside Virginia and Maria Clemm.

Homesickness

During the last year of his life, Poe's depression deepened. In the spring of 1849, he wrote to Annie Richardson, "my sadness is *unaccountable,* and this makes me the more sad. I am full of dark forebodings. *Nothing* cheers or comforts me. My life seems wasted—the future looks a dreary blank; but I will struggle on and 'hope against hope.' "[12] His hope, however, was faint and quickly faded. He kept in touch with Maria Clemm and in July published a sonnet entitled "To My Mother."

> You who are more than mother unto me,
> And fill my heart of hearts, where Death installed you
>   In setting my Virginia's spirit free.
> My mother—my own mother, who died early,
>   Was but the mother of myself; but you
> Are mother to the one I loved so dearly,
>   And thus are dearer than the mother I knew
> By that infinity with which my wife
>   Was dearer to my soul than its soul-life. (101)

His homage to his mother-in-law is, of course, an expression of his continuing love for Virginia. At the time his sonnet appeared, he was working on his last poem—"Annabel Lee." This poem is at once a eulogy and an act of mourning through which Poe attempted to work through not only the death of Virginia, but also the losses that had plagued his troubled life. As always, there is a romanticization of the feminine figure and an idealization of love.

> *I* was a child and *she* was a child,
>   In this kingdom by the sea,
> But we loved with a love that was more than love—
>   I and my Annabel Lee—
> With a love that the wingèd seraphs of Heaven
>   Coveted her and me.

The excess and hyperbole of Poe's poetry does not obscure the depth of his sense of loss and the endless longing he continued to suffer. He concludes,

> For the moon never beams, without bringing me dreams
>   Of the beautiful Annabel Lee;
> And the stars never rise, but I feel the bright eyes

> Of the beautiful Annabel Lee;
> And so, all the night-tide, I lie down by the side
>   Of my darling—my darling—my life and my bride,
> In her sepulchre there by the sea—
> In her tomb by the sounding sea. (102)

In these final lines, Poe invokes a series of associations that run through all of his works: woman, sea, tomb, burial, death. In terms Freud would invoke seven decades later, Eros and Thanatos meet in the narrator, who returns to the Mother by joining his dead lover in her watery tomb.

Art, for Poe, is a matter of life and death that expresses the infinite longing for something that forever eludes his grasp. In "The Poetic Principle," which Poe delivered as a lecture in the weeks immediately before his death but was not published until 1850, he presents his most basic aesthetic principle, which both informed the substance of his life and drove him to his death.

> An immortal instinct, deep within the spirit of man, is thus, plainly a sense of the Beautiful. This it is which administers to his delight in the manifold forms, and sounds, and odors, and sentiments amid which he exists. . . . There is still a something in the distance which he has been unable to attain. We have still a thirst unquenchable, to allay which he has not shown us the crystal springs. This thirst belongs to the immortality of Man. It is at once a consequence and an indication of his perennial existence. It is the desire of the moth for the star. It is no mere appreciation of the Beauty before us—but a wild effort to reach the Beauty above. Inspired by an ecstatic prescience of the glories beyond the grave, we struggle by multiform combinations among the things and thoughts of Time, to attain a portion of that Loveliness whose very elements, perhaps, appertain to eternity alone. And thus when by Poetry,—or when by Music, the most entrancing of the Poetic moods, we find ourselves melted into tears—we weep then—not . . . through excess of pleasure,

but through a certain, petulant, impatient sorrow at our inability to grasp *now,* wholly, here on earth, at once and for ever,
those divine and rapturous joys, of which *through* the poem,
or *through* the music, we attain to but brief and indeterminate
glimpses.[13]

Poetry, for Poe, was the antidote to "the sickness unto death." As I have
noted, in a letter to his "Mother," Poe confesses, "I am so homesick I don't
know what to do." This homesickness is an undercurrent in all of Poe's
writing.

In the first session of his last seminar, Derrida indirectly clarifies Poe's
quandary as well as its aesthetic expression by quoting a line from Novalis
that is crucial for Heidegger's interpretation of philosophy: "Philosophy
is really homesickness, an urge to be home everywhere" (B, 37). For Novalis, philosophy, poetically understood, provides the therapy Poe sees in art.
Derrida explains that art, philosophy, and religion are bound and rebound
(*re-ligere*) in a circle that is a circle of circles. He elaborates the implications
of Heidegger's reading of Novalis in his own account of *Robinson Crusoe.*
"So we are in a circle which always makes us retrace our steps. . . . And thus
to accede to the proper essence of philosophy, which is not science, or art,
or religion, one goes round in circles, either circularly or specularly, one
is sent back to oneself, to one's own point of departure, one steps in one's
own footsteps, one goes round in circles as though on an island." For
Heidegger and Derrida, the most complete formulation of the circular
narrative of philosophy is Hegel's speculative system. When Alpha and
Omega are One, the circle is closed and becoming is transformed into
Being.

The vision, which is old as Western philosophy and religion, comes
to its fullest expression in nineteenth-century German romantic poets
and idealist philosophers who prepared the way for Hegelianism. Poe read
deeply in this tradition and was influenced by figures like Friedrich and August Schlegel, Johann Fichte, and Friedrich Schiller. Perpetually suspended
between polar opposites he could neither reconcile nor collapse, Poe was
dispositionally predisposed to their unifying visions. He symbolized these

opposites, which were psychological, spiritual, metaphysical, political, and even geographical, as the North and South Poles. In his exceptionally insightful book, *American Hieroglyphics: The Symbol of the Egyptian Hieroglyphics in the American Renaissance,* John Irwin explains the importance of Poe's multivalent polar imagery. "The continuous network of differential oppositions establishes man in an essentially mediate, relational condition between the poles of primal dualities (left/right, up/down, light/ dark, and so on), poles that, because they are mutually constitutive, are always conceptually implicit in their opposites. Yet in his quest for self-definition, for the absolute limits of self-consciousness, man attempts to transcend his relational condition, to leave his position between polar opposites and, by journeying to one extreme or the other, to establish an absolute upper or lower limit through an ascent into the sublime or descent into the abyss. Both poles are, however, simultaneously the sublime and the abyss, for what one seeks in moving toward one polar opposite or the opposite, is to transcend the mediate and reach the unmediated ground where the bipolar oppositions of language are fused, to reach that totality of undifferentiated Being that, because it is without differentiation, can only be experienced as a kind of nothingness—a sublime that is an abyss."[14] For Poe, as for Blanchot and Derrida, the challenge of writing is to trace the limit of thinking and language by representing the unrepresentable in self-erasing images and ideas.

As I have suggested, two of Poe's most recurrent interrelated figures of the unfigurable are woman and the sea. "Morella" and "Ligeia," which are among his most haunting tales, are meditations on these images. "Morella" begins with an epigram from Plato's *Symposium:* "Itself, by itself solely, ONE everlasting, and single." This ONE, which Morella embodies through her death, is the ONE for which Poe eternally longs. The nameless narrator reports that the strange Morella is preoccupied with "mystical writings, which are usually considered the mere dross of the early German literature." Far from a comforting presence, this woman provokes terror, yet exercises an irresistible attraction. "Hour after hour would I linger by her side, and dwell upon the music of her voice—until, at length, its melody was tainted with terror,—and there fell a shadow upon my soul and

I grew pale, and shuddered inwardly at those too unearthly tones. And thus, joy suddenly faded into horror, and the most beautiful became the most hideous" (234, 235). Struggling to cope with his ambivalent feelings, the narrator offers a comment that illuminates all of Poe's work. "The wild Pantheism of Fichte; the modified Palingenesis of the Pythagoreans; and, above all, the doctrines of *Identity* as urged by Schelling, were generally the points of discussion presenting the most of beauty to the imaginative Morella . . . above all, the doctrines of *Identity* [Poe's emphasis] as urged by Schelling" (235). Critics have overlooked the importance of Schelling's work for Poe, but his philosophy of identity is thoroughly consistent with the metaphysical foundation of Poe's writings and illuminates his work in unexpected ways.

Schelling, who was a roommate of Hegel and Hölderlin at the Tübingen Seminary, is one of the rare figures in philosophy who developed two diametrically opposed philosophies, which both have been very influential. The *Identitätphilosophie* developed in his *System of Transcendental Idealism,* published when Schelling was only twenty-five, represents an important chapter in the history of German Idealism. Though they eventually parted ways when Hegel famously declared that Schelling's original principle was "the night in which all cows are black," Schelling's work nonetheless forms a crucial bridge between Hegelian and Fichtean Idealism. His later so-called positive philosophy represented an alternative metaphysical or, more precisely, post-metaphysical position that played a decisive role in Kierkegaard's thinking. Schelling's most interesting work for Poe's writing is *The Philosophy of Art,* which was presented in lectures during the winter term of 1802–3 at the University of Berlin, but was not published until 1859. While it is impossible to trace a direct line of influence, Schelling's formulation of the metaphysics of art clarifies the substance of Poe's aesthetic.

The foundational principle of Schelling's philosophy is the Absolute, which, he insists, is "absolutely one." Behind, beneath, or within all the differences and oppositions that plague life, there is a *point* (NB) of identity—*die Indifferenz Punkt*—where all is One and One is all. Schelling names this nameless One both the Absolute and God. "*Philosophy* emerges in its most complete manifestation only with the totality of all potencies, since it is to be an accurate image of the universe; the universe, however, = *the absolute, represented in the totality of all determinations.* God and the universe are one, or are merely different views of one and the same thing. God is the universe viewed from the perspective of identity. . . . I call this principle the *absolute point of identity* of philosophy. This point of indifference, precisely because it is such a point and because it is absolutely one, inseparable and indivisible, inheres necessarily in its own turn within every *particular* unity (also called potence). . . . We always know only the absolutely one or absolute unity, as this absolutely one only in particular forms."[15] Since this *Indifferenz Punkt* obviously excludes all differences and distinctions, it cannot be clearly and precisely articulated in concepts and language, which, as Poe realized, presuppose differential distinctions. Art conveys what reason cannot. Schelling goes so far as to argue that God or the Absolute is an artist and, thus, "*the universe is formed in God as an absolute work of art in eternal beauty.*"[16] Accordingly, human beings are works of art that are incarnations of the divine creative principle. The work of the artist mimics the work of the Artist. Individuals extend divine creativity, which is most fully revealed in the work of genius. "*The real side of genius, or that unity that constitutes the informing of the infinite in the finite,*" Schiller explains, "can be called *poesy* in the narrower sense; the ideal side, or that unity that constitutes the informing of the finite into the infinite can be called the *art* within art."[17]

The experience of beauty is the apprehension of the absolute in the relative, and the infinite in the finite. For Schelling, as for Poe, the essence of beauty is the sublime in which differences and differentiations collapse into an identity that is simultaneously original and terminal. The resulting formlessness constitutes chaos, which is the womb and tomb of all determinate existence. In Schelling's terms, "Chaos is the fundamental intuition of the sublime. . . . The fundamental intuition of chaos itself lies within the vision or intuition of the absolute. The inner essence of the absolute, that in which all resides as one and one as all, is primal chaos itself. Yet precisely here we encounter that identity of absolute form with formlessness, for that chaos within the absolute is not mere negation of form, but rather formlessness within the highest and absolute form, and, in a reverse fashion, absolute form within formlessness."[18]

This is the formlessness that Poe approaches at the North and South Poles, and the narrator sees in Morella's melancholy eyes. "I met the glance of her meaning eyes, and then my soul sickened and became giddy with the giddiness of one who gazes downward into some dreary and unfathomable abyss." As his bride fades into oblivion, she lets out a Christlike sigh, "I am dying, yet shall I live" (236). At the moment of her death this prophecy is fulfilled—her nameless daughter is born. From the time of her birth, she was an unusual child both physically and intellectually, and her father was determined to protect her from the outside world. When she, like her mother, dies prematurely, she is buried in the ancestral tomb, as "the ripples upon the sea murmured evermore—Morella" (239). Her grief-stricken father gazes into the grave that had held her mother but found no trace of his dead wife. Unsettled by the experience, the father reflects on his daughter's life. "As years rolled away, and I gazed day after day upon her holy, and mild, and eloquent face, and pored over her maturing form, day after day did I discover new points of resemblance in the child to her mother, the melancholy and the dead. And, hourly, grew darker these shadows of similitude, and more full, and more definite, and more perplexing, and more hideously terrible in their aspect. For that her smile was like her mother's I could bear; but then I shuddered at its too perfect *identity*—that her eyes were like Morella's I could endure; but then they too often looked down into the depths of my soul with Morella's own intense and bewildering meaning" (237–38). In the *Indifferenz Punkt* of this identity, mother, daughter, and father become *one* in an incestuous relationship.

This is the same abyss another nameless narrator sees in the haunting eyes of Ligeia. The story that bears her name is complicated by the suggestion that it might be an opium dream. Whatever its cause, the horror provoked by this "hideous drama of revivification" is palpable (376). "Ligeia" complements "Morella" by adding a further dimension to the experience of living death that is best described as what Blanchot labels "the terrifyingly ancient." Never fully present here-and-now, Ligeia's beauty evokes memories that remain lost in oblivion. Struggling to comprehend what repeatedly escapes his grasp, yet another nameless narrator writes, "There is no point, among the many incomprehensible anomalies of the science of mind, more thrillingly exciting than the fact—never, I believe, noticed in the schools—that, in our endeavors to recall to memory something long forgotten, we often find ourselves *upon the very verge* of remembrance, without being able, in the end, to remember. And thus how frequently, in my intense scrutiny of Ligeia's eyes, have I felt approaching the full knowledge of their expression—felt it approaching—yet not quite be mine—and so at length entirely depart! And (strange, oh strangest mystery of all!) I found, in the commonest objects of the universe, a circle of analogies to that expression" (265). As Blanchot and Derrida argue, the present is never original but is always secondary to a past that can be neither remembered nor re-collected. Once oblivion is, impossibly, recalled, it limns every person and all objects as the empty center around which they constantly revolve. Ligeia is the figure of this unfigurable void. Poe, like Schelling, realizes that the point of identity can only be "glimpsed" in poesy. That is why Ligeia is a poet.

> Mimes, in the form of God on high,
>   Mutter and mumble low,
> And hither and thither fly—
>   Mere puppets they, who come and go
> At bidding of vast formless things
>   That shift the scenery to and fro,
> Flapping from out their Condor wings
>   Invisible Wo!
>
> That motley drama!—oh, be sure
>   It shall not be forgot!
> With its Phantom chased forevermore,
>   By a crowd that seize it not,
> Through a circle that ever returneth in
>   To the self-same spot,
> And much of Madness and more of Sin,
>   And Horror the soul of the plot. (268)

"A circle that ever returneth in / To the self-same spot." This is the *point* of Poe's writing, and the placeless place of this point is the South Pole. Here lies "Horror the soul of the plot."

Poe disguised his psychological, spiritual, and metaphysical musings as captivating stories of exploration and adventure. Though he never roamed the world's oceans like Melville, he was always drawn to the sea. Two of Poe's most engaging stories, "Ms. Found in a Bottle" (1831) and *The Narrative of Arthur Gordon Pym of Nantucket* (1838), anticipate *Moby-Dick* (1851). Poe's short story presents the outline of his much longer novel in what he describes as "an incredible tale" of unlikely sur(-)vival. While ostensibly an account of a disastrous sea voyage to the South Pole, the story is actually a meditation on writing. Another nameless narrator, who takes delight in unnamed "German moralists," undertakes a journey along the archipelago of the Sunda Islands. Shortly after departing, the weather abruptly changes and a furious storm shatters the ship. There are only two survivors, the narrator and an old Swede, who live on by clinging to a fragment of the ship floating toward the South Pole. The farther South they drift, the worse the weather becomes until the sea turns even more mysterious. On the fifth day, the sun "gave out no light, properly so called, but a dull and sullen glow without reflection, as if all its rays were polarized. Just before sinking within the turgid sea, its central fires suddenly went out, as if hurriedly extinguished by some unaccountable power. It was a dim, silver-like rim, alone, as it rushed down the unfathomable ocean" (192). When the weather becomes even more violent, the abandoned pair encounters a ghost ship that is as strange as the ancient eyes of Morella and Ligeia.

Slipping into the captain's cabin, the narrator decides to record his appalling experience. "It is true," he admits, "that I may not find an opportunity of transmitting it to the world, but I will not fail to make the endeavor. At the last moment I will enclose the MS. in a bottle, and cast it within the sea" (196). As he struggles to describe the ghost ship, he sounds more like a negative theologian than a maritime storyteller. "I have made many observations lately upon the structure of the vessel. Although well armed, she is not, I think, a ship of war. Her rigging, build, and general equipment, all negative a supposition of this kind. What she *is not,* I can easily perceive; what she *is,* I fear it is impossible to say" (195–96). So impressed is the narrator with the age of the ghostly ship and its crew that he concludes the vessel is "imbued with the spirit of Eld."

As the ship rushes southward ever faster, it is surrounded by the chaos Schelling deemed sublime. The narrator records the final events in his journal. "All in the immediate vicinity of the ship, is the blackness of eternal night, a chaos of foamless water; but, about a league on either side of us, may be seen, indistinctly and at intervals, stupendous ramparts of ice, towering away into the desolate sky, and looking like the walls of the universe." At the poles, polarized opposites collapse into each other: day becomes night, white becomes black, depth becomes height. With a rush that is as much psychological as physical, the ship "howling and shrieking by the white ice, thunders on to the southward with a velocity like the headlong dashing of a cataract." Circles circulate within circles until all vanishes into a point. "Oh, horror upon horror!—the ice opens suddenly to the right, and to the left, and we are whirling dizzily in immense concentric circles. . . . The circles rapidly grow small—we are plunging madly within the grasp of the whirlpool—and amid a roaring, and bellowing, and thundering of ocean and of tempest, the ship is quivering—oh God! and—going down!" Is this a strangely destructive homecoming that reunites the orphaned son with the absent mother, who is the *arche* and *telos* of everyone and everything that exists? Final words from an impossible journal recounting an impossible experience: "To conceive the horror of my sensations is, I presume, utterly impossible; yet a curiosity to penetrate the mysteries of these awful regions, predominates even over my despair, and will reconcile me to the most hideous aspect of death. It is evident that we are hurrying onwards to some exciting knowledge—some never-to-be-imparted secret, whose attainment is destruction. Perhaps this current leads us to the southern pole itself" (198). This secret is the void, the thing, the no-thing that writing is about—always *about,* circling and circling but never arriving, defining, representing the abyss that simultaneously enables and subverts it.

Ecstasy

In the fall of 1849, Poe was both physically ill and psychologically spent. He repeatedly suffered from "moments of horror" like those described in the first sentence of "The Pit and the Pendulum." Echoing Kierkegaard and anticipating Blanchot, he writes, "I was sick—sick unto death with that long agony; and when they at length unbound me, and I was permitted to sit, I felt that my senses were leaving me. The sentence—the dread sentence of death—was the last of distinct accentuation that reached my ears" (491). When Poe collapsed on a Baltimore street, he was delirious, and the night before his death, the delirium turned violent and his sentences became death sentences.

How is this delirium to be understood? Can any delirium be understood? Was it physical, psychological, or both? Was it the result of his overwhelming sorrow? Of alcohol? Of opium? Of madness? Of ecstasy? Or of all of these factors? Might Poe's delirium foreshadow Nietzsche's madness? "The relation of the delirium to the thought of the Eternal Return that the delirium communicates," Blanchot writes, "is more important, and perhaps not anecdotal. . . . The 'delirium' most assuredly does not constitute that deliberate (or non-deliberate) simulation with which later, at the moment of manifest madness, Nietzsche's reason was credited: the 'delirium' is the form of absence in which Nietzsche's identity destroys itself—that Nietzsche who, formulating the everything returns, thus opens the circle, marks its point of singularity (point at which the non-circularity of the circle would be defined) by means of which closure and rupture coincide" (IC, 278). Poe, like Nietzsche, gazed into the void, which he found both terrifying and irresistible. The open circle is a fathomless abyss, where one sees without seeing that life begins with the trauma of loss constituting identity, and ends with the trauma of loss shattering identity. Might the instant of this loss be a/theological ecstasy?

Poe's last substantial work—*Eureka*—is his least understood. The work is dedicated to the German geographer, naturalist, and explorer Alexander von Humboldt, whose multi-volume *Kosmos* attempts to integrate different branches of science. As we will see, von Humboldt was also important for Thoreau. The initial response to Poe's work was hostile, and subsequent interpretations have been misguided. Though Poe gives the work the subtitle "A Prose Poem," it is more prose than poem, and is unlike anything else he wrote. It is not a story or tale, and it is unclear whether he intends it to be fact or fiction, if such a distinction makes sense in these uncharted waters. Many critics have misread *Eureka* as a "scientific treatise" in which Poe attempts to present a rational cosmology that anticipates modern theories of the Big Bang, black holes, and thermodynamics. This is partly Poe's own fault because he draws on the work of scientists like Galileo, Pierre-Simon Laplace, and especially Sir Isaac Newton to develop his theories.[19] Furthermore, Poe engages in astronomical speculation and mathematical calculation that seem far from poetry as it had been traditionally understood. In his preface, however, he makes perfectly clear that the truths that preoccupy him must be communicated poetically rather than scientifically.

> To these I present the composition as an Art-Product alone:—
> let us say as a Romance; or, if I be not urging too lofty a claim,
> as a Poem.
>
> *What I here propound is true.*—therefore it cannot die:—
> or if by any means it be now trodden down so that it die, it will
> "rise again to the Life Everlasting."
>
> Nevertheless it is as a Poem only that I wish this work to
> be judged after I am dead. (1259)

Many critics have argued that the seemingly wild speculations in *Eureka* testify to Poe's deteriorating mental condition, but nothing could be farther from the truth. This "prose poem" is an extraordinary work that shows a brilliant mind urgently presenting his last testament that retrospectively can be understood as the foundation of his entire *oeuvre*. This is all the more remarkable when one considers the turmoil of Poe's life at the time the work was written.

Whether or not he realized that death was near, by writing *Eureka*, he provided the key that unlocks tales and poems most readers and critics

regarded as little more than popular entertainment. It took the French—
especially Baudelaire, but also Mallarmé, and the Irish immigrant to
Paris, Beckett—to explain to Americans what a treasure they had in Poe.
Indeed, just as Derrida is an American import in France, so Poe is a
French import in America. Once Poe returned to America from abroad,
major American writers began to recognize his significance. Paul Auster,
whose own work has been deeply influenced by Poe, underscores Poe's
contribution by citing William Carlos Williams's acknowledgment of Poe's
abiding significance. "Thus Poe must suffer by his originality. . . . Invent
that which is new, even if it be made of pine from your own yard, and
there's none to know what you have done. It is because there's *no name*.
This is the cause of Poe's lack of recognition. He was American. He was
the astounding, inconceivable growth of his locality. Gape at him they
did, and he at them in amazement. Afterward with mutual hatred: he in
disgust, they in mistrust. It is only that which is under your nose which
seems inexplicable. Here Poe emerges—in no sense the bizarre, isolate
writer, the curious literary figure. On the contrary, in him American literature is anchored, in him alone on solid ground."[20] When *Eureka* is understood in this context, its importance for not only Poe's own work, but also
for American and, indeed, for world literature becomes clear. Bringing
together the perennial questions of world, self, and God, Poe's work is a
cosmology that is a psychology that is a theology, or, more precisely, an a/
theology. Writing poetic prose and prosaic poetry, he elaborates what
Heidegger described as an "ontotheological" vision that unwittingly subverts itself in its very presentation.

Poe begins *Eureka* by arguing that neither the a priori/deductive approach of continental philosophers like Kant and Schelling, nor the a
posteriori/inductive approach of British philosophers like Bacon, Hume,
and Mill is adequate to penetrate the "shadowy processes" he explores.
"We have attained a point," Poe argues, "where only *Intuition* can aid us"
(1276). Once again the point. The reason he insists on the limitation of discursive reason and the necessity of intuitive apprehension is immediately
obvious when he states his first principle. "My general proposition, then, is
this:—*In the Original Unity of the First Thing lies the Secondary Cause of*

All Things, with the Germ of their Inevitable Annihilation" (1261). All of
Poe's works presuppose a familiar pattern, which, we have seen, has been
formulated in different ways.

Unity	↔	Plurality	↔	Unity
One	↔	Many	↔	One
Simplicity	↔	Complexity	↔	Simplicity
Homogeneity	↔	Heterogeneity	↔	Homogeneity
Identity	↔	Difference	↔	Identity
Eros	↔	Reality Principle/ Pleasure Principle	↔	Thanatos
Garden	↔	Fall	↔	Kingdom

What makes Poe's elaboration of this three-part narrative distinctive is
his recognition that it can be understood cosmologically, anthropologi-
cally, theologically, epistemologically, and aesthetically. In contemporary
terms, Poe's world, like the world of German Idealists and American
Transcendentalists, is fractal; that is to say, it has the same structure at
every level. Before the beginning, there was One—absolute simplicity; the
world emerges through a mysterious act of divine will, which introduces
the separation of entities in space and the deferral of moments in time.
Though this primal unity is ruptured, a point of contact remains behind,
beneath, or within the play of differences that constitutes life. The goal of
life is to recover what was lost in the trauma of birth.

> *Oneness,* then, is all that I predicate of the originally created
> Matter; but I propose to show that this *Oneness is a principle*
> *abundantly sufficient to account for the constitution of existing*
> *phenomena and the plainly inevitable annihilation of at least*
> *the material Universe.*
>
> The willing into being the primordial Particle, has com-
> pleted the act, or more properly the *conception* of Creation. We
> now proceed to the ultimate purpose for which we are to sup-
> pose the Particle was created—that is to say, the ultimate pur-

pose so far as our considerations *yet* enable us to see it—the constitution of the Universe from it, the Particle.

The constitution has been effected by *forcing* the original and therefore normally *One* into the abnormal condition of *Many*. An action of this character implies a reaction. A diffusion from Unity, under the conditions, involves a tendency to return into Unity—a tendency ineradicable until satisfied. (1277–78)

In this scheme, the centrifugal force of diffusion, which Poe describes as "radiation," is countered by a centripetal force of reintegration, which he labels "concentralization." Poe creates a visual pyramid to illustrate his point. Echoing Newton, he explains, "we have reached the conclusion that, on the hypothesis that matter was originally radiated from a center and now is returning to it, the concentralization, in the return, proceeds *exactly as we know the force of gravitation to proceed*" (1292). Though couched in quasi-scientific language, Poe's cosmogonic narrative is a story of homecoming in which exiles return to their origin that has always already been left behind.

Since language articulates differences, this "Original Unity" is unnamable. Poe, nonetheless, offers different names for the unnamable One: "the Absolute," "the Infinite," and God. The Absolute (*ab*, away from + *solvere*, to lose) is unrelated to, and independent of everything else, and yet (impossibly) is the groundless ground of everything that exists. "In such an arrangement, under such conditions, we most easily and immediately comprehend the subsequent most feasible carrying out to completion of any such design as that which I have suggested—the design of multiplicity out of unity—diversity out of sameness—heterogeneity out of homogeneity—complexity out of simplicity—in a word, the utmost possible multiplicity of *relation* out of the emphatically irrelative *One*" (1278). Like Schelling's *Indifferenz Punkt*, Poe's Absolute is the "Absolute Irrelation" that is the origin of both every relation and all relativity. In other words, the condition of the possibility of relations is not itself relative (that is, relational).

Since the unnamable and irrelative remain inconceivable, the Infinite cannot be comprehended. Far from a determinate entity or clear and distinct idea, the Infinite is "the *thought of a thought*" that "stands for the possible attempt at an impossible conception" (1272). In this scheme, conception is ontological, epistemological, and sexual. In attempting to think the Infinite, self-consciousness tries to conceive its own inconceivable origin. While this struggle inevitably ends in failure, Poe believes, it remains unavoidable. "The human brain," he insists, "has obviously a leaning to the '*Infinite*,' and fondles the phantom of the ideal. It seems to long with a passionate fervor for this impossible conception, with the hope of intellectually believing it when conceived" (1329). Though the origin of thought is never present and, thus, cannot be represented, it is not absent. Thinking is forever shadowed by a mysterious double it can neither capture nor release. Images and ideas are never clear and distinct, but inevitably remain fuzzy. Like the navel of Freud's dream, the point of contact with the unrepresentable One is the trace of the *point* where polar opposites collapse into absolute identity. This implies that the limit of conception is internal as well as external. Paradoxically, the most complete self-consciousness presupposes the awareness of its own inadequacy and incompletion. The self, therefore, is always haunted by an other that can never be known. One of the names of this unnamable is "God."

Cosmology is epistemology is psychology is theology. Poe goes so far as to claim that "the Universe is a plot of God" (1342). This god is not the transcendent creator who manages world affairs from afar, but is the immanent/imminent origin and end of all that is. The divine realizes itself in and through evolution and involution of both the cosmos and individual selves. Matter finally "shall have returned into absolute Unity,—it will then (to speak paradoxically for the moment) be Matter without Attraction and without Repulsion—in other words, without Matter—in other words, again, *Matter no more*. In sinking into Unity, it will sink at once into that Nothingness, which, to all finite perception, Unity must be—into that Material Nihility from which alone we can conceive it to have been evoked—to have been *created* by the Volition of God." End returns to beginning. "Let us endeavor to comprehend that the final globe of globes will instantaneously disappear, and that God will remain all in all" (1355–56).

At this point, the reader is left to ponder Heidegger's question in "What is Metaphysics?"—"What about this nothing?" Recalling Schelling's *Indifferenz Punkt,* this "globe of globes" is the Nothingness Poe's nameless narrators see in the eyes of Morella and Ligeia. He indirectly suggests that this void is the trace of the lost mother he could never recover. "Nothing like *location* was conceived as their origin. Their source lies in the principle, *Unity. This* is their lost parent. This they seek always—immediately—in all directions—wherever it is even partially to be found" (1287).

As Poe approaches his end, he adds a final twist to this remarkable string of associations. "And now—this Heart Divine—what is it? *It is our own*" (1356). The recognition of the identity of God, world, and self is the "Eureka" moment, which is "the great *Now*—the awful Present" with "neither past nor future" (1353, 1313). The abyss of this ever-elusive Now is the "never-to-be-imparted secret, whose attainment is destruction" toward which the writer is forever rushing but never reaches. Every "true" work is a manuscript found in a bottle floating on a sea whose depth inevitably remains incomprehensible. In "The Imp of the Perverse," Poe writes,

> We stand upon the brink of a precipice. We peer into the abyss—we grow sick and dizzy. Our first impulse is to shrink from danger. Unaccountably we must remain. By slow degrees our sickness, and dizziness, and horror, become merged in a cloud of unnameable feeling. . . . But out of this *our* cloud upon the precipice's edge, there grows into palpability, a shape, far more terrible than any genius, or any demon of a tale, and yet it is but a thought, although a fearful one, and one that chills the very marrow of our bones with the fierceness of the delight of its horror. . . . And because our reason violently deters us from the brink, *therefore* do we the more impetuously approach it. There is no passion in nature so demonically impatient, as that of him, who shuddering upon the edge of a precipice, thus meditates a plunge. (829)

As long as writing continues, the plunge is delayed and the circle of the work remains unclosed. The paradox of writing is that it simultaneously provides glimpses of the absolute unity or identity that is the death of the self, and defers the fulfillment of catastrophic desire.

And yet, in spite of overwhelming terror, the draw of the watery void remains irresistible. Though personal immortality remains an idle dream, Poe's haunting poems, ghostly tales, and cosmic speculations turn out to be redemptive narratives for a world in which the God of Christendom has died. The last words of his last work express hope without hope.

> Think that the sense of individual identity will be gradually merged in the general consciousness—that Man, for example, ceasing imperceptibly to feel himself Man, will at length attain that awfully triumphant epoch when he shall recognize his existence as that of Jehovah. In the meantime bear in mind that all is Life—Life within Life—the less within the greater, and all within the *Spirit Divine*.
>
> THE END

Or almost the end. As if to reassure himself more than his readers, Poe adds a final supplementary footnote.

> *Note—The pain of the consideration that we shall lose our individual identity, ceases at once when we further reflect that the process, as above described, is, neither more nor less than that of absorption, by each individual intelligence, of all other intelligences (that is, of the Universe) into its own. That God may be all in all, each must become God. (1358–59)

When One is all and all are One, the circle of circles contracts into a point. This is the homecoming the orphan Poe always sought and could find only in the ecstatic delirium of death.

S E V E N

Wavering

Virginia Woolf (1882–1941): *Between the Acts*

> Lulled into such an opium-like listlessness of vacant, unconscious reverie is the
> absent-minded youth by the blending cadence of waves with thoughts, that at
> last he loses his identity; takes the mystic ocean at his feet for the visible image
> of that deep, blue, bottomless soul, pervading mankind and nature. . . . In this
> enchanted mood, thy spirit ebbs away to whence it came; becomes diffused
> through time and space; like Wickliff's sprinkled Pantheistic ashes, forming
> at last a part of every shore the round globe over.
>
> —Herman Melville, *Moby-Dick*

Civilization and Its Discontents

Freud saw it coming. As a Jew living in the heart of what became the Reich, how could he not anticipate the approaching storm that would consume the modern world? And yet, as we have seen, he stayed, and stayed, and stayed. When he and Virginia Woolf met at Mansfield Gardens on January 28, 1939, the beginning of the end was near. Eight months later, Freud died (September 23, 1939), three weeks after World War II began (September 1, 1939), and less than two years later, Woolf, who was born in 1882, would be dead (March 28, 1941).

Freud and Woolf had a vexed relationship. Just as Freud resisted reading Nietzsche, so Woolf (and Joyce) resisted reading Freud. Freud's ideas, however, pervaded Woolf's world. In 1914, just two years after her marriage, her husband Leonard Woolf wrote an appreciative review of

Freud's *The Psychopathology of Everyday Life* (1901). At the same time, Lytton and James Strachey, both members of the famous Bloomsbury Group, were discovering Freud's work. James Strachey became Freud's premier English translator, and, in 1924, persuaded Leonard to purchase Freud's works and commit Hogarth Press to publishing them. In spite of all this interest in Freud, Virginia proudly boasted, "I have not studied Dr. Freud or any psychoanalyst—indeed I think I have never read any of their books: my knowledge is merely from superficial talk. Therefore any use of their methods must be instinctive."[1] Her resistance to Freud is overstated but understandable. Woolf was critical of the implications of what she regarded as the reductionist implications of psychoanalysis for art, and was suspicious of his patriarchal proclivities. Though traces of Freud's influence can be seen in works as early as *To the Lighthouse* (1927), Woolf did not begin reading Freud seriously until after his death. On December 2, 1939, at the age of fifty-seven and with the Battle of Britain looming on the horizon, she wrote in her diary, "Began reading Freud last night; to enlarge the circumference. To give wider scope: to make it objective; to get outside. Thus defeat the shrinkage of age. Always take on new things. Break the rhythm, etc." Then she voiced her concern, "Freud is upsetting: reducing one to whirlpool; and I daresay truly. If we're all instinct, the unconscious, what's all this about civilization, the whole man, freedom, etc.?"[2]

Almost a decade earlier, Freud had asked the same question in *Civilization and Its Discontents* (1931), where he admits, "it is impossible to overlook the extent to which civilization is built up upon a renunciation of instinct, how much it presupposes precisely the non-satisfaction (by suppression, repression or some other means?) of powerful instincts. This 'cultural frustration' dominates the large field of social relationships between human beings."[3] The conflict between the pleasure principle (individual desire, or the id) and external and internal constraint (social custom and morality, or the superego) leads to repression, which, in turn, creates social and psychological tensions that must be released periodically. Mutual hostility and aggression create the constant threat of societal disintegration. The task of civilization is to maintain social and psychological order and cohesion by holding aggression in check. With the menace of Hitler be-

ginning to emerge, Freud, uncertain about the future of civilization, ended
with a question. "Men have gained control over the forces of nature to such
an extent that with their help they would have no difficulty in exterminat-
ing one another to the last man. They know this, and hence comes a large
part of their current unrest, their unhappiness and their mood of anxiety.
And now it is to be expected that the other of the two 'Heavenly Powers,'
eternal Eros, will make an effort to assert himself in the struggle with his
equally immortal adversary. But who can foresee with what success and
with what result?"[4]

As we have seen, Freud developed his instinct theory to account for
the post-traumatic stress suffered by veterans of World War I. In the course
of his investigation, he concluded that Eros and Thanatos are not simply
opposites, but are dialectically related in such a way that when each is
pushed to its limit, it turns into the other. Aggression deflects the death instinct from the self to the other; hostility directed against the other, however, is also the identification with the other. In this way, Thanatos becomes
Eros, and Eros, in turn, becomes Thanatos as the complete unity between
the self and other dissolves their differences and issues in the disappearance of both. Freud labels the experience of this unity the "oceanic feeling."

Civilization and Its Discontents begins unexpectedly with a discussion of religion rather than an analysis of war and aggression. Freud reports
that a friend had recently sent him a letter responding to *The Future of an
Illusion,* in which Freud argues that religion is a symptom of the inevitable conflict between father and child. Freud's friend offers an alternative
interpretation of the origin and function of religion in terms of what he describes as "a sensation of 'eternity,' a feeling as of something limitless, un-
bounded—as it were, 'oceanic.'"[5] Freud acknowledges that this feeling of
unity between self and world marks a necessary stage in the development
of every individual. Prior to birth, world and self are one because mother
and infant form a single organism; even after the trauma of birth, the child
is not fully differentiated from his or her surroundings. "An infant at the
breast," Freud explains, "does not as yet distinguish his ego from the external world as the source of the sensations flowing in upon him. He gradually learns to do so, in response to various promptings." The early stages

of life are marked by the increasing differentiation of self and world, but traces of this primal unity remain. "Originally the ego includes everything, later it separates off an external world from itself. Our present ego-feeling is, therefore, only a shrunken residue of a much more inclusive—indeed, an all-embracing—feeling which corresponded to a more intimate bond between the ego and the world about it. . . . The ideational contents appropriate to it would be precisely those of limitlessness and of a bond with the universe—the same ideas with which my friend elucidated the 'oceanic' feeling."[6] Freud acknowledged the importance of this experience, but nevertheless insisted that religion originates from conflicts with the father that emerge at a later stage of development.

While Woolf never mentions Freud's account of the oceanic feeling, her work is filled with images that evoke it—water, oceans, ponds, rivers, and waves. The unconscious memory of primal unity is the trace of the unrecoverable origin for which fragmented selves forever long. To recover this ancient past would be to suffer the delirium in which Eros and Thanatos become one. For Woolf, as for Freud, Melville, Poe, and others, life is lived on the edge of madness, which can be social and political as well as personal and psychological. This boundary marks the limit that her work constantly strives to present.

On April 18, 1939, five months before the outbreak of World War II and Freud's death, Woolf began to write a memoir entitled "A Sketch of the Past"; the last entry is dated November 17, 1940, four months before her death. Acknowledging the challenge anyone trying to explain a life faces, she writes, "Consider what immense forces society brings to play upon each of us, how that society changes from decade to decade; and also from class to class; well, if we cannot analyze these invisible presences, we know very little of the subject of the memoir; and again how futile life-writing becomes. I see myself as a fish in a stream; deflected; held in place; but cannot describe the stream."[7] The stream in which Woolf swam was exceptionally turbulent. Civilization's discontents erupted in barbaric violence that threatened its future. Virginia recalled the trauma of air raids and having to hide in the basement of Hogarth House during World War I.

The war not only forever changed the political landscape, but also destroyed the economy and transformed the traditional British class structure. While Woolf was uncomfortable with paternalism and social hierarchy, she could not completely break with the Victorian social system. Virginia and Leonard had two servants who managed the household and freed them to pursue their literary, political, and journalistic interests. Nonetheless, daily life presented numerous challenges. Over the years, Virginia and Leonard split their time between the city and various country retreats, which, even in peaceful times, lacked modern conveniences that made life manageable. In spite of the political and economic turmoil and disruptions of domestic life, Virginia wrote her most important works during this period: *Mrs. Dalloway* (1925), *To the Lighthouse* (1927), and *The Waves* (1931). By the mid-1930s, clouds of war once again darkened the horizon as well as Woolf's mind.

As I have noted, Hitler assumed power in 1933. As late as 1934, however, the British press was praising Hitler as a great leader. Since Leonard was a Jewish socialist who was an established journalist and a well-known political agitator, the rise of Fascism posed a serious threat for him. Years later, reflecting on his anxiety on the eve of World War II, he wrote in his autobiography, "There was in those days an ominous and threatening unreality, a feeling that one was living in a bad dream and that one was on the point of waking up from this horrible unreality into a still more horrible reality. . . . There was an incessant feeling of . . . impending disaster."[8] Virginia was far less attuned to the political and personal implications of world developments. Though she had long been involved in left-wing causes, her intellectual commitments were psychological and literary rather than political. Quentin Bell recalls that when she asked him what had gone so terribly wrong in the years leading up to Hitler's rise to power, he replied with

> the stock answer of any young socialist: the world economic crisis, of which the American stock-market crash was the grand symptom, was the prime cause; it had bred unemployment and political nationalism, hence Communism, Fascism, and war . . .

all these things were but effects of an economic cause. She was frankly amazed, neither agreed nor disagreed, but thought it a very strange explanation. To her, I think, it appeared that the horrible side of the universe, the forces of madness, which were never far from her consciousness, had got the upper hand again. This to her was something largely independent of the political mechanics of the world. The true answer to all this horror and violence lay in an improvement of one's own moral state; somehow one had to banish anger and the unreason that is bred of anger. Thus she tended, unlike Leonard, to be an out-and-out pacifist.[9]

But pacifism could not contain the violence of a world gone mad.

By 1940, the situation in Europe had become critical—on May 14, the Dutch army surrendered; on May 28, Belgium submitted; and on June 14, France fell. As the fear of invasion gripped England, Leonard recorded the growing menace he feared. "Jews were hunted down, beaten up, and humiliated everywhere publicly in the streets of towns. I saw a photograph of a Jew being dragged by storm troopers out of a shop in one of the main streets in Berlin. . . . On the man's face was the horrible look of blank suffering and despair which from the beginning of human history men have seen under the crown of thorns on the faces of their persecuted and humiliated victims. In this photograph what was even more horrible was the look on the faces of respectable men and women standing on the pavement, laughing at the victim."[10] With the Battle of Britain raging, London became the target of a sustained bombing campaign. Virginia and Leonard had recently moved to Mecklenburg Square from Tavistock Square, where they still were paying rent. When both homes were destroyed by bombs, they fled the city for Monk House in East Sussex, where some of the members of the Bloomsbury Group gathered periodically. But even this retreat was not safe from German bombs.

During the darkest days of 1940, Virginia and Leonard repeatedly considered committing suicide, and even went so far as to plan how they would do it. They would kill themselves with exhaust from their car; the backup plan was to take a lethal dose of morphine. Leonard kept a supply of gasoline and the drug for this purpose. The Woolfs, Panthea Reid explains, "were not being paranoid, only realistic: Heinrich Himmler's list for immediate arrest after the invasion of England included the names 'Woolf, Leonard, Schriftsteller' (author) and 'Woolf, Virginia, Schriftstellerin' (author). Virginia was well aware that 'capitulation will mean all Jews to be given up. Concentration camps. So to our Garage.' "[11] Faced by the prospect of death by bombing, suicide, or life in a concentration camp, it is hardly surprising that Virginia wrote, "I can't conceive that there will be a 27th June 1941."[12]

The chaos of war exacerbated emotional and psychological problems that plagued Woolf throughout her life. Her family life and childhood were filled with traumas that created conflicts she continuously struggled to resolve. Her father, Leslie Stevens, and mother, Julia Duckworth (née Jackson), had both been previously married. Leslie studied theology and became a clergyman, but, after suffering a crisis of faith, left the ministry and went on to a distinguished career in journalism and writing.[13] His support for the Union army during the Civil War led to a trip to the United States, where he interviewed Abraham Lincoln and became a lifelong friend of Oliver Wendell Holmes, Charles Eliot Norton, and James Russell Lowell, who became Virginia's godfather. Leslie's success as a journalist led to his appointment as the editor of the prestigious *Dictionary of National Biography*. His first wife, Harriet Marian, was the granddaughter of William Thackeray. They had one daughter, Laura, who was mentally ill and lived with her father and his family until 1891. When Harriet died, Leslie suffered profound depression, from which he emerged only after meeting the widow Julia Duckworth. Julia was born in British India and was the niece of the noted photographer Julia Margaret Cameron. She had married Herbert Duckworth, an Indian civilian, and the couple had three children—George, Stella, and Gerald. Leslie and Julia also had three children of their own—Vanessa, Thoby, and Virginia, who was unplanned but not unwanted. While simple oppositions always tend to be reductionistic, Quentin Bell correctly identifies two sides of Virginia's psychological and literary inheritance, which, he insists, were "real enough in her imagination . . . : sense and sensibility, prose and poetry, literature and art."[14]

There were predictable tensions among the children in this extended family, but the marriage was relatively happy and stable until the pressures of Leslie's editorial responsibilities led to serious psychological and physical problems. Between 1888 and 1891, he had three breakdowns, during which he suffered from what he described as "fits of the horrors."[15] As his condition worsened, Julia persuaded Leslie to resign his editorial position. Though this provided some relief from daily pressures, growing financial problems made Julia increasingly anxious. While struggling to keep her family together and afloat, she contracted rheumatic fever and died on May 5, 1895. With the death of his second wife, Leslie once again slipped into a deep depression, and this time relied on his daughters to support him.

Family turmoil and death surrounding Virginia's childhood were unsettling, but it was Julia's death that led to her first breakdowns. The trauma of the loss of her mother was deepened by Leslie's interminable mourning and the unreasonable demands he made on his daughters. To make matters even worse, after Julia's death, Virginia's half-brother George appears to have been a sexual predator who molested her. Needless to say, this experience complicated the issue of sexuality for Virginia throughout her life. The loss of her mother and the ideal world of childhood she represented continued to haunt Virginia. "What a jumble of things I can remember," she wrote, "if I let my mind run about my mother; but they are all of her company; of her surrounded; of her generalized; dispersed, omnipresent, of her as the creator of that crowded merry world which spun so gaily in the center of my childhood." The morning of her death, she recalls, "I got a feeling of calm, sadness, and finality. It was a beautiful spring morning, and very still. That brings back the feeling that everything had come to an end" (MB, 84). Looking back near the end of her life, Virginia recounts the moment of her mother's death.

> I remember very clearly how even as I was taken to the bedside
> I noticed that one nurse was sobbing, and a desire to laugh came
> over me, and I said to myself as I have often done at moments

of crisis since, 'I feel nothing whatever.' Then I stopped and kissed my mother's face. It was still warm. She [had] only died a moment before. Then we went upstairs into the day nursery.

Perhaps it was the next evening that Stella took me into the bedroom to kiss mother for the last time. She had been lying on her side before. Now she was lying straight in the middle of her pillows. Her face was immeasurably distant, hollow and stern. When I kissed her, it was like kissing cold iron. Whenever I touch cold iron the feeling comes back to me—the feeling of my mother's face, iron, cold, and granulated. (MB, 92)

One moment there is life, the next moment there is death; what disappears in that brief instant in between?

In spite of the distress her mother's death caused, all was not lost. Just as moments of great beauty often harbor terrifying darkness, so moments of darkness sometimes afford a glimpse of great beauty. Woolf recalls standing on the Paddington railway platform with her brother Thoby at the time of her mother's death. "It was sunset, and the great glass dome at the end of the station was blazing with light. It was glowing yellow and red and the iron girders made a pattern across it. I walked along the platform gazing with rapture at this magnificent blaze of color, and the train slowly steamed into the station. It impressed and exalted me. It was so vast and so fiery red. . . . Also it was partly that my mother's death unveiled and intensified; made me suddenly develop perceptions, as if a burning glass had been laid over what was shaded and dormant. Of course this quickening was spasmodic. But it was surprising—as if something were becoming visible without any effort" (MB, 93). In later years, she attempted to capture these "spots of time" (William Wordsworth), which she labeled "moments of Being," in her writing.

These rapturous moments, which interrupted the boredom of daily routines, were rare, and were always surrounded by the darkness of mental illness. Virginia suffered from a variety of physical and psychological maladies—severe headaches, insomnia, eating disorders, sexual problems, anxiety, and depression. Periods of stability were punctuated by episodes of instability. As her writing progressed, a pattern emerged—after completing a new work, Woolf often suffered a mental breakdown, which sometimes required extended hospitalization. Her diary and letters are filled with excruciating accounts of her mental anguish. During the decade of the 1920s, Woolf enjoyed considerable professional and social success, but her diary reveals inner turmoil. While working on *To the Lighthouse* and beginning to imagine *The Waves,* her two most successful novels, she went through a very dark period. On September 15, 1926, she wrote an entry in her diary entitled "A State of Mind."

> Woke up perhaps at 3. Oh it's beginning, it's coming—the horror—physically like a painful wave swelling about the heart—tossing me up. I'm unhappy, unhappy! Down—God, I wish I were dead. Pause. But why am I feeling this? Let me watch a wave rise. I watch. Vanessa. Children. Failure. Yes; I detect that. Failure, failure. (The wave rises). . . .
>
> Wave crashes. I wish I were dead! I've only a few years to live, I hope. I can't face this horror any more. (This is the wave spread out over me.) This goes on; several times, with varieties of horror. Then, at the crisis, instead of the pain remaining intense, it becomes rather vague. I wake with a start. The wave again! The irrational pain; the sense of failure; generally some specific incident, as for example my taste in green paint, or buying a new dress . . . tacked on. (MB, 110)

In such moments, suicide was never far from her mind. As the world raced toward the vortex of total war during the following decade, inner and outer madness collided to create an abyss she could neither fathom nor escape.

Moments of Being

One of the ways Woolf attempted to sustain a semblance of balance in her troubled life was to create different kinds of retreats where she could withdraw. Some were geographical like Monk House, and others were social and intellectual like the Bloomsbury Group, and still others were mental like reading and writing. Behind all of these sanctuaries was her childhood retreat—the seaside town in southern Cornwall, St. Ives, where her father rented Talland House during summers from 1882 to 1894. Though in later life she idealized her early years, the memories of her experience in St. Ives not only provided solace during difficult periods, but also shaped all of her writing. Woolf begins her late autobiographical sketch by recalling her very first memories, which she associated with St. Ives.

> Perhaps we were going to St. Ives; more probably, from the light it must have been evening, we were coming back to London. But it is more convenient artistically to suppose that we were going to St. Ives, for that will lead to my other memory, which also seems to be my first memory, and in fact it is the most important of all my memories. If life has a base that it stands upon, if it is a bowl that one fills and fills and fills—then my bowl without a doubt stands upon this memory. It is of lying half asleep, half awake, in bed in the nursery at St. Ives. It is of hearing waves breaking, one, two, one, two, sending a splash of water over the beach; and then breaking, one, two, one, two, behind a yellow blind. It is of hearing the blind draw its little acorn across the floor as the wind blew the blind out. It is of lying and hearing this splash and seeing this light, and feeling, it is almost impossible that I should be here; of feeling the purest ecstasy I can conceive.
>
> I could spend hours trying to write that as it should be written, in order to give the feeling which is even at this moment very strong in me. But I should fail (unless I had some wonderful luck). (MB, 64–65)

The waves that shatter and scatter also heal and mend. The second memory is of the garden at Talland House.

> The next memory—all these color-and-sand memories hang together at St. Ives—was much more robust; it was highly sensual. It was later. It still makes me feel warm; as if everything

were ripe; humming; sunny; smelling so many smells at once;
and all making a whole that even now makes me stop—as I
stopped then going down to the beach; I stopped at the top to
look down at the gardens. They were sunk beneath the road.
The apples were on a level with one's head. The gardens gave
off a murmur of bees; the apples were red and gold; there were
also pink flowers; and the grey and silver leaves. The buzz,
the croon, the smell, all seemed to press voluptuously against
some membrane; not to burst it; but to hum round one such a
complete rapture of pleasure that I stopped, smelt; looked. But
again I cannot describe that rapture. It was rapture rather than
ecstasy. (MB, 66)

Water and garden—waves and apples. In a manner reminiscent of Thoreau
gathering autumn apples, Woolf is transported by ripe fruit hanging in a
summer garden in the midst of flowers and bees. In the distance she hears
the rhythmic sound of waves lapping the shore. Like Kierkegaard's *Øjeblikket* and Blanchot's instant, these moments of Being are in time as a certain
outside that disrupts temporal succession with a more profound unity that
eludes precise articulation.

   Suffering inward fragmentation in the midst of a world torn apart by
the brutalities of war, Woolf was consumed by what Geoffrey Hartman
aptly describes as "a voracious desire for continuity."[16] Like Rhona in *The
Waves,* she longs to "live wholly, indivisibly and without caring in the moment."[17] In her personal life as well as her work, Woolf relentlessly pursued
this moment. However, as we have seen, the here-and-now of such a moment is always already past—as soon as "I" am aware of the moment, it has
vanished. The challenge of writing is not to represent this unrepresentable
moment, but to cultivate a performative style that affords the occasion for
both the writer and the reader to experience moments of Being. Woolf repeatedly describes such experiences as "mystical." When literature is understood as the cultivation of such experience, it displaces religious texts
and rituals as the expression of spiritual striving in a world where God has
grown distant or completely disappeared. Woolf's stylistic innovations re-

flect her effort to break with traditional narrative structure and discursive forms. In the words of Bernard in *The Waves*, "How tired I am of stories, how tired I am of phrases that come down beautifully with all their feet on the ground! Also, how I distrust neat designs of life that are drawn upon half sheets of notepaper. I begin to long for some little language such as lovers use, broken words, inarticulate words, like the shuffling of feet on the pavement. I begin to seek some design more in accordance with those moments of humiliation and triumph that come now and then undeniably" (W, 238–39).

Woolf's works have neither linear plots nor consistently identifiable characters. A different temporal rhythm structures her fiction; the lines between and among characters tend to be fuzzy. There is no omniscient narrator, and it is often unclear where one person ends and the other begins. Moreover, different characters sometimes appear to be alternative aspects of a single person. Woolf also blurs the line between poetry and prose. Like Poe, her most successful works can best be described as "prose poems." The most distinctive characteristic of Woolf's style is, of course, what is often too quickly labeled "stream of consciousness." Bernard's description of himself recalls the multiple personae of Melville's confidence-man. "I am not one and simple, but complex and many. Bernard in public, bubbles; in private, is secretive. That is what they do not understand, for they are now undoubtedly discussing me, saying I escape them, am evasive. They do not understand that I have to effect different transitions; have to cover the entrances and exits of several different men who alternately act their parts as Bernard" (W, 76). To capture the protean character of subjectivity, Woolf develops a style that is as fluid as human consciousness itself. Most of the time people are distracted—they live un-self-consciously; awareness is endlessly mobile, flitting from object to object and occasion to occasion without resting long enough to become self-aware. For this reason, the mind appears to be something like a rushing stream, a meandering river with momentary eddies, and a vast ocean with rhythmic waves.

It is important to stress that Woolf's aim is not to *represent* either the cadences of the mind or the moment of Being; rather, she seeks to create the occasion for the actual experience of what eludes words. When successful, writing becomes a retreat from the dispersion and distraction of everyday life, which she identifies as "non-being." "Every day life," Woolf acknowledges, "includes much more non-being than being. . . . A great part of every day is not lived consciously. One walks, eats, sees things, deals with what has to be done; the broken vacuum cleaner; ordering dinner; writing orders to Mabel; washing; cooking dinner; bookbinding. When it is a bad day the proportion of non-being is much larger" (MB, 70). In Woolf's psychic economy, Being shatters non-being in "exceptional moments" that disclose an overwhelming "whole."

Always arriving unexpectedly, the shock of Being is as unsettling as it is reassuring. In what is, perhaps, her most revealing comment on her "philosophy of composition," Woolf writes,

> I still have the peculiarity that I receive these sudden shocks, they are now always welcome; after the first surprise, I always feel instantly that they are particularly valuable. *And so I go on to suppose that the shock-receiving capacity is what makes me a writer* [emphasis added]. I hazard the explanation that a shock is at once in my case followed by the desire to explain it. I feel that I have had a blow; but it is not, as I thought as a child, simply a blow from an enemy hidden beneath the cotton wool of daily life; it is or will become a revelation of some order; it is a token of some real thing behind appearances; and I make it real by putting it into words. It is only by putting it into words that I make it whole; this wholeness means that it has lost its power to hurt me; it gives me, perhaps because by doing so I take away the pain, a great delight to put the severed parts together. Perhaps this is the strongest pleasure known to me. It is the rapture I get when in writing I seem to be discovering what belongs to what; making a scene come right; making a character come together. From this I reach what I might call a philosophy; at any rate it is a constant idea of mine; that behind the cotton wool is hidden a pattern; that we—I mean all human beings—are connected with this; that the whole world is a work of art; that we

are parts of the work of art. *Hamlet* or a Beethoven quartet is
the truth about this vast mass that we call the world. But there
is no Shakespeare, there is no Beethoven; certainly and emphatically there is no God; we are the words; we are the music; we
are the thing itself. And I see this when I have a shock. (MB, 72)

The "philosophy" that underlies and informs Woolf's writing is surprisingly familiar. In a manner similar to philosophers like Hegel and Schelling
and writers like Poe and Thoreau, Woolf sees life as wavering between polar
opposites: dispersion/gathering, discord/harmony, fragmentation/unity,
differences/identity, discord/harmony, many/One.[18] The most persistent
image for this philosophical conception is the ambiguous motion of waves.
Woolf ends *The Waves* with a sentence whose simplicity masks its complexity. "*The waves broke on the shore*" (W, 297).

How is the word "broke" to be understood in this context? The sea
is, of course, the ancient image of the origin and end of life—it is the indeterminate matrix from which all determinate beings emerge and to which
they inevitably return. Life begins and ends with a break, or, in psychoanalytic terms, with trauma. The first break is the moment of rupture in
which individuality emerges from the condition of undifferentiation, and
the second break is the shattering of individuality in the return to what
Schelling, as we have seen, describes as the *Indifferenz Punkt*. "With
intermittent shocks, sudden as the springs of a tiger," Woolf writes, "life
emerges heaving its dark crest from the sea. It is to this we are attached;
it is to this we are bound, as bodies to wild horses" (W, 64). This abiding connection with the sea is what Freud describes as the trace of the
lost maternal matrix that creates the insatiable longing of the oceanic
feeling. Recalling the death of her beloved Percival, Rhoda, like Blanchot's Thomas the Obscure, expresses the seemingly eternal draw of *la
mer(e)*.

Walking on the embankment, I prayed that I might thunder
forever on the verge of the world where there is no vegetation,
but here and there a marble pillar. I threw my bunch into the

spreading wave. I said, "Consume me, carry me to the furthest limit." The wave has broken; the bunch is withered. . . . There is only a thin sheet between me now and the infinite depths. . . . We launch out now over the precipice. Beneath us lie the lights of the herring fleet. The cliffs vanish. Rippling small, rippling grey, innumerable waves spread beneath us. I touch nothing. I see nothing. We may sink and settle on the waves. The sea will drum in my ears. The white petals will be darkened with sea water. They will float for a moment and then sink. Rolling me over the waves will shoulder me under. Everything falls in a tremendous shower, dissolving me. (W, 206)

Suspended between the trauma of birth and the trauma of death, life remains inescapably liminal. The shore, strand, beach is the margin, boundary, limit that simultaneously joins and separates land (differentiation, individuality) and sea (undifferentiation, anonymity). In one of the most suggestive and disturbing passages in all her work, Woolf graphically describes the opposites between which life wavers. The rhythm of the waves is punctuated by intervals that follow the movement of the sun during a single day. "*The sun, risen, no longer couched on a green mattress darting a fitful glance through watery jewels, bared its face and looked straight over the waves.*" As the sun continues to rise, the waves' "*shapes took on mass and edge.*" Gradually a garden appears, but this is not the idealized garden that lifted Woolf into rapture when she was a child; rather it is a garden riven by divisions.

> *In the garden where trees stood thick over flower-beds, ponds, and greenhouses the birds sang in the hot sunshine, each alone. One sang under the bedroom window; another on the topmost twig of the lilac bush; another on the edge of the wall. Each sang stridently, with passion, with vehemence, as if to let the song burst out of it, no matter if it shattered the song of another bird in harsh discord. . . . They sang as if the song were urged out of them by the pressure of the morning. They sang as if the edge of being were*

*sharpened and must cut, must split the softness of the blue-green
light, the dampness of the wet earth.*

Beneath the kitchen window was a pile of rotting garbage seething with life.
The fluid vitality of the rubbish stands in stark contrast with the aridity of
the *"dry-beaked, ruthless"* birds that descended from the sky and *"tapped
furiously, methodically, until the shell broke and something slimy oozed
from the crack."*

> *They swept and soared sharply in flights high into the air, twit-
> tering short, sharp notes, and perched in the upper branches of
> some tree and looked down upon leaves and spires beneath, and
> the country white with blossom, flowing with grass, and the sea
> which beat like a drum that raises a regiment of plumed and tur-
> baned soldiers. Now and again their songs ran together in swift
> scales like the interlacings of a mountain stream whose waters,
> meeting, foam and then mix, and hasten quicker and quicker
> down the same channel brushing the same leaves. But there is a
> rock; they sever.* (W, 108–9)

Hard and soft, dry and wet, edged and porous. Opposites emerge, separate, mingle, dissolve, and then start the cycle over again in what appears
to be a process that returns eternally.

This pattern is found not only in the rhythms of nature, but also in the
pulsating rhythms of the modern city. Pausing to ponder a London train returning from the countryside, Bernard sounds like David Foster Wallace describing life in the hyper-connected twenty-first century. "I am become part
of this speed, this missile, hurled at the city. . . . All are merged in one turning wheel of single sound. All separate sounds—wheels, bells, the cries of
drunkards, of merrymakers—all churned into one sound, steel, blue circular" (W, 111, 135). Lost in the pulsating crowd, Bernard's sense of identity
vanishes. "We insist, it seems, on living. Then again, indifference de-
scends. The roar of the traffic, the passage of undifferentiated faces, this
way and that way, drugs me into dreams; rubs the feature from faces. People

might walk through me. . . . Time has been whizzed back an inch or two on its reel; our short progress has been cancelled. I think also that our bodies are in truth naked. We are only lightly covered with buttoned cloth; and beneath these pavements are shells, bones and silence" (W, 113). Under the hustle and bustle of the city lie the remains of a past as ancient as time itself. Shells, bones, silence. Before the beginning . . . after the end there is nothing . . . nothing but silence.

One of the most profound paradoxes of human life is that for many intelligent and creative people, self-consciousness is most completely realized in and through its own self-negation. In biblical terms, the only way to find yourself is to lose yourself. If loss is truly loss, there is no return from the void in which the self disappears. In ecstatic moments, the self becomes "porous," and, Woolf explains, "life is not confined to one's body and what one says and does; one is living all the time in relation to certain background rods or conceptions." She proceeds to confess that "it struck me, on my walk yesterday, that these moments of being of mine were scaffolding in the background; were the invisible and silent part of my life as a child" (MB, 73). Second childhood, like the first, is sheer immediacy, or, in Kierkegaard's terms, is "immediacy after reflection" in which there is "no past, no future; merely the moment in its ring of light, and our bodies; and the inevitable climax, the ecstasy" (W, 252). In this moment, the boundary separating self and world, self and other, and subject and object dissolves and two become One. Recalling the childhood memories that form the foundation of her life and work, Woolf writes, "The peculiarity of these two strong memories is that each was very simple. I am hardly aware of myself, but only of the sensation. I am only the container of the feeling of ecstasy, of the feeling of rapture" (MB, 67). No longer a separate self, one becomes a vessel through which the currents of Being flow.

If, as Nietzsche insists, Midnight is Midday, Midday is also Midnight. When divisive walls crumble and separating membranes become permeable, light becomes darkness. Always on the way to the lighthouse, this darkness is inward as well as outward. "Our apparitions, the things you know us by, are simply childish. Beneath it is all dark, it is all spreading, it is unfathomably deep." In the depths of this darkness, self-realization is self-annihilation. Mrs. Ramsey speaks for Woolf when she reflects, "Losing personality, one lost the fret, the hurry, the stir; and there rose to her lips always some exclamation of triumph over life when things came together in this peace, this rest, this eternity."[19] And yet, Woolf admits, "many of these exceptional moments brought with them a peculiar horror and a physical collapse" (MB, 72). This horror is a response to the death of the self. Overwhelmed by an oceanic feeling, womb becomes tomb, and Eros becomes Thanatos. To imagine this moment is, impossibly, to conceive the instant of one's death. This impossibility is the beginning and end of writing.[20]

Interlude: Marking Time

Eros . . . Thanatos. Love . . . Hate. Peace . . . War. Country . . . City. Light . . . Dark. One . . . Many. Identity . . . Difference. Unifiers . . . Separators. Victorians . . . Moderns. Traditional . . . Avant-garde. Being . . . Non-being. Permanence . . . Transience. Ecstasy . . . Horror. Depth . . . Surface. Sea . . . Land. Flow . . . Ebb. Da . . . Fort. Sanity . . . Madness. Life . . . Death. Death . . . Life. Suspended . . . always wavering between . . . Between . . . Between the Acts. Tick . . . Tock. Between . . . always between fleeting moments.

"Marking time," said old Oliver beneath his breath.
    "Which don't exist for us," Lucy murmured.
    "We've only the present."
    "Isn't that enough?" William asked himself. Beauty—isn't that enough? But here Isa fidgeted. Her bare brown arms went nervously to her head. She half turned in her seat. "No, not for us, who've the future," she seemed to say. The future disturbing our present.[21]

" 'I'm here, in the place of my grandfather or great grandfather,' as the case might be. At this very moment, half-past three on a June day in 1939" (B, 76). Virginia Woolf was always marking time by writing about the impossible gift of presence. Her most important works are structured by temporal rhythms. Like Joyce's *Ulysses, The Waves, Mrs. Dalloway,* and *Between the Acts* are confined to a single day. In the absence of a sustained plot, Woolf is as interested in what happens between the tick and the tock as in the events, thoughts, and snapshots of conversations she narrates. In *The Waves,* the interval is natural—the movement of the sun throughout the day; in *Between the Acts,* it is artistic—the interlude between acts in a play. As the title suggests, *Between the Acts* is thoroughly liminal; the interval expands to encompass the entire work. Woolf might well have said of all her characters what she said of those in her last work. "They were neither one thing nor the other; neither Victorians nor themselves. They were suspended, without being, in limbo. Tick, tick, tick went the machine" (B, 178). The moments this "between" joins and separates are as multiple as the lives of people living in limbo: war and peace, madness and sanity, conflict and harmony, modern and traditional, separation and unity, dispersion and gathering, and, most important, non-being and Being.

Going with the Flow

What if the last work is not a novel, poem, painting, or symphony but a suicide? Just as each work of art is distinctive, so each suicide has its own style: Freud's sigh, Wallace's scream, Hemingway's bravado. When death is a choice, it does not remain silent. The manner of suicide reveals something about the life it ends.

The events in *Between the Acts* take place in 1939. The original title of the work was *Pointz Hall,* which was the name of a country retreat quite unlike the Talland House of Woolf's childhood memories. Northrop Frye has gone so far as to call *Between the Acts,* written under difficult circumstances, Woolf's "most profound work."[22] She first conceived the novel in April 1938 and completed it November 23, 1940, one year after the start of World War II and just four months before her death. She was also working on a history of literature and a biography of her late Bloomsbury colleague Roger Fry at the time. Though this was a precarious time for England, Woolf remained strangely calm. Describing her mood in August 1940, Bell writes, "By that time, the Battle of Britain was approaching its climax and Virginia was passing from a mood of apprehension to one of quiet imperturbability. Her serenity was perhaps a necessary prelude to the storm—by which I mean the workings of Virginia's mind may have been such that she had to pass from the terror of June 1940 to the final agony of March 1941 by way of an euphoric interval, and that this may have been just as much a part of her mental illness. . . . Never had a novel of hers flowed so rapidly, so effortlessly from her pen; there were no checks, doubts, despairs, struggles or revisions."[23] Her tranquility and productivity were all the more remarkable when one realizes that the war was drawing close to Monk House, where she was writing. In November, as she was finishing the novel, a bomb fell, destroying the bank of the River Ouse, flooding nearby meadows and her garden.

As I have noted, when Woolf finished a novel, she often became mentally unstable. As soon as she completed *Between the Acts,* confidence gave way to uncertainty, doubt, and anxiety. Pressed for money and with groceries scarce during wartime, she wrote to a friend on October 31, 1940, "I never heard a more absurd 'business proposition' as you call it. A month's milk and cream in return for an unborn and as far as I can tell completely worthless book. I've lost all power over words, cant do a thing with them."[24] Even more revealing, four days before her death, Woolf wrote to John Lehmann, the managing editor of Hogarth Press, withdrawing *Between the Acts* from publication. "I'd decided, before your letter came, that I cant publish that novel as it stands—its too silly and trivial. What I will do is to revise it, and see if I can pull it together and so publish it in the autumn. If published as it is, it would certainly mean a financial loss; which we dont want. I am sure I am right about this."[25] Woolf's wish was not honored, and the book was published posthumously on July 17, 1941.

Between the Acts is structured around the age-old tradition of a summer village pageant held at Pointz Hall. This estate is owned by Bartholomew Oliver, who traces his lineage back three centuries. Every year villagers present a different play written for the occasion. This year, the play, written by the very untraditional Miss La Trobe, has different acts that reflect Woolf's preoccupation with the history of literature: after a prologue, a Shakespearean scene, followed by a parody of restoration comedy and the age of reason, which lead up to the Victorian era. The main characters include Bart Oliver, a retired Indian army officer; Lucy Swithin, his unmarried sister who is a devout Christian; his son Giles, a discontent London businessman; his wife Isabel (Isa), who is a frustrated poet; Mrs. Manresa, a sexually charged outsider to whom Giles is attracted; her gay companion, William Dodge; and Rupert Haines, a gentleman farmer to whom Isa is drawn. Sexual innuendo and intrigue, which never reach a climax, are staged with war literally on the horizon.

La Trobe's play is set against the backdrop of the larger history of England dating back to prehistoric times, recorded in a book Lucy and Isa are reading. A play within a historical narrative within a novel. With the protective walls of civilization crumbling around them, villagers turn to art for a sense of meaning and reassurance that religious texts and rituals once provided. "Now Miss La Trobe stepped from her hiding. Flowing, and streaming, on the grass, on the gravel, still for one moment she held them together—the dispersing company. Hadn't she, for twenty-five minutes, made them see? A vision imparted was relief from agony . . . for one moment . . . one moment. Then the music petered out on the last word *we*" (B, 98). Miss La Trobe raises expectations only to frustrate them; art, she believes, should disturb rather than reassure. As we will see, she ends by turning a mirror on the audience, and everyone and everything falls apart.

Between the acts. Two moments separated by a decade—1929 . . . 1939. Two very different summer evenings.

1929. The first, recounted in "The Moment: Summer's Night," begins:

> The night was falling so that the table in the garden among the trees grew whiter and whiter; and the people round it more indistinct. An owl, blunt, obsolete looking, heavy weighted, crossed the fading sky with a black spot between its claws. The trees murmured. An aeroplane hummed like a piece of plucked wire. . . . Yet what composed the present moment? If you are

old, the past lies upon the present, like a thick glass, making it waver, distorting it. All the same everybody believes that the present moment is something, seeks out the different elements in this situation in order to compose the truth of it, the whole of it.[26]

Like every moment of Being, this moment "is largely composed of visual and sense impressions . . . the surface of the body is opened, as if all the pores were open and everything language exposed, not sealed and contracted as in cold weather." What is most characteristic of such a moment is a reassuring feeling of centeredness and rootedness that lends life pattern and meaning. Life, in other words, is grounded. In this moment, "One becomes aware that we are spectators and also passive participants in a pageant. And as nothing can interfere with the order, we have nothing to do but accept, and watch. . . . Thus then the moment is laced about with these weavings to and fro, these inevitable downsinkings, flights, lamp lightings." But rapture, Woolf always insists, is inevitably laced with the prospect of the dread that comes from the death of the self. After ecstasy "comes the terror, the exultation; the power to rush out unnoticed, alone; to be consumed; to be swept away to become a rider on the random wind; the tossing wind; the trampling and neighing wind . . . ; to be part of the eyeless dark, to be rippling and streaming, to feel the glory run molten up the spine, down the limbs, making the eyes glow, burning, bright, and penetrate the buffeting waves of wind."

1939. Much has changed in a decade. Though set thirty-five, one hundred, three hundred miles from the sea, *Between the Acts* is framed by water, or its lack—two visions of a polluted pond. In the beginning: "It was a summer's night and they were talking in the big room with the windows open to the garden, about the cesspool. The county council had promised to bring water to the village, but they hadn't." At the end:

> Lucy still gazed at the lily pool. "All gone," she murmured, "under the leaves." Scared by shadows passing, the fish had withdrawn. She gazed at the water. Perfunctorily she caressed her cross. But her eyes went water searching, looking for fish. The

lilies were shutting; the red lily, the white lily, each on its plate
of leaf. Above, the air rushed; beneath was water. She stood
between two fluidities, caressing her cross. Faith required
hours of kneeling in early morning. Often the delight of
the roaming eye seduced her—a sunbeam, a shadow. Now the
jagged leaf at the corner suggested, by its contours, Europe.
(B, 204)

Gone are lapping waves, rushing streams, and flowing rivers. Water is as
absent from *Between the Acts* as it is present in *To the Lighthouse* and *The
Waves*. When there is water, it is polluted and dangerous. The stagnant
pond is surrounded by legend. The servants are convinced that bones
found in the mud at the bottom are the remains of a girl who drowned herself because her lover had forsaken her. The girl's ghost haunts the house
as Europe floats fragilely on a sea seething with discontent.

   Though it is not one of England's grand estates, Pointz Hall, which
had been in the Bartholomew family for centuries, has a venerable history.
The cesspool is on what was once a Roman road, and in the surrounding
fields, wheat had been grown during the Napoleonic wars. The barn is
tinged with numinosity. "It was as old as the church, and built from the
same stone, but it had no steeple. . . . Those who had been to Greece always said it reminded them of a temple" (B, 26). The garden surrounding
the house is five hundred years old. Caught in a time warp with the modern world in the grip of madness that threatened the future of civilization,
Pointz Hall was a refuge designed to provide a sense of security.

   The Guide Book still told the truth. 1830 was true in 1939. No
   house had been built; no town had sprung up. Hogben's Folly
   was still eminent; the very flat, field-parceled land had changed
   only in this—the tractor had to some extent superceded the
   plough. The horse had gone; but the cow remained. . . . So they
   always said when in summer they sat there to drink coffee, if
   they had guests. When they were alone, they said nothing. They
   looked at the view; they looked at what they knew, to see if what

they knew might perhaps be different today. Most days it was the same.

"That's what makes a view so sad," said Mrs. Swithin, lowering herself into the deck chair which Giles had brought her. "And so beautiful. It'll be there," she nodded at the strip of gauze laid upon the distant fields, "when we're not." (B, 52–53)

But the times were changing. "The clock ticked. The house gave little cracks as if it were very brittle, very dry. Isa's hand on the window felt suddenly cold. Shadow had obliterated the garden. Roses had withdrawn for the night" (B, 217). And this night would be long. The snake in the garden foreshadows the darkness falling on the world. On this dry summer day, Giles took a shortcut to the barn, which passed through the garden. "There, couched in the grass, curled in an olive green ring, was a snake. Dead? No, choked with a toad in its mouth. The snake was unable to swallow; the toad was unable to die. A spasm made the ribs contract; blood oozed. It was birth the wrong way round—a monstrous inversion. So, raising his foot, he stamped on them. The mass crushed and slithered. The white canvas on his tennis shoes was bloodstained and sticky" (B, 99). Rather than the scene of birth and generativity, this garden has become a place of death and decay. The trace of blood lingers as a sign of violence looming on the horizon.

Reflections on/of Ending

Echoes of Kierkegaard: "Such works are mirrors: when an ape looks in, no apostle can look out." A play within a play within a history within a novel traces "stages on life's way" from the dawn to what might be the end of civilization. In the last act of the play, the actors turn mirrors toward the audience. "The hands of the clock stopped at the present. It is ourselves. So that was her little game! To show us up, as we are here and now" (B, 186). In the final scene, La Trobe, speaking for Woolf, tips her hand. "She wanted to expose them, as it were, to douche them, with present-time reality" (B, 179). The actors as well as the characters in the novel are divided between "unifiers and separatists," and action repeatedly wavers between gathering and dispersing. The festival is designed to bring the community together to renew communal bonds. The improvised outdoor theater, like the ancient barn, appears to be a "cathedral" that evokes memories of a religious past modernity is destroying.

When the audience is drawn into the play as actors they did not realize they were, confusion erupts. The dialogue degenerates into the cacophonous noise of actors reciting disconnected fragments. Gazing into a mirror of jumbled words, "the audience saw themselves not whole by any means, but at any rate sitting still" (B, 185). As noise without signal increases, no one is sure whether the play has ended. With people growing impatient and Miss La Trobe nowhere to be found, it is left to the country pastor, Rev. G. W. Streatfield, to summarize what he takes to be the point of the play. "'I will offer, very humbly, for I am not a critic . . . my interpretation. . . . Am I treading, like angels, where as a fool I should absent myself? To me at least it was indicated that we are members of one another. Each is part of the whole. . . . Dare we, I asked myself, limit life to ourselves? May we not hold that there is a spirit that inspires, pervades . . .' (The swallows were sweeping round him. They seemed cognizant of his meaning. Then they swept out of sight)" (B, 191–92). His faithful parishioner, Lucy Swithin, emphatically reinforces this interpretation. She "was off . . . on a circular tour of the imagination—one-making. Sheep, cows, grass, trees, ourselves—all are one. If discordant, producing harmony—if not to us, to a gigantic ear attached to a gigantic head. And thus—she was smiling benignly—the agony of the particular sheep, cow, or human being is necessary; and so—she was beaming seraphically at the gilt vane in the distance—we reach the conclusion that *all* is harmony, could we hear it" (B, 175). Once again, circles within circles within circles—like ripples on the surface of water left when a stone is thrown into a pond.

Though neither Rev. Streatfield nor Lucy realizes it, these words are, of course, bitterly ironic—their reading of the play is completely wrong and is met with derisive laughter. "Scraps, orts and fragments! Surely, we should unite?" (B, 192). These words echo a refrain that is repeated throughout the play, and, with the end approaching, becomes louder—"*Dispersed are we."* As the audience scatters, the villagers, unable to identify a coherent plot, express bafflement about the play's meaning. The pastor's mistaken interpretation of the play only compounds their confusion. Swallows were not the only thing sweeping through the sky. An anonymous voice from the audience asks, "if one spirit animates the whole, what about the aeroplanes?" (B, 197). With Western civilization in ruins, the line separating man from brute dissolves. Art offers no refuge from bombs and the madness of brutal violence; the crumbling walls of civilization cannot be rebuilt by *"orts and fragments like ourselves"* (B, 188). When her work is met with uncomprehending chatter, Miss La Trobe despairs, thinking all her efforts have been for naught and the play was an utter failure. "Panic seized her. Blood seemed to pour from her shoes. This is death, death, death, she noted in the margin of her mind; when illusion fails" (B, 180). Withdrawing to the local tavern to drown her humiliation and despair in ale, she struggles to envision a new work, but her hopes are suffocated as the words she imagines sink in the ancient mud at the bottom of a polluted cesspool.

Civilization and its discontents. "The church bells always stopped, leaving you to ask: Won't there be another note?" (B, 207). As Woolf had once feared, it is not certain that there will be a June 27, 1941. "The doom of sudden death hangs over us," William Dodge laments. "There's no retreating and advancing." Nowhere to run, nowhere to hide—every retreat has been shattered, every exit blocked. The last word, or almost the last words, of the last work. "The window was all sky without color. The house had lost its shelter" (B, 219). *The house had lost its shelter.*

> The gramophone gurgled *Unity—Dispersity.* It gurgled
> *Un . . . dis . . .* And ceased. (MB, 201)
> Dis(-)ceased

April 3, 1941. Special cable to the *New York Times.* "Virginia Woolf Believed Dead." "It was reported that her hat and cane has been found on the bank of the Ouse River." After finishing *Between the Acts,* Woolf characteristically succumbed to depression. During the early weeks of 1941, Leonard became very concerned and persuaded her to see a doctor, but she resisted both responsible treatment and hospitalization. The possibility of her committing suicide had haunted Leonard for years, and this time concern was deepened by her despair about her writing. On February 26, Virginia wrote in her diary, "My 'higher life' is almost entirely the Elizabethan play. Finished Pointz Hall, the Pageant: the Play—finally Between the Acts this morning. . . . No walks for ever so long. People daily. And rather a churn in my mind. And some blank spaces. Food becomes an obsession. I grudge giving away a spice bun. Curious—age, or the war? Never mind. Adventure. Make solid. But shall I ever write again one of those sentences that gives me intense pleasure?"[27] A week before she died, Woolf declared, "I can't write. I've lost the art." Leonard realized her condition was critical because he no doubt remembered her saying two years earlier, "if I cant write . . . one may as well kill oneself."[28] It would not be the first time that Virginia had attempted suicide; indeed, she had tried years before and may even have attempted it again three days before her death. If her last work proved to be her death, she knew it would elude words. Anticipating Blanchot and Derrida, she confessed that death would be "the one experience I shall never describe."[29] Like David Foster Wallace decades later, Virginia could not quiet the voices driving her mad. No longer able to go on, she left two notes—one for her sister, Vanessa, the other for Leonard, to whom she wrote,

> Dearest,
>
> I feel certain I am going mad again. I feel we can't go through another of those terrible times. And I shan't recover this time. I begin to hear voices, and I can't concentrate. So I am doing what seems the best thing to do. You have given me the greatest possible happiness. You have been in every way all that anyone could be. I don't think two people could have been happier till this terrible disease came. I can't fight any longer. I know that I am spoiling your life, that without me you could work. And you will I know. You see I can't even write this properly. I can't read. What I want to say is I owe all the happiness of my life to you. You have been entirely patient

with me and incredibly good. I want to say that—everybody knows it. If anybody could have saved me it would have been you. Everything has gone from me but the certainty of your goodness. I can't go on spoiling your life any longer.

I don't think two people could have been happier than we have been.

V.[30]

Leaving the letters to be found after her death, Virginia walked to the River Ouse, filled her pockets with stones, and slipped into "the water and sank into a tidal current, hoping to find 'rest on the floor of the sea.' "[31]

Every suicide is, of course, as incomprehensible as the life of the individual it ends. Woolf's final note to Leonard is not the only, and perhaps not even the most revealing clue she left. Comments throughout her fiction raise the question of whether her decision to kill herself was simply an act of despair. Was she attempting to escape the unbearable pain and impossible pressure of her illness, or could she have been seeking the ecstasy of one final moment of Being? Was she searching for "the mystic sense of completion" for which she had always longed? (W, 251). Given the importance of water in her work, it is significant that she chose death by drowning. In *The Waves,* friends scattering after an evening of genuine community reflect,

> "We have destroyed something by our presence," said Bernard, "a world perhaps."
>
> "Yet we scarcely breathe," said Neville, "spent as we are. We are in that passive and exhausted frame of mind when we only wish to rejoin the body of our mother from whom we have been severed. All else is distasteful, forced and fatiguing. Jinny's yellow scarf is moth-colored in this light. Susan's eyes are quenched. We are scarcely to be distinguished from the river." (W, 232-33)

The mother . . . once again the mother. And the river . . . the river that is the undercurrent of human life.

Like Poe, Virginia—but which Virginia?—seems to be rushing toward "some never-to-be-imparted secret whose attainment is destruction." The friends gathered for a communal meal waver between unity and dispersion. "Half-way through dinner, we felt enlarge itself round us the huge blackness of what is outside us, of what we are not. The wind, the rush of wheels became the roar of time, and we rushed—where? . . . But we—against the brick, against the branches, we six, out of how many millions, for one moment out of what measureless abundance of past time and time to come, burnt there triumphant. The moment was all; the moment was enough" (W, 277–78). Before going their separate ways, they pause to gaze at the river below. Bernard, who is a storyteller always trying to express the inexpressible, speaks for all of the friends.

> I could not collect myself; I could not distinguish myself; I could not help letting fall the things that had made me a minute ago eager, amused, jealous, vigilant and hosts of other things into the water. I could not recover myself from that endless throwing away, dissipation, flooding forth without our willing it and rushing soundlessly away out there under the arches of the bridge, round some clump of trees or an island, out where seabirds sit on stakes, over the roughened water to become waves in the sea—I could not recover myself from that dissipation. So we parted.
>
> "Was this then, this streaming away mixed with Susan, Jinny, Neville, Rhoda, Louis, a sort of death? A new assembly of elements? Some hint of what was to come? (W, 279)

The moment of Being is always "a sort of death" that borders on the religious. Was Virginia speaking for herself through the words of Clarissa's reflection on Septimus's suicide? "Death was an attempt to communicate; people feeling the impossibility of reaching the center, which mystically, evaded them; closeness drew apart; rapture faded, one was alone. There was an embrace in death." Questions remain, always remain. Is death the end or the beginning? Is there a next act? Is suicide the last work? When

Virginia Woolf's grave

Virginia slipped into the flowing river, was she thinking of Clarissa, who, sitting on a bus going up Shaftesbury Avenue and feeling herself "everywhere; not 'here, here, here'" had "intimations of immortality"?

> It ended in a transcendental theory which, with her horror of death, allowed her to believe, or say that she believed (for all her skepticism), that since our apparitions, the part of us which appears, are so momentary compared with the other, the unseen part of us, which spreads wide, the unseen might survive, be recovered somehow attached to this person or that, or even haunting certain places after death . . . perhaps—perhaps.[32]

. . . Perhaps . . . Perhaps . . . Perhaps . . .

Intensity

Ernest Hemingway (1899–1961): *The Dangerous Summer*

The thought of suicide is a great consolation: by means of it one
gets through many a dark night.
—Friedrich Nietzsche

Deadly Legacy

Imagine, just try to imagine that your inheritance was the gun your father
had used to kill himself. Immediately after the father was buried, both sons
asked the mother to give them the gun, which the family had dubbed "Long
John," as a memento of the father. The mother resisted but eventually passed
on the gun to her older son. Was the father's suicide his gift of death that
his sons and daughters were destined to bear? Was the gun the mother's
gift of death to the son who hated her? Can the gift of death ever be
denied?

On December 6, 1928, Clarence Edmonds Hemingway told his wife, Grace,
he was tired, withdrew to their bedroom, and shot himself in the right
temple with a Civil War .32-caliber Smith and Wesson revolver he had inherited from his father two years earlier. At the time, Edmonds was under
considerable pressure created by financial and health problems. He suffered
from diabetes and feared he was developing gangrene, which could lead to
amputation. There were also questions about his mental stability—he suffered abrupt mood swings and might have been a manic-depressive. When

Edmonds shot himself, his thirteen-year-old son, Leicester, was lying sick in a nearby bedroom. He rushed into his parents' bedroom and found his dying father. Leicester, like his father, had diabetes, and in 1982, when informed that his legs would have to be amputated, he also took his life with a single shot to the head. Writing in an autobiographical novel, *The Sound of the Trumpet,* years earlier, Leicester recalled the traumatic moment that forever changed his life. The door "opened and in the darkened room, all shades drawn except one, there on the bed lay his father making hoarse breathing noises. His eyes were closed, and in that first instant he saw him there in the half-dark, nothing looked wrong. He put his hand under his father's head. His hand slipped under easily and when he brought it out again, it was wet-warm with blood."[1] Edmonds's suicide was the inescapable legacy he left not only for his own children but also for later generations of his family as well. Three of his six children committed suicide; in addition to Leicester and Ernest, Ursula killed herself in 1966, after learning she had cancer, and in 1996 his great-granddaughter, Margaux, took her life at the age of forty-one.

At the time of his father's death, Ernest Hemingway, who was twenty-nine, was en route from New York City to Key West. He returned to Chicago and took responsibility for funeral arrangements. Even though he later admitted to a friend, "what makes me feel the worst is that my father is the one I cared about," his response was far from sympathetic.[2] Hemingway's biographer, Kenneth S. Lynn, reports that "he infuriated Marcelline by saying that Catholicism had taught him that suicide was a mortal sin and that consequently their father would languish in hell forever. On the other hand, he comfortingly assured young Leicester and Carol that there was nothing to be ashamed of in their father's death. Because of all his ailments, the old boy had been temporarily knocked in the head and wasn't responsible for what he had done."[3] His father's suicide left an indelible mark on Hemingway; he was both terrified by death and irresistibly drawn to it. The thought of suicide was constantly on his mind, and, as Nietzsche suggests, got him through many sleepless nights. His father's death remained an unresolved puzzle that he repeatedly probed in his fiction. A passage deleted from *Green Hills of Africa* (1935) might have been too revealing to include in the novel. "My father was a coward. He shot himself without necessity. At least I thought so. I had gone through it myself until I figured it in my head. I knew what it was to be a coward and what it was to cease being a coward. Now, truly, in actual danger, I felt a clean feeling as in a shower. Of course it was easy now. That was because I no longer cared what happened. I knew it was better to live it so that if you died you had done everything that you could do about your work and your enjoyment of life up to that minute, reconciling the two, which is very difficult."[4] Hemingway's lifelong obsession with courage and manliness is at least in part a function of what he perceived to be his father's weakness and cowardice. Over the years, however, his understanding of his father's death slowly changed.

Hemingway and his siblings had a complicated relationship with their strict and mercurial father. Edmonds was an avid outdoorsman who was an expert marksman. He passed on to his two sons and four daughters his love for the woods, and taught them to hike, hunt, and fish. He never seemed happier than when leading his band of young initiates through the brush. Edmonds's mood, however, could change abruptly. As Marcelline, his oldest daughter, expressed it, Lynn reports, "'Sometimes the change from being gay to being stern was so abrupt that we were not prepared for the shock that came, when one minute Daddy would have his arm around one of us or we would be sitting on his lap, laughing and talking, and a minute or so later—because of something we had said or done, or some neglected duty of ours he suddenly thought about—we would be ordered to our rooms and perhaps made to go without supper. Sometimes we were spanked hard, our bodies across his knee. Always after the punishment we were told to kneel down and ask God to forgive us.' For serious infractions, she added, he went at them with a razor strap that he kept in his closet. Washing their mouths out with bitter-tasting soap and refusing to speak to them for days at a time were other devices he resorted to for making them pay for their transgressions."[5]

Edmonds's volatility was the result of a combustible combination of mental instability and religious constraints. In addition to his physical ailments, he suffered depression, which periodically became incapacitating. His obsessive and repressive religious beliefs reflected the time and place where he lived and the family in which he was raised. In the early twentieth century, Oak Park was a bastion of conservative Protestantism. The sale of alcohol had been illegal since 1870, and the community took measures to exclude African Americans, Catholics, and Jews. In an effort to protect themselves from the changing face of America, town officials went so far as to refuse to become part of Chicago, and actually withdrew from Cicero because of the growing working class in the town.

Edmonds's father-in-law, Ernest Hall, was a committed Congregationalist and successful businessman who insisted on conducting daily family worship services during the years Edmonds and Grace lived in his home. His own father, Anson Hemingway, was even more devout. A close friend of the evangelist Dwight Lyman Moody, who founded the still-influential Moody Bible Institute, Anson found his calling as the secretary of the Chicago Young Men's Christian Association. The strict moralism of Hemingway's father and grandfather came to represent everything he spent his life rebelling against.

Grace Hall Hemingway's version of Protestantism was considerably more lenient than that of her husband. Though they attended a liberal Congregational church, Edmonds quietly resented his wife's acceptance of music, dancing, and card playing. While Ernest rejected his father's repressive moralism, he could not accept his mother's easy Christianity, which repressed the pain and suffering that he believed were an unavoidable part of human life. When Hemingway converted to Catholicism in 1926 to appease his second wife, Pauline, it was the blood of the crucified Christ that attracted him. The mother's lasting influence on her son was, however, more psychological than religious. Grace enjoyed a privileged childhood, which led to her becoming a social climber, who considered herself and her children superior to their neighbors in Oak Park. A devotee of the arts, she had fantasies of becoming an opera star. When her dreams of a musical career did not materialize, she projected her ambition onto her son by insisting that Ernest learn to play the cello. But another of Grace's fantasies proved devastating for her older son. She had long imagined having twins, and when Ernest was born one and a half years after Marcelline, their mother decided to raise her children as female twins. For several years, she dressed Ernest in girl's clothing and pretended he was a girl. The mother's sexual games remained a family secret for almost fifty years, when an embittered Marcelline revealed her mother's cross-dressing pranks. While it is too simple to reduce Hemingway's obsession with masculinity to these experiences, there is no doubt that his early childhood years had a lasting impact on him. His preoccupation with questions of sexual identity and fascination with androgynous fantasies can be traced to the confusions his mother engendered.[6]

Hemingway's problems with his mother were not limited to her early manipulation of his relationship to his sister. As he grew older, he began to recognize how his mother harassed and dominated his father. In 1936, suffering from depression and insomnia, Hemingway wrote to his mother-in-law, with whom he, like Poe, had such a close relationship that he called her "Mother," "Had never had the real old melancholia before, and am glad to have had it so I know what people go through. It makes me more tolerant of what happened to my father."[7] Rather than an act of cowardice, Hemingway eventually came to see his father's suicide as a desperate attempt to escape from a woman who had made his life unbearable. John Dos Passos, who was one of Hemingway's close friends, said that "Ernest was the only man he had ever known who really hated his mother."[8]

Though Edmonds and Grace did not have the same ambition for their son, they both expected Ernest to attend college. A long line of Hemingways had gone to Oberlin College, and when Marcelline enrolled, Edmonds hoped his son would join her. But Ernest had other ideas; eager to escape his family and small-town Midwestern life, he wanted to see more of the world. His father eventually agreed to let him accept a position at the Kansas City *Star*, where Hemingway learned the craft of journalism and developed what would become his signature style. When he expanded his repertoire from journalism to fiction, his parents, especially his mother, were upset by his work. On his twenty-first birthday, Grace wrote a devastating letter to her son that reveals many of the problems with which Hemingway was wrestling at the time. Describing a mother's love as a bank with seemingly inexhaustible reserves, she declared that her son's excesses had overdrawn his account. In this family's closed economy, there was no investment without the expectation of a profitable return. Rarely has the interplay between debt and guilt in family relations been more graphically described. In the end, Hemingway would learn, it is impossible to repay some debts.

In 1934, Hemingway wrote to F. Scott Fitzgerald, "We are all bitched from the start and you especially have to be hurt like hell before you can write seriously. But when you get the damned hurt use it—don't cheat with it. Be as faithful to it as a scientist."[9] Though his words were intended to console his friend and competitor, Hemingway knew he was speaking to himself. He made good use of the troubling legacy his parents had left him, but it took a heavy toll. As early as 1934, he wrote to Dos Passos, "I felt that gigantic bloody emptiness and nothingness like couldn't ever fuck, fight write and was all for death."[10] With thoughts of mortality constantly pursuing him, it is often hard to tell if Hemingway is running from or toward his death. Joyce Carol Oates's comment about Poe might well be applied to Hemingway. "As Pascal observed in the 139th Pensée: '. . . all the unhappiness of men arises from one single fact, that they cannot stay quietly in their own chamber.'"[11] By this measure, Hemingway was, indeed, a very unhappy person. He was constantly on the move—Chicago, New York, Paris, Key West, Cody, Cuba, Africa, Spain, Sun Valley . . . . His relationships were as mobile as his life: four wives—Elizabeth Hadley Richardson, 1921–27; Pauline Pfeiffer, 1927–40; Martha Gellhorn, 1940–45; and Mary Welsh, 1946–61—and countless lovers and liaisons.

Throughout his life, Hemingway was obsessed with war. Eager to join the war to end all wars, he tried to enlist in the army but was rejected because of poor eyesight. Undeterred, he signed up for the Red Cross ambulance corps and served in Italy, where he was seriously wounded by shrapnel from an exploding shell. He was awarded the Silver Medal of Military Valor for his service. The firsthand experience of combat forever changed Hemingway. In a short story entitled "A Natural History of the Dead" (1933), he describes the shock of his face-to-face encounter with the obscene brutality of war. The setting is the 1918 Austrian offensive in Italy. Arriving shortly after a munitions factory had been blown up, the narrator recalls collecting fragments of men, women, children, and animals that had been scattered across the fields.

> Until the dead are buried they change somewhat in appearance each day. The colour change in Caucasian races is from white to yellow, to yellow-green, to black. If left long enough in the heat the flesh comes to resemble coal-tar, especially where it has been broken or torn, and it has quite a visible tar-like irides-cence. The dead grow larger each day until sometimes they become quite too big for their uniforms, filling these until they seem blown tight enough to burst. The individual members may increase in girth to an unbelievable extent and faces fill taut and globular as balloons. . . . The heat, the flies, the indicative positions of bodies in the grass, and the amount of paper scat-tered are impressions one retains. The smell of a battlefield in hot weather one cannot recall. You can remember that there was such a smell, but nothing ever happens to you to bring it back. It is unlike the smell of a regiment, which may come to you sud-denly while riding in the street car and you will look across and see the man who has brought it to you. But the other thing is gone as completely as when you have been in love; you remember things that happened, but the sensation cannot be recalled.[12]

Hemingway's two obsessions, love and death, Eros and Thanatos, are fleet-ing moments whose intensity does not last and can hardly be remembered.

Neither wounds nor the vile smell of death could deflect Hemingway's insatiable desire to be in the midst of the chaos of war. Like a junkie need-ing a fix, he sought the heat of battle, and journalism was his excuse for courting death in World War II, the Spanish Civil War, and the Cuban Revolution. Though always on the move, Hemingway could not outrun the demons that relentlessly pursued him. The list of physical and psycho-logical ailments he suffered throughout his life is truly staggering: malaria, anthrax, appendicitis, kidney trouble, bronchial pneumonia, amoebic dysentery, blood poisoning, severe liver problems, hypertension, skin cancer, nephritis, hepatitis, arteriosclerosis, diabetes, hepatitis, overweight, underweight, impotence, loss of memory, and, most devastating, alcoholism, depression, and paranoia. Some of these maladies were self-inflicted, others were not. Like an ancient alchemist, Hemingway sublimated the material of his suffering into the pure gold of literature.

Real Fake

Strange though it may seem, Hemingway's life and work are best understood as a prolonged religious quest. His ceaseless restlessness was a symptom of his constant search for something that always eluded both his comprehension and grasp. His religion was the polar opposite of the gospel he heard preached from the Congregational pulpit during his youth. Where his parents found the sacred, he found the profane, and what he regarded as sacred, his parents, and many others, regarded as profane.

Eager to escape the stifling world of early twentieth-century American suburbia, Hemingway rushed off to war in search of something real. War, he believed, could provide the intensity of experience that many people once found in religion. He abhorred everything that appeared to be fake, and relentlessly searched for what he took to be real, or, in a more recent idiom, authentic. His search for the real was not unique; indeed, many modernist writers and artists were preoccupied with escaping bourgeois life, subverting traditions, and shattering forms and styles they were convinced repressed the rich immediacy of experience. Hemingway's life spanned the dominance of the military-industrial complex and the emergence of the information-media-entertainment complex. Modernity and its extension in postmodernity have created the disenchantment of the world first through the mechanization and standardization, and then the digitization and virtualization of experience. When representations displace things, images absorb the body, and the map replaces the territory, the real disappears in the ether of what eventually would be called "the cloud." At this point, something unexpected occurs—the real returns with a vengeance to disrupt simulations designed to replace it. The real, in other words, becomes an obsession at the moment it seems to be disappearing.

Hemingway's quest for the real took him to the battlefields of Europe and Cuba, boxing rings with professional prizefighters, bullfighting arenas in Spain, the jungles of Africa, the beds of countless women, and the mountains of Idaho, where his journey tragically ended. He was a man whose contradictions were as grand as his appetites. Hemingway was one of the first celebrity artists whose fame at its height surpassed even that of Andy Warhol, who became the modern master of media manipulation. The celebrity role was not only projected onto Hemingway, but was also calculatedly cultivated by him. The transition from being a well-known writer to a celebrity was largely the result of a profile written by Dorothy Parker and published in the *New Yorker* on November 30, 1929. Mired in the depth of the Great Depression, readers were eager for glamor and glitter. Parker wrote, "People so much wanted him to be a figure out of a saga that they went to the great length of providing the saga themselves." It was her conclusion, however, that highlighted the phrase with which Hemingway would forever be associated.

> That brings me to the point I have been trying to reach all this time: Ernest Hemingway's definition of courage—his phrase that, it seems to me, makes Barrie's "Courage is immortality" sound like one of the more treble trillings of Tinker Bell. Mr. Hemingway did not use the term "courage." Ever the euphemist, he referred to the quality as "guts," and he was attributing its possession to an absent friend.
>
> "Now just a minute," somebody said, for it was one of those argumentative evenings. "Listen. Look here a minute. Exactly what do you mean by 'guts'?"
>
> "I mean," Ernest Hemingway said, "grace under pressure."
>
> That grace is his. The pressure, I suppose, comes in, *gratis,* under the heading of the Artist's Reward.[13]

From this moment on, wherever Hemingway went, members of the media were sure to follow. He was complicit in this mythmaking, often to the detriment of his work. Edmond Wilson once went so far as to suggest that Hemingway had "become imprisoned by his myth."[14] Reporters and the public they served had a vested interest in seeing the Hemingway myth continue to grow. During the late 1930s, articles consistently glorified his exploits during the Spanish Civil War. Lynn reports, "Hemingway created the impression that enemy aircraft and artillery bombardments, along with curtains of machine-gun and automatic-rifle fire, were constantly threatening his life. Even when he went to bed he was in danger, for his suite in the Hotel Florida in Madrid was on the front side of the building, facing squarely toward the Nationalists' big guns two miles away, he explained to his readers."[15] By the 1940s, Hemingway and the media were engaged in a game of mutual exploitation. Countless articles about him appeared in magazines like *Time, New York Sunday Mirror, American Weekly, New York Post Weekend Magazine,* and, above all, *Life,* which was the most influential publicity machine at the time. *Life* commissioned journalist, novelist, poet, and literary critic Malcolm Cowley to write an article about Hemingway. By this time Hemingway had become weary of all the attention from the media, but eventually agreed to be interviewed at his home in Cuba. When "A Portrait of Mr. Papa" appeared on January 10, 1949, it further contributed to the credulous exaggeration of Hemingway's exploits, which had begun twenty years earlier. To make matters worse, from Hemingway's point of view, the article made virtually no mention of his works.

Hemingway had turned into precisely what he had long abhorred—a fake. In 1953, he sought to recapture precious moments of earlier years by returning first to Spain and then to Africa. In Spain, he and Mary retraced the bullfighting circuit he had followed while writing *Death in the Afternoon.* During this trip, he began to think about a revised version of the book that eventually would become his last work. From Spain, the couple and their entourage proceeded to Kenya, where they were met by Philip Percival, who had taken Hemingway on a safari in 1934. In the intervening years, everything had changed. Percival was sixty-nine and suffering from typhus, and Hemingway had too many ailments to list. Rather than a dangerous journey into the heart of darkness to test himself by confronting wild beasts, the safari had become a carefully orchestrated event staged for the media. *Look* magazine sent a photographer, Earl Theisen, to compile a photo essay for the magazine. The Kenyan government, hoping to revive the tourist industry after recent tribal violence, was eager to cooperate. As a young man, Hemingway had been a crack shot and avid hunter of small and big game. Now at the age of fifty-four, his eyesight was weak, his hand unsteady, and his shot unreliable. In order to avoid embarrassment that would shatter the Hemingway myth, his African hosts staged kills for the American audience eager for more tales of "grace under pressure." During the following weeks, this sorry scene, made to order for Theisen, was repeated several times. The *Look* photo essay, of course, hid the behind-the-scenes manipulation and presented the image of a bold and triumphant Papa.

Though his body was failing and the world he had created was crumbling, the Hemingway myth continued to flourish. After the safari, Hemingway and Mary stayed in Kenya, where they camped at the base of Mount Kilimanjaro. In an effort to help the government convince people that it was safe to travel to Kenya, he agreed to serve as the honorary game warden and ranger. To break the monotony of life so far from civilization, he and Mary sometimes accompanied their bush pilot friend, Roy Marsh, on low-flying trips across the vast African wilderness. In January 1954, while flying over the famous Murchison Falls, the Cessna crashed, injuring both Hemingway and Mary. Another plane spotted the wreckage and reported that there were no survivors. By the evening, newspapers around the world carried headlines reporting Hemingway's death. Marsh was not injured and was able to charter a boat to ferry the couple to what they thought was safety. They boarded another plane to be airlifted from the jungle, when, shortly after takeoff, an engine caught fire and the entire plane was quickly engulfed in flames. Once again, Hemingway and Mary escaped, but this time not without serious injuries. Though in considerable pain, Hemingway summoned his characteristic swagger to meet with the press. This time headlines reported his resurrection, and the legend, it seemed, lived on. While the world continued to believe that Hemingway was the real deal, he knew he had become a fake. And he was not alone—

others had begun to suspect that Hemingway was not what he appeared to be.

To be a fake in life is bad enough, but for a writer to be regarded as a fake in his work is even worse. On September 16, 1926, Virginia Woolf published "An Essay in Criticism" in the *Times Literary Supplement.* Ostensibly a review of Hemingway's recently released *The Sun Also Rises,* this essay presents Woolf's clearest and most concise statement of her understanding of modernism. "The moderns," she writes, "make us aware of what we feel subconsciously; they are truer to our own experience; they even anticipate it, and this gives us a particular excitement."[16] Above all else modernism was preoccupied with the new, and, measured by this standard, Hemingway, Woolf insists, is not a modernist. "Nothing new is revealed about any of the characters in *The Sun Also Rises.* They come before us shaped, proportioned, weighed, exactly as the characters of Maupassant are shaped and proportioned. They are seen from the old angle; the old reticences, the old relations between author and character are observed." Woolf then proceeds to quote parenthetically a passage that, we will see below, was very important for Hemingway. "Romero never made any contortions, always it was straight and pure and natural in line. The others twisted themselves like corkscrews, their elbows raised and leaned against the flanks of the bull after his horns had passed, to give a faked look of danger. Afterwards, all that was faked turned bad and gave an unpleasant feeling. Romero's bullfighting gave real emotion because he kept the absolute purity of line in his movements and always quietly and calmly let the horns pass close each time." It was the aversion to the fake and search for the real that had drawn Hemingway to the bullfighting arenas of Spain. This made Woolf's conclusion all the more bitter to swallow. Analyzing the characters in Hemingway's novel, she writes,

> If we place them . . . against Tchekov's people, they are flat as cardboard. If we place them . . . against Maupassant's people they are crude as a photograph. If we place them . . . against real people, the people we liken them to are an unreal type. They are people one may have seen showing off at some café;

talking in a rapid, high-pitched slang, because slang is the speech of the herd, seemingly much at their ease, and yet if we look at them a little from the shadow not at their ease at all, and, indeed, terribly afraid of being themselves, or they would say things simply in their natural voices. So it would seem that the thing that is faked is character; Mr. Hemingway leans against the flanks of that particular bull after the horns have passed.

"The thing that is faked is character"—no criticism could have been more devastating. Hemingway's search for the real ends with him becoming a fake in the eyes of some of his most accomplished fellow writers, and, perhaps, even his own.

Violence and the Sacred

Georges Bataille (1897–1962) was an exact contemporary of Hemingway. Though they never met, to my knowledge, Bataille's provocative writings uniquely illuminate Hemingway's life and work. A member of the Parisian circle of Surrealists and a close associate of Freud's successor, Jacques Lacan, Bataille's literary and critical position was decisively shaped by Alexander Kojève's well-known lectures on Hegel's *Phenomenology of Spirit,* which were delivered in Paris in the late 1930s. In a 1953 review of Hemingway's *Old Man and the Sea,* suggestively entitled "Hemingway in the Light of Hegel," Bataille approached Hemingway's fiction from the perspective of Kojève's influential reading of Hegel's account of the master-slave relationship in the *Phenomenology.* The master, in contrast to the slave, is willing to pursue the struggle for recognition, through which self-consciousness emerges, to the point of death. The slave, by contrast, values life more than recognition and, therefore, chooses servitude rather than possible annihilation. Bataille labels the master's wager of death "sovereignty." The sovereign is willing to violate every limit and transgress all taboos in pursuit of the "impossible intensity of experience." Far from a fake who creates cardboard characters, as Woolf had argued Hemingway did, Bataille claims his work actually stages the return of the real in a world the gods have fled. "Literature is not poetry, but that which, in its very way, strives with passion toward honesty, drawing us to the inaccessible . . . from the moment when we will no longer be subjected. Hemingway may be limited, but there is no trickery in his work, nor is there any concession to the cowardliness that leads us to dominate others as if they were things."[17]

For Bataille, the death of God is the birth of the sacred. In contrast to the traditional transcendent God, who is a quasi-personal being, the sacred is the immanent creative-destructive milieu in which everything arises and passes away. While profane experience is characterized by the separation and opposition of independent subjects and discrete objects, the sacred is a continuity in which differences and oppositions dissolve in a primal unity.

> The Sacred and the divine are essentially identical notions, apart from the relative discontinuity of God as a person. God is a composite being possessed of the continuity I am talking about on the affective plane in a fundamental way. God is nevertheless represented by biblical and rational theology alike as a personal being, as a creator distinct from the generality of things created. I will say just this about continuity of existence: it is not in my opinion knowable, but it can be experienced in such fashions, always somewhat dubious, as hazard allows. Only negative experience is worthy of our attention, to my thinking, but this experience is rich enough. We ought never to forget that positive theology is matched by a negative theology founded on mystical experience.[18]

So understood, the experience of the sacred is inseparable from violence, which pushes beyond every fixed limit and ruptures the boundaries separating entities. Self and other, subject and object, love and death, man and animal, human and sacred become one in this violence. "The act of violence that deprives the creature of its limited particularity and bestows on it the limitless, infinite nature of sacred things is with its profound logic an intentional one. It is intentional like the act of the man who lays bare, desires and wants to penetrate his victim. The lover strips the beloved of her identity no less than the blood-stained priest his human or animal victim."[19]

Over the course of history, the experience of violence associated with the sacred has been ritualistic. Bataille was preoccupied with animal and human sacrifice, and once even went so far as to seriously propose to his colleagues at the College of Sociology the actual performance of a human sacrifice. In his provocative book *Erotism: Death and Sensuality,* he writes, "Mystical experience seems to me to stem from the universal experience of religious sacrifice. . . . In sacrifice, the victim is divested not only of clothes but of life (or is destroyed in some way if it is an inanimate object). The victim dies and the spectators share in what his death reveals. This is what religious historians call the element of sacredness. This sacredness is the revelation of continuity through the death of a discontinuous being to those who watch it as a solemn rite. A violent death disrupts the creature's discontinuity; what remains, what the tense onlookers experience in the succeeding silence, is the continuity of all existence with which the victim is now one."[20] Beyond the bounds of religion, the sacred can be experienced in erotism, intoxication, war, and some sports. It is important to distinguish erotism from more customary forms of sexuality. The defining characteristic of erotism is that it is non-productive; that is to say, it has no purpose other than itself. Erotism does not issue in off-spring, but is, in Bataille's apt phrase, an "expenditure without return." Unlike the closed family economy in which Hemingway was raised, there is no return on the investment (that is, cathexis) of love—no children, no assurances, no gratitude. Erotism pushes sensuality beyond all limits to the point of absolute loss. This is why erotism is inseparable from death. The climax of the erotic relationship is the "privileged instant," the "sacred instant" in which, like Blanchot's "instant of death," Poe's "delirium," and Woolf's "moment of Being," two become One. The loss of independent entities creates "anguish" in which "terror and awe" are indistinguishable.[21] This is the negative pleasure some writers and artists associate with the sublime.

Bataille follows Freud in understanding aggression as the deflection of the death instinct from self to other. As we have seen, Eros and Thanatos are inseparable because hostility toward the other is at the same time identification with the other. Sexuality, therefore, always entails a certain violence, and violence is always in some sense erotic. In war, like love, differences dissolve in the undifferentiated flow of blood. War is "organized violence" whose climax is death that is no longer *petite.* In a passage that recalls Hemingway's young soldier searching for body fragments among swollen, putrefying bodies as well as Woolf's rotting garden, Bataille writes,

> . . . decay summed up the world we spring from and return to, and horror and shame were attached to both our birth and death. That nauseous, rank and heaving matter, frightful to look upon, a ferment of life, teeming with worms, grubs, and eggs is at the bottom of the decisive reactions we call nausea, disgust or repugnance. Beyond annihilation to come, which will fall with all its weight on the being I now am, which still waits to be called into existence, which can even be said to be about to exist rather than to exist, death will proclaim my return to seething life. Hence I can anticipate and live in expectation of that multiple putrescence that anticipates its sickening triumph in my person.[22]

To face death honestly, it is necessary to admit that in the end, everyone becomes meat that nourishes worms. At this moment, the human returns to humus, which is never really left behind.

In the modern world, religious rituals have become ossified and no longer provide the occasion for liberating ecstatic experience. Since neither self nor society can survive without the periodic release of tensions created by social taboos, new forms of sacrificial rituals have emerged. In a brief essay entitled simply "The Sacred," Bataille includes a photograph of "the Torrero Villalta before the bull he has just killed," under which there is the following caption. "Modern bullfights, owing to their ritual enactment and their tragic character, represent a form close to ancient sacred games."[23] From the caves of Lascaux and the ancient Gilgamesh epic to the Egyptian god Apsis, the Greek god Dionysus, and the cult of Mithra, which is a precursor to the Christian Eucharist, the bull has been regarded as a sacred animal. Though historians of religion have written extensively on the ritual significance of bulls, Bataille returns to Hegel's account of the master-slave relationship to explain the significance of bullfighting for Hemingway. "Starting with Hegel (with the Hegelian notion of 'master'), I have defined the world of archaic values illustrated by Hemingway's work. His heroes excel in hunting or fishing, their only occupation being war. . . . Of all games, bullfighting is the one that suits them. . . . Or, to put it another way, nothing suits them which is not a game, on the condition that, in some way, the game is one of life and death."[24]

In a review of Hemingway's letters, Edward Mendelson claims, "Hemingway's deepest wish, concealed by his self-asserting mask, was to become one with someone or something else, to live without the burden of a self. Denis de Rougemont observed that 'lovers like Tristan and Isolde who wish to dissolve their separate selves by merging into each other instead find themselves trapped in their separate bodies, and can escape the trap only by dying.'"[25] As I have argued, for Hemingway, in the disenchanted modern world, the two escapes from the separate self are war and love. His obsession with being in the midst of the most violent military action and countless string of lovers are symptoms of his overwhelming desire to lose himself in a whole larger than his separate self.

    For many people who engage in combat, war becomes a sacred time set apart from the tedium of everyday life. Facing mortal danger, the shackles separating actors snap and individuals merge to create what anthropologist Victor Turner calls "communitas." Communitas is a liminal phenomenon that only emerges at the limit of quotidian experience, where individual differences disappear and individuals merge in the anonymity of their shared humanity.[26] Far from paralyzing, life on the edge releases "creative effervescence" that religious rituals once produced.[27] In his most accomplished war novel, *For Whom the Bell Tolls,* Hemingway describes participation in combat as a "crusade." "It was a feeling of consecration to a duty toward all of the oppressed of the world which would be as difficult and embarrassing to speak about as religious experience and yet it was as authentic as the feeling you had when you heard Bach, or stood in Chartres Cathedral or the Cathedral at Leon and saw the light coming through the great windows; or when you saw Mantegna and Greco and Brueghel in the Prado. It gave you a part in something that you could believe in wholly and completely and in which you felt an absolute brotherhood with the others who were engaged in it."[28] Though war obviously is traumatic, it can also be addictive. For those who have experienced the high of absolute brotherhood, life often becomes a futile *recherche du temps perdu.*

According to Hemingway, one of the two things more intense than the camaraderie of combat is love in the time of war. In writing *For Whom the Bell Tolls,* he drew on his experience as a reporter for the North American Newspaper Alliance during the Spanish Civil War. Between 1937 and 1938, he traveled to Spain four times, and met Martha Gellhorn, whom he eventually married. The two main characters in the novel are thinly disguised versions of Hemingway and Gellhorn. Hemingway's journalistic activities were an excuse that concealed more complicated motives for his immersion in combat. During these years, suicide was never far from his mind, but the experience of his father's death had created a disdain for the cowardice he thought taking one's own life represented. Furthermore, having suffered his father's deadly legacy, he was for many years reluctant to set a bad example for his own children. In 1936, he wrote to Archibald MacLeish, "Me I like life very much. So much it will be a big disgust when I have to shoot myself. Maybe pretty soon I guess although will arrange to be shot in order not to have bad effect on kids."[29] By recklessly throwing himself into extremely dangerous situations, Hemingway seemed to be tempting death by daring others to do to him what he could not do to himself.

The action of the novel is limited to four days and three nights and centers on the relationship between Robert Jordan, a Spanish teacher from Missoula, Montana, and Maria, a young Italian woman, raped by the fascists who had killed her parents. Jordan is an explosives expert, who, along with Maria, joined a republican guerilla unit. Their mission is to blow up a key bridge near Segovia with the help of local anti-fascists in an effort to prevent reinforcements from joining government troops. Facing overwhelming odds on the ground and in the air, divisions within rebel ranks complicate an already difficult situation. Jordan is responsible for placing the explosives under the bridge. With no mechanized artillery, insufficient ammunition, and riding on horseback, Jordan and Marie, as well as their fellow guerrillas, realize their chances of surviving are slim. The most important scene in the novel occurs the night before the final battle. Acknowledging to Maria that time is running out, Jordan reflects, "I suppose it is possible to live as full a life in seventy hours as in seventy years; granted that your life has been full up to the time that the seventy hours start and that you have reached a certain age" (BT, 166). The shorter the time, the more intense experience becomes—life, paradoxically, appears to expand as it contracts. Past and future collapse into the present, which seems to become eternal. "There is nothing else than now. There is neither yesterday, certainly, nor is there any tomorrow. How old must you be before you know that? There is only now, and if now is only two days, then two days is your life and everything in it will be in proportion. This is how you live a life in two days" (BT, 169).

How long *does* it take to learn that? A lifetime, it seems, no matter how long or how short that lifetime is. At the end of the day, at the end of every day, we only have the present. Knowing that this will be their last night together and suspecting it might well be their last night alive, Jordan says to himself, "if you love this girl as much as you say you do, you had better love her very hard and make up in intensity what the relation will lack in duration and in continuity" (BT, 168). That night they make love as never before. Drawing together, their bodies become one in a rhythmic embrace, and they both tremble—yes, tremble not because of fear or falling bombs but because they both realize that the price of love is death. "I die each time," Maria moans. "Do you die?" (BT, 160). And then in a remarkable passage bordering on poetry that violates every principle of his spare style, Hemingway offers his most revealing comment on the obsession that possessed him throughout his life.

This, that they were not to have, they were having. They were
having now and before and always and now and now and now.
Oh, now, now, now, the only now, and above all now, and
there is no other now but thou now and now is thy prophet.
Now and forever now. Come now, now, for there is no now but
now. Yes, now. Now, please now, only now, not anything else
only this now, and where are you and where am I and where is
the other one, and not why, not ever why, only this now; and
on and always please then always now, always now, for now always one now; one only one, there is no other one but one now,
one, going now, rising now, sailing now, leaving now, wheeling
now, soaring now, away now, all the way now, all of all the
way now; one and one is one, is one, is one, is one, is still one,
is still one, is one descendingly, is one softly, is one longingly, is
one kindly, is one happily, is one in goodness, is one to cherish,
is one now on earth with elbows against the cut and slept-on
branches of the pine tree with the smell of the pine boughs and
the night; to earth conclusively now, and with the morning of
the day to come. Then he said, for the other was only in his
head and he had said nothing, "Oh, Maria, I love thee and I
thank thee for this."[30] (BT, 379)

"Oh, now, now, now, the only now, and above all now, and there is no other
now. . . . Now and forever now. Come now, now, for there is no now but
now. Yes, now." For all their differences in personality, style, and substance,
Ernest Hemingway and Virginia Woolf shared a passion for the intense moment of Being that finally drove them to an early death.

After this moment, everything is anti-climactic. Dawn breaks and
Jordan and Maria go their separate ways to a battle they know is futile.
Jordan succeeds in blowing up the bridge, but with planes dropping
bombs and tanks shelling the hillside, the advance of the fascists cannot
be halted. He sends Maria ahead, disingenuously promising to meet her in
Madrid. He stays behind to allow others to do to him what he cannot do to
himself. Lying in the same pine needles as he was described in the first

sentence of the book, at peace with himself and the world, Jordan awaits death.

> He was completely integrated now and he took a good long look at everything. Then he looked up at the sky. There were big white clouds in it. He touched the palm of his hand against the pine needles where he lay and he touched the bark of the pine trunk that he lay behind.
>
> Then he rested as easily as he could with his two elbows in the pine needles and the muzzle of the submachine gun resting against the trunk of the pine tree. . . . He could feel his heart beating against the pine needle floor of the forest. (BT, 471)

Dancing with Death

Hemingway never stopped dancing with death. *Death in the Afternoon* (1932) was the first book he published after his father's suicide. Not needing any reminders of the trauma that transformed his life, Hemingway was deeply shaken when the galleys for the book arrived and each page was tagged "Hemingway's Death." The book received an unusually hostile reception. Writing in the *New Yorker,* Robert Coates described it as "almost a suicidal book," and Max Eastman's review in the *New Republic* was entitled "Bull in the Afternoon."[31] Critics were more concerned about what they thought was Hemingway's obsession with his own virility than with the importance of this work for his literary vision. He had long been interested in bullfighting for aesthetic and artistic reasons as much as sport. He saw bullfighting as a reflection of the vexing existential issues he faced as well as an art form that reflected his understanding of writing. In the opening chapter, Hemingway writes, "The only place where you could see life and death, *i.e.*, violent death now that the wars were over, was the bull ring and I wanted very much to go to Spain where I could study it. I was trying to learn to write, commencing with the simplest things, and one of the simplest things of all and the most fundamental is violent death."[32]

In 1959, Scribner decided to reissue *Death in the Afternoon* and Hemingway wanted to update it. To prepare for this task, he and his then-wife Mary followed a full season of bullfights, which featured a series of *mano a mano* contests between an aging veteran matador, Luis Miguel Domínguín, and his aspiring young rival, Antonio Ordóñez. Originally intending the book to be a relatively modest revision of his earlier work, Hemingway, in a manner similar to David Foster Wallace decades later, lost control of both his manuscript and his life. When the editors of *Life* magazine heard about Hemingway's plans, they commissioned him to write an article. Once he started writing, however, he could not stop; it was as if he feared what was on the other side of the final period. Again like Wallace, he could not organize his reams of writing into a coherent article. That task was left for his editor at *Life,* Aaron Edward Hotchman; on September 5, 1960, the first of three installments was published. The heavily edited book version did not appear until 1985, twenty-four years after his death. Though separated by several decades, *Death in the Afternoon* and *The Dangerous Summer* form a single book, which was Hemingway's last work.[33]

By the time Hemingway and Mary sailed for Spain on the S.S. *Constitution,* his health had deteriorated to a critical condition. As early as the late 1940s, he had developed cirrhosis of the liver and also lived in constant fear of madness. The 1950s proved a particularly difficult decade. The growing public acknowledgment of his work deepened his despair that he might never again be able to write as he once had. In 1953, he received the Pulitzer Prize for *The Old Man and the Sea,* and in 1954, he was awarded the Nobel Prize for Literature. As his sixtieth birthday approached, he was drinking heavily in spite of worsening liver problems. He was also taking tranquilizers, heart medicine, and testosterone steroids. His mental state was no better than his physical condition. Paranoia paralyzed him; he was convinced the FBI was following him, and was constantly worried that he was running out of money. When one of his doctors urged him to go to the Menninger Clinic in Topeka, Kansas, he refused because he did not want the press he had so long courted to discover that he had mental problems. He finally agreed to go to the Mayo Clinic in Rochester, Minnesota, where it was reported that he was being treated for physical rather than psychological problems. During his two visits to the clinic, Hemingway underwent two rounds of electroconvulsive therapy. The sicker and more disturbed he became, the more he feared he would never again be able to write.

Hemingway's decision to return to Spain to follow another bullfighting season appears to have been motivated by his desire to recapture his lost youth as much as journalistic concerns. There was, however, another factor that was even more important than either of these reasons—having gone to Spain to learn to write after his father's death, he hoped his return would help him recover his lost craft. What others regarded merely as blood sport, Hemingway always saw as a distinctive art form. What made bullfighting an art was its proximity of death—the closer death draws, the more accomplished the artist. The art form to which he most often compares bullfighting is sculpture. "I know of no other sculpture, except Brancusi's," he writes, "that is in any way the equal of the sculpture of modern bullfighting. But it is an impermanent art as singing and the dance are, one of those that Leonardo advised men to avoid, and when the performer is gone the art exists only in the memory of those who have seen it and dies with them. . . . It is an art that deals with death and death wipes it out. . . . Suppose a painter's canvases disappeared with him and a writer's books were automatically destroyed at his death and only existed in the memory of those who had read them. That is what happens in bullfighting" (DA, 99).

The art of bullfighting assumes religious significance for Hemingway. The carefully choreographed drama allows spectators to participate in the ritual by identifying with the matador. At the moment of death, the flow of blood joins bull, fighter, and crowd in an elemental unity. Paradoxically, the moment of death is the most profound experience of the moment of Being in which time is arrested and participants in the ritual become immortal.

> If the spectators know the matador is capable of executing a
> complete, consecutive series of passes with the muleta in which
> there will be valor, art, understanding and, above all, beauty
> and great emotion, they will put up with mediocre work, cow-
> ardly work, disastrous work because they have the hope sooner

or later of seeing the complete faena; the faena that takes a man out of himself and makes him feel immortal while it is proceeding, that gives him an ecstasy that is, while momentary, as profound as any religious ecstasy; moving all the people in the ring together and increasing in emotional intensity as it proceeds, carrying the bullfighter with it, he playing on the crowd through the bull and being moved as it responds in a growing ecstasy of ordered, formal, passionate, increasing disregard for death that leaves you, when it is over, and the death administered to the animal that has made it possible, as empty, as changed and as sad as any major emotion will leave you.[34]

Hemingway devoted his life and work to the search for this moment of "emotional and spiritual intensity" (DS, 207). Sometimes he found it in war, sometimes in sex, sometimes in bullfighting, and sometimes in writing. As he explains to Antonio, bullfighting is a form of writing, and writing sometimes becomes ecstatic.

"All right. Let's walk some more. Tell me about everything that's happened. Did you write well?"

"Some days very well. Some days not so good."

"I'm the same way. There are days when you can't write at all. But they have paid to see you so you write as well as you can."

"You've been writing all right lately."

"Yes. But you know what I mean. You have days too when it isn't there."

"Yes. But I always force it and use my head."

"So do I. But it's wonderful when you really write. There's nothing better."

He was very pleased, always, to call the faena writing.
(DS, 102–3)

When the moment of ecstasy passes, the writer, like the bullfighter, is left empty and sad.

At the time Hemingway returned to Spain, physical and psychological illnesses combined with anxiety about his ability to write left him feeling profoundly empty. James A. Michener begins his introduction to *The Dangerous Summer,* "This is a book about death written by a lusty sixty-year-old man who had reason to fear his own death was imminent. It is also a loving account of his return to those heroic days when he was young and learning about life in the bull rings of Spain" (DS, 3). The art of bullfighting had changed in many ways during the fourteen years Hemingway had been away. What he regarded as the purity of the ritual had been tainted by tricks designed to appeal to the crowd and to make fights safer for matadors. Hemingway had known the fathers of Luis Miguel and Antonio and had written about the younger man's father in *The Sun Also Rises.* Luis Miguel had always been the number-one bullfighter, but by 1959, his younger brother-in-law, Antonio, was challenging his reputation. Luis Miguel remained convinced that he was still the better fighter and, though he was quite wealthy, came out of retirement to defend his reputation. Hemingway realized that Luis Miguel's ability was no longer what it once had been; at the same time, Antonio's mastery of the art was soaring. It is obvious that Luis Miguel's story is Hemingway's own, but he could not admit this to himself or to others. Forsaking any pretense of neutrality, he sided with Antonio, which deeply hurt Luis Miguel. In Luis Miguel he saw the sad man he had become, and in Antonio, he saw the proud man he once was and desperately wanted to be again. As the season unfolded and Hemingway followed the fighters from city to city, it became clear that, while Luis Miguel was a great fighter, Antonio was "an all-time great bullfighter," and would do whatever was necessary to prove it.

In the course of the contest, both matadors were seriously gored, but pride and ambition made them refuse to take sufficient time off to recover. As Antonio continued to demonstrate his superiority, Luis Miguel lost his confidence and became overwhelmed by anxiety. Hemingway finally admitted that his longtime friend "was becoming truly tragic," and was even "seeing ghosts" (DS, 178, 186). As his skill continued to fade, Luis Miguel became haunted by death; Antonio, by contrast, "made poetry of movement," as he danced with death. "It was the complete naturalness and the classical simplicity as he watched the death go by him as though he were overseeing it and helping it and making it his partner all in one ascending rhythm that made it so moving" (DS, 170–71). The final denouement came during the last *mano a mano* in Bilbao. Luis Miguel was severely gored and the wound appeared to be fatal. As was the custom, Antonio stepped into the ring and completed what his rival could not finish; he then faced his own bull with a memorable flourish. Hemingway concludes his last work with a telling description of the end of the rivalry.

> Antonio's feet had not moved and the bull and he were one now and when his hand came flat onto the top of the black hide the horn had passed his chest and the bull was dead under his hand. The bull did not know it yet and he watched Antonio standing before him with his hand raised, not in triumph but as though to say good-bye. I knew what he was thinking but for a minute it was hard for me to see his face. The bull could not see his face either but it was a strange friendly face of the strangest boy I ever knew and for once it showed compassion in the ring where there is no place for it. Now the bull knew that he was dead and his legs failed him and his eyes were glazing as Antonio watched him fall. That was how the duel between Antonio and Luis Miguel ended that year. There was not any true rivalry anymore to anyone who was present in Bilbao. (DS, 204–5)

"The bull and he were one." Defeated and wounded, though not fatally, "Miguel was standing looking across the ring at nothing" (DS, 188). Staring into Luis Miguel's vacant eyes, Hemingway saw his own face reflected.

For Hemingway, there are no happy endings in fiction or life; the victorious Antonio stayed too long and eventually became a sad parody of his once triumphant self. Michener ends his introduction to *The Dangerous Summer* by reporting,

> The taurine reader will want to know what happened to the conqueror Ordoñez after his incandescent triumphs during that dangerous summer of 1959. In subsequent years I saw him fight perhaps two dozen times and invariably it was disgraceful. Although others saw him fight well after 1959, the times I saw him

he was pudgy and evasive, apparently terrified of any real bull he faced. He took refuge in every ugly trick that Hemingway despised, accomplishing nothing with the cape or muleta and killing with a shameful running swipe from the side. And yet we crowded into the arenas to see him, hoping in vain for one final afternoon of honest triumph. It never came. Instead we saw debacles, heard boos and whistles, ducked as cushions came showering down upon him, and watched as the police prepared to rescue him if outraged fans tried to invade the arena. Hemingway was spared these indignities. He had traveled with Ordoñez when the matador was incomparable, and it was of this greatness that he wrote. (DS, 39–40)

For the proud matador who has lost his touch and proud writer whose muse has gone silent, death might be preferable to such an end. An important lesson in leaving.

Marked for Death

As the darkness that soon would swallow him was gathering, a melancholy Hemingway reflected on his dangerous summer, "Finding the country unspoiled and being able to have it again and share it with the people that were together that July I was as happy as I had ever been and all the overcrowding and the modernizations at Pamplona meant nothing" (DS, 139). But the moment never lasts, and when it passes, the darkness can be worse than ever. In *A Moveable Feast*, Hemingway recalls a conversation with the Irish poet Ernest Walsh that took place in Ezra Pound's Paris studio. Walsh bemoans James Joyce's deteriorating eyesight.

"I wish his eyes were better," Walsh said.
    "So does he," I said.
    "It is the tragedy of our time," Walsh told me.
    "Everybody has something wrong with them," I said, trying to cheer up the lunch.

"You haven't." He gave me all his charm and more, and then he marked himself for death.

"You mean I am not marked for death?" I asked. I could not help it.

"No, you are marked for Life." He capitalized the word.

"Give me time," I said.[35]

By the fall of 1960, his time had come.

The worse Hemingway's physical and psychological condition became, the more he drank, and the more he drank, the worse his health became. Ever since his father's death, he had regarded suicide as an act of cowardice, but, with his demons raging out of control, ending his life became an irresistible temptation. He sometimes tormented Mary by staging his suicide for horrified onlookers.[36] By November 1960, his condition had gotten bad enough for a second round of electroshock therapy at the Mayo Clinic. During his stay, he was deeply shaken one day when he looked in the mirror and saw his own face superimposed on his father's face. "Anguish," Joyce Carol Oates writes, "shone in this face. Yet it was a handsome face, the face of a general. The face of a leader of men. The face of a man crucified, who does not cry out as the nails are hammered into the flesh of his hands and feet. It was an astonishment, to see his father's face in his face and to see such anguish."[37]

The treatment did not alleviate the symptoms of depression for long. After returning to his recently purchased home in Sun Valley, Hemingway, unable to write, withdrew into silence. Realizing that suicide had become a realistic possibility, Mary locked the guns in the basement but, for some inexplicable reason, left the key unattended in the kitchen. On July 2, 1961, Hemingway rose as dawn was breaking across Sun Valley, found the key to the basement storeroom, and retrieved his favorite twelve-gauge double-barreled shotgun. Sitting beside the empty gun rack with Mary sleeping upstairs, he placed the gun between his legs, put the barrel in his mouth, just as he had previously practiced, and pulled the trigger.

Traveling through Spain during the summer that was the happiest time of his life, Hemingway recalled his experience during the Spanish Civil War.

The poignant passage carries echoes of his account of the last night Jordan
and Marie spent together, and anticipates the obscenity of his own death.

> Seeing the terrain did not bring back the fight. That had never
> gone away. But it helped a little, as always, to purge some things
> that happen on the earth to see how little difference it has made
> to the dry hills that once were all-important to you. Riding
> along the road toward Segorbe that morning I thought how a
> bulldozer does more violence to a hill than the death of a bri-
> gade and that a brigade that was left to hold a height so that it, the
> brigade, might be destroyed, may enrich the soil for a short time
> and add some valuable mineral salts and a certain amount of
> metal to the hill but the metal is not in mineable quantities and
> any fertilization made will be washed away from the infertile soil
> in the rains of spring and fall and in the run-off of the snow of
> winter. (DS, 119–20)

Earth, fertile earth, the end and the beginning of life.

NINE

Speed

David Foster Wallace (1962–2008): *The Pale King,*
"Good Old Neon"

Boredom rests upon the nothing that interlaces existence; its dizziness is
infinite, like that which comes from looking down into a bottomless abyss.
—Kierkegaard, *Either/Or*

Duplicity

GEORGE: Everybody's doing something, we'll do nothing.

JERRY: So, we go into NBC, we tell them we've got an idea for
a show about nothing.

GEORGE: Exactly.

JERRY: They say, "What's your show about?" I say, "Nothing."

GEORGE: There you go.[1]

Every day walking to and from my office, I pass Tom's Restaurant on
the corner of Broadway and 112th Street, where some version of this conversation takes place. Most days, people are standing in front of Tom's taking selfies to send family and friends, and occasionally a couple, usually
from a foreign country, asks me to take a picture of them. *Seinfeld,* which
ran from June 6, 1989, to May 14, 1998, with reruns continuing worldwide,
not only captured prevailing attitudes during the decade of the 1990s, but

also expressed the mood of a generation that still resonates today. The show's timing was perfect. It launched the year the Berlin Wall fell. With the subsequent collapse of the Soviet Union, followed by the explosion of the information and media revolution, which ushered in the frenzy of the Dot.com bubble, pundits were confidently declaring that the triumph of global capitalism marked nothing less than the end of history. As Marx had predicted in *The Communist Manifesto* over one hundred and fifty years earlier, everything solid seemed to be melting into thin air. The rules of the game were changing or even disappearing faster than most people realized. Hip became cool and an ironic wink signaled that savvy players were in the know. What better way to represent this endlessly fluid world that was emerging at the end of the millennium than a TV show as well as a fragmentary novel about nothing?

But there is nothing and there is nothing: Nietzsche's silent stare, Melville's silence, Poe's polar abyss, Woolf's water, Blanchot's neuter, Derrida's *différance*, Heidegger's *Nichts*, Kierkegaard's irony, and David Foster Wallace's irony.

Postmodern irony is the cultural symptom of the closure of a trajectory that defined modernity. When Luther turned from the heavens to his inner self, and Descartes reduced objective truth to subjective certainty (that is, *cogito ergo sum*), they prepared the way for Kierkegaard to declare, "truth is subjectivity." As objectivity folded back into subjectivity, the creator God morphed into the creative subject, who fashions the world in his own image. Far from abstract religious and philosophical ideas, these developments implicitly and explicitly affect all aspects of everyday life. As Heidegger points out, modern science and technology mark the end of Western theology and philosophy by translating Nietzsche's death of God and will to power into the will to mastery for which the world as well as other people are a "standing reserve" awaiting exploitation for utilitarian ends. "Man," Heidegger argues, "exalts himself to the posture of lord of the earth. In this way the impression comes to prevail that everything man encounters exists only insofar as it is his construct. This illusion gives rise to the final delusion: It seems as though man everywhere and always encounters only himself."[2] As modernity passes into postmodernity, self-certainty and security give way to uncertainty and insecurity. Foundations that had long grounded thinking and acting begin to tremble and, like Kierkegaard's ironist, people fall prey to a dizziness that "comes from looking down into a bottomless abyss."[3]

David Foster Wallace was a student of philosophy and mathematics before he was a writer. His father, James D. Wallace, was a professor of philosophy at the University of Illinois at Urbana-Champaign, and wrote several books on moral philosophy. Wallace followed in his father's footsteps, attending Amherst College, where he too studied philosophy. Reflecting on his interest in philosophy, he recalls, "Return with us now to Deare Olde Amherst. For most of my college career I was a hard-core syntax weenie, a philosophy major with a specialization in math and logic. I was, to put it modestly, quite good at the stuff, mostly because I spent all my free time doing it. Weenieish or not, I was actually chasing a special sort of buzz, a special moment that comes sometimes." Hooked on this buzz, he started a doctoral program in philosophy at Harvard at a pivotal moment in the history of Western philosophy. He explains that when he began studying philosophy, "it was the beginning of the infiltration by kind of continental deconstruction on analytic philosophy and the world was full of recursion, and involution, and things bending back on themselves, and various incarnations of Gödel's proof, and I think some of that kind of affected me at a spinal level. I really like recursions, and I really like contradictions and paradoxes and statements that kind of negate themselves in the middle."[4] As the loops proliferated, he could not find the fix he needed in philosophy and realized that literature and writing provided an even better buzz. Nevertheless, the questions he discovered in deconstruction and poststructuralism continued to be an obsession and, when he could not find Ariadne's thread, eventually became a labyrinth he could not escape.

The two major works of fiction that Wallace published during his lifetime (*The Broom of the System,* 1987, and *Infinite Jest,* 1996) span the heyday of postmodernism. The writers to whom he was initially drawn—Gaddis, Nabokov, Barthelme, DeLillo—had experimented with various versions of meta-fiction that took the self-reflexivity of modernism to a new level. Wallace saw in their work imaginative explorations of the enigmas and paradoxes of self-consciousness that had preoccupied many modern philosophers. While his Harvard professors were immune to deconstruction and postmodernism, they did expose Wallace to Wittgenstein, in whose work he discovered many of the questions post-structural philosophers were asking but analytic philosophers were ignoring. In a 1993 interview, he reported indirectly drawing on Wittgenstein's work for his understanding of language. "In order for language both to be meaningful and to have some connection to reality, words like 'tree' and 'house' have to be like little pictures, representation of little trees and houses. Mimesis. But nothing more. Which means we can know and speak of nothing more than little mental pictures. Which divides us, metaphysically and forever, from the external world. If you buy such a metaphysical schism, you're left with only two options. One is that the individual person with her language is trapped in here, with the world out there, and never the twain shall meet. Which, even if you think language's pictures are really mimetic, is an awfully lonely proposition. And there is no guarantee that pictures 'are' mimetic, which means you're looking at solipsism. One of the things that makes Wittgenstein a real artist to me is that he realized that no conclusion could be more horrible than solipsism."[5] This conclusion is what Wallace struggles, finally unsuccessfully, to avoid in his personal life as well as his writing.

With the shift from consciousness to self-consciousness, the opposition between subject (self) and object (world) turns inward and becomes the opposition between self (as subject) and self (as object). In this endlessly recursive loop, the self-conscious subject is inwardly divided and, thus, unavoidably duplicitous. Wallace is profoundly ambivalent about the hyper-awareness that this level of self-consciousness involves. On the one hand, he sees the post-industrial mediated world as dehumanizing because it relentlessly programs consciousness and routinizes behavior to serve the interests of postmodern consumer and financial capitalism. Just as Kierkegaard, who, we have seen, was the first critic of modern media, argued that the popular press anesthetizes awareness in a way that represses individuality, so Wallace insists that today advertising, TV, the Internet, video games, and iPhones create pernicious distractions that divert attention from the vital importance of personal decisions. In his wildly popular commencement address delivered at Kenyon College on May 21, 2005, he tells graduating students the value of a liberal arts education is the cultivation of critical self-awareness that teaches the importance of paying attention so that you "will know there are other options. It will actually be within your power to experience a crowded, hot, slow consumer-hell type situation as not only meaningful, but sacred, on fire with the same force that made the stars: love, fellowship, the mystical oneness of all things deep down."[6] Such heightened self-awareness is only the propaedeutic to free decisions in which individuals take responsibility for controlling their attention, rather than blindly following a script someone else has written.

But Wallace was too smart, too skeptical, too tormented, and, perhaps, too cynical to heed his own advice, however desperately he might have wanted to do so. All too often canny carnies hawking mystical oneness turn out to be confidence-men duping gullible seekers. In an essay entitled "*E Unibus Pluram:* Television and U.S. Fiction," published in 1993, he admits, "Jacking the number of choices and options up with better tech will remedy exactly nothing, so long as no sources of insight on comparative worth, no guides to *why* and *how* to choose among experiences, fantasies, beliefs, and predilections, are permitted serious consideration in U.S. culture."[7] As Kierkegaard and Derrida repeatedly insist, when there are no rules to choose the rules by which to choose, you face "the madness of decision." Forever suspended on a tightrope above a bottomless abyss, individuals are compelled to choose without any foundational principles or secure norms to guide their decisions.

Paradoxically, the very hyper-awareness necessary for responsible decisions creates a hall of mirrors that makes deciding nearly impossible. Caught in the "infinity of reflection," the will becomes paralyzed. In the most suggestive chapter in *The Pale King,* a prototypical postmodern student, Chris Fogel, finds himself in the double-bind that acute self-consciousness creates.

> *"Now I am aware that I am aware that I'm sitting up oddly straight, right now I'm aware that I feel an itch on the left side of my neck, now I'm aware that I'm deliberating whether to*

*scratch or not, now I'm aware of paying attention to that delib-
eration and what the ambivalence about scratching feels like and
what those feelings and my awareness of them do to my awareness of the intensity of the itch.*" Meaning that past a certain
point, the element of choice of attention in doubling could get
lost, and the awareness could sort of explode into a hall of mirrors of consciously felt sensations and thoughts and awareness
of awareness of awareness of these. This was attention without
choice, meaning the loss of the ability to focus in and concentrate on just one thing . . . [8]

Like Heidegger's masters of the universe, everywhere Wallace and
his characters turn, they see only themselves. But Fogel's story, like
Wallace's own life, is not a tale of the mighty and powerful, but of everyday people struggling to negotiate the demands of a world in which nothing seems all too real and meaning is swallowed up by the surrounding
cacophony.

Wallace's works are filled with doubles—buildings that are mirror images of each other, ghosts of ghosts of ghosts, different characters with the
same name, and multiple authors named David Foster Wallace, who offer
purportedly non-fictive asides in works of fiction. Even when they seem to
be talking straight, these characters remain duplicitous. The reader, and
one suspects, the writer, become caught in an echo chamber where the
words of Melville's confidence-man continue to reverberate, "I don't know,
I don't know . . . there's so many marks of all sorts to go by, it makes it a
kind of uncertain."[9] Sitting on a couch watching *As the World Turns* on TV,
Fogel admits, "I knew, sitting there, that I might be a real nihilist, that it
wasn't always just a hip pose. That I drifted and quit because nothing meant
anything, no one choice was really better. That I was, in a way, too free, or
that this kind of freedom wasn't actually real—I was free to choose 'whatever' because it didn't really matter" (225).

"Whatever"! This single word effectively captures the attitude of
postmodern ironists whose nothing Kierkegaard presciently described almost two hundred years ago. "With irony . . . , when everything else be-

comes vain, subjectivity becomes free. And the more vain everything becomes, so much the lighter, more vacuous, more evanescent becomes subjectivity. Whereas everything else becomes vain, the ironic subject does not himself become vain but saves his own vanity. For irony everything becomes nothingness, but nothingness may be taken in several ways. The speculative nothingness is that which at every moment is vanishing for concretion, since it is itself the demand for the concrete. . . . The mystical nothingness is a nothingness for representation, a nothingness which yet is as full of content as the silence of the night is eloquent for one who has ears to hear. Finally, the ironic nothingness is that deathly stillness in which irony returns to 'haunt and jest.' "[10] A novel about a sitcom about nothing. What could be more boring?

Total Noise

"The great thing about irony," Wallace explains, "is that it splits things apart, gets up above them so we can see all the flaws and hypocrisies and duplicates. . . . Sarcasm, parody, absurdism and irony are great ways to strip off stuff's mask and show the unpleasant reality behind it. The problem is that once the rules of art are debunked, and once the unpleasant realities the irony diagnoses are revealed and diagnosed, 'then' what do we do?"[11] Using a word borrowed from Kierkegaard, the ironist, Wallace observes, "hovers" above himself watching himself watching as the world turns. Looking at himself as if from above, the ironist sees oppositions he cannot reconcile: self vs. world, inner vs. outer, authentic vs. inauthentic, real vs. fake, self vs. self. While such duplicity is as old as self-consciousness itself, Wallace is convinced that the malaise it creates is the distinctive plague of our postmodern media culture and information society. In a world where everything is for sale and people are transformed into "targets" for relentless customized ads bombarding them with images and information that disclose neither pattern nor meaning, everything that once seemed real vaporizes in worldwide webs of high-speed simulations that have neither ground nor purpose. As the outer world becomes a senseless swirl, people turn inward only to discover a void as vast as the universe.

The impact of these large social, economic, and cultural dynamics on Wallace was compounded by his deep psychological problems. He was, in many ways, an extreme example of the inward fragmentation that Hegel described as "unhappy consciousness." Like Poe and Woolf, Wallace was confined to psychiatric hospitals, and, like Hemingway, he was put on countless regimens of drugs and even subjected to electroconvulsive therapy. His problems were even deeper than those diagnosed by Hegel and explored by Kierkegaard. Whereas for modern unhappy consciousness the real, however it is defined, is believed to be elsewhere—in the past or the future, in the heavens or beneath the earth—and life becomes an endless pursuit of what is not present but still remains elsewhere, for postmodern unhappy consciousness the real is not merely hiding, but appears to have been a deceptive fantasy that has never been present here or elsewhere. In the absence of the real, there is nothing meaningful or valuable to pursue. Absolutely nothing.

From a young age, Wallace suffered severe psychological distress and was prone to bouts of depression, which often incapacitated him, and on several occasions required hospitalization. He turned to philosophy to help him come to terms with the questions that were tormenting him, but the more he studied, the deeper his depression became. During both his undergraduate years at Amherst and his graduate years at Harvard, he suffered mental breakdowns and had to be institutionalized. Persistent alcohol addiction exacerbated his difficulties. A short story entitled "The Planet Trillaphon as It Stands in Relation to the Bad Thing," written while he was still an undergraduate at Amherst, offers one of the most gut-wrenching accounts of what Kierkegaard described as "the sickness unto death" that has ever been written. Under the guise of a troubled adolescent, who is on antidepressants and has been subjected to "Electro-Convulsive Therapy (E.C.T.)," he explains, "imagine that every single atom in every single cell in your body is sick like that, sick, intolerably sick. . . . Just imagine that, a sickness spread utterly through every bit of you, even the bits of the bits. So that your very . . . very essence is characterized by nothing other than the feature of sickness; you and the sickness are, as they say, 'one.' "[12] Powerful drugs like Nardil were prescribed to alleviate Wallace's symptoms, but

the side effects actually deepened his depression. Suffering seemingly incurable mental anguish from a very young age, he considered suicide at
regular intervals throughout his life. When he was twenty-eight, he admitted that taking his life was "a reasonable if not at this point desirable option with respect to the whole wretched problem."[13]

"Good Old Neon," which is one of Wallace's most revealing works,
is about a young advertising agent named Neal who commits suicide. As
the tale unfolds, it becomes clear that it is actually a ghost story told from
beyond the grave. Toward the end of the story, Neal's high school friend
David Wallace appears as an important character. TV again plays a crucial role in the narrative. Neal, who confesses he is haunted by personal
demons, is slouched on the couch watching an episode of *Cheers* when Fra-
sier's fiancée Lilith, who is a psychoanalyst, returns from her office com-
plaining about her privileged yuppie clients. Seeing himself in the mirror
of the TV screen, Neal no longer can bear the lie he is living and finally
decides to kill himself by crashing his car into a bridge abutment in the
middle of a Midwestern cornfield. But this is not the end of the story,
because his ghost returns to report what everyone wants to know—what is
it like to die? Looking back on his life after his death, Neal identifies two
closely related reasons for the decision: fraudulence and speed. Trapped
in endless loops of self-reflection, he was constantly hovering above himself. The story begins with Neal admitting that he had always been a fraud
who tried to impress other people.[14] As the opposition between his inner
self and outer appearance deepens, Neal is finally driven to consult with a
rather pathetic psychologist, Dr. Gustafson, who has intestinal cancer. Assuming he knows more than his doctor, Neal diagnoses his condition as
being an inveterate poseur who suffers from a feeling of inescapable inauthenticity.

Gustafson doesn't reject this diagnosis but ups the ante by introduc-
ing a psychological variation of Epimenides's Liar's Paradox—the Fraudulence paradox. The admission of fraud, he argues, is self-negating. Just
as the claim "I am not telling the truth" proves that I am telling the truth,
so the claim "I am a fraud" proves that I am not a fraud. As paradoxes proliferate, Neal's despair deepens. His sense of inauthenticity is not merely

the result of intentional deception; rather, it is also a symptom of the "tornado" in his head, which makes it impossible to fathom his own inwardness and truly to express himself to others. Voices, countless voices rushing through his mind too fast to be processed until he is uncertain about what is real and what is fake.

The problems created by the opposition between the inner and the outer, the real and the fake, and the authentic and inauthentic are, then, structural rather than simply the result of deliberate deception. The mind is simply too big and too fast for the brain to process what is constantly circulating through it. Drugs like Ritalin, Adderall, and Dexedrine prescribed to relieve his symptoms make them worse. One might say of both Neal and Wallace what Virginia Woolf writes of Lily Briscoe in *To the Lighthouse*, "to follow her thought was like following a voice which speaks too quickly to be taken down by one's pencil."[15] Neal's moment of revelation occurs at the instant of death, and he is compelled to return from the grave to explain what really drove him to suicide. Was it his inability to comprehend and express to others the enormity of what was rushing through his mind at a speed too fast to process? We will see in what follows that the inadequacy of language was one of the factors contributing to Wallace's decision to kill himself.

What makes Wallace's fiction so powerful is the way in which the psychological complexities he suffers reflect the psycho-social dynamics of the high-speed mediascape of postmodern society and culture. Information overload creates a condition he describes as "Total Noise." In today's hyper-connected world, reality, he explains, has become "overwhelmingly, circuit-blowingly huge and complex." Total Noise is "the seething static of every particular thing and experience, and one's total freedom of infinite choice about what to choose to attend to and to represent and to connect, and how, and why, etc."[16] About the same time that attention deficit hyperactivity disorder (ADHD) was becoming a fashionable diagnosis for the children of anxious helicopter parents, Wallace was suffering from the malaise he realized was, in part, a function of postmodern network culture. Commenting on the work of two of his postmodern heroes, he observes, "The seminal novels of Pynchon and DeLillo revolve metaphorically off the concept of interference: the more connections, the more chaos, and the harder it is to cull any meaning from the seas of signal."[17] In the decades since *Gravity's Rainbow* (1973), *White Noise* (1985), and *Underworld* (1997), whose repeated refrain is "everything is connected," were published, connectivity and the accompanying noise have increased exponentially, creating what Wallace describes as a "torrential flow of information" (242). While he concentrated on television, advertising, and mass media more than on the Internet, Google, and social media, the pertinence of his diagnosis increases with each passing year. Information and media overload create distractions that make it increasingly difficult to concentrate and to remain attentive for long periods. Information that cannot be processed becomes noise that fragments attention and scatters awareness. In order to distinguish signal from noise, filters are required to process the data stream.

In this media- and information-saturated world, attention requires deliberate effort. The stakes of attention could not be higher. Wallace insists that to which you give your attention defines who you are. He elaborates this point in the opening pages of *The Pale King:* "The whole ball game was perspective, filtering, the choice of perception's objects" (PK, 14). Filters screen information by both showing what merits attention and hiding what does not. But how can one choose a filter in a world of infinite screens? With screens screening other screens, the problem is not so much the lack of meaning, as Sartre, Ionesco, and Camus had worried, as the infinite proliferation of meanings with no sure way to sort them out. Who could blame the pomo hipster for throwing up his or her hands and declaring, "Whatever!"

With this twist, we are right back in the recursive loops of postmodern irony. Today the best and the brightest want to go to Wall Street, where they sit all day surrounded by screens monitoring signs of signs that refer to nothing real. Wallace reports that when he was in school, many of his "hip, cynical, cool" friends went into advertising and earned millions of dollars manipulating people to spend money they didn't have to buy stuff they didn't need. As media become more effective and pervasive, and their manipulators more sophisticated, it is even harder to break out of echo chambers created by programmed pitchmen pushing new deals faster and faster. In an economic system that has the infinite capacity to turn what is designed to oppose it to its own advantage, resistance becomes almost impossible. For Wallace, the virus of commerce and finance invades the body politic and leaves what previously were citizens isolated and infected. Artists who once took responsibility for social criticism have been displaced by artists who, as Andy Warhol was the first to admit, are businessmen hustling for a piece of the action. When everything is for sale, nothing is real. Absolutely nothing.

Bored to Death

With the publication of *Infinite Jest,* David Foster Wallace came to be regarded as precisely the kind of super-cool hipster about whom he had developed so many reservations. Three years before his magnum opus appeared, he concluded the essay on the deleterious effects of TV by suggesting, "The next real literary 'rebels' in this country might well emerge as some weird bunch of 'anti-rebels,' born oglers who dare to back away from ironic watching, who have the childish gall actually to endorse single-entendre values. Who treat human troubles and emotions in U.S. life with reverence and conviction. Who eschew self-consciousness and fatigue. . . . The new rebels might be the ones willing to risk the yawn, the rolled eyes, the cool smile, the nudged ribs, the parody of gifted ironist, the 'How banal.'"[18] What could possibly be more banal than an IRS facility in Peoria, Illinois?

Wallace began research on his last work in 1997 and started writing in 2000. When he died in 2008, *The Pale King* was still unfinished. This work does not have a coherent narrative with a discernible plot, but is a collection of vignettes in which characters, who lack depth, but not always complexity, appear, disappear, and reappear, telling tales that often intersect and collide in unexpected ways. In addition to the pile of manuscript pages Wallace left at his death, he also wrote countless notes, additions, and corrections. Michael Pietsch includes a small selection of these notes in an appendix to the published novel. One note in particular indicates the structure of the work Wallace envisioned, two "broad arcs"—one describing the problem of boredom and the difficulty of focusing attention, and the other considering the vexed relationship between the individual and the group in an increasingly anonymous world. A novel, like a sitcom, in which nothing actually happens. Obviously, even though Wallace had become disillusioned with ironic disillusionment, he cannot free himself from postmodernism's hyper-consciousness. One of the leading characters in the novel is a person named David Wallace, who, upon arriving at the Regional Education Center (REC), is mistaken by Ms. Neti-Neti for a high-ranking agent also named David Wallace. The ensuing comedy of errors is compounded by the way Wallace plays with "proper" names. In Jnana Yoga and Advanta, the Sanskrit term *neti-neti* means "not this, not this," and is used in meditative practices to help "devotees comprehend what Brahman is by understanding what it is not."[19] In other contexts, as well as his personal life, David Foster Wallace explores the possibility that non-Western meditative practices might offer a way out of the cage of hyper-awareness.

As if the convolutions of all these references and cross-references were not enough, David Foster Wallace compounds the duplicity of the narrative by doubling the doubles with yet another David Wallace. In the "Author's Foreword," inserted as chapter nine, David Wallace claims to be "the real author, the living human holding the pencil, not some abstract narrative person." This "real" Wallace insists that though *The Pale King* is a work of fiction, "All of this is true. This book is really true." Like *House of Cards*, with Frank Underwood calling a timeout to talk into the camera, Wallace proceeds to address the reader directly to explain that he has to claim the work is fiction for legal purposes. "I need this legal protection in order to inform you that what follows is, in reality, not fiction at all, but substantially true and accurate. That *The Pale King* is, in point of fact, more like a memoir than any kind of made-up story." Needless to say, this only compounds the problem, and both "David Wallace" and David Wallace know it. They admit, "This might appear to set up an irksome paradox. The book's legal disclaimer defines everything that follows it as fiction, including this Foreword, but now here in this Foreword I'm saying that the whole thing is really nonfiction; so if you believe one you can't believe the other,

& c., & c." And, then, with the wink of an irrepressible ironist, "Please know that I find these sorts of cute, self-referential paradoxes irksome, too—at least now that I'm over thirty I do—and that the very last thing this book is is some kind of clever metafictional titty-pincher" (68, 69). But at one level, though there are many others, a "metafictional titty-pincher" is precisely what all of these Wallaces have created.

The setting and time of the novel underscore these thematic preoccupations. The IRS facility is located in a hive-like building on Self-Storage Parkway, where agents, known as wigglers, tucked away in their cubicles, slave silently day in and day out processing tax returns. The building is fiendishly designed to create confusion—it is virtually impossible to tell the back from the front, and signs that appear to provide direction actually point to other signs that lead nowhere. The façade of the main building is decorated with a large mosaic representation of a 1978 IRS Form 1040 with two pages completely filled out. Another architectural detail is even more suggestive: "The whole elaborate façade assembly was reflected—though in an angled and laterally foreshortened way that made the edge's glyph and motto look closer together than they actually were—by the garishly mirrored exterior side of the REC's other structure, a.k.a. the 'REC Annex'" (284). It is as if Wallace were mimicking Jean Baudrillard's "precession of simulacra": mirrors reflecting mirrors create endless series of copies with no originals.[20]

Wallace underscores the importance of this mirror effect by providing the backstory for the IRS facility. Not all the doubles in this story are living—the REC building is haunted by two ghosts. In contrast to phantoms, which are hallucinations that appear when wigglers cross "a certain threshold of concentrated boredom," these ghosts are "real." The first ghost haunting the REC was an examiner named Blumquist, who died at his desk in 1980 but was not noticed for four days. The second was Garrity, who worked for the Mid West Mirror Works, which previously occupied the building currently housing the REC. His responsibility was to inspect mirrors for flaws by "examining his face's reflection at very close range. He did this three times a minute, 1,440 times per day, 365 days a year, for eighteen years. . . . In 1964 or 65, he had apparently hanged himself from a steam pipe in what is now the north hall off the REC Annex's wiggle room" (317–18). With mirrors mirroring mirrors and signs disorienting more than orienting, not only the REC but also *The Pale King* becomes, in "the Author's" words, "some kind of ur-bureaucratic version of Kafka's castle" (263).

The time of the novel is no less important than the place. In preparing to write, Wallace studied accounting and immersed himself in the U.S. Tax Code, which by April 15, 2014, had exploded to 73,954 pages and now has an average of 500 changes every year. In the first "authorial" intervention, "David Wallace" comments in one of Wallace's signature footnotes, explaining that he had worked at the IRS during a break in college from May 1985 to June 1986. He stresses that this was a very important period because the IRS was undergoing a dramatic change from a "moral" agency that fulfilled a civic responsibility by providing financial resources, which were the life blood of government, to a money machine whose primary purpose was to maximize profit. The change was the result of the Reagan revolution, which rested on two pillars: cutting taxes and increasing defense spending. Wallace tells this story in a series of interviews with IRS employees that were taped for a PBS film intended to humanize and demystify the organization. To close the gap between falling revenue from tax reductions and increased spending for defense, Treasury officials developed policies based on a 1960s paper by a bureaucrat named Spackman in which he argued that the deficit could be covered by increasing the efficiency of collection. Spackman is obviously a stand-in for Reagan's director of the Office of Management and Budget, David Stockman, who was the leading cheerleader for the supply-side policies that lie at the heart of neo-liberal economics. As Wallace realizes, it was never clear whether these conservative economists were as concerned about deficits as they claimed to be because their most cherished unspoken goal was to starve what they regarded as the "beast" of the social welfare system.

Wallace shrewdly draws a direct connection between the agenda of conservatives in the 1980s and the interests of many members of the counterculture in the 1960s. While sixties rebels opposed the corporation and the military-industrial complex, hippies and yippies were also deeply suspicious of government interference in their lives. Reagan effectively appropriated the rhetoric of rebellion to support the very corporate and defense interests the counterculture vehemently opposed. By so doing, he created the conditions for a new form of financial capitalism that has been transforming the world ever since. As financial, media, and information webs spread, the very nature of reality changes. If consumer capitalism is postmodern, financial capitalism is postmodernism on steroids. The most important difference between consumer and financial capitalism is speed. In previous forms of capitalism, wealth is created by selling labor or stuff; in financial capitalism, wealth is created by trading signs backed by nothing other than other signs circulating around the world in global networks at speeds that exceed any possibility of human intervention. Like tornadoes racing across Midwestern cornfields, these whirling signs create a sense of vertigo that is utterly disorienting, and often leave massive destruction in their wake. In this wired world, it becomes as impossible to distinguish signal from noise as it is to tell the difference between fiction and nonfiction. With total noise roaring in his head, Wallace asks, Is it possible to slow down long enough to overcome the anxieties generated by hypermediated culture and to heal the inner and outer divisions that are tearing us apart?

In an effort to answer this question, he turns his attention to the unlikely subject of boredom. In an etymological digression, he notes that the word "boredom" does not appear until 1766. "Philologists say it was a neologism—and just at the time of industry's rise, too, yes? Of the mass market, the automated turbine and drill bit and bore, yes? Hollowed out?" (386). Kierkegaard was the first writer to suggest that boredom is a symptom of the deadening routinization brought about by mass media and modern industrial society. He regarded the experience of boredom as so important that he began the all-important first book of his pseudonymous authorship, *Either/Or,* with an analysis of its devastating effects. "How dreadful boredom is—how dreadfully boring. . . . I lie prostrate, inert; the only thing I see is emptiness, the only thing I live is emptiness; the only thing I move in is emptiness. . . . My soul is like the Dead Sea, over which no bird is able to fly; when it has come midway, it sinks down, exhausted, to death and destruction."[21] Wallace's view of boredom is more nuanced. Whereas Kierkegaard regarded boredom as a mark of the inauthenticity and spirit-lessness of modernity, Wallace suggests that boredom might unexpect-edly have a therapeutic effect that could lead to spiritual bliss.

It is difficult to imagine a more boring job than being an IRS agent who spends all day poring over tax returns. With the emergence of net-worked computers in the 1980s, Fredrick Winslow Taylor's principles of scientific management were extended from the physical labor of industrial production to the mental labor of information processing. Industrial and postindustrial technologies involve a complex interplay of distraction and attention. We have seen that Wallace is very critical of the way TV, the Internet, video games, and other digital media scatter attention and frag-ment selves. But this centrifugal action is countered by a centripetal action— the same technologies that are so distracting also require considerable concentration. Kids playing video games, Wall Street traders surrounded by screens tracking global financial markets, and wigglers processing as many tax returns as possible must block out noise and focus their attention for endless periods of time. During Ms. Neti-Neti's tour of the REC, David catches a glimpse of "The Immersive Room," where men and women sit in-tently working in total silence. Looking back on this moment, he admits, "there was something about the silent, motionless intensity with which everyone in that opened door's instant was studying the tax-related doc-uments before them frightened and thrilled me" (292). It was frightening because David, like Kierkegaard, realizes that such overwhelming bore-dom can smother the soul. The sting of boredom is the awareness of nothingness. "Boredom," Kierkegaard explains, "rests upon the nothing that interlaces existence; its dizziness is infinite, like that which comes from looking into a bottomless abyss. That eccentric diversion is based upon boredom is seen also in the fact that the diversion sounds with reso-nance, simply because in nothing there is not even enough to make an echo possible."[22]

For Wallace, by contrast, the preoccupation with repetitious routines of everyday life can both distract from the void boredom exposes and to-tally immerse one in the moment in a way that approximates spiritual oneness. In an exchange about the contemporary culture of distraction, a wiggler named Stuart Nicholas explains, "Everything is on fire, slow fire, and we're all less than a million breaths away from an oblivion more total than we can even bring ourselves to try to imagine, in fact, probably that's why today the manic US obsession with production, produce, produce, impact the world, contribute, shape things, to help distract us from how little and totally insignificant and temporary we are" (145–46). For a person with Wallace's restless self-awareness, distractions deliberately pursued inevitably failed to distract from the urgent existential issues that obsessed him.

With his thoughts spinning faster and faster in loops he could not break, Wallace desperately sought ways to turn off his mind. As biographer D. T. Max observes, "Wallace had now spent half a decade trying to slow down not just literature's pulse but his own." Searching for a way to quiet the noise of his mind, he turned to mystics east and west like Meister Eckhart, Krishnamurti, and pop psychologist Alan Watts. He even went on a two-week meditation retreat with Zen master Thich Nhat Hanh in Bordeaux, France, but, predictably, left before it was over.[23] The effort to immerse himself in silent meditation failed for two reasons: first, Wallace could not calm his mind long enough to focus his attention, and second, he kept being distracted by imagining how other members of the class were thinking about him. The account of Neal in "Good Old Neon" undoubtedly reflects Wallace's own experience. The recognition that when practicing meditation he was still striking a pose deepened Neal and Wallace's sense of being a fraud. Ever vigilant, Wallace suspects that the very effort to confirm one's authenticity makes one even more inauthentic.

With all avenues of escape short of death closed, Wallace tried to turn the problem into the solution by suggesting that boredom might do what meditation could not do—cultivate a mindfulness that would lead to bliss. In an appendix to *The Pale King*, Pietsch published a paragraph Wallace wrote but did not include in the novel. "Ability to pay attention. It turns out that bliss—a second-by-second joy + gratitude at the gift of being alive, conscious—lies on the other side of crushing, crushing boredom. Pay close attention to the most tedious thing you can find (tax returns, televised gold), and, in waves, a boredom like you've never known will wash over you and just about kill you. Ride these out, and it's like stepping from black and white into color. Like water after days in the desert. Constant bliss in every atom" (548).[24] The middle-aged Wallace dreams that such bliss might cure "The Bad Thing" he so poignantly described as a young college student. "Now imagine that every single atom in every single cell in your body is sick like that, sick, intolerably sick. . . . You are the sickness yourself. It is what defines you."[25] The dream that boredom can lead to bliss is, however, nothing more than a soothing illusion and Wallace knew it. His paean to boredom does not ring true; it appears to be either an act of desperation, or an expression of the very corrosive irony he was struggling to overcome.

End of the Line

Sometimes the end of the line is the end of a rope. In his classic study *The Sense of an Ending*, Frank Kermode observes, "men die because they cannot join the beginning and the end."[26] Over the years, Wallace and Jonathan Franzen became friendly competitors, carrying on an extensive correspondence. In an essay about Wallace's death, Franzen writes, "David had died of boredom and in despair about his future novels." Admitting to having been hurt by his suicide, Franzen delayed responding for several months, until he had finished a new novel. A lifelong birdwatcher, he packed binoculars, a two-way radio, GPS, notebook, a copy of *Robinson Crusoe,* and some of Wallace's ashes to scatter, and set out on a birding trip to Masafuera, an island five hundred miles off the coast of Chile, where the Scottish seaman Alexander Selkirk, whose account of his solitary life was the most likely basis of Defoe's novel, spent his life. Wrestling with his own anger and sense of betrayal, Franzen composed an eloquent homage to his dead friend that highlights many of the themes Derrida explored in his comments on *Robinson Crusoe* during his last seminar.

> To the extent that each of us is stranded on his or her own existential island—and I think it's approximately correct to say that his [Wallace's] most susceptible readers are the ones famil-

iar with the socially and spiritually isolating effects of addiction or compulsion or depression—we gratefully seized on
each new dispatch from the farthest-away island which was
David. At the level of content, he gave us the worst of himself: he
laid out with an intensity of self-scrutiny worthy of comparison
to Kafka and Kierkegaard and Dostoyevsky, the extremes of
his own narcissism, misogyny, compulsiveness, self-deception,
dehumanizing moralism and theologizing doubt in the possibility of love, and entrapment in footnotes-within-footnotes self-
consciousness. At the level of form and intention, however, this
very cataloguing of despair about his own authentic goodness
is received by the reader as a gift of authentic goodness: we feel
the love in the fact of his art, and we love him for it.[27]

Franzen's conclusion is a variation of Wallace's fraudulence paradox: what
was most authentic about his life and work was his honest admission of the
impossibility of being authentic.

Wallace's suicide should not have come as a surprise to either his
friends or readers. Like Woolf and Hemingway, he often spoke and wrote
about suicide as both a release from incurable despair and a way of shutting off the relentless noise wracking his mind. Death became the final version of what he called "Thought Stopping" (17). The inability to write
during the last years of his life was not simple writer's block; rather, it was
a symptom of his continuing mental illness as well as the result of his growing awareness of the limitations of language. As his anxieties became more
profound, he was less able to write, and the longer he could not write, the
more anxious he became. His most revealing exploration of the dilemma
that made it impossible for him to write and all but inevitable that he would
take his own life is his account of Neal's suicide in "Good Old Neon." In a
manner reminiscent of Blanchot's "The Instant of My Death," Neal narrates
the moments immediately preceding his death. With death approaching
faster than he can comprehend, Neal muses, it's "as if we are all trying to
see each other through these tiny keyholes. . . . And you think it makes you
a fraud, the tiny fraction anyone else ever sees?"[28] The problem, as we have

seen, continues to be speed and time—the mind is too vast and too fast to be captured in words. Human subjectivity can never be integrated because the I is always a we whose inner conflicts create a cacophony that cannot be silenced. Thought is fast, speech and writing are slow; thought is non-linear, language is linear. All expression, therefore, is unavoidably deceptive, and, thus, concealment lies at the heart of every self-revelation. Since interiority and exteriority never coincide, personality is a persona that hides more than it shows, and agents are actors playing roles that cannot be decoded.

For Wallace, literature was literally a matter of life and death. In one of his more reflective moments, he muses, "Fiction's about what it is to be a fucking human being."[29] But what does it mean to be a fucking human being in a world where the real has virtually disappeared in a play of images and signs, and authenticity has become an advertising gimmick for political and financial gain? One of the reasons Wallace's fiction remains so powerful is that his work, more than any other writer of his generation, captures the overwhelming psychological, social, political, and economic tensions created by today's high-speed, hyper-connected world. With too much interference generating static and too many filters from which to choose, it becomes impossible to distinguish signal from noise. As disorder increases, entropy becomes a psychological as well as a cosmological reality. In an email to Franzen, Wallace confesses, "I am tired of myself it seems; tired of my thoughts, associations, syntax, various verbal habits that have gone from discovery to technique, to tic. It's a dark time workwise."[30] His fragmented and incomplete works are mirrors in which we see our own distracted and scattered selves reflected.

If Wallace had any hope, it came from his belief that literature could be redemptive. His literary ambitions were as enormous as the psychological distress he suffered. "I had a teacher," he recalled, "who used to say that good fiction's job was to comfort the disturbed and disturb the comfortable. I guess a big part of serious fiction's purpose is to give the reader, who like all of us is sort of marooned in her own skull, to give her imaginative access to other selves. Since an ineluctable part of being a human self is suffering, part of what we humans come to art for is an experience of suffering. . . .

We all suffer alone in the real world; true empathy's impossible. But if a piece of fiction can allow us imaginatively to identify with a character's pain, we might then also more easily conceive of others identifying with our own. This is nourishing, redemptive; we become less alone inside."[31] Wallace wanted to do nothing less than create new literature that would purge the world of cynicism and corrosive postmodern irony. By cultivating the old-fashioned virtues of sincerity and authenticity in single-entendre prose about everyday struggles in the real world, he hoped to reground experience for himself as well as others. But he failed because he could not turn off the switch to his own mind. If sincerity and authenticity have to be cultivated, they are no longer real. Once infected with the virus of hyper-consciousness, it is impossible to return to a primary naiveté in which meaning is transparent, values are secure, the world is ordered, and the self is unified. Trapped like a caged rat spinning on a wheel, suicide became Wallace's final out.

"It's a dark time workwise," but then he added, "and yet a very light and lovely time in all other respects. So overall, I feel I'm ahead and pretty happy."[32] The year before his death was particularly difficult. In the summer of 2007, Wallace decided to go off Nardil after twenty-two years.[33] At this time his personal life was more stable than it had been in years. He was married to Karen Green, who was an accomplished artist, and was enjoying teaching creative writing at Pomona College. The relief domestic tranquility brought proved to be short-lived. By the following spring, his depression had returned with a vengeance and doctors put him on a new regimen of antidepressants. The drugs prescribed to alleviate his symptoms deepened the despair and anxiety they were supposed to cure. No longer able to sustain the struggle, he sent Karen a suicide note, checked into a motel, and took an overdose of pills he had collected. The pills, however, were not enough; when he awoke, he called Karen and she took him to the hospital. During the following weeks, he agreed to undergo another round of electroconvulsive therapy, and eventually went back on Nardil. None of these measures helped, and, as his condition became progressively worse, he became more and more reclusive. The words of encouragement Karen and Franzen constantly offered were not enough—on September 12,

2008, David Foster Wallace hanged himself in the garage of his Claremont home. He left a two-page suicide note, and on his desk Karen found a neatly ordered pile of two hundred pages of what eventually became *The Pale King*. Max reports, "In his final hours, he had tidied up the manuscript so that his wife could find it. Below it, around it, inside his two computers, on old floppy discs in his drawers were hundreds of other pages—drafts, character sketches, notes to himself, fragments that had evaded his attempt to integrate them into the novel over the past decade."[34] Looking back, Karen recalls, "It was terrible. I think he was so panicked that it was not working that it was self-defeating in a way. . . . I have these visual cues where it all comes back to me, and if there is any way you can make that stop then you will do. If it means bashing your head against the wall, or whatever. The fear that you won't get out of it is worse than the thing itself. I think that is where he was that afternoon. He couldn't see a way to be."[35] She recognized all too well the bitter irony in Wallace's death—by committing suicide, he became "the celebrity writer dude" he always had struggled to avoid.

Wallace's death left countless questions unanswered. Was the decision to edit and publish his unruly manuscript an act of loyalty or betrayal? The inability to edit his own work was a symptom of both his psychological condition and the mental stress created by entanglement in high-speed worldwide webs. When images and information circulate faster than the human mind can comprehend them, excess data become noise. If this noise is to be rendered intelligible, it must be edited through processes of screening or filtering, which, like Plato's demiurge or the Christian Logos (that is, Word), create worlds by forming order out of chaos. A successful editor is something like what Wallace describes as a "data mystic," who discerns coherent patterns where others see only senseless flux. As connectivity increases, patterns proliferate and it becomes difficult to distinguish what is meaningful from what is meaningless. The very empathetic identification that Wallace saw as potentially therapeutic and even redemptive compounds the problem of editing by disclosing countless filters that appear to be equally plausible. Without a reliable "counterfeit detector," Wallace becomes Melville's helpless dupe who cannot be sure what is real and what is fake, and what is authentic and what is inauthentic.

Inasmuch as Wallace's ambition was, among other things, to write realistic fiction for an era in which the real has disappeared, the best way to remain faithful to his work would have been not to edit his literary remains, but to publish everything just as he left it. Everything—hundreds of unedited manuscript pages, drafts, sketches, fragments, footnotes, footnotes to footnotes—the whole disorderly mess. Pulling it all together into a coherent story with quasi-identifiable characters to create what once was called a novel is the final act of betrayal. Wallace's inability to find the narrative line that organizes the whole is actually the "story" of our time. What could be a more realistic depiction of the contemporary world than a jumble of information that resists every effort to organize it? His failure was actually his success.

A footnote to one of Wallace's end-less footnotes, marked by an asterisk. When literature could not provide the redemption for which he so desperately longed, Wallace was at the end of his rope. But what if the end is not the end? What if the end always returns to the beginning without necessarily bringing everything full circle? As the end (of this work) approaches, the remaining question is the same as it was at the beginning: What is the relation between "time and self"?[36]

"Good Old Neon" ends before it ends with a footnote about speed and time. Neal interrupts his narrative about his suicide with a meta-narrative aside to the reader that raises a lingering question: What if the end is not really the end? Speaking from beyond the grave, Neal's ghost recalls a conversation with Dr. Gustafson in which they imagined that before his death. "We'd both died and were outside linear time and in the process of dramatic change, you can bet on that. (*Outside time* is not just an expression or manner of speaking, by the way.)"[37] How is this parenthetical remark to be read? Is it just one more postmodern ironic gesture, or does Wallace sincerely mean it? Is there an outside time beyond time, or perhaps even in time? As the instant of death approaches, Neal pauses to recall his confession that he is a fraud, and then asks the reader, "What if no time has passed at all?* . . . What if there's really no movement at all? . . . Meaning that what if in fact this *now* is infinite and never really passes in the way your mind is supposedly wired to understand *pass,* so that not only your whole life but every single humanly conceivable way to describe and account for life has time to flash like neon shaped into those connected cursive letters that businesses' signs and windows love so much to use through your mind all at once in the literally immeasurable instant between impact and death, just as you start forward to meet the wheel at a rate no belt ever made could restrain—THE END."[38]

What is this "infinite now"? What is its relation to Kierkegaard's Moment, Nietzsche's Eternal Return, Melville's whiteness, Poe's polar abyss, Freud's navel, Derrida's *différance,* Woolf's moments of Being, Hemingway's Now, or Thoreau's autumn apples? THE END. To experience the end that is not the end is like dying without dying. After the end, the question is whether Wallace's final answer to all these unanswered questions must be ours, or is there another ending?

Silence

Herman Melville (1819–1891):
The Confidence-Man, Billy Budd

> The sentence leads the one who lets himself be taken by it without his
> knowing where he is going and where he is losing himself. It transports
> sparkling images that fall back with a voluptuous violence, having clarified
> nothing, leaving the landscape that they have illumined more somber
> with the fire that they have cast on it in vain. It draws attention into its
> sinuous wake; it forces it to a complete obeisance; it makes it familiar
> with a voyage without hope and without escape; and shipwreck itself
> is nothing more than an insignificant accident at the expense of this
> cruel madness of language that says everything and says nothing,
> condemned finally to silence, after these orgies of cries and images,
> by the simplicity of its mystery.
>
> —Maurice Blanchot, "The Secret of Melville," *Faux Pas*

Place Matters

What one writes is to a great extent a function of when and where one
writes. I am writing these words before dawn on a winter morning in the
barn that has been my studio for many years. Stone Hill is a ridge in the
Berkshire Mountains that runs along the road joining western and eastern
Massachusetts. Twenty miles to the south is Arrowhead, where Melville
lived and wrote during the most productive period of his career. One
hundred and thirty-one miles to the east is the cabin beside Walden
Pond, where Thoreau wrote his best-known work. On my desk is a flower

252

pot with ivy clipped from Melville's grave, and on the nearby wall is a photograph of Thoreau's simple grave in Concord. For more years than I can remember, I have been thinking, writing, and, indeed, living *between* Melville and Thoreau. In ways that are not immediately obvious, Melville and Thoreau are the heirs of Kierkegaard and Hegel, respectively. Melville and his mentor Hawthorne were what Hegel aptly described as poets of "unhappy consciousness." Unhappy consciousness, as I have explained, is a form of awareness for which the real is radically other and, thus, always elsewhere—in the heavens or the depths, in the past or the future. Life becomes the restless search for what can be neither comprehended nor attained. For Hegel, the only cure for unhappy consciousness is a form of life that negates such altarity by affirming what is real here-and-now. This affirmation does not necessarily overlook or deny the darker side of life, but does insist that negativity, though inescapable, is not the last word. In a manner reminiscent of Hegel, Thoreau, following Emerson, who was his friend and neighbor in Concord, believes that the real is neither wholly other nor radically transcendent, but is immanent in the world, and, thus, fulfillment and even redemption are possible here-and-now in this world.

While not mistaken, this way of posing the issue is, nonetheless, too simple. As we have discovered, opposites are never merely opposite, but are codependent in such a way that neither can be itself apart from the other. There are Hegelian moments in Melville, and Kierkegaardian moments in Thoreau. At the end of his life, standing beside Lake Pontoosuc in nearby Pittsfield, Melville glimpsed immanence in what Virginia Woolf described as a "moment of Being," and, recalling his canoe trip along the Merrimack River with his brother, John, Thoreau encountered powers of nature dark enough to cloud Emerson's transparent eyeball.

Transcendence or immanence, negation or affirmation, absence or presence, elsewhere or here, Midnight or Midday, Nay or Yea. Kierkegaard or Hegel, Melville or Thoreau. Perhaps Melville can be read through Thoreau, and Thoreau through Melville in a way that makes it possible to discern a third way that avoids every oppositional either/or without collapsing differences into an identity in which Thanatos and Eros become one. This Middle Way might reveal something like Nietzsche's "Gay Wisdom."

Night is also day, and day is also night. As I am writing, dawn is slowly breaking on the Berkshire Mountains. For more than two decades, I have begun each day in silence, watching first light gradually dispel lingering darkness. The most intriguing moment in this ritual process is not when the sun's rays first touch the mountain, but the instant just before dawn when all of what will be creation hovers on the edge of emergence. I am never sure whether light makes the mountains appear, or the mountains make light visible. In the twinkling of an eye, betwixt and between not appearing and appearing, reality remains virtual and all things seem possible. This moment never lasts because it can appear only by disappearing. As soon as light falls on the mountaintop, it begins a gradual descent to the valley. If you are patient, the eye can glimpse the sun's movement in the steady withdrawal of shadows. Light, however, is not simply light—illumination creates a residual obscurity more impenetrable than the darkness it displaces but does not eliminate.

Annual rhythms repeat daily cycles that are as disturbing as they are reassuring. On the evening of the summer solstice, the sun sets directly in front of my study window, and then immediately starts its southward journey toward Arrowhead. The first day of summer marks the end of increasing light and the beginning of growing darkness. By the winter solstice the sun has moved so far south in the sky that I can no longer see it set. Then, in an instant, everything is reversed once again—on the longest night of the year light begins to wax and darkness wane as the sun begins its northern journey toward Walden Pond. Darkness in the midst of light and light in the midst of darkness. As Nietzsche insists, Midnight is also Midday, and Midday is also Midnight.

This morning there is no sunrise—clouds shroud the mountain and a cold rain pelts the earth. The darkness recalls the day without dawn twenty-seven years ago when my mother died five nights before before the Christianized celebration of the winter solstice, and nine days before her fiftieth wedding anniversary. It took me many years to realize that in reading, writing, and teaching between Kierkegaard and Hegel, and between

Melville and Thoreau, I have been living between my mother, the literature teacher whose greatest curse and gift to me was her melancholy, and my father, the science teacher and sometimes poet whose greatest gift to me was his love of the earth. In one way or another, everything I have written over the years has been an effort to overcome the melancholy of unhappy consciousness. This melancholy lingers, perhaps even deepens, in last works. Completion never seems to satisfy, and the end so eagerly anticipated invariably proves to be disappointingly empty. The book is finished, the class ended, the career complete, and it is finally time for celebration, but when family and friends gather, there is an uninvited guest. Melancholy disrupts the moment—the person in its grip can never be fully present. While others are immersed in the moment, the vision of the melancholic is split, her consciousness always double. The most profound melancholy is invisible to the eyes of others. The melancholic spirit often travels incognito—while seeming to be absorbed in the moment, he floats slightly above, watching from without, knowing the moment will pass, and uncertain it will ever arrive again. In melancholy the present is never fully present but always already past—even before it arrives. This trace of the impending past is most haunting in precisely those moments that are supposed to be complete.

Time and place. On this winter morning, I hear the whispers of the ghosts who haunt the Berkshire Mountains. Along the crest of Stone Hill behind the barn I can see Mount Greylock just as Melville saw it while sitting at his desk in Arrowhead, rising from the valley to the highest point in Massachusetts. He said that on winter days, when he gazed at Greylock covered with snow, he saw "the pyramidal hump" of Moby-Dick.

Over the years, Mount Greylock came to have a religious, even metaphysical, significance for Melville. The mountain was so important to him that he dedicated his first book after *Moby-Dick* (1851), *Pierre; or, The Ambiguities* (1852), to "Greylock's Most Excellent Majesty."

> In old times authors were proud of the privilege of dedicating their works to Majesty. A right noble custom, which we of Berkshire must revive. For whether we will or no, Majesty is all around us here in Berkshire, sitting as in a grand Congress of Vienna of majestical hill-tops, and eternally challenging our homage.

Melville's desk at Arrowhead

But since the majestic mountain, Greylock—my own more immediate sovereign lord and king—hath now, for innumerable ages, been the one grand dedicatee of the earliest rays of all Berkshire mornings, I know not how this Imperial Purple Majesty (royal-born: Porphyrogenitus) will receive the dedication of my own poor solitary ray.

Nevertheless, forasmuch as I, dwelling with my loyal neighbors, the Maples and the Beeches, in the amphitheater over which his central majesty presides, have received his most bounteous and unstinted fertilizations, it is but meet, that I here devoutly kneel, and render up my gratitude, whether, thereto, The Most Excellent Purple Majesty of Greylock benignantly incline his hoary crown or no.[1]

Pierre. Pierre. How is this title, this name, this word to be understood? Book, person, or thing? Subject or object? English, French, perhaps
both? *Pierre* is not only a proper name, but can also mean stone, rock. If it
is *le nom proper,* then which Pierre? There is, of course, another Pierre,
who is a character in a different story—Pierre, the rock upon whom Jesus
promised to build his church. In Melville's tale, Pierre appears to be something like the anti-Christ, who is the rock upon which the church of his
anti-gospel of nothing will be built. The question that remains after the
book is finished is whether this anti-Christ prefigures Nietzsche's anti-Christ
whose unbelief is more faithful than the devotion of those who claim to
follow Jesus.

Epigrams are always enigmatic. Neither inside nor outside the work,
they seem to offer clues but give no clear solutions. How is "Greylock's Most
Excellent Majesty" to be understood? What sermon did this mountain
preach to Melville as he gazed at it in the distance while feverishly writing?

"For whether we will or no, Majesty is all around us here in Berkshire,
sitting as in a grand Congress of Vienna of majestical hill-tops, and eternally
challenging our homage." Far from a reassuring presence, Mount Greylock
"eternally challenges our homage." This majesty is sublime rather than
beautiful, and, as such, provokes terror more than comfort. While fleeing
to the forest, Pierre stumbled on a strange rock he "fancifully christened
the Memnon Stone." This name suggests the Colossi of Memnon, which
are two huge statues of the Egyptian pharaoh Amenhotep III, located at
the entrance to the Thebian necropolis beside the Nile near Luxor. According to legend, this stone had oracular powers and could be heard to sing
during the hours prior to dawn. Pierre discovers an indecipherable hiero-
glyph inscribed on his Memnon Stone. As he ponders this massive outcropping, it becomes so menacing that he renames it the "Terror Stone." In an
effort to unearth what lay beneath, Pierre throws himself "upon the wood's
last year's leaves" and slides "straight into the horrible interspace and lay
there as dead." Waiting for the stone to reveal its secrets, he falls into a
deadly trance, and when he awakes cries out in despair. "If Duty's self be
but a bugbear, and all things are allowable and unpunishable to man;—then
do thou, Mute Massiveness, fall on me! Ages thou hast waited; and if these

things be thus, then wait no more; for whom better canst thou crush than him who now lies here invoking thee?"

Pierre's questions remain unanswered—nothing breaks the stony silence. How is this "profound silence" to be understood? Is it perhaps the echo of the absence or even the death of God? Or is it, as Pierre suggests elsewhere, "the only Voice of our God, which I before spoke of; from that divine thing without a name, those impostor philosophers pretend somehow to have got an answer; which is as absurd, as though they should say they had got water out of stone; for how can a man get a Voice out of Silence?"[2]

Near the barn where I write there is a massive outcropping of Berkshire marble, which, like Poe's purloined letter, was hiding in plain sight for two decades. When I unearthed it several years ago, it emerged gradually like the hump of a whale breaching the sea.

Four million years ago this stone lay off the coast of Nantucket, where the *Pequod* one day would moor. The stone is furrowed and, like Pierre's Terror Stone, is covered with markings too ancient to decipher. Chip away the beige surface, and dazzling white stone is revealed. This stone, which harbors frightful secrets, is the marble with which Hawthorne's lime-burner filled his kiln on the side of Mount Greylock across the valley. Returning from his search for "the unpardonable sin," to tell what he had learned from his journey, Ethan Brand reports that what he was looking for was all the while within himself. "It is a sin that grew within my own breast. A sin that grew nowhere else! The sin of an intellect that triumphed over the sense of brotherhood with man and reverence for God, and sacrificed everything to its own mighty claims! The only sin that deserves a recompense of immortal agony! Freely, were it to do again, would I incur the guilt. Unshrinkingly I accept the retribution!"[3] This knowledge proves unbearable, and, with darkness encroaching within as well as without, Brand throws himself into the lime kiln. In the morning, townspeople from the village at the foot of Greylock discover Brand's bones transformed into lime. Within what once were his ribs, there is a piece of lime in the shape of a heart. When a villager taps the remains, they crumble. Marble, lime, bones. There is nothing mystical about these bones—dust to dust, ashes to ashes.[4] A garden made of

Berkshire Marble, Stone Hill

such bones would be no Eden, but a memorial to a world where mortals are destined to dwell with no hope of redemption.

Stone teaches us that everything solid has its faults and that the ground beneath us is not secure. Unexpected and uncontrollable tectonic shifts change everything. The apparent beauty of stone is more troubling than reassuring because it is utterly gratuitous and completely spontaneous. No mind conceived its designs; no hand carved its figures. Hieroglyphs etched in marble represent nothing and are without meaning. This is what makes stone sublime. For readers patient enough to listen, Melville's art allows Berkshire stone to speak words of silence.

The Failure of Success

Herman Melville's parents both came from families with rich military backgrounds dating back to the Revolutionary War.[5] His mother, Maria Gansevoort, was from a prominent Dutch Calvinist family, who lived in Albany and Troy. Her father, Peter Gansevoort, who was the commander of Fort

Bone Garden, Stone Hill

Stanwix during the British battle in 1777, was honored for his successful defense of this important outpost. Herman's most lasting inheritance from his mother was her brooding Calvinism, which burdened him throughout his life. In contrast to his wife's severe faith, Allan Melville was a Unitarian whose lenient religion allowed him to indulge his fantasies in ways that proved disastrous for his family. He became a merchant who trafficked in French luxury goods, which were anathema to frugal Calvinists. After moving his family from Boston to New York City to advance his business interests, Allan's social ambition exceed his financial resources. Continuously borrowing to expand his business, while at the same time moving his family into ever more expensive homes, eventually led to financial ruin. In 1830, when Herman was only eleven, his father's business collapsed, and Allan, accompanied by Herman, fled New York for Albany, where they joined

Maria and their three other sons and four daughters. In his definitive biography, Andrew Delbanco reports, "Two months later, he presented the undignified spectacle of a middle-aged man and father of eight begging his own father for help. 'I am destitute of resources and without a shilling,' he wrote to the old Major on December 4, and 'may soon be prosecuted for my last quarter's rent . . . without immediate assistance I know not what will become of me.'"[6] Allan's father and brother-in-law, Peter Gansevoort, supported him, but the reprieve was brief. In January 1832, Herman's father sank into delirium, and a few days later died a broken man.

Allan's death left Maria in dire straits. While in New York, Herman had attended the New York Male High School for four years and had gone on to study at Columbia College's grammar school for a year. With the death of his father and impoverishment of his mother, Herman had to drop out of school and work as an errand boy for an Albany bank to help to support his family. This marked the premature end of Melville's formal education. Peter once again stepped in to support Maria by offering his farm in Pittsfield, Massachusetts, as a retreat. The family settled in the Berkshires in 1838, but rural life was too confining for the young Melville. Within a year, at the age of twenty, restless and still unsettled by his father's decline into madness, he left his family and secured a job as a cabin boy on a merchant ship sailing between New York City and Liverpool. Ishmael speaks for Melville when he declares, "And, as for me, if, by any possibility, there be any as yet undiscovered prime thing in me; if I shall ever deserve any real repute in that small but high hushed world which I might not be unreasonably ambitious of; if hereafter I shall do anything that, upon the whole, a man might rather have done than to have left undone; if at my death, my executors, or more properly my creditors, find any precious MSS. in my desk, then here I prospectively ascribe all honor and glory to whaling; for a whale-ship was my Yale College and my Harvard."[7] Thus began the informal education that informs all of Melville's writings and transformed modern literature.

On January 3, 1841, Melville boarded the whaleship Acushnet, bound for the South Seas. Six months later, while harbored in Nuku Hiva in the Marquesas Islands, he and some of his shipmates deserted and spent a month living with the natives. When island life proved less idyllic than Melville had imagined, he escaped and signed on with the Australian whaler *Lucy Ann*. For the next several years, he roamed the seas hunting whales and gathering material for what would become one of the most remarkable creative outbursts in American literary history. While Kierkegaard was furiously writing in distant Copenhagen, Melville was obsessively writing in New York City and the Berkshires. Both men were extraordinarily young when they completed their most important works—Kierkegaard 38–42, and Melville 27–39. Between 1846 and 1857, Melville published an astonishing twelve novels, including *Moby-Dick,* which remains the most important *theological* work any American has produced. With his mission accomplished, Kierkegaard was suddenly stricken and died; Melville, having glimpsed "naught beyond," fell silent and lived for nearly four decades in total obscurity.

Melville's first books, *Typee* (1846) and *Omoo* (1847), drew on his South Seas experiences and were both popularly and financially successful. However, his endlessly probing mind was not satisfied with more-or-less light-hearted adventures. With the country expanding rapidly and edging toward civil war, Melville began to address pressing social issues like industrialization, urbanization, and slavery. As his work improved and grew more serious, his readership declined and income plummeted. He became increasingly cynical about critics, the press, and the reading public, and was deeply discouraged about the prospect of writing the kind of serious fiction he thought was important. In the summer of 1850, dispirited and with financial pressures mounting, Melville left New York City and retreated to the Berkshires. When he moved to Arrowhead in the summer of 1850, both his life and his writing changed.

Melville was familiar with the Berkshires from his childhood days when his widowed mother took her family to her brother's farm to spend the summer in the mountains. Lizzie's father, Lemuel Shaw, was chief justice of the Supreme Judicial Court of Massachusetts, and had the financial resources to help his daughter and her family through difficult times. With his father-in-law's support, Herman and Lizzie purchased the 160-acre Arrowhead farm, which lay at the base of Mount Greylock. In an essay de-

voted to the importance of Hawthorne's contributions, Melville described
the room where he wrote his most important works. "A papered chamber
in a fine old farm house—a mile from any other dwelling, and dipped to
the eaves in foliage—surrounded by mountains, old woods, and Indian
ponds,—this, surely, is the place to write of Hawthorne. Some charm is in
this northern air, for love and duty seem both impelling and to the task. A
man of deep and noble nature has seized me in this seclusion. His wild,
witch voice rings through me; or, in softer cadences, I seem to hear it in
the songs of the hillside birds that sing in the larch trees at my window."[8]

These years were productive in ways other than literary. Between
1849 and 1855, Herman and Lizzie had four children—two sons, Malcolm
and Stanwix, both of whom died before their parents, and two daughters,
Elizabeth and Frances. With a growing family and frequent visits from his
mother and sisters, it was difficult for Herman to find quiet time for reflection and writing. His relation to Lizzie was practical but not passionate, and
family life often seemed more a burden than a pleasure. For him, as for Bar-
tleby, the walls closed in and all too often he muttered, "I would prefer not
to." In addition to coping with family tensions, Melville had to spend hours
laboring in the fields and tending livestock. Whenever possible he would
retire to his second-floor study to find the solitude he needed to write. As
these periods of seclusion lengthened, his family became concerned about
his mental stability. They never appreciated his genius and did not realize
that solitude was, as Blanchot insists, essential for his most important work.

The move from the city to the country was not as intellectually dis-
ruptive as it might seem. In the middle of the nineteenth century, direct
rail lines connected both Boston and New York City to Pittsfield. Then as
now, the Berkshires were a popular retreat for writers and cultural figures.
Fanny Kemble, Oliver Wendell Holmes, and James Russell Lowell all lived
in nearby Lenox, and Henry Wadsworth Longfellow visited Pittsfield. Thoreau hiked Mount Greylock, and, most important, Hawthorne and his
family lived in a cottage near Melville's farm for several decisive years. By
the time Melville settled in Arrowhead, an early draft of *Moby-Dick* was half
finished. This work, like *The Confidence-Man,* took a historical event as
its point of departure. On August 12, 1819, a whaling ship named the *Essex*

left Nantucket for what was supposed to be a two-and-a-half-year trip to the whaling grounds off the coast of South America, but the voyage was interrupted when the ship was attacked by a sperm whale and sank. Twenty members of the crew were stranded at sea for several months and eventually were forced to resort to cannibalism; only eight of the men survived. Thomas Nickerson, who was one of the crew members, wrote an account of the disaster, which Melville drew on while writing *Moby-Dick*.[9] With Nickerson's narrative and his personal experience, Melville had more than enough material for a novel; however, by 1850, his writing had stalled. He initially envisioned *The Whale* as a popular romance like his early works, but his ambition was growing. Preoccupied with establishing a distinctively American literature that would leave behind the literary traditions of the Old World, he declared, "Let us boldly condemn all imitation, though it comes to us graceful and fragrant as the morning; and foster all originality, though, at first, it be crabbed and ugly as our own pine knots. . . . The truth is, that in our point of view, this matter of a national literature has come to such a pass with us, that in some sense we must turn bullies, else the day is lost, or superiority so far beyond us, that we can hardly say it will ever be ours."[10] The book he was struggling to imagine would be precisely such an original work and would not fit into any established genre. Though he did not realize it at the time, his work as well as his life was at a turning point.

The pivotal event in Melville's life occurred on August 5, 1850, when he met Hawthorne for the first time. He was only thirty-one; Hawthorne was fifteen years his senior and was enjoying a growing reputation. Melville's new neighbor, David Dudley Field, a prominent New York attorney, arranged a picnic hike up nearby Monument Mountain. In addition to Field, Melville, and Hawthorne, the party included Oliver Wendell Holmes, Harvard professor of medicine, writer, and poet; Evert Duyckinck, a New York critic and editor of *Literary World;* Cornelius Mathews, a writer and associate of Duyckinck; and James T. Fields, Hawthorne's Boston publisher. When a thunderstorm broke out, Melville and Hawthorne took shelter and engaged in a long conversation. While neither recorded the substance of the exchange, in 1879 J. E. A. Smith writing in *Taghconic* reconstructed this decisive moment in modern literary history. "One day it chanced that when they were out on a picnic excursion, the two were compelled by a thunder-shower to take shelter in a narrow recess of the rocks of Monument Mountain. Two hours of enforced intercourse settled the matter. They learned so much of each other's character and found that they held so much of thought, feeling and opinion in common, that the most intimate friendship for the future was inevitable."[11] While Smith overstates the case for intimacy, the two men did develop such an important relationship that Melville eventually dedicated *Moby-Dick* to Hawthorne as a "token of my admiration for his genius."

In Hawthorne, Melville found a kindred spirit, and in Melville, Hawthorne found a younger writer whose talent he must have suspected might one day eclipse his own. Hawthorne was impressed enough to invite Melville to visit him in Lenox. Their conversations continued until Hawthorne left the Berkshires to settle in Concord, where Emerson and Thoreau were living. Hawthorne encouraged Melville to have the strength of his convictions. He counseled him to give up the adventure tale and to write a novel that probed the difficult and complex psychological and theological questions that preoccupied both of them. Somewhat overwhelmed by Hawthorne, Melville took his sage advice and decided to delay returning to his stalled opus in order to read more of Hawthorne's work. Reflecting on what he discovered, Melville realized that what drew him to Hawthorne was the dark Puritan heritage they shared. "For spite of all the Indian-summer sunlight on the hither side of Hawthorne's soul, the other side—like the dark half of the physical sphere—is shrouded in a blackness, ten times black. . . . Certain it is, however, that this great power of blackness in him derives its force from its appeals to that Calvinist sense of Innate Depravity and Original Sin, from whose visitations, in some shape or other, no deeply thinking mind is always and wholly free. For, in certain moods, no man can weigh this world, without throwing in something, somehow like Original Sin, to strike the uneven balance. At all events, perhaps no writer has ever wielded this terrific thought with greater terror than this same harmless Hawthorne."[12] Having recognized in Hawthorne's work the "great power of blackness" that had always haunted his own imagination, Melville was freed to rewrite the novel that became *Moby-Dick*. More precisely, the work that had been simmering on the edge of his imagination for years was freed to write itself. *The Whale* possessed the author as much as the author expressed the Whale.

Predictably, Melville's spectacular accomplishment was a critical and commercial failure. Critics savaged the work and the public ignored it. The first edition of 3,000 copies did not sell out, and Melville's lifetime income from the novel was $556.37.[13] With financial pressures greater than ever, Melville quickly began writing *Pierre, or The Ambiguities,* which was published a year later (1852). In this novel, Melville attempted the impossible task of combining in one work what the public wanted to read and what he needed to write. Critics once again trashed his work. Delbanco reports, "When *Pierre* was published in 1852, it bore its author's own name and the critics savaged it. The *New York Day Book* reviewed it under the headline 'HERMAN MELVILLE CRAZY,' and the *American Whig Review* agreed, declaring that his 'fancy is diseased.' The respected critic Fitz-James O'Brien, playing on the pun of *Pierre* with *pierre* (the French word for stone), was more polite but still severe: 'Let Mr. Melville stay his step in time. He totters on the edge of a precipice, over which all his hard-earned fame may tumble with such another weight as *Pierre* attached to it.'"[14] It did not occur to any of Melville's critics that the precipice on which he was teetering harbored what Poe had described as "some never-to-be-imparted secret, whose attainment is destruction."[15] Just when it seemed matters could not get any worse, on December 10, 1853, the warehouse of Melville's publisher, Harper & Brothers, burnt down, destroying all unsold copies of his works. With his literary career in ashes, financial affairs in ruin, and personal life in shambles, the "great power of blackness" engulfed him and his despair deepened.

Masks

What do masks betray? What do they show? What do they hide? What if masks mask nothing? No tin . . . notin? Nothing but nothing. How is nothing figured? Is it possible to mask nothing? Is it possible to unmask notin?

If the void around which (the) all revolves is nothing, words are hollowed-out words and the writer is a confidence-man.

The Confidence-Man was the last prose work Melville published during his lifetime. In the years between 1857 and his death in 1891, he wrote some poetry, which was published at his own expense, and wrote, but left unfinished, *Billy Budd,* which was found in a tin container after his death, and was finally published in 1924. Melville wrote this last work during a particularly dark period of an unusually troubled life. Though he was only thirty-eight, Lizzie reported to her father that Herman was not only suffering from failing eyesight and physical pain brought on by rheumatism and sciatica, but was also subject to "ugly attacks" that made her worry about his mental state. As his condition worsened, he withdrew further, leading his neighbor, Sarah Morewood, to say what others could not openly admit. Melville, she declared, is "slightly insane."[16]

"Shrouded in a blackness, ten times black," Melville's last work expresses his most profound doubts about religion, life, and, most important, writing. Like others before and after him, literature had become his gospel. With the "failure" of *Moby-Dick* and frustration brought by the hostile response to *Pierre,* he began to fear that words were betraying him. Perhaps fiction could no more tell the truth than words once deemed divine. He began to suspect that the only truth left to tell is that truth is unknowable and certainty is an idle fantasy. While the questions plaguing Melville were religious, psychological, and literary, he realized that their broader implications were also economic and political. His genius in *The Confidence-Man: His Masquerade* was to weave together such diverse strands to create a text that asks whether it is possible for individuals as well as economic and political systems to survive without the confidence that faith alone can provide.

The time is April 1; the place, a latter-day ship of fools named *Fidèle,* sailing down the Mississippi from St. Louis to New Orleans; the characters, a motley crew, which, the narrator avers, resembles nothing so much as "Chaucer's Canterbury pilgrims."[17] As the story opens, a young man who appears to be deaf and dumb boards the ship. "His cheek was fair, his chin downy, his hair flaxen, his hat a white fur one, with a long fleecy nap. He had neither trunk, valise, carpet-bag, nor parcel. No porter followed him. He was unaccompanied by friends. From the shrugged shoulders, titters, whispers, wonderings of the crowd, it was plain that he was, in the extremist sense of the word, a stranger."[18] Though the identity of this seemingly innocent youth remains obscure, this description evokes the image of the lamb whose sacrifice is essential to the Christian economy of salvation. This point is reinforced when the youth repeatedly writes verses from Saint Paul's ode to charity on a slate he displays to the assembled passengers (I Corinthians 13).

Between the innocent's initial appearance and his scriptural citation, Melville inserts an episode that provides the dramatic tension for the entire narrative. Making his way through the crowd on the lower deck, the youth "chanced to come to a placard nigh the captain's office, offering a reward for the capture of a mysterious impostor, supposed to have recently arrived from the East" (1). What follows is a catalogue of the disguises the alleged impostor is supposed to have assumed as well as a warning to passengers to beware of this trickster. Though apparently intended to counter doubts raised by the possible presence of a swindler, the actions of this ostensibly Christlike figure leave the unavoidable impression that he himself might actually be a confidence-man. Suspicions grow as the drama unfolds.

In the midst of the clamor and confusion created by voyagers struggling to read the cautionary placard and charitable citations, the ship's barber prepared to open his shop for the day. "Pushing people aside and jumping on a stool, he hung over his door, on the customary nail, a gaudy sort of illuminated pasteboard sign, skillfully executed by himself, gilt with the likeness of a razor elbowed in readiness to shave, and also, for the public benefit, with two words not unfrequently seen ashore gracing other shops besides barbers':

"No TRUST." (3)

With the suspension of the barber's sign both on the door and between quotation marks, it becomes clear that *The Confidence-Man* is not only a book whose plot hinges on the duplicity of signs, but, more important, is a text that raises the question of the reliability or unreliability of words. This work is simultaneously a narrative and a metanarrative whose textual strategies question themselves in their very deployment. In the first three chapters, the reader encounters three different signs that are explicitly identified as such: the placard, the slate, and the gilded pasteboard sign. The sign that Melville names a sign is no ordinary sign, for it raises doubts about the very meaning and significance of all signs. Were one to follow the counsel of the sign by refusing trust, it would be foolhardy to have confidence in any sign. If, however, no sign is to be trusted, then it is impossible to have confidence even in the sign that reads "No TRUST." The challenge of the sign creates a double bind: on the one hand, signs are not to be trusted, but on the other hand, the barber's sign bends back on itself to create a distrust of distrust. The sign, in other words, discredits itself by encouraging an attitude that is precisely the opposite of what it seems to promote. When one distrusts distrust, it once again becomes possible to credit signs.[19] Whether Melville is urging confidence or no confidence, belief or disbelief, trust or mistrust remains completely undecidable. Trafficking in signs that cannot be trusted, the confidence-man prefigures postmodern ironists who dupe credulous believers. The gilded sign and the paradoxes it engenders return later in the narrative to discredit accounts that once seemed settled.

It is significant that the sign upon which Melville's questions turn is "gilt." A gilded sign is almost as good as gold: its surface is gold but its substance a matter of little value. This play of surface and substance inverts the customary relation of signifier and signified to create a simulation whose value is uncertain. Throughout human history, gold is not so much a sign as the transcendental signified that is supposed to ground the meaning and value of other signs. Gold, in other words, is a sign constructed to erase its status as a sign, and thereby serve as a credible referent for all other signs. Within this system of exchange, religious and economic redemption depend upon a foundational referent (that is, go[l]d) that secures meaning and value by rendering signs credible. In the absence of any such transcendental referent, signs are merely freely floating signifiers of other signifiers that can never be trusted.

From 1825 to 1875, debate about the gold standard raged throughout the United States. With increasing economic demands created by the approaching Civil War, pressures to forsake the gold standard became overwhelming. Nevertheless, many people were reluctant to lift anchor and set sail in the uncharted waters of floating signifiers. Concerns about the threat of the devaluation of currency, which the shift to paper not backed by gold seemed to pose, ranged across the political spectrum. While politicians and bankers debated the practical effects of lifting the gold standard, some of the era's most important writers realized the broader religious, philosophical, aesthetic, and linguistic implications of these economic changes. No one was more sensitive to these questions than Edgar Allan Poe. Fourteen years before the appearance of *The Confidence-Man,* Poe published "The Gold-Bug," which anticipates many of Melville's concerns as well as his literary strategy for addressing them.[20]

In Poe's tale, an amateur entomologist, William Legrand, and his faithful Negro servant, Jupiter, happen to find a gold bug. Describing the precious bug, Legrand observes:

> "It is of a brilliant gold color—about the size of a large hickory-nut—with two jet black spots near one extremity of the back, and another, somewhat longer, at the other. The *antennae* are—"
>
> "Dey aint *no* tin in him, Massa Will, I keep a tellin' on you," here interrupted Jupiter; "dey bug is a goole-bug, solid, ebery bit of him, inside and all, sep him wing—neber feel half so hebby a bug in my life."[21]

Truth—such as it is—is spoken by the fool. "Dey aint *no* tin in him." All gold, no tin. The gold bug, Poe suggests, is no tin, notin, nothin, nothing. As the story unfolds, the focus shifts from bugs and gold to language and signs. While writing about gold, Poe makes it clear that his interest is really language. Having been bitten by the gold bug, Legrand becomes obsessed with finding buried treasure. In his quest for hidden riches, the gold bug turns out to be less valuable in itself than as a sign that points to even greater reserves of wealth. After tracing the outline on a fragmentary parchment, Legrand notices an obscure image emerging on the underside of his drawing. Teasing out the hidden figure with heat and moisture, he discerns a series of signs that are initially unintelligible. In spite of the seeming arbitrariness of the signifiers, Legrand believes in their profound significance and has confidence in his ability to decipher it. Displaying skills as sophisticated as any contemporary cryptographer, he eventually decodes the script and, following its instructions, unearths the treasure for which he had long been searching. Legrand explains his interpretive procedure:

> In the present case—indeed in all cases of secret writing—the first question regards the language of the cipher; for the principles of solution, so far, especially, as the more simple ciphers are concerned, depend upon, and are varied by, the genius of the particular idiom. In general, there is no alternative but experiment (directed by probabilities) of every tongue known to him who attempts the solution, until the true one be attained. But, as with the cipher now before us, all difficulty is removed by the signature. The pun on the word "Kidd" is appreciable in no other language than the English. But for this consideration I should have begun my attempts with the Spanish and French, as the tongues in which a secret of this kind would most naturally have been written by a pirate of the Spanish main. As it was, I assumed the cryptograph to be English. (587–88)

Poe's irony is unmistakable. If Legrand's assumption proves correct and the cryptograph is English, his decipherment of the message establishes nothing or, in Jupiter's terms, no tin. Like the barber's sign, Kidd is a joker whose code erases itself in its very inscription. If Kidd means kid, then only a person who does not get the joke or is totally bugs would have confidence in signs.

Legrand's faith in his cryptographic skills rests upon his assumptions about the relationship between the mind and the signs it fabricates. "Circumstances, and a certain bias of mind," he admits, "have led me to take interest in such riddles, and it may well be doubted whether human ingenuity can construct an enigma of the kind which human ingenuity may not, by proper application, resolve" (587). In this version of the hermeneutic circle, Poe insists that human beings can always decipher the codes they create. But this leaves a critical question unasked: What if some signs are not created by human beings, or are formed by an intelligence that does not remotely resemble the human mind? What if some signs or all signs are not created by any intelligence? What if signs are arbitrary traces of notin?

Legrand's faith in signs and their comprehensibility seems to be confirmed by his discovery of long-lost treasures. Following the trail marked by Kidd's signs, he eventually discovers their referent, which turns out to be nothing other than gold. "There was not a particle of silver. All was gold of antique date and of great variety—French, Spanish, and German money, with a few English guineas, and some counters, of which we had never seen specimens before. There were several large and heavy coins, so worn that we could make nothing of their inscriptions" (579–80). Gold, pure gold; coins, some worn beyond recognition, others French, Spanish, German, and a few English guineas. If, however, Kidd is kidding, how are we to read these signs? What, after all, is a guinea? A guinea is, of course, a former British coin worth one pound and one shilling. But the currency named "guinea" sometimes takes forms other than precious metal. Profiting from the exchange of this inhuman currency was on the verge of tearing the United States apart.

Poe's text raises questions that take us back to the deck of the *Fidèle*. The young man peddling his scriptural wares disappears as suddenly as he appears. His place is taken by "a grotesque negro cripple, in tow-cloth attire and an old coal-sifter of a tamborine in his hand, who, owing to something wrong about his legs, was, in effect, cut down to the stature of a Newfoundland dog; his knotted black fleece and good-natured, honest black face rubbing against the upper part of people's thighs as he made shift to shuffle about, making music, such as it was, and raising a smile even from the gravest" (7). As white turns to black, the fleece seems to become a sign that is more diabolical than holy. Suspicions having been raised by the signs posted by the captain and barber, many of the passengers fear being fleeced by the confidence-man who is supposed to be roaming the ship.

> "What is your name, old boy?" said a purple-faced drover, putting his large purple hand on the cripple's bushy wool, as if it were the curled forehead of a black steer.
> "Der Black Guinea dey calls me, sar." (7)

Few passengers have confidence in the Guinea. When he attempts to defend himself by offering what he insists is indisputable proof of his identity, a fellow cripple explodes: "He can walk fast enough when he tries, a good deal faster than I; but he can lie yet faster. He's some white operator, betwisted and painted up for a decoy. He and his friends are all humbugs" (10). A credulous Methodist clergyman rushes to the defense of the poor Guinea by urging a more charitable response to his entreaties, but the master of suspicion remains unconvinced and responds:

> "Charity is one thing, and truth is another, . . . he's a rascal, I say."
> "But why not, friend, put as charitable a construction as one can upon the poor fellow?" said the soldier-like Methodist . . . "he looks honest, don't he?"
> "Looks are one thing, and facts are another," snapped out the other perversely; "and as to your constructions, what construction can you put upon a rascal, but that a rascal he is?" (1)

In an effort to resolve the conflict of interpretations created by the alternative constructions projected on the Black Guinea, an Episcopal clergyman, "with a clear face and blue eyes; innocence, tenderness, and good sense triumvirate in his air," intervenes to ask whether anyone on board can testify to the identity of the beggar. "Der Black Guinea" replies by listing many of the personae he later assumes. Seeing through the charade staged by the confidence-man, the person bearing the "true" prosthesis counsels the Episcopal priest not to waste his time on a "wild goose chase." The advice seems to be reliable because a search produces nothing.

As personae proliferate, the ambiguities deepen; indeed, even the title of the novel becomes obscure. *The Confidence-Man: His Masquerade.* His? Who is this confidence-man? Is he one or many? Cultivating uncertainty with every twist in his tale, Melville offers a mirror in which everyone can see himself or herself reflected. "And yet self-knowledge is thought by some not so easy. Who knows, my dear sir, but for a time you may have taken yourself for somebody else? Stranger things have happened" (15). If facts are looks, if reality is nothing more than appearance, if the self is nothing other than roles that are played, then are knowledge and self-knowledge even possible? The problem of the one and the many, which, we have seen, is both theological and anthropological, once again returns. Are God and self one or many? Is there a unified reality beneath the surface or behind the multiplicity of appearances that unites everyone and everything by reconciling differences? Melville expresses his doubts, "Upon the whole, it might rather be thought, that he, who, in view of its inconsistencies, says of human nature the same that, in view of its contrasts, is said of the divine nature, that it is past finding out, thereby evinces a better appreciation of it than he who, by always representing it in a clear light, leaves it to be inferred that he clearly knows all about it" (59).

Two years before Melville wrote these words at Arrowhead, Thoreau was writing *Walden* at the other end of the state. Along with other Transcendentalists like Emerson and Whitman, Thoreau was deeply influenced by English Romantics, who, in turn, drew inspiration from German idealists like Schiller, Hegel, Schelling, and Fichte. Emerson's essay "Nature" (1836) set forth what became the creed of Concord. "In the woods, we return to reason and faith. There I feel that nothing can befall me in life—no disgrace, no calamity (leaving me my eyes), which nature cannot repair. Standing on the bare ground—my head bathed by the blithe air and uplifted into infinite space—all mean egotism vanishes. I become a transparent eyeball; I am nothing; I see all; the currents of the Universal Being circulate through me; I am part or parcel of God."[22] In this vision of divine immanence, the writer becomes the mask of God whose words are a transparent extension of the divine gospel.

Nothing could be farther from Melville's dark vision than Emerson's transparent eyeball, which purportedly illuminates everything. The vestiges of strict Calvinism led to Melville's relentless criticism of every vision of life that is confident of redemption. In a letter to Hawthorne dated June [1?], 1851, he wrote, "In reading some of Goethe's sayings [which, we will see were very important for Thoreau], so worshipped by his votaries, I came across this, '*Live in the all.*' That is to say, your separate identity is but a wretched one,—good; but get out of yourself, spread and expand yourself, and bring to yourself the tinglings of life that are felt in the flowers and the woods, that are felt in the planets Saturn and Venus, and the Fixed Stars. What nonsense! Here is a fellow with a raging toothache. 'My dear boy,' Goethe says to him, 'you are sorely afflicted with that tooth; but you must *live in the all,* and then you will be happy!'"[23]

Melville divides his novel into two parts—daylight (chapters 1–23), in which the confidence-man appears in seven guises, and nighttime (chapters 24–45), in which he appears only as the cosmopolitan. He returns to his disagreement with Emerson and Thoreau in the second half of *The Confidence-Man* through the character of the cosmopolitan. Melville's trickster, like Goethe's Mephistopheles, assumes whatever role is necessary to achieve his nefarious ends. Like Socrates exposing the ignorance of those who claim to know, Melville stages an ironic Socratic dialogue with the cosmopolitan, Mark Winsome, who represents Emerson, and his "practical" disciple, Egbert, who speaks for Thoreau. The issues the interlocutors discuss are the reality of evil and the possibility of true friendship. Winsome appears on the scene confidently declaring the virtues of the "beautiful soul" idealized by both Romantics and Transcendentalists. For a person "full of all love and truth . . . where beauty is, there must those be." "'A pleasing belief,' rejoined the cosmopolitan, beginning with an even air, 'and to confess, long ago it pleased me. Yes, with you and Schiller, I am pleased to believe that beauty is at bottom incompatible with ill, and therefore am so eccentric as to have confidence in the latent benignity of that beautiful creature, the rattle-snake, whose lithe neck and burnished maze of tawny

gold, as he sleekly curls aloft in the sun, who on the prairie can behold without wonder?'" (162). A lengthy exchange about the danger of the venom-
ous serpent and its place in the divine scheme of things follows. The
cosmopolitan turns Winsome's logic against him to expose the absurdity
of his pollyannish insistence that apparent evil is really nothing more than
the partial guise of a greater good. To rationalize or justify evil, the cosmopolitan insists, is to deny its reality.

    When the debate shifts to friendship, Egbert attempts to defend his
mentor's position. The cosmopolitan's criticisms undercut the views Emerson presented in his essay "Friendship" and Thoreau developed in *A
Week on the Concord and Merrimack Rivers* and *Walden*. Melville frames
the discussion in terms of his broader argument in *The Confidence-Man*—
credit, credibility, and credulity. Egbert, who is preoccupied with "ser-
viceable knowledge," is "the last person in the world one would take for
any disciple of Transcendental philosophy" (171). Nevertheless, he is the
spokesperson for the Romantic Transcendentalism that was thriving at the
other end of the state. In the course of the debate, Egbert appears to be less
an Emersonian self-reliant individual than a "ventriloquist" channeling the
thoughts of his master.

    Melville further complicates an already confusing scene by multiply-
ing masks. The cosmopolitan proposes that for the purpose of debate he
and Egbert assume the personae of Frank Goodman and Charlie Noble,
respectively. Frank, of course, is anything but frank, and Charlie turns out
to be less noble than the philosophy he espouses. To expose what he believes to be the deceit of Emerson and Thoreau, the cosmopolitan poses
the question of whether it is advisable to loan a friend money. Through
Frank's dramatic performance, the contradictions in Egbert and Winsome's
philosophy emerge. When Charlie ends by affirming what he had set out
to deny, both he and his mentor are exposed as confidence-men peddling
counterfeit goods. "Yet the difference between this man and that man,"
Charlie maintains, "is not so great as the difference between what the same
man be today and what he may be in days to come. For there is no bent of
heart or turn of thought which any man holds by virtue of an unalterable
nature or will. Even with those feelings and opinions deemed most identi-

cal with eternal right and truth, it is not impossible but that, as personal persuasions, they may in reality be but the result of some chance tip of Fate's elbow in throwing her dice. . . . As particular food begets particular dreams, so particular experiences or books particular feelings or beliefs" (191). In a world where everything is "chance caught on a wing," the pursuit of absolute truth and value is madness.[24] We have all been cast adrift on a ship of fools drifting aimlessly on a sea whose depths are impossible to fathom. This is the conclusion toward which *The Confidence-Man* and, indeed, Melville's entire oeuvre has been relentlessly moving.

On the most obvious level, Frank Goodman presents a fierce satire of every form of spirituality that turns a blind eye to the inexplicability and inescapable darkness of life. What Emerson and Thoreau sell as sophisticated metaphysics is for Melville nothing more than New Age pabulum marketed for personal gain. But Melville's point is considerably broader and more disturbing than a disagreement about two popular nineteenth-century philosophers. Having tricked Egbert into expressing his own views, the cosmopolitan, whose words admittedly can never be trusted, abruptly ends the conversation.

> With these words and a grand scorn the cosmopolitan turned on his heel, leaving his companion at a loss to determine where exactly the fictitious character had been dropped, and the real one, if any, resumed. If any, because, with pointed meaning, there occurred to him, as he gazed after the cosmopolitan these familiar lines.
>   "All the world's a stage,
>   And all the men and women merely players,
>   Who have their exits and their entrances,
>   And one man in his time plays many parts."[25] (192)

". . . the real one, if any . . ." Once again, questions remain. The next time the cosmopolitan appears, he is staging yet another elaborate hoax. While deeply immersed in a theological conversation with an old man, a juvenile *marchand,* clad in a yellow coat, which "flamed about him like the

painted flames in the robes of a victim in *auto-da-fe*," interrupts him (210).[26]
Playing on the elderly man's fear and distrust, the youth sells him a trav-
eler's lock and a money belt to secure his possessions. As a bonus, he throws
in a "Counterfeit Detector." Though insisting that he does not lack confidence in the economic system in which he has invested more than his
money, the old man nonetheless examines several of his bills "just to pass
the time." Goodman, who disingenuously claims to take considerable pride
in his faith in other people, asks,

"Well, what say you, Mr. Foreman; guilty, or not guilty?—Not
guilty, ain't it?"

"I don't know, I don't know," returned the old man, per-
plexed, "there's so many marks of all sorts to go by, it makes it
a kind of uncertain. Here, now, is this bill," touching one, "it
looks to be a three dollar bill on the Vicksburgh Trust and Insurance Banking Company. Well, the Detector says—"

"But why, in this case, care what it says? Trust and Insurance! What more would you have?"

"No; but the Detector says, among fifty other things, that,
if a good bill, it must have, thickened here and there into the
substance of the paper, little wavy spots of red. . . ."

"Well, and is—"

"Stay. But then it adds, that sign is not always to be
relied on; for some good bills get so worn, the red marks get
rubbed out. And that's the case with my bill here—see how old
it is—or else it's a counterfeit, or else—I don't see right—or
else—dear, dear me—I don't know what else to think."

"What a peck of trouble that Detector makes for you now;
believe me, the bill is good; don't be so distrustful. . . ."

". . . Stay, now, here's another sign. It says that, if the bill
is good, it must have in one corner, mixed in with the vignette,
the figure of a goose, very small, indeed, all but microscopic;
and, for added precaution, like the figure of Napoleon outlined
by the tree, not observable, even if magnified, unless the atten-

tion is directed to it. Now, pore over it as I will, I can't see this goose."

"Can't see the goose? why, I can; and a famous goose it is. There" (reaching over and pointing to a spot in the vignette).

"I don't see it—dear me—I don't see the goose. Is it a real goose?"

"A perfect goose; beautiful goose."

"Dear, dear, I don't see it." (213–14)

A real goose? A perfect goose? A beautiful goose? Since faith is a matter of vision, seeing is believing. It remains unclear whether one believes because one sees, or one sees because one believes. If, as the Counterfeit Detector claims, "the sign is not always to be relied on," then the search for faith based on vision, and vision based on faith, might be a wild goose chase![27]

In an effort to advance his cynical deceit by spreading seeds of doubt, Frank enters into an agreement with the barber, whose name we now learn is William Cream, to take down his "No TRUST" sign and serve his customers in good faith. Frank, in turn, pledges to provide compensation for any losses resulting from this willing suspension of disbelief. To justify his insistence on the establishment of an escrow account as security against the possibility of lost income, Cream cites lines from "Wisdom of Jesus, the Son of Sirach": "I recalled what the son of Sirach says in the True Book: 'An enemy speaketh sweetly with his lips'; and so I did what the son of Sirach advises in such cases: 'I believed not his many words'" (202). Feigning unwillingness to believe that "such cynical sort of things are in the True Book," Frank consults the old man who is absorbed in Scripture, and discovers, or claims to discover, that the troubling words are not precisely in the Bible, but are in a book that is not truly incorporated within the holy text. The words the barber cites are part of a textual supplement that falls *between* the Old and New Testaments and, as such, remains marginal to the text proper. "Ecclesiasticus or the Wisdom of Jesus son of Sirach" is part of the Apocrypha.

Apocrypha (Latin *apocryphys,* hidden, from Greek *apokruptein,* to hide away) was the Greek word used to designate writings that were so

important that they had to be hidden from the general public and were
disclosed only to initiates or the inner circle of believers. When used in a
biblical context, *Apocrypha* designates the books of the Septuagint included in the Vulgate but considered uncanonical by Protestants. The
more general sense of the word reflects the biblical usage. *Apocryphal*
also means "of questionable authorship; false, counterfeit." The status of
the Apocrypha remains subject to dispute. While customarily composed
of fourteen books, there is no universal agreement about which texts belong to the Apocrypha. The books designated "apocryphal" are not included in the Jewish canon of the Hebrew scripture. In 1534, Luther
gathered a collection of apocryphal texts and published them in a separate section at the end of the Old Testament. The Reformed tradition in
which Melville was raised was more suspicious of the Apocrypha. The
Geneva Bible omitted the Apocrypha after 1599, and the Westminster
Confession of Faith (1646–48) went so far as to identify these texts as
"secular literature." Catholics affirmed the Apocrypha and at the Council
of Trent (1546) declared anathema anyone who did not accept the entire
Vulgate as canonical.

The references to the Apocrypha raise broader questions about
the reliability of scripture. Might the Author of the Book of books be a
confidence-man whose Word cannot be trusted? After all, God reveals himself by concealing himself with the masks of not one but three personae.
As John Irwin explains, "To distinguish a true god from false gods is
no guarantee that the nature of the true god is absolute truth. Or rather,
there is only such a guarantee in a tradition like the Platonic-Christian
one of God as the Logos, a tradition in which God is logically incapable
of falsehood. But is it a falsehood to wear a mask and play a role? When
the Maker of the universe masked himself as the son of a Jewish carpen-
ter, was that a falsehood?"[28] Perhaps deceit is the only way to trick people
into seeing the truth, or, perhaps, deceit exposes the lack of any truth to
be revealed.

Suspicions raised in this appendix spread to the book proper. Is
scripture canonical or heretical? Reliable or deceitful? Credible or incredible? True or false? Genuine or counterfeit? Frank Goodman admits what

he has known all along. "Fact is, when all is bound up together, it's some-times confusing. The uncanonical part should be bound distinct. And, now that I think of it, how well did those learned doctors who rejected for us this whole book of Sirach. I never read anything so calculated to destroy man's confidence in man. . . . And to call it wisdom—the Wisdom of the Son of Sirach! Wisdom, indeed! What an ugly thing wisdom must be! Give me the folly that dimples the cheek, say I, rather than the wisdom that curdles the blood. But no, no; it ain't wisdom; it's apocrypha, as you say, sir. For how can that be trustworthy that teaches distrust?" (209).

"Fact is, when all is bound up together, it's sometimes confusing." As the margin that both separates and joins the Old and New Testaments, the Apocrypha contains or attempts to contain doubt. For thoughtful readers, however, the apocryphal doubt is uncontainable; the margin inevitably overflows its bounds and contaminates the whole book as if from within. Uncertainty about the Apocrypha discloses the undeniable arbitrariness of the entire text. Once doubts about the authority of the book have been raised, only those whose faith is blind can fail to wonder whether every canon is apocryphal.

Though always shrouding his thoughts in duplicity, Melville appears to leave little doubt about his own doubt. On the penultimate page of the book, he returns to the exchange between Frank Goodman and the Mas-ter of Faith. Having just claimed to have had a vision of the goose that lays the golden egg by securing his confidence in the Vicksburgh Trust and Insurance Banking Company, Frank addresses the old man, who, in yet another reversal of roles, is now the one who needs reassurance. "Ah, sir, though every one must be pleased at the thought of the presence in public places of such a book, yet there is something that abates the satisfaction. Look at this volume; on the outside, battered as any old valise in the baggage-room; and inside, white and virgin as the hearts of lilies in bud" (215). This is the second time that a "gilt inscription" appears. The first, I have noted, is the barber's gilded sign "No TRUST." By returning to the image of gold at the conclusion of his work, Melville extends the questions raised by the sign to the book as a whole. The Word of God, like William Cream's sign, is not pure gold but is only gilded; its gold is perhaps fool's gold, which, though it might contain no tin, is nevertheless notin but a thin veneer that is utterly superficial. In his description of the Bible, Melville plays on the contrasts between surface and depth as well as inside and outside: "Look at this volume; on the outside, battered as any old valise in the baggage-room; and inside, white and virgin." How is such a book to be read? On the one hand, Melville implies that superficial corruption obscures a deeper purity; on the other hand, the worn cover and virgin pages suggest that the book is never opened and thus only surfaces matter.

The Bible, however, is not the only book contaminated by William Cream's duplicitous sign. Questions about the sign invade every book—even the book supposedly authored by Melville. Is *The Confidence-Man* a reinscription of the gilded sign that is notin? Can we bank on Melville's words? Does he attempt to credit faith or discredit confidence by counseling readers to distrust trust and/or trust distrust? The book is prefaced with a brief inscription: "Dedicated to victims of Auto da Fe." *Auto-da-fè* refers to both "the public announcement of the sentences imposed on persons tried by the Inquisition" and "the public execution of these sentences by the secular authorities, especially the burning of heretics at the stake." Melville's book, then, appears to be dedicated to heretics who have died for their lack of confidence. But *auto-da-fè* can also be read in another way. The Portuguese phrase means act (*auto,* Latin *actus*) of (*da*) faith (*fè*). When read more "literally," which, in this case, means more literarily, Melville seems to dedicate his work to "victims of the act of faith." Is faith, then, the ultimate confidence game?

How is the exergue to be read? *Exergue,* it is important to note, means not only that which is outside of (*ex*) the work (*ergon*), but also "the space on the reverse of a coin or medal, below the central design." The underside of currency, we have discovered, is faith, and the currency of faith is an economy in which there is a profitable return on every investment. This is what redemption is all about. But what role does *The Confidence-Man* play in the economy of faith? Is Melville's missive sent to believers or heretics? Does he counsel confidence or doubt? Is *Melville*'s book a gilded sign that reads "No TRUST"? Is it a narrative that is a metanarrative calling all signs—even the sign "No TRUST"—into question? If the book is "inwardly" faulted in a way that discredits it, can we have confidence in Melville's work? Is his book the incarnation of words in which we can have faith? Is Melville a confidence-man, perhaps *the* confidence-man? Or is he the pale shadow of a confidence-man who never appears in person without a mask?

Melville does not directly answer these questions and, thus, leaves his readers hanging. Just as the sign "No TRUST" turns back on itself to counsel distrust in distrust, so radical doubt bends back on itself to counsel doubt about doubt. Ambiguity and uncertainty have the last word, which means there is no last word, and, perhaps, no last work. There is little consolation in a conclusion that is inconclusive. In the darkest passage of his entire corpus, and, indeed, one of the darkest passages in all American literature, Melville goes so far as to suggest that confidence, be it religious or economic, is a pile of shit.[29] With light fading, the old man searches for the life-preserver his son had given him before he set sail. Unlike Ishmael, no buoy appears to support him in the sea of doubt. Searching beneath the bunk, the cosmopolitan finds "a curved tin compartment," and declares "this, I think, is a life-preserver, sir; and a very good one." Less than fully convinced, the old man responds,

> "Why, indeed, now! Who would have thought it? *that* a life-preserver? That's the very stool [i.e., shit or a chamber pot] I was sitting on, ain't it?
>
> "It is. And that shows that one's life is looked out for, when he ain't looking out for it himself. In fact, any of these stools here will float you, sir, should the boat hit a snag, and go down in the dark. But, since you want one in your room, pray take this one," handing it to him. "I think I can recommend this one; the tin part," rapping it with his knuckles, "seems so perfect—sounds so very hollow." (216)

If every life-preserver is notin, the Word that "seems so perfect sounds so very hollow." This would be the ultimate betrayal, which might or might not betray the Ultimate.

"Naught Beyond"

All visible objects, man, are but pasteboard masks. But
in each event—in the living act, the undoubted deed—there,
some unknown but still reasoning thing puts forth the mould-
ings of its features from behind the unreasoning mask. If man
will strike, strike through the mask! How can the prisoner reach
outside except by thrusting through the wall? To me, the white
whale is that wall, shoved near to me. Sometimes I think that
there's naught beyond.[30]

Critics attacked *The Confidence-Man* even more vehemently than they
had *Moby-Dick*. One went so far as to declare, "Mr. M.'s authorship is
toward the nadir rather than the zenith, and he has been progressing in the
form of an inverted climax."[31] Another added, "The sum and substance of
our fault-finding with Herman Melville is this. He has indulged himself in
a trick of metaphysical and morbid meditations until he has almost per-
verted his fine mind from its healthy productive tendencies."[32] By this time,
Melville was no longer surprised by such uncomprehending responses, he
was, nonetheless, discouraged. In an 1857 letter to his son Sam, living in Europe, Lemuel Shaw reported, "Herman says he is not going to write any
more at present and wishes to get a place in the N.Y. Custom House." Melville was only thirty-eight at the time. The judge was worried enough about
his son-in-law's physical and psychological condition to underwrite a trip to
Europe and the Middle East. Melville began his journey with a three-day
visit to Hawthorne, who was living in Liverpool. His erstwhile Berkshire
neighbor found him "depressed and aimless." Reflecting on their conversations, Hawthorne offered a penetrating account of his friend.

Melville, as he always does, began to reason of Providence and
futurity, and of everything that lies beyond human ken, and informed me that he had "pretty much made up his mind to be
annihilated"; but still he does not seem to rest in that anticipation; and, I think, will never rest until he gets hold of a definite

belief. It is strange how he persists—and has persisted ever since I knew him, and probably long before—in wandering to-and-fro over these deserts, as dismal and monotonous as the sand hills amid which we were sitting. He can neither believe, nor be comfortable in his unbelief; and he is too honest and courageous not to try to do one or the other. If he were a religious man, he would be one of the most truly religious and reverential; he has a very high and noble nature, and better worth immortality than the rest of us.[33]

"He can neither believe, nor be comfortable in his unbelief . . . ." No better description of the mental turmoil that fueled Melville's creativity and plunged him into abyssal despair has ever been written. Neither . . . Nor. Neither belief nor unbelief—this is the boundary along which Melville forever roamed throughout his life.

His pilgrimage to the Holy Land was a search for the reassurance he would never find. In an account of the trip in *Journal of a Visit to Europe and the Levant, October 11, 1856–May 6, 1857,* the desolation of the landscape he described reflected his parched soul. An entry entitled "The Barrenness of Judea" recalls Ethan Brand's infernal lime kiln.

Whitish mildew pervading whole tracts of landscape—bleached—leprosy—encrustation of curses—old cheese—bones of rocks,—crunched, knawed, & mumbled—mere refuse & rubbish of creation—like that lying outside of Jaffa Gate—all Judea seems to have been accumulations of this rubbish.—You see the anatomy compares with ordinary regions as skeleton with living & rosy man.—So rubbishy, that no chiffonier could find any thing all over it.—*No moss as in other ruins—no grace of decay—no ivy—the unleavened nakedness of desolation*—whitish ashes—lime kilns.[34]

Ten years later Melville transformed these musings into the 18,000 verses of his epic philosophical poem *Clarel.* There were other poetic works—

some unpublished, some published at his own expense—but none could compare with the magisterial works he completed as a young man. The weakness of his poetry underscores the strength of his prose.

After returning from his sojourn, Melville found farm work increasingly difficult. Unable to sell Arrowhead, in 1863, he traded the farm to his brother Allan for a house in New York City on East 26th Street, only a few blocks from where he had been born. Melville did not secure a job at the New York Customs House for three years, a decade after he had finished *The Confidence-Man.* For almost twenty years, Delbanco reports, "he took the horse car down Broadway six times a week, then headed west, where he walked the docks along the Hudson down to the Battery. (Later he was assigned to an East River pier uptown at Seventy-ninth Street and traveled to work on the new Third Avenue El.)"[35] Bound to a mind-numbing job and surrounded by corruption he abhorred but could not change, his mood once again darkened. Approaching his sixtieth birthday, he wrote to his Pittsfield friend, John Hoadley, "I am verging on three-score, and at times a certain lassitude steals over one—in fact, a disinclination for doing anything but the indispensable. At such moments the problem of the universe seems a humbug, and epistolary obligations mere moonshine, and the— well, the nepenthe [i.e., a drug, or anything that brings oblivion and eases the pain of sorrow] seems all-in-all."[36] During these difficult years, Melville was surrounded by death. Only one year after he started working at the Customs House, his favored son, Malcolm, committed suicide; twenty years later, his ne'er-do-well son, Stanwix, died alone in a San Francisco hotel room. The intervening decades were filled with darkness that rarely lifted. As deaths of family and friends mounted, depression became despair, which Kierkegaard had diagnosed as "the sickness unto death."

Melville drank too much, but he rarely spoke about what mattered most deeply to him. He tried to get water out of stone one last time. *Billy Budd* began as a poem, "Billy in the Darbies," and ended as a novella Melville could not complete. While many critics have read this work as a political allegory, it is better understood as an act of interminable mourning for Melville's dead sons. The counterpart of Ahab, Billy represents humanity before the fall; Billy is without duplicity—inner and outer, surface and depth, and appearance and reality are one for him. Even such innocence, however, turns out to be infected with what Captain Vere, citing Saint Paul, describes as "the mystery of iniquity" (2 Thessalonians 2:7).

Though the captain loves Billy like a father, he feels duty bound to fulfill the law by executing the youth, who might well be his son. Melville acknowledged that Captain Vere's relation to Billy recalls Abraham's relation to Isaac. "He was old enough to have been Billy's father. The austere devotee of military duty, let himself melt back into what remains primeval in our formalized humanity, may in the end have caught Billy to his heart, even as Abraham may have caught young Isaac on the brink of resolutely offering him up in obedience to the exacting behest."[37] But this association with the biblical parable is misleading. Kierkegaard's rendering of this biblical parable in *Fear and Trembling* makes it clear that there are two important differences between the dilemmas Vere and Abraham face. First, the captain is bound by a human law or custom rather than a command issued by a radically transcendent God; and second, in Melville's tale, God remains silent and does not intervene to stay the executioner's hand. For Kierkegaard's Abraham and his people, Isaac represented the future; for Melville, the death of the son was the end of hope. Whether this impenetrable silence betrays God's lasting inscrutability, or is the echo of God's non-existence, remains undecidable. Unable to finish the work, Melville sealed it in a tin box and left it for others to discover after his death.

Twelve years of astonishing creativity, followed by forty-one years of silence as profound as Nietzsche's vacant stare. Never before or never since has a writer produced so much in such a short time, and then fallen silent for so long. What was Melville thinking all those years as he trudged off to work day after day and drank himself to sleep night after night? As early as 1851, he had written to Hawthorne, "Though I wrote the Gospels in this century, I should die in the gutter."[38] Melville did not die in a gutter, but he did die unknown. On September 28, 1891, at the age of seventy-two, he suffered a heart attack and died at home. Most people, including younger writers, assumed he had been dead for many years. The *New York Times*

Herman Melville's grave

death notice listed his name as "Henry Melville." Melville was buried in Brooklyn's Woodlawn Cemetery beside Malcolm. His grave is covered with ivy.

Everything remains uncertain and unresolved. Melville's poems were as inconclusive as his prose. "The Conflict of Convictions" (1860–61) ends with lines that anticipate Nietzsche's Zarathustra.

> YAY AND NAY—
> EACH HATH HIS SAY;
> BUT GOD HE KEEPS THE MIDDLE WAY.
> NONE WAS BY
> WHEN HE SPREAD THE SKY;
> WISDOM IS VAIN, AND PROPHESY.[39]

The Middle Way: between belief and unbelief. But what is this middle way that Melville is tracing? What does it mean to believe, and what does it mean to believe not? Perhaps belief is really unbelief, and unbelief is truly belief. At the edge, along the border, near the margin, polar opposites reverse. The most haunting chapter of *Moby-Dick*, "The Whiteness of the Whale," suggests that atheism might be true belief.

> But not yet have we solved the incantation of this whiteness, and learned why it appeals with such power to the soul; and more strange and far more portentous—why, as we have seen, it is at once the most meaning symbol of spiritual things, nay, the very veil of the Christian's Deity; and yet should be as it is, the intensifying agent in things the most appalling to mankind.
>
> Is it that by its indefiniteness it shadows forth the heartless voids and immensities of the universe, and thus stabs us from behind with the thought of annihilation, when beholding the white depths of the milky way? Or is it, that as in essence whiteness is not so much a color as the visible absence of color, and at the same time the concrete of all colors; is it for these reasons that there is such a dumb blankness, full of meaning, in a wide landscape of snows—a colorless, all-color of atheism from which we shrink?[40]

The terrifying whiteness of the Whale is the figure of "mystical, inscrutable divineness." This blinding whiteness strikes the writer dumb.

Or almost dumb. Published and unpublished fragments remain. Though never as powerful as his prose, a few of Melville's poems imply that revelations are not always terrifying and sometimes can even be reassuring. On rare occasions, Melville seems to have experienced what we have seen Virginia Woolf describe as "moments of Being." Pierre experiences such a moment in the midst of confusion created by his futile struggle to fulfill his moral obligation. "Now, that vague, fearful feeling stole into him, that, rail as all atheists will, there is a mysterious, inscrutable divineness in the world—a God—a Being positively present everywhere;—nay, He is now in this Room; the air did part when I here sat down. I displaced the Spirit then—condensed it a little off from this spot."[41] The closest Melville

himself seems to have come to experiencing such a moment of positive presence occurred beside a lake that lies halfway between Arrowhead and the
barn where I am writing. He recorded his vision in a poem entitled simply
"Pontoosuce." Gazing across the lake, the poet sees "fields, pastoral fields,
and barns."

> As dreamy Nature, feeling sure
> Of all her genial labor done,
> And the last mellow fruitage won,
> Would idle out her term mature;
> Reposing like a thing reclined
> In kinship with man's meditative mind.[42]

Though this "autumnal noon-tide" is not bathed in melancholy, the poet
realizes that "evanescence will not stay." As the poet feels the passage of
time, harmony slowly gives way to dissonance.

> A year ago was such an hour,
> As this, which but foreruns the blast
> Shall sweep these live leaves to the dead leaves past.
> All dies!

With clouds beginning to gather and his mood darkening further, a nameless lady appears and, while kissing the poet, assures him that the leaves
rotting at the base of the Terror Stone are not the only leaves that fill books.

> Dies, all dies!
> The grass it dies, but in vernal rain
> Up it springs and it lives again;
> Over and over, again and again
> It lives, it dies and it lives again.
> Who sighs that all dies?
> Summer and winter, and pleasure and pain
> And everything everywhere in God's reign,

They end, and anon they begin again:
Wane and wax, wax and wane:
Over and over and over amain
End, ever end, and begin again—
End, ever end, and forever and ever begin again!

A moment of light in a life of darkness? A glimpse of hope in the midst of despair? Midday. These words, which are so uncharacteristic of Melville, might have been written by Thoreau. Though the awful Lord of the heavens might be shrouded in silence, the poet momentarily sees not death but renewal in the cycles of nature. Dead leaves return to earth to nourish new life. These leaves return in "Autumnal Tints," which Thoreau wrote less than three months before he died.

Earth

Henry David Thoreau (1817–1862):
Wild Fruits, "Walking"

The apples were on a level with one's head. The gardens gave off a murmur
of bees; the apples were red and gold; there were also pink flowers; and the grey
and silver leaves. The buzz, the croon, the smell, all seemed to press
voluptuously against some membrane; not to burst it; but to hum round one
such complete pleasure that I stopped, smelt, looked. But again I cannot
describe the rapture. It was rapture rather than ecstasy.
—Virginia Woolf, *Moments of Being*

Retirement

Nothing seals death more than questions you no longer can ask. My mother
taught American literature and my father taught biology and physics in the
suburban New Jersey high school I attended. I never asked them if they ever
discussed the relationship between literature and science. Nor did I ask
them how, in the depth of the Depression, they found their way from a small
Pennsylvania coal-mining town to Duke University, where they received
master's degrees in literature and botany. My father published one book,
Activities Units in Biology (1954), and one booklet, *Brightwood Park:
Westfield, N.J.* (1981). My mother never published a book—her classes
were her publications. What is most surprising about my father's book is
that it begins with poetry rather than science—with Alfred Lord Tennyson's "Flower in the Crannied Wall." "In these simple lines," he com-

ments, "the poet Tennyson expressed the idea that even the humblest and most common form of life contains within it all the secrets and wonders of nature. That is not only a poetic but also a scientific truth. A knowledge of living things brings us a better understanding and appreciation of the world around us, of other people, of ourselves, and of the ultimate forces in the universe."[1] I do not remember my father reading much literature and never recall him reading poetry. I suspect my mother suggested the poem and perhaps even wrote the beginning of the book with lines from Tennyson.

Having grown up on a farm during the first two decades of the twentieth century, my father studied animals and plants as if they were literature. Until the day he died, he knew the Latin name of every plant we found while hiking, hunting, and gardening. He appreciated their subtle differences and reveled in their extravagant beauty. But what seemed most to draw him to plants was their bond with the earth—their roots rooted him. He never lost his love of earth that he had first learned on the Gettysburg farm of his youth, and he was determined to pass on to me the lessons his father had conveyed to him. Craft cherishes tradition more than innovation. He taught me how to dig, rake, hoe, plant, fertilize, weed, and harvest. Though not always a willing worker, even at a young age I realized that gardening was about more than gardening. The garden was my father's classroom, where he taught by showing and I learned by doing. His lessons remain etched not only in my mind, but also in my muscles and bones.

What my father knew about Thoreau, he learned from my mother. One of my most cherished possessions is the anthology from which she taught American literature to high school juniors, and all of her class notes on cards and small scraps of paper. She always claimed that Emerson and Thoreau were her favorites, but her notes and, indeed, her life revealed another story. Her melancholy soul resonated more with Berkshire Calvinists than Concord Transcendentalists. My father's connection with Thoreau was more visceral than intellectual. When he spent hours walking through towns and woods, he was following in Thoreau's footsteps.

As I approach the end of my professional life, I am coming to appreciate my father's lessons in leaving. In today's high-speed, 24/7, wired world, retirement is no longer possible or desirable for many people. For some, financial pressures and social insecurity make retirement impossible; for others, refusing to retire is a strategy for avoiding the void idleness opens. Such evasion can suffocate the soul. Though routine is sometimes reassuring, it dulls the imagination, and makes it impossible for people to conceive of thinking and living otherwise. When every tomorrow is a repetition of yesterday, what appears to be life is actually living death.

My father did not want to stop teaching, but, when New Jersey law forced him to retire at the age of seventy, he transformed necessity into possibility. Having studied botany and taught biology most of his adult life, he was a dedicated environmentalist before it was fashionable. For many years, he regularly included units on ecology in his biology courses. Having moved to a New Jersey suburb in 1945, he was acutely aware of the problems excessive development creates. By the late 1970s, there was only one undeveloped area left in our hometown. When the local town council presented a plan to use the land for tennis and basketball courts, my father, who had never been politically active, led a movement to preserve the area as a natural park. The plan included woods, marsh, swamp, a pond, and a nature trail. After a long struggle, he secured funding from the state of New Jersey, and today Taylor Park is a quiet sanctuary surrounded by noisy suburban sprawl.

While his political activity was impressive, what my father did next is more intriguing. A lifelong teacher, he devoted his retirement years to studying the area that became the park and writing a booklet about it. In his text, he explained the geology, history, and ecology of the area. He also identified all the flora and fauna in the park. His catalog recorded eighty-four different species of birds and two hundred and twenty-seven varieties of plants, shrubs, and trees. The booklet included drawings of many of the flora.

Almost all the drawings are finely drawn leaves with all kinds of shapes, stems straight, bending, sometimes prickly, and veins tangled and twisting like capillaries on the back of an aging hand. Why was he so interested in leaves? What lessons do they teach? What did my father teach young people through leaves? This booklet became a resource for

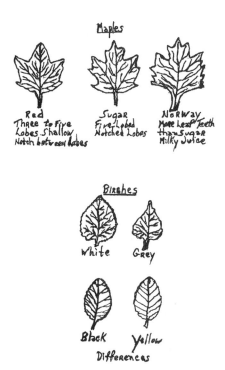

Noel A. Taylor, *Brightwood Park,* Westfield, New Jersey

the next phase of his project—he developed a K–12 curriculum for studying ecology by doing fieldwork in the park. During the last years of his life, he spent many hours working with teachers and students in the field.

Though my father never read much philosophy, he would have understood Nietzsche's point when he wrote, "Books.—What good is a book that does not even carry us beyond all books?"[2] My father's last work was both a "book" and a garden. Neither alone was sufficient, and taken together, they formed two complementary parts of a single work. The "book" articulates the vision the garden made real by grounding ideas in earth. As I ponder my father's last work, the epigram for his booklet gives me pause.

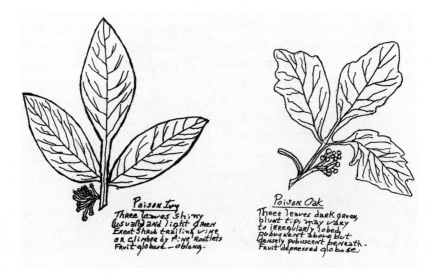

Noel A. Taylor, *Brightwood Park*

A quiet sanctuary for all lovers of nature where one can relax
and listen to the sounds of nature, enjoy its beauty or begin to
understand the lesson that man depends on wildlife for survival.

If one understands that man does depend on nature for
his existence, one can also understand that man cannot continue to subdue the whole planet earth.

Man and living things must learn to live together.

The final line is inscribed on the plaque at the entrance to the park that
bears his name.

Though these words are attributed to my father, I suspect they were
not his alone; I also hear the murmur of my mother's voice in these lines.
While Thoreau is not quoted directly, his vision echoes in the words that
bring together the literature teacher and the science teacher, who defined
my life's vocation long before I understood the lessons their lives and deaths
have taught me.

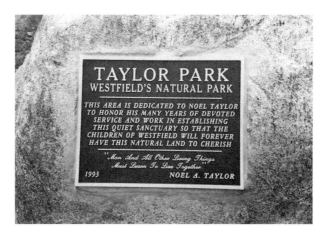

Taylor Park

Concord

If I could time travel, there are two places I would go—Jena from 1790 to 1800, and Concord from 1840 to 1862. Concord during the middle decades of the nineteenth century was for American literature, art, philosophy, and theology what Jena during the last decade of the eighteenth century was for European culture. Never before or since have so many extraordinary thinkers and writers gathered together for such a productive period. Jena: Hegel, Fichte, Schelling, Schiller, Schleiermacher, Novalis, Holderlin, August and Friedrich Schlegel, and Ludwig Tieck; Concord: Emerson, Thoreau, Hawthorne, Margaret Fuller, William Ellery Channing, and Bronson and Louisa May Alcott. There is a direct line joining Jena and Concord—Concord is where German Idealism and Romanticism took root in American soil. The literary tradition that resulted from this remarkable synthesis of art, philosophy, and religion became the polar opposite of the literary tradition that was forming in the Berkshires at the same time. During the years all of these writers were working, the road connecting Lenox and Concord passed along the edge of my property on Stone Hill where I am writing this book. The name of the town captures my father's vision. Concord: "Man and living things must learn to live together."

To understand the beginning of any human life, the best place to start is the end—the cemetery, which, in Danish, is *den kirkegaard*. The Sleepy Hollow Cemetery in Concord was dedicated on September 29, 1855. William Ellery Channing, a friend and hiking companion of Thoreau, read his poem "Sleepy Hollow," and Emerson delivered the address in which he expressed his confidence that all would be reconciled in the Over-Soul. "We give our earth to earth. We will not jealously guard a few atoms under immense marbles, selfishly and impossibly sequestering it from the vast circulations of Nature but, at the same time, fully admitting the divine hope and love which belong to our nature, wishing to make one spot tender to our children, who shall come hither in the next century to read the dates of these lives."[3] In this quiet preserve, all are gathered for eternity—the Alcotts, Hawthorne, Emerson, and Thoreau—as if engaged in what Blanchot describes as an "infinite conversation."[4] Emerson's gravestone is a large boulder with a plaque bearing an inscription from his poem "The Problem." "The passive master lent his hand to the vast soul which o'er him planned." Not far away lie the mortal remains of Henry David Thoreau, marked by nothing more than a modest stone with a single word: Henry.

When the town was incorporated in 1635 as Musketaquid, it was the first Puritan settlement that was not organized primarily around trans-Atlantic commerce. Shortly thereafter the village was renamed Concord to commemorate what was purported to be the peaceful agreement in which Native Americans exchanged six square miles for wampum.[5] While Concord was well known for its illustrious history during the Revolutionary War, memorialized in Emerson's "Concord Hymn," it was not until leading writers gathered there during the middle decades of the nineteenth century that the town assumed its true place in world history. Located at the confluence of the Sudbury and Assabet Rivers and the intersection of the Boston and Lexington roads, Concord became an important hub for the exchange of ideas as well as goods.

David Henry Thoreau was born in Concord on July 12, 1817, and lived there almost his entire life. He never ventured abroad and only made it as far west as Minnesota. His foreign travel was through books; always a voracious reader, Thoreau was particularly intrigued by books about travel

in foreign countries. Like Kierkegaard during imaginary walks with his
father, Thoreau journeyed to distant lands through his imagination. When
he did actually travel, it was by foot—he walked the state of Massachusetts
from Mount Greylock to Cape Cod, and ventured as far north as New
Hampshire, Maine, and Canada. His imaginary travels took him to places
he could not reach by walking. On these trips, he developed a genuine appreciation for other cultures and religions. He was especially drawn to India, where he discovered Hinduism and Buddhism. James Eliot Cabot's
article "The Philosophy of the Ancient Hindoos," published in the *Massachusetts Quarterly,* edited by Emerson, was especially important for Thoreau. Biographer Robert D. Richardson reports, "Cabot takes pains to
show the similarity between Hindu idealism and that of Kant and Fichte,
especially the latter. Cabot, in other words, understands Hinduism as a
major version of transcendental idealism, couched in different terms and
originating in another culture. But Cabot notes important differences too.
Where Western thought works in terms of antitheses (thought and being,
mind and nature), oriental thought, Cabot contends, reflects a prior way of
thinking. . . . 'To the Hindoos the highest description of God is as the One
Soul.'"[6] What Cabot describes as "the Hindu One Soul" became Emerson's "Over-Soul." Encouraged to learn more about Hinduism, Thoreau
concentrated primarily on *The Laws of Manu* and the *Bhagavad Gita,* but
also studied *Icvara Krsna* and *Sacontala.* He was so impressed by what he
discovered that he went so far as to experiment with a rice diet and yoga.[7]

Thoreau remained both physically and emotionally close to his
family throughout his life. His father, John, worked as a sign painter before
establishing his own pencil factory, where Thoreau worked on and off. His
mother, Cynthia, encouraged her children to read and was active in the
anti-slavery movement. She even made their home a stop on the Under-
ground Railroad. Thoreau's unwavering support of John Brown and anti-
slavery tracts were extensions of his mother's political work. John and
Cynthia had three other children in addition to David Henry—Helen, who
died at age thirty-seven, Sophia, and John, who died at age twenty-seven.

David Henry Thoreau left Concord to attend Harvard at the age of
sixteen and returned four years later as Henry David Thoreau. At Harvard,

he continued to study mythology and classics (Greek and Latin), which he had begun in secondary school, and expanded his language study to Italian, French, and German. His interest in literature, especially poetry, began during a course he took with Longfellow, who, after traveling extensively throughout Europe, had recently arrived at Harvard. Though they did not remain close, Longfellow had a lasting impact on Thoreau. In 1836, the year Thoreau graduated from Harvard, the United States was facing a financial crisis that led to a decade-long depression. He was fortunate enough to secure a job teaching in the Concord public schools; however, within several weeks he was fired for refusing to subject his students to corporeal punishment.

During the years Thoreau was in Cambridge, Concord was transformed by Emerson's arrival. After his first wife, Ellen, died, Emerson resigned his pulpit in an influential Boston church and traveled in Europe before settling in Concord. Emerson's flourishing reputation in the United States and abroad drew people to Concord. Thoreau was quite taken with Emerson, and they developed a close and sometimes difficult relationship. Over the years, Thoreau lived in Emerson's home, where he tutored his children and worked as a handyman. What Hawthorne was for Melville, Emerson was for Thoreau—Thoreau found in Emerson a lifelong mentor, and Emerson found in Thoreau a protégé who could help to promote his version of Transcendentalism.

Thoreau's introduction to Emerson's thought was Emerson's famous Phi Beta Kappa address delivered at Thoreau's Harvard graduation. A short time later, he read *Nature,* where he discovered what would become the rudiments of his mature vision. In Concord, Emerson introduced Thoreau to many influential writers, one of the most important of whom was Margaret Fuller, the first important American feminist writer. Thoroughly conversant with German philosophy, she was at the time translating Johann Peter Eckermann's influential *Conversations with Goethe.* When Emerson and Fuller established a journal entitled *The Dial* to spread their transcendentalist gospel, they drew Thoreau into the enterprise as a sometimes editor and contributor. Emerson's most important influence on Thoreau, however, was his encouragement to start writing a journal, which he began in 1837. Though he published only two books in his life—*A Week on the Concord and Merrimack Rivers* (1849) and *Walden* (1854)—Thoreau religiously kept his journal throughout his life. At the time of his early death at the age of only forty-four, it numbered twenty volumes, precisely the same as Kierkegaard's journal, when he died at the young age of forty-two. Though certain tensions inevitably developed over the years, Emerson and Thoreau remained close until the end. At Thoreau's funeral in Sleepy Hollow Cemetery, Emerson presented a eulogy, which was subsequently published in the *Atlantic Monthly*.

> It was a pleasure and a privilege to walk with him. He knew the country like a fox or a bird, and passed through it as freely by paths of his own. He knew every track in the snow or on the ground, and what creature had taken this path before him. One must submit abjectly to such a guide, and the reward was great. Under his arm he carried an old music-book to press plants; in his pocket, his diary and pencil, a spy-glass for birds, microscope, jack-knife, and twine. . . . He was equally interested in every natural fact. The depth of his perception found likeness of law throughout Nature, and I know not any genius who so swiftly inferred universal law from the single fact. He was no pedant of a department. His eye was open to beauty, and his ear to music. He found these, not in rare conditions, but wheresoever he went.[8]

German philosophy came to America by way of England.[9] Samuel Taylor Coleridge studied the works of Kant, Schelling, and especially Fichte, and reported his interpretation of German Idealism and Romanticism in *Biographia Literari* (1817). Richardson correctly maintains, "For Emerson and the circle of liberal intellectuals around him, Kant and Fichte were simply more important than Locke or Hume or the Scottish Common Sense school in philosophy; Goethe and Novalis were more important than Wordsworth or Keats in literature, and the work of Herder, Coleridge (himself strongly influenced by German thought), and Schleiermacher was more important in theology than Jonathan Edwards and the American Puritan tradition."[10] Longfellow had introduced Thoreau to Goethe's concept of *Bildung* in his lectures at Harvard. This led to Thoreau's life-long preoccupation with different forms of self-cultivation in both his writings and his personal life.[11] After Harvard, Thoreau's interests expanded to Goethe's speculative investigation of plant morphology, which became especially important during the final decade of his life and informs his last work.

In *Nature*, Emerson presents a thoroughly idealistic interpretation of life in which he integrates theology (God), anthropology (self), and cosmology (world). The foundation of his position is the insistence that "Nature is the vehicle for thought." This argument turns on the claim that epistemology (subjectivity) and ontology (objectivity) are not antithetical but, to the contrary, are codependent mirror images of each other. "Mind is a part of the nature of things; the world is a divine dream, from which we may presently awake to the glories and certainties of day." In a manner completely consistent with Hegel's absolute idealism, human consciousness becomes aware of itself in nature, and the natural world comes to completion in and through human self-consciousness. When taken as a whole, this process is for both Hegel and Emerson divine. In a passage that could have been written in the cabin Thoreau built on land Emerson loaned him beside Walden Pond, Emerson writes, "In the woods, we return to reason and faith. There I feel that nothing can befall me in life—no disgrace, no calamity . . . , which nature cannot repair. Standing on the bare ground—my head bathed by the blithe air and uplifted into infinite space—all mean egotism vanishes. I become a transparent eyeball; I am nothing; I see all; the currents of the Universal Being circulate through me; I am part or parcel of God."[12] The reconciliation of God, self, and world in the "Hegelian" vision of Emerson and eventually Thoreau is the antidote to the suffering of unhappy consciousness expressed in the "Kierkegaardian" vision of Melville. For Thoreau, "it is the marriage of the soul with Nature that makes the intellect fruitful, that gives birth to imagination."[13]

It is, however, misleading to label Thoreau simply an idealist; he was in important ways also a realist. In his eulogy, Emerson actually referred to him as a realist, though his explanation sounds like a combination of Kierkegaardian and Hegelian dialectics. "The habit of a realist to find things the reverse of their appearance inclined him to put every statement in a paradox. A certain habit of antagonism defaced his earlier writings,—a trick of rhetoric not quite outgrown in his later, of substituting for the obvious word and thought its diametrical opposite. He praised wild mountains and winter forests for their domestic air, in snow and ice he would find sultriness, and commended the wilderness for resembling Rome and Paris. 'It was so dry, that you might call it wet.' "[14] It is worth noting that while at Harvard, Thoreau took a course on the history of philosophy in which he studied Locke's *Essay on Human Understanding.* The empirical and the practical bent of his mind distinguishes him from other speculative Transcendentalists and Idealists. For Thoreau, the real and the ideal are unified in such a way that one neither excludes nor absorbs the other. Unlike American Transcendentalists and many, though not all, German Idealists, Thoreau was genuinely interested in the natural sciences.[15] He read extensively in the fields of biology, geology, and especially botany, and was conversant with the important scientific debates of the day. While he was intrigued by Alexander von Humboldt's magisterial five-volume study *Kosmos,* it was Darwin above all others who engaged Thoreau's attention. He read *Journal of the Voyage of the Beagle* when it was published in New York in 1846, and followed the controversies surrounding his work. Thoreau was as impressed by Darwin's powers of observation and patient descriptions of what he saw as he was by his grand theory. The works of Darwin's most important American follower, Harvard botanist Asa Gray, were also very important for Thoreau. The same taxonomic impulse in Gray's *Natural System of Botany* (1837) and *Manual of the Botany of the Northern United States,* known simply as *Gray's Manual* (1848), is also present in the research of the great Swedish botanist Carl Linnaeus, who was responsible for establishing the principles for defining the genera and species of organisms. The uniform system he created is the binomial nomenclature that is still used today. Thoreau read Linnaeus's summary of his system, *Philosophia Botanica* (1751), and drew on it in *Wild Fruits.* While he appreciated Linnaeus's accomplishment in defining differences and relations among various flora and fauna, he did not think his system adequately accounted for the interaction of plants, animals, and humans.

The commitment to the real as well as the ideal or, in different terms, to both science and art, shapes the distinctive style of Thoreau's mature work—his writing style creatively integrates prosaic description and poetic reflection. When formulating this important point that lies at the heart of all his work, he turns not to British empiricists and natural philosophers, but to the German philosophical and aesthetic tradition as formulated by Goethe. "We can never safely exceed the actual facts in our narratives. Of pure invention, such as some suppose, there is no instance. To write a true work of fiction even, is only to take leisure and liberty to describe some things exactly as they are. A true account of the actual is the rarest poetry, for common sense always takes a hasty and superficial view. Though I am not much acquainted with the works of Goethe, I should say that it was one of his chief excellencies as a writer, that he was satisfied with giving an exact description of things as they appeared to him, and their effect upon him."[16] Goethe's appreciation for the rarest poetry of real things led Thoreau to translate his *Italian Journey,* and to use it as the model for his first book, *A Week on the Concord and Merrimack Rivers.*

Flows

One of the most common misunderstandings of Thoreau is that he was something of a proto–New Ager, who had a naïve interpretation of nature's beneficence. Nothing could be farther from the truth. As much a realist as an idealist, he always acknowledged nature's destructive, even fatal power. Richardson goes so far as to describe Thoreau as "one of our great poets of loss."[17] In his late essay "Walking," Thoreau makes this point with words Melville could have written, "Genius is a light that makes darkness visible."[18] Unlike Melville, however, for whom darkness rarely lifted, Thoreau cultivated the ability to rise above pain, depression, and loss by putting these experiences in a more comprehensive perspective.

Thoreau knew darkness well. Suffering both physically and psychologically throughout his life, he described himself as "a diseased bundle of nerves straining between time and eternity, like a withered leaf."[19] The figure of the leaf returns frequently in his writings, especially at the end of his life. In addition to his own frailty, Thoreau's life was haunted by death. In 1842, his brother, John, with whom he had a complicated relationship, unexpectedly died when he was only twenty-seven. After cutting himself while shaving, he contracted tetanus, which quickly spread and developed into lockjaw. A few days later, John died in his brother's arms. Two weeks later, Thoreau had a sympathetic reaction and developed the physical symptoms of lockjaw. The day his symptoms disappeared, Emerson's son, Waldo, with whom Thoreau was very close, came down with scarlet fever and was dead in three days. Thoreau and Emerson were bound together in grief, but responded in very different ways. Though terribly shaken by Waldo's death, Emerson dealt with it by resuming normal activity as quickly as possible. Thoreau, by contrast, did not come to terms with John's death for several years, when he wrote *A Week on the Concord and Merrimack Rivers,* which is a work of mourning for the loss of his brother.

In addition to the pain of disease and death, Thoreau observed and experienced the violence of nature on both a microscopic and a macroscopic scale. Two of his most memorable experiences were encounters with death along the Atlantic shore. He traveled to Cape Cod four times during his life. On his first trip in 1849, he arrived to discover the beach strewn with bodies from the wreck of the ship *St. John,* which was arriving from Galway, Ireland. Twenty-seven or twenty-eight bodies had been recovered and were being placed in wooden coffins; others were still in the sea or on the rocky coast. Less than a year later, another shipwreck proved even more difficult for him to accept. On July 19, 1850, Margaret Fuller was returning to the United States from Europe, where the *New York Tribune* had sent her as its first female correspondent, when the ship on which she was traveling sank less than one hundred yards off the coast of Fire Island. Margaret and her family perished in the wreck. At Emerson's urging, Thoreau traveled to New York to search the shore, but her body was never recovered. As always, Thoreau recorded his thoughts in his journal, and his account is included in his posthumous book *Cape Cod.* "Alone with the sea and the beach, attending to the sea, whose hollow roar seemed addressed

to the ears of the departed—articulate speech to them. It was as conspicuous on that sandy plain as if a generation had labored to pile up a cairn
there. Where there were so few objects, the least was obvious as a mauso-
leum. It reigned over the shore. That dead body possessed the shore as
no living one could. It showed a title to the sands which no living ruler
could."[20]

It was not the shoreline of Cape Cod but the summit of Mount Greylock at the other end of the state that opened the perspective that allowed
Thoreau to come to terms with these experiences and to overcome moments
of despair. In July 1844, Thoreau began a walking trip from Concord to
the Catskills. He planned to meet Ellery Channing at the base of Saddleback Mountain, which was the name of Mount Greylock at the time. While
Melville pondered Mount Greylock for hours while writing, he never
climbed the mountain. An inveterate hiker, Thoreau relished the challenge
of finding the most difficult route to the top of the highest mountain in Massachusetts. Though he recorded the climb in his journal, he did not publish his thoughts for five years, when he described the ascent in religious
terms. "It seemed a road for the pilgrim to enter upon who would climb
to the gates of heaven."[21] Though Thoreau attended Harvard, the woods
and the mountains were the whaleship where he received his real education.
Tired and thirsty, he arrived at the summit of Mount Greylock in the dark;
with no blanket, he built a fire, ate some rice, and fell asleep. He woke before
dawn, climbed an observation tower that had been "erected by the students
of Williamstown College" (that is, Williams College, where I taught for
thirty-seven years), and waited for the sun to rise.

With light gradually falling on the Berkshire Mountains, Thoreau
had a transformative epiphany.

> As the light increased I discovered around me an ocean of mist,
> which by chance reached up exactly to the base of the tower,
> and shut out every vestige of the earth, while I was left floating
> on this fragment of the wreck of a world, on my carved plank,
> in cloudland; a situation which required no aid from the imag-
> ination to render it impressive. As the light in the east steadily

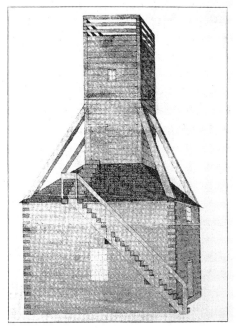

The Old Greylock Tower of 1840.
(By permission of Mrs. Wm. H. Phillips of Amherst.)

1841 Observation Tower, Mount Greylock

increased, it revealed to me more clearly the new world into which I had risen in the night. . . . All around beneath me was spread for a hundred miles on every side, as far as the eye could reach, an undulating country of clouds, answering in the varied swell of its surface to the terrestrial world it veiled. It was such a country as we might see in dreams, with all the delights of paradise. . . . As there was wanting the symbol, so there was not the substance of impurity, no spot nor stain. It was a favor for which to be forever silent to be shown this vision. The earth beneath had become such a flitting thing of lights and shadows as the clouds had been before. It was not merely veiled to me, but it had passed away like the phantom of a shadow . . . , and this new platform was gained. As I had

climbed above storm and cloud, so by successive days' journeys
I might reach the region of eternal day, beyond the tapering
shadow of the earth.

"Heaven itself shall slide,
And roll away, like melting stars that glide
Along their oily threads."

While Thoreau does not mention the death of his brother, it is clear
that his experience on the top of Mount Greylock contributed significantly
to his acceptance not only of John's death, but also of the dark side of nature.
After recounting his experience, he adds one of the most revealing comments in all his works.

The inhabitants of earth behold commonly but the dark and
shadowy underside of heaven's pavement; it is only when seen
at a favorable angle in the horizon, morning or evening, that
some faint streaks of the rich lining of the clouds are revealed.
But my muse would fail to convey an impression of the gorgeous
tapestry by which I was surrounded, such as men see faintly reflected afar off in the chambers of the east. Here, as on earth, I
saw the gracious God.

"Flatter the mountain tops with sovereign eye,
Gilding pale streams with heavenly alchemy."

When Thoreau returned to the valley, he brought his vision down to earth,
where he "discovered God in flowing streams." While Melville glimpsed a
fleeting moment of Being beside Pontoosuce Lake at the base of Mount
Greylock, he never climbed the mountain, and, thus, only ever saw "the
dark and shadowy underside of heaven's pavement."

Writing *A Week on the Concord and Merrimack Rivers,* Thoreau completed what began at the top of Saddleback Mountain that July morning.
While Thoreau was traumatized by John's untimely death, the relationship

between the brothers was fraught. The tensions arose because of their mutual love for a young girl. In 1839, Ellen Sewall spent two weeks in Concord visiting her brother, who was a student in the school John founded
and where Henry taught. Both brothers fell in love with the seventeen-year-
old girl. A few weeks after Ellen's visit, Henry and John set out on their trip
up the Concord and Merrimack Rivers. When they returned, John immediately went to nearby Scituate to visit Ellen. Whether because of brotherly
loyalty or his awkward shyness, Henry did not interfere with John's court-
ship of Ellen. A year later, John proposed to Ellen; Richardson reports the
ensuing confusion. "Ellen at first accepted, then either because of family
pressure or because she suddenly realized she cared more for Henry than
for John, she refused him. Thoreau couldn't openly exult over John's failure,
but his journal clearly records his eternity of suspenseful waiting and his
unconcealed joy at the outcome."[22] Four months later Thoreau proposed to
Ellen. Having been chastised for accepting John's proposal without consulting her parents, this time she asked her father's permission to marry and
he refused. Ever the obedient daughter, Ellen accepted her father's decision, and two years later married another man. Thoreau never fell in love
again, and on his deathbed confessed to his sister Sophia that he had "always loved" Ellen.

  A Week on the Concord and Merrimack Rivers, a book framed by
death, is about the alternating rhythms of decay and renewal. Thoreau's
first published work is suspended between the death of his brother, John,
and the death of his sister, Helen, two weeks after the work appeared.
Though Helen suffered from tuberculosis for many years, her death at the
age of thirty-six was unsettling for Thoreau. His first book came neither
easily nor quickly; indeed, he wrestled with *A Week* for seven years. He completed the first draft at Walden Pond in 1835, but the work was not published for four more years. At the time of the trip with John, he had not taken
extensive notes in his journal, and over the years his memories faded. In
addition to his physical and psychological problems, and the complexities
of his relationship with John, he was struggling to find what he believed
would be a new genre. The final version of the work proved to be as baf-
fling to publishers as it was to readers. After repeated rejections, Thoreau

finally found a printer who agreed to issue the book on the condition that
Thoreau would cover expenses if it did not sell enough copies. The
initial review of *A Week* was appreciative of the descriptions of nature,
but critical of what was described as Thoreau's "pantheistic" attack on
Christianity.

The turning point that enabled Thoreau to forge his scattered notes
and memories into a coherent work was his recognition of the importance
of Goethe's work and its place in the German philosophical tradition to
which Emerson had introduced him. Thoreau took as his model Goethe's
Italian Journey (1816–1817). "In his Italian Travels," he writes, "Goethe
jogs along at a snail's pace, but always mindful that the earth is beneath and
the heavens above him. His Italy is not merely the fatherland of lazzaroni
and virtuosi, and scene of splendid ruins, but a solid turf-clad soil, daily
shined on by the sun, and nightly by the moon. Even the few showers are
faithfully recorded. He speaks as an unconcerned spectator, whose object
is to faithfully describe what he sees, and that, for the most part, in the order in which he sees it" (326).[23] Goethe's challenge "to faithfully describe
what he sees" becomes the aim of Thoreau's writing. But he does not see
what other people see because his vision is as poetic as it is prosaic. "A true
account of the actual," he insists, "is the rarest poetry" (325). For Thoreau,
science and literature, the real and the ideal, earth and heaven are one. Like
Poe's *Eureka* and Woolf's *The Waves,* Thoreau's *A Week* can best be described as a prose poem.

Thoreau solved his organizational problem by structuring the book
as a week-long river journey. In all of his writing, he is preoccupied with
the passage of time, which, he believed, heals the wound it inflicts. "There
is something even in the lapse of time by which time recovers itself. . . . The
constant abrasion and decay of our lives makes the soil of our future growth"
(321). The ebb and flow of the river and tidal marshes suggest the passing
and the renewal of time. Henry and John's actual trip was a two-week
canoe-and-hiking journey from Concord to the White Mountains in
New Hampshire, where they climbed Mount Washington. Epigrams from
Ovid, Emerson, and his own poetry, leave no doubt about the philosophical and spiritual stakes of the venture. The outward trip up the rivers

and back figures his inward "journey to selfhood."[24] As he spins his tale, Thoreau develops an expansive interpretation of poetry that weaves God, world, and self into a seamless tapestry. For those who know how to read the book of nature, furrows in the earth are lines of poetry. Describing farmers and manual laborers working along the river, Thoreau writes, "Look at their fields, and imagine what they might write, if ever they should put pen to paper. Or what have they not written on the face of the earth already, clearing, and burning, and scratching, and harrowing, and plowing, and subsoiling, in and in, and out and out, and over and over, again and again, erasing what they had already written for want of parchment." These earthly lines are, in Thoreau's fine phrase, "faint revelations of the Real" (8, 385). Such revelations are not, however, evident to the untutored eye because they hide as well as show and, therefore, fail to dispel earth's mystery.

On the last day of August in 1835, Henry and John launched the boat they had made in a late-summer drizzle and headed north toward the Middlesex Canal. His eventual account of their seven days and seven nights recasts the original creation story as parable of renewal, even if not of redemption. "The Musketaquid, or Grass-ground River," Thoreau begins, is "probably as old as the Nile or Euphrates," and is as grand as the Ganges and Mississippi (5, 12). Ancient and modern worlds intersect in the flow of rivers across time. Familiar fields, farms, and villages appear strange from the river, and sounds never noticed on land echo across the water. After a long day of rowing, the brothers stop and make camp for the night. When they awake the next morning, the river, like the Berkshire Mountains, is shrouded in fog. As they were preparing to set out on the second day, "the sun arose and the fog rapidly dispersed, leaving a slight steam only to curl along the surface of the water. It was a quiet Sunday morning, with more of the auroral rosy and white than of the yellow light in it, as if it dated from earlier than the fall of man, and still preserved a heathenish integrity" (43). In this seemingly idyllic prelapsarian world everything appears to be connected, though not necessarily transparent. As Thoreau struggles to understand what he had experienced on the Concord and Merrimack Rivers, he repeatedly turns to Goethe for guidance.

Goethe (1749–1832) lived during one of the most important periods of Western cultural history. His artistic, philosophical, and scientific writings contributed significantly to creating the world in which we still live today. In his *Italian Journey,* Goethe recounts the revelatory moment that led to the mature vision that was so influential for European Romanticism and Idealism, as well as American Transcendentalism. "It had become apparent to me that in the plant organ we ordinarily call the leaf, a true Proteus is concealed, who can hide and reveal himself in all formations. From top to bottom, a plant is all leaf, unified so inseparably with the future bud that one cannot be imagined without the other. To grasp, to endure such a concept, to detect it in nature, is a task that puts us into a sweet torment."[25] Three years later, he published his controversial and influential *The Metamorphosis of Plants* in which he elaborated the far-reaching implications of his vision.

The intellectual and artistic transition from the eighteenth to the nineteenth century was marked by a shift from mechanistic to organic images, metaphors, and concepts for interpreting God, self, and world. The atomism of Newton and British empiricists as well as Descartes's dualism led to a deistic understanding of the world in which a distant transcendent God governs by imposing mechanistic laws that regulate independent entities that have no intrinsic relation to each other. By the end of the eighteenth century, this line of analysis was being questioned by leading philosophers, theologians, writers, and artists. Two of the most influential works for what became the intellectual revolution that prepared the way for the nineteenth and twentieth centuries were Goethe's *The Metamorphosis of Plants* and Kant's *Critique of Judgment,* both published in 1790. Critics who claimed to be empiricists condemned Goethe for being too speculative and failing to provide adequate experimental evidence. Almost three decades later, Goethe published several essays in which he responded to critics by providing more detailed descriptions of his observations and evidence for his argument. In the intervening years, philosophers, writers, and artists appropriated many of the insights of Goethe and Kant to develop the Idealism and Romanticism that were so influential for Thoreau. Goethe's analysis of plants and especially leaves deepened what

Thoreau had learned from Emerson's *Nature* and formed the foundation of his mature position developed in *Walden* and *Wild Fruits.*

Goethe's argument turns on his distinction between "the atomistic point of view" and "dynamic points of view."[26] Whereas atomists regard every object and subject as an independent entity and insist that relations are externally imposed, dynamists maintain that objects and subjects are codependent and are constituted through internal relationships. For dynamists, the world does not resemble a mechanistic clock that operates according to unbending laws, but is a vital organism in which everything is inextricably interrelated. The specificity of all entities as well as the identity of every subject is a function of their place in the whole of which they are integral members. Accordingly, subjects and objects are not, as Descartes had argued, separate opposites, but are inseparably interconnected, and, thus, mutually constitutive. The structure of this whole is, in a contemporary idiom, fractal; that is to say, it has the same structure from the smallest part to the most encompassing whole. This comprehensive and comprehensible dynamic structure is both synchronic and diachronic. Within this web or network, objects and subjects are constituted by their interrelation at a particular moment as well as their development over time. *The Metamorphosis of Plants* begins with a poem, in which Goethe uses the image of the stems and veins of leaves to suggest currents flowing through all natural systems. To illustrate this point, he includes drawings, which are very similar to those in Thoreau's *Wild Fruits* and my father's booklet.

Prior to Goethe's work, the most important botanist was Linnaeus. While Thoreau was initially impressed by Linnaeus's classification system, Goethe was critical of it for two closely related reasons. First, his classifications drew distinctions effectively but could not adequately define the interrelations between and among individual plants and different species; second, Linnaeus's system was static and could not give a satisfactory account of the dynamic development of living plants and organisms. To overcome these problems, Goethe developed what he described as "a higher law of the organism." "When we study forms, the organic ones in particular," he argues, "nowhere do we find permanence, repose, or termination.

We find rather that everything is in ceaseless flux. . . . This is why our language makes such frequent use of the term '*Bildung*' to designate what has been brought forth and likewise what is in the process of being brought forth" (23).

Goethe's use of the term *Bildung* in this context is very significant. *Bildung* has a rich history; it means not only formation, creation, production, growth, form, shape, structure, and organization, but also education and culture. In other words, *Bildung* specifies both natural and cultural processes of development. Goethe suggests the isomorphism of natural and cultural processes in his highly influential *Bildungsroman Wilhelm Meister* (1795). When this work is taken together with *The Metamorphosis of Plants,* it becomes clear that Goethe sees the same formative process at work in plants, animals, human beings, history, and culture. He writes, "These organisms are partly united by origin; partly they discover each other and unite. They separate and seek each other out again, thus bringing about endless production in all ways and in all directions" (24). The common origin is the *Urphanomen* (original or primal phenomenon, archetype, pattern), or, in the case of botany, the *Urpflanz* (original or primal archetypal plant) from which all other plants derive. Goethe triumphantly declared, "The primordial plant is turning out to be the most marvelous creation in the world, and nature itself will envy me because of it."[27] Since his system is fractal, the same developmental pattern operates in all individual plants and organisms as in species and, indeed, is at work in the totality of nature and history. Within this framework, the development of each individual plant as well as nature as a whole is a unified unfolding that can, in principle, be retraced to its point of origin.

It is important to note that we have observed this developmental pattern in other writers we have considered. There is a progression from unity to diversity, which tends to become opposition, and then either a return to primal unity, or an advance to an integration, which issues in unity-in-diversity. As we have seen, writers interpret this process differently—it can be understood ontologically, cosmologically, psychologically, theologically, or in all of these ways at once. In a manner reminiscent of Hegel's process of sublation (*Aufhebung*) in which later forms preserve earlier stages they negate, the development of the plant, for Goethe, preserves the *Ur-plantz* through all its later stages. Development is, therefore, a continuous process.

This organic unity is not immediately obvious and can only be grasped through the cultivation of the imagination. Goethe develops his interpretation of the imagination by elaborating a pivotal passage from the *Critique of Judgment*. Kant draws a distinction between two modalities of the imagination, which illuminate the difference between Goethe's atomism and dynamism. "In contrast to our own analytic intellect, we can conceive of an intuitive one which proceeds from the synthetically universal (the concept of the whole as such) and advances to the particulars, in other words, from the whole into its parts. At this point it is not necessary to prove such an *intellectus archetypus* is possible, but merely that we are inevitably led to it when we contrast our own analytical, image-requiring intellect (*intellectus ectypus*) with its own fortuitous character, and that the idea of an *intellectus archetypus* would contain no condition" (232). While the *intellectus ectypus* grasps particulars in their concrete specificity, the *intellectus archetypus* comprehends the whole in which all parts are interrelated. The imagination is what Coleridge aptly labeled "the esemplastic power," which both discerns relations and forges connections that overcome divisive oppositions. When understood in this way, Goethe suggests, the imagination appears to be nothing less than divine. Commenting on Kant's argument, he continues, "To be sure, the author seems to be referring here to godlike understanding; yet since it is possible in the moral realm to ascend to a higher plane, drawing close to the Supreme Being through faith in God, virtue, and immortality, the same might well hold true in the intellectual realm. Through contemplation of ever-creative Nature, we might make ourselves worthy of participating intellectually in her productions" (233). For Goethe, the transcendent creator God dies and is reborn as the immanent creative principle operating through nature and the imagination of finite human beings. In other words, the divine is "the supreme artist" and the world is a work of art. "She [i.e., Nature] is eternal life, eternal becoming, eternal change, yet she does not move forward. She ever transforms herself, without pausing to rest. She is constant, yet

impatient with anything static, and has set her curse on stagnation"
(242–43).

Goethe's writings resonated with Thoreau and provided a way for
him to bring unity to the diversity and plurality of his insights and writerly fragments as well as his life and world. *A Week on the Concord and
Merrimack Rivers* became his *Bildungsroman* in which an outward trip
became an inward journey. Goethe's protean vision dissolves oppositions
and reveals a vital relational web in which everything is interrelated. With
his voyage of discovery drawing to a close, Thoreau recorded the most
important lesson he had learned. "The hardest material seemed to obey the
same law with the most fluid, and so indeed in the long run it does. Trees
were but rivers of sap and woody fiber, flowing from the atmosphere, and
emptying into the earth by their trunks, as roots flowed upward to the surface. And in the heavens there were rivers of stars, and milky-ways, already beginning to gleam and ripple over our heads. There were rivers of
rock on the surface of the earth, and rivers of ore in its bowels, and our
thoughts flowed and circulated, and this portion of time was but the current hour."[28] "No wonder," Thoreau adds five years later in *Walden*, "that
the earth expresses itself outwardly in leaves, it so labors with the idea inwardly. The atoms have already learned this law, and are pregnant with it.
The overhanging leaf sees here its prototype."[29] The veins of leaves figure
rivers through which sap, pulp, blood, even earthly rocks and heavenly
stars eternally flow.

Apples

Why does a person spend the last years of his life cataloging plants? What
is the draw of lists? What is the weight of the catalogue? And why plants?
Why fruits? Why wild fruits? What secrets do these plants and fruits harbor? What stories do they tell? What lessons in leaving do they teach?

My father never read *Wild Fruits*, but, if he had, I am sure he would
have quoted Thoreau's words in his booklet. "I think that each town should
have a park, or rather a primitive forest, of five hundred or a thousand acres,
either in one body or several, where a stick should never be cut for fuel, nor

for the navy, nor to make wagons, but stand and decay for higher uses—a common possession forever, for instruction and recreation."[30] In the years after my mother died, my father walked every day; after his death, neighbors reported that he often was gone one, two, three, even four hours. Much of this time he spent in the park cataloging all the flora and fauna he could identify. When cleaning out the house after he died, I found in the garage the container he carried for the plants he collected and two plant presses he used to preserve specimens. I never asked him why it was so important to collect, name, and catalog so many plants.

In an essay about Rousseau in his book *A Place in the Country,* W. G. Sebald suggests an answer to the question about lists and catalogs. Rousseau, like Kierkegaard, Nietzsche, Thoreau, and my father, was a tireless walker. Nietzsche speaks for all these pedestrians when he insists, "Sit as little as possible; give no credence to any thought that was not born outdoors while one moved about freely. . . . The sedentary life . . . is the real *sin* against the holy spirit."[31] In *Reveries of the Solitary Walker,* Rousseau explains that leisurely, aimless, even "errant" walking is a form of thinking.[32] Suffering ill health, besieged by critics, and fearful of political unrest, Rousseau fled to the Ile Saint-Pierre in the autumn of 1765. On this island retreat, he attempted to regain some semblance of order and stability by studying botany. In the reverie of his fifth walk, he writes,

> Not wanting to spend the time on serious work, I needed some agreeable pastime which would give me no more trouble than an idler likes to give himself. I set out to compose a *Flora Pertinsularis* and to describe every single plant on the island in enough detail to keep me busy for the rest of my days. . . . I could have written [a book] about every grass in the meadows, every moss in the woods, every lichen covering the rocks—and I did not leave even one blade of grass or atom of vegetation without a full and detailed description. In accordance with this noble plan, every morning after breakfast . . . I would set out with a magnifying glass in my hand and my *Systema Naturae* under my arm to study one particular section of the island.[33]

Sebald stresses the Apollonian motivation for Rousseau's efforts. "The central motif of this passage is not so much the impartial insight into the indigenous plants of the island as that of ordering, classification, and the creation of a perfect system. Thus this apparently innocent occupation—the deliberate resolve no longer to think and merely to look at nature—becomes, for the writer plagued by the heroic need to think and work, a demanding rationalistic project involving the compiling of lists, indices, and catalogs, along with the precise description of, for example, long stamens of self-heal, the springiness of those of nettle and of wall-pellitory, and the sudden bursting of seed capsules of balsam and of beech."[34] I am more impressed by the Dionysian effect plants had on Rousseau. He concludes his reverie by adding, "Nothing could be more extraordinary than the raptures and ecstasies I felt at every discovery I made about the structure and organization of the sexual parts in the process of reproduction, which was completely new to me at this time."[35]

Thoreau shared Rousseau's passion for walking and often was enraptured by plants, leaves, and wild fruits he discovered in untended fields and woods. In his essay "Walking," published shortly before his death, he described the art of walking in religious terms. "I have met with but one or two persons in the course of my life who understood the art of Walking, that is, of taking walks—who had a genius, so to speak for SAUNTERING, which word is beautifully derived 'from idle people who roved about the country in the Middle Ages, and asked charity, under the pretense of going a la Saint Terre' to the Holy Land."[36] For Thoreau, the Holy Land is not a distant realm, but is all around him. On September 7, 1851, as he was beginning the decade-long project that would result in his posthumous last work, *Wild Fruits*, he explained the religious motivation for his life's work in words well worth heeding in today's high-speed world.

> The art of spending a day! If it is possible that we may be addressed, it behooves us to be attentive. If by watching all day and all night, I may detect some trace of the Ineffable, then will it not be worth the while to watch? Watch and pray without ceasing? . . .

> If by patience, if by watching I can secure one new ray of
> light, can feel myself elevated for an instant upon Pisgah, the
> world which was dead prose to me become living and divine,
> shall I not watch ever—shall I not be a watching man hence-
> forth? . . . We are surrounded by a rich and fertile mystery.
> May we not probe it, pry into it, employ ourselves about it—a
> little? To devote your life to the discovery of the divinity in
> Nature or to the eating of oysters: would they not be attended
> with very different results? . . .
>
> My profession is to be always on the alert to find God in
> nature—to know his lurking places.[37]

Thoreau's spiritual preoccupations did not overshadow his scientific interests; to the contrary, he always believed religion, art, and science are complementary and mutually illuminating.

Like Rousseau, Thoreau was obsessed with knowing "the species of
every twig and plant."[38] Place matters as much, indeed, perhaps more, for
Thoreau as for Melville. His ambition was to develop a comprehensive
natural history of Concord and the surrounding area. Toward this end, he
read widely in the history of natural philosophy as well as recent scientific
literature. Following Goethe, he gathered his observations during long
walks and recorded them in his journal. The fields and woods around Concord were for Thoreau what the South Seas and distant islands were for
Melville. Traveling far and wide while rarely leaving home, he begins
Wild Fruits, "As I sail the unexplored sea of Concord, many a dell and
swamp and wooded hill is my Ceram and Amboyna. Famous fruits imported from the East or South and sold in our markets—as oranges, lemons,
pine-apples, and bananas—do not concern me so much as many an unnoticed
wild berry whose beauty annually lends a new charm to some wild walk or
which I have found to be palatable to an outdoor taste. We cultivate imported
shrubs in our front yards for the beauty of their berries, while at least equally
beautiful berries grow unregarded by us in the surrounding fields."[39] As this
remark suggests, Thoreau is less concerned with the exotic than with the local, and is more interested in wild than in cultivated fruits. He was always

suspicious of whatever was civilized, and was constantly drawn to the wild. As he famously declared in "Walking," again using a nautical metaphor, "Wildness is the preservation of the World. Every tree sends its fibers forth in search of the Wild. The cities import it at any price. Men plow and sail for it. From the forest and wilderness come the tonics and barks which brace mankind." In his last work, Thoreau confronts, but does not acknowledge, a fundamental paradox: in naming and cataloging wild fruits, he negates the very wildness he is dedicated to preserving.

Wild Fruits is the strangest work I have considered in this book. Neither simply fact nor fiction, prose nor poetry, science nor literature, it combines all this and more to create a parable that, like *Walden,* plots the course of life and death according to the rhythms of changing seasons. Ten years of hiking, writing, and reflecting lie behind this work. In the early 1850s, Thoreau began collecting information about all the plants, flowers, trees, and fruits in and around Concord. After identifying the flora and fauna in the area, he recorded the annual life cycle of plants, trees, flowers, and fruits from 1852 to 1861. This material eventually grew to seven hundred and fifty pages for trees, and six hundred pages for wild fruits.[40] He organized the data in large charts, which he used when writing about what he had discovered. His records are meticulous, noting the precise day leaves begin to change their color, fall, and start to bud again year after year. There is neither an overarching narrative nor an overall theory to integrate what he observed. The work is more of a compendium with separate sections devoted to different plants and fruits than a book with a consistent argument. He labels each specimen with both its Latin and English names, and records his observations in impressive detail. In the published version of the work, many of the entries are accompanied by elegant drawings.

While interested in all plants and fruits, Thoreau was especially intrigued by wild apples. He spent the last weeks of his life completing an article entitled "Wild Apples," which was published only one month before he died, and was included in his posthumous *Wild Fruits.* In this essay, he departs from the style of scientific field notes and lets his imagination roam more freely.

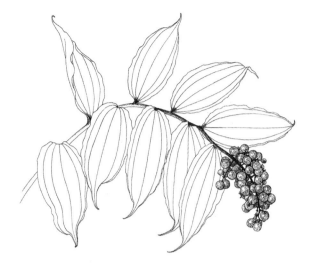

From Henry David Thoreau, *Wild Fruits* (pen and ink drawing by Abigail Rorer)

From my experience with wild apples, I can understand that there may be reasons for a savage's preferring many kinds of food which the civilized man rejects. The former has the palate of an outdoor man. It takes a savage or wild taste to appreciate a wild fruit. What a healthy out-of-door appetite it takes to relish the apple of life, the apple of the world, then! . . .

So there is one thought for the field, another for the house. I would have my thoughts, like wild apples, to be food for walkers and will not warrant them to be palatable if tasted in the house. . . .

Apples, these I mean, unspeakably fair—apples not of Discord but of Concord. (87)

As a result of grafting, by the 1850s, there were at least one thousand different kinds of apples in the United States.[41] Most people at the time did not know, or had forgotten the names of these apples. In addition to the known varieties, there were countless wild apples that had never been named. Like Adam standing in the Garden of Eden, Thoreau gave these wild apples Latin names, but unlike Linnaeus, he was less interested in advancing scientific knowledge than in reveling in nature's extraordinary prodigality.

Thoreau's ambition was as excessive as nature "herself." His aim was to write a new scripture for the New World by translating the Book of Nature into his own words. It is important to stress that he saw this exercise as exegesis rather than eisegesis; that is to say, he sought to uncover instead of impose the universal laws by which nature operates. He believed this is possible because he was convinced that mind and matter are not opposites, as Descartes and many others had argued, but are correlative embodiments of the same universal structural and developmental principles. For Thoreau, as for Hegel and his idealistic followers, mind comes to know itself in matter, and matter becomes self-conscious in mind. When interpreted in religious and artistic terms, this is a sacramental process in which the finite and the infinite are brought together through an eternal incarnational process. Referring to English writer and gardener John Evelyn's *Kalendarium Hortense, or Gardner's Almanack* (1664), which was an important resource for him, Thoreau writes, "There will be some reference to it, by way of a parable or otherwise, in my New Testament. Surely, it is a defect in our Bible that it is not truly ours, but a Hebrew Bible. The most pertinent illustrations for us are to be drawn, not from Egypt or Babylonia, but from New England."[42] The most pertinent illustration of this new gospel in *Wild Fruits* is the wild apple. In the much-overlooked wild apple, Thoreau sees heaven on earth. If renewal is to be found, it will not be in an otherworldly redemption, but in a reconciliation with the cycles of nature embodied in "the gnarliest" apple. In Thoreau's parable, the apple is the symbol of renewal, rather than of evil temptation—his "apples not of Discord but of Concord." "Bring me an apple from the tree of life," he sings (87).

Thoreau sees in wild apples what Nietzsche discovered in Dionysian grapes. Anticipating Nietzsche's critique of nihilism, Thoreau confidently declares, "Talk of heaven! ye disgrace earth."[43] Thoreau's gospel is the cure for unhappy consciousness; the Real, he insists, is not elsewhere—in the heavens or depths, in the past or the future—but is utterly pedestrian and, thus, is present here-and-now on, and, indeed, in *earth*. "Above all," Thoreau warns in a moment of terrible suffering with his life slipping away, "we cannot afford not to live in the present. He is blessed over all mortals who loses no moment of the passing life in remembering the past. Unless our philosophy hears the cock crow in every barnyard within our horizon, it is belated. That sound commonly reminds us that we are growing rusty and antique in our employments and habits of thoughts. His philosophy comes down to a more recent time than ours. There is something suggested by it that is a newer testament,—the gospel according to this moment. He has not fallen astern; he has got up early and kept up early, and to be where he is is to be in season, in the foremost rank of time. It is an expression of the health and soundness of Nature, a brag for all the world,—healthiness as of a spring burst forth, a new foundation of the Muses, to celebrate this last instant of time."[44] To live "the gospel according to this moment" even at "the last instant of time" is to realize that

The miracle is, that what is *is*.[45]

The present of this presence, which is outside of time in time, is what Virginia Woolf described as a moment of Being. She might have been thinking of Thoreau's last work when she wrote, "To watch a leaf quivering in the rush of air was an exquisite joy."[46] For Thoreau, not even the shadow of death could dispel this joy. In a passage I have quoted above, Nietzsche summarizes the vision toward which Thoreau as well as I have been steadily moving. Sometimes it takes a madman to speak the truth.

> Did you ever say "Yes" to one joy? Oh my friends, then you also said "Yes" to *all* pain. All things are entwined, enmeshed, enamored—
>
> —did you ever want Once to be Twice, did you ever say "I love you, bliss—instant—flash—" then you wanted *everything* back.
>
> —Everything anew, everything forever, everything entwined, enmeshed, enamored—oh, thus you love the world—

—you everlasting ones, thus you love it forever and for
all time; even to pain you say: Refrain but—come again! *For joy
accepts everlasting flow!*[47]

Leaves

"The purest October light everywhere," Nietzsche reflected with the end
approaching, "I am the most grateful man in the world, in an autumnal
mood in every good sense of the word; it is my great harvest time."[48] For
Thoreau, as for Nietzsche, autumn and winter came early. Thoreau died at
forty-four, the same age Nietzsche went mad. Thoreau knew he was dying,
and Nietzsche must have known he was losing his mind. Even with darkness
descending, the glow of autumn light was no longer merely melancholy.

Thoreau suffered ill health much of his life. On April 12, 1861, the
Civil War broke out. An ardent supporter of John Brown, Thoreau was dedicated to the abolitionist cause, but health problems prevented him from
joining other volunteers from Concord. What was diagnosed as bronchitis
was actually tuberculosis.[49] When his doctor recommended that he spend
time in a better climate, Thoreau, incongruously, decided to travel to Minnesota. When he returned to Concord, his health was worse than ever.
Nonetheless, he continued to collect material for his grand project until
January 1862, and sent his final four articles to the *Atlantic Monthly* between
February 20 ("Autumnal Tints") and April 2, 1862 ("Wild Apples"). News
of his failing health was widespread throughout New England and beyond.
When he no longer was able to write, he dictated his thoughts to his sister
Sophia. "Autumn leaves," he quietly reflected, "teach us how to die." Too
weak to read by himself, he asked his last surviving sibling to read to him
from *A Week on the Concord and Merrimack Rivers.* When death finally arrived, his sister knew what to do. With time running out, her brother had
written, "I confess that I love to be convinced of this inextinguishable vitality in Nature. I would rather that my body should be buried in a soil thus
wide awake than in a mere inert dead earth."[50] His last hope was that others
might learn from his life what he had learned from autumn leaves—"We
are all the richer for their decay."

We end where we began—in a cemetery; no iron fence surrounds this final resting place, and matters are not quite as grave as they once seemed.[51] "Autumnal Tints" is one of Thoreau's most beautiful and memorable essays. Though he began working on it in 1857, the essay was not published until four months before his death. Clearly aware that the end was near, Thoreau once again turned to leaves to learn what lessons in leaving they teach. I quote it at length not only because it is an effective summary of Thoreau's final vision, but also because it draws together so many of the issues I have been probing throughout *Last Works*.

It is pleasant to walk over the beds of these fresh, crisp, and rustling leaves. How beautifully they go to their graves! How gently lay themselves down and turn to mold!—painted of a thousand hues, and fit to make the beds of us living. So they troop to their last resting place, light and frisky. They put on no weeds, but merrily they go scampering over the earth, selecting the spot, choosing the lot, ordering no iron fence, whispering all through the woods about it,—some choosing the spot where the bodies of men are moldering beneath, and meeting them half-way. How many flutterings before they rest quietly in their graves! They that soared so loftily, how contentedly they return to dust again, and are laid low, resigned to lie and decay at the foot of the tree, and afford nourishment to new generations of their kind, as well as to flutter on high! They teach us how to die. One wonders if the time will ever come when men, with their boasted faith in immortality, will lie down as gracefully and as ripe,—with such an Indian-summer serenity will shed their bodies, as they do their hair and nails.

When the leaves fall, the whole earth is a cemetery pleasant to walk in. I love to wander and muse over them in their graves. Here are no lying nor vain epitaphs. What though you own no lot at Mount Auburn? Your lot is surely cast somewhere in this vast cemetery, which has been consecrated from of old. You need attend no auction to secure a place. There is room

Henry David Thoreau's grave

enough here. The Loose-strife shall bloom and the Huckleberry-
bird sing over your bones. The wood man and hunter shall be
your sextons, and the children shall tread upon the borders as
much as they will. Let us walk in the cemetery of the leaves,—
this is your true Greenwood Cemetery.[52]

All that now remains is a simple gravestone bearing the name "Henry."
And, of course, the leaves of his books.

Works Last

Lessons Learned

W H Y   W R I T E ?   W H Y   N O T   W R I T E ? When to begin? When to end? How to begin? How to end?

The writing that matters—and much does not, especially when time is, as always, short—is not a choice. It is the response to a demand, a demand whose origin is obscure and whose end never arrives. The demand, which seems to approach from elsewhere, is distant in its nearness; it is not expressed in words that can be clearly understood; rather, it appears as a rustling that is difficult to distinguish from noise, white noise whose silence cannot be silenced. The unending murmur of this noise creates an infinite restlessness that leaves everything unfinished.

The demand "Write!" summons but cannot be summoned. Serious writing is always a matter of timing, though time is not at the disposal of the writer, or anyone else. The moment of writing cannot be planned, plotted, or projected. It arrives unexpectedly as a gift that both astonishes and unsettles. This gift imposes an obligation that cannot be avoided because refusal is as much a response as acceptance.

If one listens long enough to writers who matter, it seems that when the moment comes, it is impossible for them not to write. Indeed, the only writers really worth reading are writers who cannot not write. True writers are obsessed, even possessed by something or someone they can neither know nor name. This obsession, this possession borders on delirium, which allows no rest. Writers tend to be insomniacs whose minds speed up until they approach the tipping point. Just as there is no on-switch for the demand to write, so there is no off-switch when thoughts become overwhelming. Ideas whirl and swirl, creating a fatigue no rest relieves. Moments, hours, days, nights of wakefulness while others sleep are intervals of solitude essential for writing. In a world filled with distractions, solitude is what everyone finally shares. Each individual arrives and departs alone, even when in the presence of others. The writer cultivates rather than avoids solitude because significant work must be done alone, in a room of one's own, facing a blank page whose emptiness words never fill.

In the depths of solitude, the writer hears voices of the ghosts who haunt him. Words are never merely one's own, but are always also the words of others both remembered and forgotten. In this way, words resurrect the dead who live through the writer, even as the writer lives through them. Spirits haunt the interstices of memory, allowing writers to write, and preventing them from revealing their ghosts' secrets. Though not all ghosts are holy, writing is the incarnation and reincarnation of what once was called the Word.

When those closest to the writer ask what keeps him awake, all he can say is, "Nothing." Nothing but nothing. If nothing becomes an obsession by becoming everything, if the void fills life by emptying it, if (the) all is *about* nothing, the writer—but not only the writer—is seized by dread. Fear and trembling infect and inflect her words, making them oscillate, alternate, waver. When writing *about* nothing, communication inevitably becomes indirect. Never simple or straightforward, words are complex, nuanced, and (k)not(-)ted in webs within webs that create labyrinths with no exits. Like dreams that always harbor something else, indirect communication throws everything and everyone off center through a play of *fort-da*.

Real writing is fraught with paradox—its failure is success, its success is failure. This failure is not merely the author's, but also the failure of language itself. The challenge of writing is to make language fail revealingly. What keeps writing in play is not what can be known, but what remains unknowable, not what can be said, but what cannot be said, not what can be named, but what is never named. When writing works, it occasions the impossible experience of what repeatedly slips away from thought and language. The writer struggles to represent the unrepresentable with words that are never adequate. The lack of words is the tear in the text that delays and defers its closure. Writers who claim to mend this tear, wipe away this tear are confidence-men peddling counterfeit notes. True writers know we live in a world without redemption where there is no cure short of death.

With the end always approaching, the writer must learn to wait, to wait without expectation for the arrival of what cannot be imagined. Writing can never be rushed; it requires piety, patience, and practice. Thoughts must simmer until they reach the boiling point; there is no recipe for this process—it either happens, or it does not. If the moment arrives, writing becomes urgent, for the writer knows that this moment, like life itself, vanishes as quickly as it appears, and when it is gone it can never be recovered.

Passion moves the writer; she does not write so much as she is written. Words she did not know she knew arrive unexpectedly from an elsewhere that now is near, but no more than near. In the heat of the moment, hand cannot keep up with mind. It is as if the writer were taking dictation from someone speaking faster than any human being can record. The writer neither possesses nor processes words; rather, words that cannot be processed possess the writer. In the intensity of the moment, the writer does not know what, if anything, comes next.

Writing is always a lesson in leaving, and every book is a house of leaves. Page after page, book after book, the leaves pile up until the slightest breeze sweeps them away unread. All too often, letters do not arrive at their destination, and either end up in the dead letter box, or are returned to the sender unopened. A mere four hundred copies of the greatest American novel ever written! What writer would not fall silent?

What is the work of art? Where is the work of art? What is art's end? What does it mean for (a) work to end? What does it mean for (a) work to last?

Far from a finished product, the work of art is an unending process whose infinite demand leaves it forever unfinished. The gift of the demand creates a debt that imposes guilt whose other name is desire. Desire is the presence of absence, and the absence of presence that keeps the writer working. For the writer, research is always the search for an uncanny something that can never be found as long as life continues. Completion, Immanence, Waiting, Ghosts, Trembling, Delirium, Wavering, Speed, Silence, Earth. Eros becoming Thanatos, Thanatos becoming Eros. In this moment, the writer does not write about experience—writing becomes the experience that obsesses the writer. No matter how high the high, the moment inevitably passes, leaving a sweet melancholy that always longs for more. This is as close to the Real as the writer gets in a world the gods have fled. The draw of this instant makes writing addictive, and the dream of the return of this here-and-now is what makes it so difficult to stop writing.

Last works. Works last. Since the end arrives unexpectedly, like a thief in the night, every work written, every work read might be the last work. Works that last are as demanding as the demand to which they respond. They must be read and reread because with every return, they reveal something that had gone unnoticed. Writers worth reading do not throw readers a lifeline. Their words are not designed to close the gap, fill the hole, erase the void; to the contrary, their tangled lines draw readers toward "some never-to-be-imparted secret, whose attainment is destruction." The most important works come from troubled lives, and trouble the lives of mindful readers. These works should give readers pause, for they are dangerous and can become labyrinths with neither center nor exit. When writing works, and usually it does not, it changes both writer and reader in ways that cannot be predicted. Readers beware: approach such works with caution because they take you elsewhere and make it impossible to return to where you thought you were.

True works of art cannot be skimmed or summarized; the reader must be as patient as the writer. Reading, like writing, has a pace, a rhythm of its own; it must be slow, deliberate, reflective. Pauses become as pregnant as phrases. Errant words, sentences, paragraphs are masks of what cannot be unmasked. They show the way by leading astray, like woodland paths leading nowhere.

The purpose of writing is writing. The book is not one but many— the writer rewrites the works of others who haunt him, and his hope is that his work will haunt others he will never know. While the book ends, the work is unending. Works that matter last—they have an afterlife in other

Mark C. Taylor, *neXus*

writers and readers. Incarnation becomes the reincarnation of words in a process that is eternal, even if the writer is not.

Words both reveal and conceal the silence that is our beginning and our end. "We know not yet what we have done," Thoreau muses, "still less what we are doing. Wait till evening, and other parts of our day's work will shine than we had thought at noon, and we shall discover the real purport of our toil. As when the farmer has reached the end of the furrow and looks back, he can tell best where the pressed earth shines the most."[1] With the end that never arrives approaching, it might be possible to return to the beginning and know unknowing for the first time.

P. S.

December 5, 2015

Memento mori. These words were written very early this morning, as light once again slowly dispelled darkness on the Berkshire Mountains, where I live and work. Today is the tenth anniversary of my first death day, and eight days before the seventieth anniversary of my birth day. Threescore ten. The past decade has been life after death for me. I did not plan to write today, but during the night I awoke, as I often do, and jotted a note on the pad of paper beside my bed. When I got up this morning, I read: "Writing is not a choice, it is the response to a demand whose origin is obscure and whose end never arrives." For more years than I remember, for more pages than I can count, I have been trying to understand that demand. By the time I settled at my desk in the barn that is my study, the words that have been written were there waiting for me.

Not all writing is truly writing; when words are real, they arrive from elsewhere, leaving the writer passive even when he appears active. As I have explained, I thought I had written my last work years ago, but I was granted a temporary reprieve—by whom or by what, I have no idea. Nor do I know if this is my last work, if these are my last words. No one ever knows. The biggest surprise of having died without dying has been the discovery of how liberating the experience or non-experience of death has been. "Death," Kierkegaard wrote, "is a good dancing partner." Sometimes the dance is fatal, but sometimes the dance imparts a gay wisdom that allows you to say "Yes! Yes! Yes!" to what little time remains. In this moment, at this instant, the gift of death is the gift of life. This, I believe, is the meaning of grace.

Notes

In translations and works where multiple editions exist, I have sometimes used a variant of the cited source.

Errant Reflections

1. Ernest Hemingway, *Death in the Afternoon* (New York: Scribner, 2003), 278.
2. Ray Kurzweil, *Fantastic Voyage: Live Long Enough to Live Forever* (New York: Plume, 2005).

Chapter 1. Completion

1. Søren Kierkegaard, *The Soul of Kierkegaard: Selections from His Journals,* ed. Alexander Dru (Mineola, NY: 2003), 121.
2. Kierkegaard, *Journals and Papers,* trans. Howard and Edna Hong (Princeton, NJ: Princeton University Press, 1966ff.), no. 5645.
3. Quoted in Josiah Thompson, *Kierkegaard* (New York: Knopf, 1973), 27.
4. Quoted in Thompson, *Kierkegaard,* 37.
5. Kierkegaard, *Journals and Papers,* no. 5430.
6. Kierkegaard's birthday was May 5, 1813.
7. Søren Kierkegaard, *Stages on Life's Way,* trans. Walter Lowrie (New York: Schocken Books, 1967), 236–37.
8. Søren Kierkegaard, *The Concept of Anxiety,* trans. Reidar Tomte (Princeton, NJ: Princeton University Press, 1980). Kierkegaard's analysis of dread anticipates Freud's famous interpretation of the uncanny. See Freud, "The Uncanny," *The Second Edition of the Complete Psychological Works of Sigmund Freud,* vol. 17, ed. J. Strachey (London: Hogarth Press, 1964).
9. Kierkegaard, *Journals and Papers,* no. 5149.
10. Karl Abraham and Maria Torok, *The Wolf Man's Magic Word,* trans. Nicolas Rand (Minneapolis: University of Minnesota Press, 2005), xxv.
11. Kierkegaard, *Soul of Kierkegaard,* 22.
12. Kierkegaard, *Journals and Papers,* II A 243; Joakim Garff, *Søren Kierkegaard: A Biography,* trans. Bruce Kirmmse (Princeton, NJ: Princeton University Press, 2005), 131.

13. Søren Kierkegaard, *Attack upon Christendom,* trans. Walter Lowrie (Princeton, NJ: Princeton University Press, 1968), 139.

14. Søren Kierkegaard, *Two Ages: The Age of Revolution and the Present Age, A Literary Review,* trans. Howard and Edna Hong (Princeton, NJ: Princeton University Press, 1978), 88.

15. Kierkegaard, *Attack upon Christendom,* 139.

16. Søren Kierkegaard, *The Present Age,* trans. Howard and Edna Hong (Princeton, NJ: Princeton University Press, 1978), 104.

17. Kierkegaard, *Journals and Papers,* no. 6511.

18. Søren Kierkegaard, *The Point of View of My Work as an Author: A Report to History,* trans. Walter Lowrie (New York: Harper Torchbooks, 1962), 24–25.

19. Søren Kierkegaard, *Stages on Life's Way,* trans. Howard and Edna Hong (Princeton, NJ: Princeton University Press, 1988), 8.

20. Kierkegaard, *Papers and Journals,* no. 654.

21. Søren Kierkegaard, *Concluding Unscientific Postscript,* trans. David Swenson and Walter Lowrie (Princeton, NJ: Princeton University Press, 1971), 550. The pseudonymous authorship includes: *Either/Or* I, II (1843), *Fear and Trembling* (1843), *Repetition* (1843), *Philosophical Fragments* (1844), *The Concept of Anxiety* (2844), and *Stages on Life's Way* (1845).

22. Søren Kierkegaard, *Philosophical Fragments,* trans. David F. Swenson (Princeton, NJ: Princeton University Press, 1967), 89.

23. Kierkegaard, *Journals and Papers,* no. 4806.

24. Søren Kierkegaard, *Training in Christianity,* trans. Walter Lowrie (Princeton, NJ: Princeton University Press, 1967), 134.

25. Kierkegaard, *Journals and Papers,* no. 4087.

26. The following biographical details about Kierkegaard's life are drawn primarily but not exclusively from Garff, *Søren Kierkegaard.*

27. Quoted in Garff, *Søren Kierkegaard,* 729.

28. Søren Kierkegaard, *The Moment,* trans. Howard and Edna Hong (Princeton, NJ: Princeton University Press, 1998), 5–6.

29. Kierkegaard, *The Moment,* 101. "Both-and" is Kierkegaard's shorthand for Hegel's reconciliation of opposites.

30. Kierkegaard, *Journals and Papers,* no. 4680.

31. Kierkegaard, *Journals and Papers,* no. 4711.

32. Jacques Derrida, *The Beast and the Sovereign,* II, trans. Geoffrey Bennington (Chicago: University of Chicago Press, 2010), 68.

33. Kierkegaard, *The Moment,* 212.

34. Peter Sloterdijk, *You Must Change Your Life,* trans. Wieland Hoban (Malden, MA: Polity, 2013), 203.

35. Kierkegaard, *Journals and Papers,* no. 6969.

36. Quoted in Garff, *Søren Kierkegaard,* 789. I have followed Garff in this account of Kierkegaard's death.

37. Quoted in Garff, *Søren Kierkegaard,* 811.

Chapter 2. Immanence

1. Friedrich Nietzsche, *Ecce Homo: How One Becomes What One Is,* trans. Walter Kaufmann (New York: Random House, 1969), 303. Hereafter, references to this work are given in the text.

2. Ernest Hemingway, *Death in the Afternoon* (New York: Scribner, 1960), 4.

3. In summarizing the biographical details of Nietzsche's life, I have drawn on: R. J. Hollingdale, *Nietzsche: The Man and His Philosophy* (New York: Cambridge University Press, 1999); David Krell and Donald Bates, *The Good European: Nietzsche's Work Sites in Word and Image* (Chicago: University of Chicago Press, 1997); and Lesley Chamberlin, *Nietzsche in Turin: An Intimate Biography* (New York: Picador, 1996), as well as details from Nietzsche's own writings.

4. Quoted in Hollingdale, *Nietzsche,* 9–10.

5. Dimitri Hemelsoet et al., "The Neurological Illness of Friedrich Nietzsche," http://www.researchgate.net/profile/Dimitri_Hemelsoet/publication /5279485_The_neurological_illness_of_Friedrich_Nietzsche/links /09e415140c32673eb0000000.pdf, 13.

6. Krell and Bates, *The Good European,* 205. In addition to a narrative of Nietzsche's life, this work includes beautiful photographs of places Nietzsche visited and lived.

7. Hollingdale, *Nietzsche,* 220.

8. Quoted in Krell and Bates, *The Good European,* 209.

9. See Chamberlin, *Nietzsche in Turin,* 212–18, for further details.

10. Quoted in Hollingdale, *Nietzsche,* 238.

11. *The Portable Nietzsche,* ed. Walter Kaufmann (New York: Penguin, 1980), 685, 687.

12. Hemelsoet et al., "The Neurological Illness of Friedrich Nietzsche," 11.

13. Quoted in Hollingdale, *Nietzsche,* 246, 247.

14. Quoted in Hollingdale, *Nietzsche,* 253.

15. Chamberlin, *Nietzsche in Turin,* 186.

16. This passage and the previous one are quoted in Chamberlin, *Nietzsche in Turin.* I have followed Chamberlin's account of the final chapter in Nietzsche's troubled relationship with Elisabeth.

17. Friedrich Nietzsche, *The Gay Science,* trans. Walter Kaufmann (New York: Random House, 1974), 181.

18. This reading of the relation between Nietzsche and Hegel runs counter to the interpretation popularized by Derrida and Deleuze. See Jacques Derrida, *Spurs: Nietzsche's Styles,* trans. Barbara Harlow (Chicago: University of Chicago Press, 1978), and Gilles Deleuze, *Nietzsche and Philosophy* (New York: Columbia University Press, 1983).

19. Friedrich Nietzsche, *The Anti-Christ: The Portable Nietzsche* (New York: Penguin, 1980), 612.

20. Søren Kierkegaard, *Concluding Unscientific Postscript,* trans. David Swenson (Princeton, NJ: Princeton University Press, 1968), 182.

21. Friedrich Nietzsche, *The Will to Power,* trans. Walter Kaufmann (New York: Random House, 1967), 267.

22. Nietzsche, *The Will to Power,* 302.

23. Nietzsche, *The Will to Power,* 323.

24. Nietzsche, *The Will to Power,* 7, 9.

25. G. W. F. Hegel, *Phenomenology of Spirit,* trans. A. V. Miller (New York: Oxford University Press, 1977), 455.

26. Hegel, *Phenomenology of Spirit,* 126, 127. Translation modified.

27. Friedrich Nietzsche, *Twilight of the Idols,* trans. Walter Kaufmann (New York: Penguin Books, 1968), 627.

28. Nietzsche, *The Anti-Christ,* 573, 630.

29. Nietzsche, *Twilight of the Idols,* 535.

30. Hegel, *Phenomenology of Spirit,* 27, 19.

31. Friedrich Nietzsche, *The Birth of Tragedy,* trans. Francis Golffing (New York: Doubleday, 1956), 9, 41.

32. Nietzsche, *The Birth of Tragedy,* 23–24.

33. Nietzsche, *Twilight of the Idols,* 481.

34. Nietzsche, *The Will to Power,* 542–43.

35. Nietzsche, *Twilight of the Idols,* 605, 554.

36. Nietzsche, *The Anti-Christ,* 616, 609.

37. Nietzsche, *The Will to Power,* 99.

38. Nietzsche, *Dionysos Dithyrambs,* http://www.thenietzschechannel.com/works-pub/dd/dd.htm.

39. These sculptures are part of a multi-faceted work entitled *neXus,* which was part of an exhibition, *Sensing Place,* at the Francis and Sterling Clark Institute (July 4–October 10, 2016). I discuss this work in *Recovering Place: Reflections on Stone Hill* (New York: Columbia University Press, 2014).

40. Friedrich Nietzsche, *Thus Spoke Zarathustra,* trans. Marianne Cowan (Chicago: Henry Regnery, 1957), 335.

Chapter 3. Waiting

1. Throughout this chapter, references to Blanchot's works are given in the text. These are the editions and abbreviations I have used:

   D: *The Instant of My Death*/Jacques Derrida, *Demeure: Fiction and Testimony,* trans. Elizabeth Rottenberg (Stanford, CA: Stanford University Press, 1998).

   F: *Friendship,* trans. Elizabeth Rottenberg (Stanford, CA: Stanford University Press, 1997).

   G: *The Gaze of Orpheus and Other Literary Essays,* trans. Lydia Davis (Barrytown, NY: Station Hill Press, 1981).

   I: "The Instant of My Death," trans. Elizabeth Rottenberg (Stanford, CA: Stanford University Press, 1998).

   IC: *The Infinite Conversation,* trans. Susan Hanson (Minneapolis: University of Minnesota Press, 1993), 278.

   O: *Awaiting Oblivion,* trans. John Gregg (Lincoln: University of Nebraska Press, 1997).

   PA: *The Step/Not Beyond,* trans. Lycette Nelson (Albany: State University of New York, 1992).

   SL: *The Space of Literature,* trans. Ann Smock (Lincoln: University of Nebraska Press, 1982).

   TO: *Thomas the Obscure,* trans. Robert Lamberton (New York: David Lewis, 1973).

   WD: *The Writing of the Disaster,* trans. Ann Smock (Lincoln: University of Nebraska Press, 1986).

2. *Récit* means account, story, narrative, and report. It derives from *reciter,* which means recite, rehearse, repeater, and recount. *Citer* means quote, name, and point out. The "re" of *récit* suggests that the work is not original but is secondary to something that is antecedent to it. Writing, therefore, is always an afterword to something that forever eludes it. Blanchot's *Thomas l'obscur* was first published in 1941 as a *roman*; in 1950 Blanchot revised it and made it into a *récit.*

3. http://www.egs.edu/library/maurice-blanchot/biography.

4. Jacques Derrida, "A Witness Forever," *Nowhere Without No,* ed. Kevin Hart (Sydney: Vagabond Press, 2003), 42.

5. Maurice Blanchot, "Kierkegaard's 'Journals,'" *Faux Pas,* trans. Charlotte Mandell (Stanford, CA: Stanford University Press, 2001), 18.

6. Blanchot, "Kierkegaard's 'Journals,'" 19, 20.

7. Maurice Blanchot, "The Essential Solitude," *The Space of Literature,* trans. Ann Smock (Lincoln: University of Nebraska Press, 1982), 27.

8. Blanchot, "Kierkegaard's 'Journals,'" 19.

9. John Updike, "Some Nachtmusik, from All Over," *Hugging the Shore* (New York: Knopf, 1983), 546.

10. Friedrich Nietzsche, *Twilight of the Idols,* trans. Walter Kaufmann (New York: Penguin Books, 1968), 468.

11. Jacques Derrida, *Positions,* trans. Alan Bass (Chicago: University of Chicago Press, 1972), 77; *The Writing of the Disaster.*

12. G. W. F. Hegel, *Phenomenology of Spirit,* 19.

13. Hegel, *Phenomenology of Spirit,* 59–60.

14. This is one of the reasons the book is theological. One of the likely origins of the word "religion" derives from the Latin *religare,* to bind back: *re* (back) + *ligare* (to bind). Of course, as Blanchot teaches, one must always be suspicious of origins.

15. Throughout his works, Blanchot and Derrida play with associations among a "host" of words related to *"hotel"—hostile, hostilite, hospice, hôte,* which designates, among many other things, the communion wafer, and, by extension, the English word "ghost." For a helpful analysis of the implications of these words, see J. Hillis Miller, "The Critic as Host," *Deconstruction and Criticism* (New York: Continuum, 1984), 217–53; and Michel Serres, *The Parasite* (Baltimore: Johns Hopkins University Press, 2007).

16. Maurice Blanchot, *L'Attente l'oubli* (Paris: Gallimard, 1962), 158.

Chapter 4. Ghosts

1. Mark St. Germain, *Freud's Last Session* (Dramatists Play Service, 2010), 12–13.

2. Freud's rebellious sons included, among others, Otto Rank, Carl Jung, Karl Abraham, and Sandor Ferenczi.

3. Quoted in Peter Gay, *Freud: A Life for Our Time* (New York: Norton, 2006), 46. In developing this account of Freud's life, I have drawn on Gay's superb biography as well as Mark Edmundson, *The Death of Sigmund Freud: The*

Legacy of His Last Days. While I disagree with Edmundson's interpretation of *Moses and Monotheism,* his study includes valuable biographical information.

4. Otto's father, Ludwig, founded the Bellevue Clinic in 1857, which was located on the grounds of an Augustinian monastery and remained in the control of the family until 1980. Otto's nephew, also named Ludwig, was a leading existential analyst who was influenced by Husserl, Heidegger, and Buber.

5. Cited in Gay, *Freud,* 12, 9.

6. Gay, *Freud,* 118.

7. Gay, *Freud,* 618.

8. Gay, *Freud,* 619.

9. Gay, *Freud,* 58, 59, 156.

10. Quoted in Edmundson, *The Death of Sigmund Freud,* 156.

11. Gay, *Freud,* 417–18.

12. Quoted in Gay, *Freud,* 422.

13. Quoted in Gay, *Freud,* 624.

14. Quoted in Gay, *Freud,* 640.

15. Virginia Woolf, *The Diary of Virginia Woolf,* vol. 5: *1936–1941,* ed. Anne Bell (New York: Harcourt Brace Jovanovich, 1984), 202.

16. Quoted in Gay, *Freud,* 641.

17. Quoted in Gay, *Freud,* 643.

18. Sigmund Freud, *The Interpretation of Dreams,* trans. James Strachey (New York: Avon Books, 1965), 311–12, 143 n.

19. Sigmund Freud, *Beyond the Pleasure Principle,* trans. James Strachey (New York: Norton, 1961), 1.

20. Freud, *Beyond the Pleasure Principle,* 14, 15, 26, 27.

21. Freud, *Beyond the Pleasure Principle,* 52.

22. Freud, *Beyond the Pleasure Principle,* 28, 30, 32, 33, 34–35, 47.

23. G. W. F. Hegel, "Love," *Early Theological Writings,* trans. T. M. Knox (Chicago: University of Chicago Press, 1948), 307.

24. Sigmund Freud, *Moses and Monotheism,* trans. Katherine Jones (New York: Random House, 1967), 132. Throughout this section, citations to this work are given in the text in parentheses.

25. Gay, *Freud,* 608.

26. Sigmund Freud, *Moses and Monotheism: The Standard Edition of the Complete Psychological Works of Sigmund Freud,* trans. James Strachey (London: Hogarth Press, 1981), vol. 23, 43.

27. For an elaboration of this point, see the brilliant paper by my colleague Gil Anidjar, "Jesus and Monotheism," *Southern Journal of Philosophy* 50, Spindel

suppl. (2013): 158–83. In developing the following analysis, I have benefited from Anidjar's writings as well as lengthy personal discussions.

28. Sigmund Freud, *Totem and Taboo*, trans. James Strachey (New York: Norton, 1950), 153.

29. Freud, *Totem and Taboo*, 154–55.

30. Jack Miles, *Christ: A Crisis in the Life of God* (New York: Knopf, 2001), 166.

31. Freud's argument on this point is an example of a strategy he uses repeatedly. He selects a later event to analyze an earlier event, and then uses that earlier event to explain the later event. Such arguments are thoroughly circular and explain very little, if anything at all.

32. Anidjar, "Jesus and Monotheism." While I am in agreement with Anidjar's argument and have been instructed by it, my own interests are somewhat different. He is concerned with the fascinating but strangely overlooked subject of the history of murder. The question motivating his study is whether the origin of society is necessarily violent, as Freud's argument obviously suggests.

33. Freud, *Totem and Taboo*, 155, 158.

34. Gay, *Freud*, 650–51. Edmundson also stresses how important Anna was for Freud. "Freud loved Anna for herself; he passionately wanted her happiness—that much is certain. But he also loved her as a guarantor of the only kind of immortality that Freud, the self-professed godless Jew, could believe in." Edmundson, *The Death of Sigmund Freud*, 65. Edmundson does not, however, make any effort to explain Freud's concern about immortality in terms of his psychoanalytic theory.

Chapter 5. Trembling

1. References to Derrida's works in this chapter are given in the text. These are the editions and abbreviations I have used:

B: *The Beast and the Sovereign*, vol. 2, trans. Geoffrey Bennington (Chicago: University of Chicago Press, 2011).

G: *Glas*, trans. John Leavey (Lincoln: University of Nebraska Press, 1986).

GD: *The Gift of Death*, trans. David Wills (Chicago: University of Chicago Press, 1995).

GT: *Given Time: I. Counterfeit Time*, trans. Peggy Kamuf (Chicago: University of Chicago Press, 1992).

LF: *Learning to Live Finally*, trans. Pascale-Anne Brault and Michael Naas (Hoboken, NJ: Melville House, 2007).

S: *For Strasbourg: Conversations of Friendship and Philosophy,* trans. Pascale-Anne Brault and Michael Naas (New York: Fordham University Press, 2004)

TP: *The Truth in Painting,* trans. Geoffrey Bennington and Ian McLeod (Chicago: University of Chicago Press, 1987)

2. Sylviane Agacinski, *Aparté: Conceptions and Deaths of Søren Kierkegaard* (Tallahassee: Florida State University Press, 1988).

3. Edmond Jabès, *The Book of Questions: El, or The Last Book,* trans. Rosmarie Waldrop (Middletown, CT: Wesleyan University Press), 16, 15.

4. Roland Barthes, *Camera Lucida: Reflections on Photography,* trans. Richard Howard (New York: Hill and Wang, 1981), 96.

5. For a discussion of the implications of this figure, see Mark C. Taylor, *Recovering Place: Reflections on Stone Hill* (New York: Columbia University Press, 2014).

6. See Taylor, *Recovering Place.*

7. Derrida frequently associates his initials, J.D., with the word *déjà.*

8. Mark C. Taylor, *Field Notes from Elsewhere: Reflections on Dying and Living* (New York: Columbia University Press, 2009).

9. His eulogies are included in *The Work of Mourning,* ed. Pascale-Anne Brault and Michael Naas (Chicago: University of Chicago Press, 2001).

10. Quoted in Benoit Peeters, *Derrida: A Biography,* trans. Andrew Brown (New York: Polity, 2013), 541. I have drawn the details of Derrida's final months from this book. Pierre Derrida is also a philosopher. Ostensibly a study of the fourteenth-century philosopher William of Ockham, his book *Guillaume D'Ockham: Le Singulier,* published under his mother's maiden name, Alferi, is actually an illuminating study of his father's work. Pierre's interpretation of Ockham's account of God's absolute power (*potential absoluta*) illuminates the notions of *Walten* and *Gewalt* that preoccupy his father in his last seminar.

11. Jonathan Kandell, "Jacques Derrida, Abstruse Theorist, Dies at 74," *New York Times,* October 10, 2004.

12. Mark C. Taylor, "What Derrida Really Meant," *New York Times,* October 14, 2004.

13. For Stoics and Neoplatonists, the *logos spermatikos* is the generative principle of the universe.

14. The apophatic logos is a central notion in what is sometimes misleadingly described as negative theology. In this tradition, God is ineffable and, therefore, cannot be described but can be suggested by the repeated denial of

positive traits or attributes. Accordingly, God, like Derrida's *différance* and khora, is *neither* this *nor* that.

15. For a thoughtful commentary on *The Beast and the Sovereign,* II, see Michael Naas, *The End of the World and Other Teachable Moments: Jacques Derrida's Final Seminar* (New York: Fordham University Press, 2015).

16. Jacques Derrida, *Cinders,* trans. Ned Lukacher (Minneapolis: University of Minnesota Press, 1991).

17. Maurice Blanchot, *The Unavowable Community* (Barrytown, NY: Station Hill Press, 1989); Jean-Luc Nancy, *The Inoperative Community,* trans. Christopher Fynsk (Minneapolis: University of Minnesota Press, 1991).

18. Mark C. Taylor and Christian Lammerts, *Grave Matters* (London: Reaktion Books, 2002). For those who were cremated, we photographed where their ashes had been spread. When I wrote *Grave Matters,* I was surprised to discover how few of the people whose graves we photographed had been cremated. Of the one hundred and fifty people included in the book, only five were cremated: Friedrich Engels, Walter Benjamin, Alfred Stieglitz, Bertrand Russell, Georgia O'Keeffe, and Joseph Beuys.

19. See Jacques Derrida, *Archive Fever: A Freudian Impression,* trans. Eric Prenowitz (Chicago: University of Chicago Press, 1996).

20. See Peeters, *Derrida,* 537–39.

21. Martin Heidegger, "What Is Metaphysics?" *Basic Writings,* trans. David Krell (New York: Harper and Row, 1977), 104, 105.

22. Peeters, *Derrida,* 553.

23. Derrida, "Comment ne pas trembler?," *Annali della Fondazione europea del disegno,* 2006, 91–104. All quotations in the following pages are from this article. The translations are my own.

Chapter 6. Delirium

1. In spite of its popularity, Poe received only $9 for the poem.

2. Throughout this chapter, all references to Poe's works are given in the text and are from *Poe: Poetry and Tales* (New York: The Library of America, 1984).

3. See Benjamin Waldman and Andy Newman, "After a Part in Poe's 'Raven,' the Dust of Obscurity," *New York Times,* August 11, 2012.

4. Arthur Hobson Quinn, *Edgar Allan Poe: A Critical Biography,* with a foreword by Shawn Rosenheim (Baltimore: Johns Hopkins University Press, 1998), 508–9. Quinn's work remains the best biography on Poe. I have drawn on it in developing my account of Poe's life.

5. "Virginia Eliza Clemm Poe," Wikipedia.com, https://en.wikipedia.org/wiki/Virginia_Eliza_Clemm_Poe.

6. Quoted in Quinn, *Edgar Allan Poe,* 510.

7. Quinn, *Edgar Allan Poe,* 524.

8. Quoted in "Virginia Eliza Clemm Poe."

9. Quoted in Quinn, *Edgar Allan Poe,* 618, 619.

10. Quoted in Quinn, *Edgar Allan Poe,* 638.

11. Quinn, *Edgar Allan Poe,* 640.

12. Quoted in Quinn, *Edgar Allan Poe,* 604.

13. Edgar Allan Poe, "The Poetic Principle," *Home Journal,* August 31, 1850, http://www.eapoe.org/works/essays/poetprnb.htm.

14. John Irwin, *American Hieroglyphics: The Symbol of the Egyptian Hieroglyphics in the American Renaissance* (Baltimore: Johns Hopkins University Press, 1980), 51.

15. F. W. J. Schelling, *The Philosophy of Art,* trans. Douglas Scott (Minneapolis: University of Minnesota Press, 1989), 88–89. The term "potence" refers to any individual entity.

16. Schelling, *Philosophy of Art,* 31.

17. Schelling, *Philosophy of Art,* 85.

18. Schelling, *Philosophy of Art,* 88.

19. It is important to recall that Newton wrote more theological than scientific treatises. His speculation about the relationship between absolute and relative space in what he describes as the "divine sensorum" bears a family resemblance to Poe's account of space in *Eureka.*

20. Paul Auster, "Going Home," in Isaac Gewirtz, *Edgar Allan Poe: Terror of the Soul* (New York: New York Public Library, 2013), 7–8.

Chapter 7. Wavering

1. Quoted in Julia Briggs, "Virginia Woolf Meets Sigmund Freud," http://www.charleston.org.uk/virginia-woolf-meets-sigmund-freud/.

2. Quoted in Briggs, "Virginia Woolf."

3. Sigmund Freud, *Civilization and Its Discontents,* trans. James Strachey (New York: Norton, 1961), 44.

4. Freud, *Civilization and Its Discontents,* 92.

5. Freud, *Civilization and Its Discontents,* 11.

6. Freud, *Civilization and Its Discontents,* 13, 15.

7. Virginia Woolf, *Moments of Being,* ed. Jeanne Schulkind (New York: Harcourt, 1985), 80 (hereafter MB).

8. Leonard Woolf, *The Journey Not the Arrival Matters: An Autobiography of the Years 1939–1969* (London: Hogarth, 1969), 53.

9. Quoted in Quentin Bell, *Virginia Woolf: A Biography* (New York: Harcourt, 1972), II, 187.

10. Quoted in Virginia Woolf, *The Diary of Virginia Woolf,* vol. 5: *1936–1941,* ed. Anne Oliver Bell (New York: Harcourt Brace Jovanovich, 1984), II, 216.

11. Panthea Reid, *Art and Affection: A Life of Virginia Woolf* (New York: Oxford University Press, 1996), 425.

12. Quoted in Woolf, *Diary,* II, 217.

13. I have drawn these biographical details primarily from Woolf, *Diary,* and Reid, *Art and Affection.*

14. Woolf, *Diary,* II, 20.

15. Woolf, *Diary,* II, 39.

16. Geoffrey Hartman, "Virginia's Web," *Chicago Review* 14 (1961): 28.

17. Virginia Woolf, *The Waves* (New York: Harcourt, 1959), 131 (hereafter W).

18. There is no conclusive evidence that Woolf read philosophy seriously, but these issues preoccupied some of the members of the Bloomsbury Group. As I have noted, Eliot, whose work Leonard and Virginia published, wrote his undergraduate thesis at Harvard on the British Hegelian F. H. Bradley. While Poe exercised no direct influence on Woolf, his French reception increased the appreciation for his work in the English-speaking world.

19. Virginia Woolf, *To the Lighthouse* (New York: Harcourt, 1981), 62.

20. Woolf anticipates Blanchot's account of the instant of death in *To the Lighthouse* in a scene in which Andrew tries to explain his father's philosophy to Lily:

> "Oh, but," said Lily, "think of his work!"
>
> Whenever she "thought of his work" she always saw clearly before her a large kitchen table. It was Andrew's doing. She asked him what his father's books were about. "Subject and object and the nature of reality," Andrew had said. And when she said Heavens, she had no notions of what that meant. "Think of a kitchen table then," he told her, "when you're not there." (23)

> To imagine one's absence is to imagine one's death, and this, as Blanchot explains, is impossible. When I am there, death is not, and when death is there, I am not.

21. Virginia Woolf, *Between the Acts* (New York: Harcourt, 1969), 82 (hereafter B).

22. Northrup Frye, *Anatomy of Criticism* (New York: Athenaeum, 1967), 67.

23. Woolf, *Diary,* II, 221–22.

24. Virginia Woolf, *The Letters of Virginia Woolf*, vol. 6: *1936–1941*, ed. Nigel Nicolson and Joanne Trautman (New York: Harcourt Brace, 1980), II, 456.

25. Woolf, *Letters*, II, 486.

26. Virginia Woolf, *The Moment, and Other Essays* (New York: Harcourt Brace, 1929), 3. All quotations in the following paragraphs are from this essay.

27. Woolf, *Diary*, 356–57.

28. Reid, *Art and Affection*, 443, 416.

29. Woolf, *Diary*, II, 226.

30. Woolf, *Letters*, 486–87.

31. Reid, *Art and Affection*, 454.

32. Virginia Woolf, *Mrs. Dalloway* (New York: Harcourt Brace, 1981), 184, 153.

Chapter 8. Intensity

1. Quoted in Kenneth S. Lynn, *Hemingway* (Cambridge, MA: Harvard University Press, 1987), 379. I have drawn on Lynn's work for the details of Hemingway's life.

2. Quoted in Lynn, *Hemingway*, 379–80.

3. Lynn, *Hemingway*, 379.

4. Quoted in Lynn, *Hemingway*, 415.

5. Lynn, *Hemingway*, 36–37.

6. Hemingway's most explicit exploration of sexual experimentation can be found in *The Garden of Eden*, published posthumously in 1986.

7. Quoted in Lynn, *Hemingway*, 427.

8. Lynn, *Hemingway*, 395.

9. Quoted in Lynn, *Hemingway*, 117–18, 10.

10. Quoted in Lynn, *Hemingway*, 427.

11. Joyce Carol Oates, *Wild Nights: Stories About the Last Days of Poe, Dickinson, Twain, James, and Hemingway* (New York: HarperCollins, 2008), 11.

12. Ernest Hemingway, "A Natural History of the Dead," http://www.24gra mmata.com/wp-content/uploads/2014/08/Hemingway.

13. Dorothy Parker, "The Artist's Reward," *The New Yorker*, http://www .newyorker.com/magazine/1929/11/30/the-artists-reward.

14. Quoted in Lynn, *Hemingway*, 426.

15. Lynn, *Hemingway*, 445.

16. All quotations from this essay are from *The Story About the Story: Great Writers Explore Great Literature*, ed. J. C. Hallman (New York: Tin House Books, 2009), 35–41.

17. Georges Bataille, "Hemingway in the Light of Hegel," *Semiotext(e)* 2, no. 2 (1976): 14.

18. Georges Bataille, *Eroticism: Death and Sensuality* (San Francisco: City Lights Books, 1986), 22–23.

19. Bataille, *Erotism,* 90. As this passage makes clear, Bataille's interpretation of the relationship between ritual violence and eroticism has disturbing implications for sexual relations, which, I think, are not unintended.

20. Bataille, *Erotism,* 22, 23.

21. Bataille, *Erotism,* 69.

22. Bataille, *Erotism,* 57.

23. Georges Bataille, "The Sacred," *Visions of Excess: Selected Writings, 1927–1939,* trans. Allan Stoekl (Minneapolis: University of Minneapolis Press, 1985), 243.

24. Bataille, "Hemingway in the Light of Hegel," 11.

25. Edward Mendelson, "Who Was Ernest Hemingway?" *New York Review of Books,* August 14, 2014, 31.

26. Victor Turner, *The Ritual Process: Structure and Anti-Structure* (New York: Aldine de Gruyter, 1995).

27. Emile Durkheim, *The Elementary Forms of Religious Life,* trans. Karen Fields (New York: Free Press, 1995).

28. Ernest Hemingway, *For Whom the Bell Tolls* (New York: Scribner, 1968), 235 (hereafter BT).

29. Quoted in Lynn, *Hemingway,* 441.

30. Throughout *For Whom the Bell Tolls,* Hemingway uses "thou," "thee," and "ye," which in English seem to be excessively formal. His intent is actually the opposite. As in German, French, and Italian, the plural came to be the formal or polite form, the singular restricted to intimates, close friends, small children, and animals. Hemingway is imitating in English the use of the familiar form in Spanish.

31. Lynn, *Hemingway,* 398–99.

32. Ernest Hemingway, *Death in the Afternoon* (New York: Scribner, 1960), 2 (hereafter DA).

33. Hemingway left other works unfinished, which were also published posthumously—most notably *A Moveable Feast* (1964) and *The Garden of Eden* (1986).

34. Ernest Hemingway, *The Dangerous Summer* (New York: Scribner, 1960), 99, 206–7 (hereafter DS). The muleta is the heart-shaped red cloth draped over a wooden stick with a sharp metal end. The faena is the work with the muleta that the matador performs during the third and final act of the bullfight.

35. Ernest Hemingway, *A Moveable Feast* (New York: Scribner, 1965), 127–28.

36. Lynn, *Hemingway,* 582.

37. Oates, *Wild Nights,* 219.

Chapter 9. Speed

1. "The Pitch," *Seinfeld,* September 16, 1992, http://www.seinfeldscripts.com /ThePitch.htm

2. Martin Heidegger, *The Question Concerning Technology,* trans. William Lovitt (New York: Harper, 1977), 27.

3. Søren Kierkegaard, *Either/Or,* 2 vols., trans. Howard and Edna Hong (Princeton, NJ: Princeton University Press, 1987), 2:291.

4. David Foster Wallace, "Some Kind of Terrible Burden," *The Last Interview and Other Conversations* (Brooklyn: Melville House, 2012), 106–7.

5. Wallace, "Some Kind of Terrible Burden."

6. David Foster Wallace, "Kenyon Commencement Address," May 21, 2005, http://web.ics.purdue.edu/~drkelly/DFWKenyonAddress2005.pdf.

7. David Foster Wallace, "*E Unibus Pluram:* Television and U.S. Fiction," *Review of Contemporary Fiction* 13, no. 2 (1993): 151, http://jsomers.net/DFW _TV.pdf, 189.

8. David Foster Wallace, *The Pale King,* ed. Michael Pietsch (New York: Back Bay Books, 2012), 190 (hereafter PK).

9. Herman Melville, *The Confidence-Man: His Masquerade,* ed. Hershel Parker (New York: Norton, 1971), 213.

10. Søren Kierkegaard, *The Concept of Irony with Constant Reference to Socrates,* trans. Lee M. Capel (Bloomington: Indiana University Press, 1965), 275.

11. David Foster Wallace, "An Interview with Larry McCaffery," *Review of Contemporary Fiction* 13, no. 2 (1993): 127–50.

12. David Foster Wallace, "The Planet Trillaphon as It Stands in Relation to the Bad Thing," *Amherst Review* 12 (1984): 29.

13. D. T. Max, "The Unfinished," *The New Yorker,* March 9, 2009, 53.

14. David Foster Wallace, "Good Old Neon," *Oblivion* (New York: Back Bay Books, 2004), 141 (hereafter O). The figure of Lilith, first mentioned in the Babylonian Talmud, derived from earlier female demons in Mesopotamian religion. In the Jewish tradition, she is the first wife of Adam, who, unlike Eve, was created at the same time he was. She played an important role in Jewish mysticism and is often depicted as a fantastic and horrifying figure in occult traditions.

15. Virginia Woolf, *To the Lighthouse* (New York: Harcourt, 1981), 24.

16. David Foster Wallace, "Deciderization 2007—A Special Report," http:// www.neugierig.org/content/dfw/bestamerican.pdf. 2.

17. Wallace, "*E Unibus Pluram*," 188.

18. Wallace, "*E Unibus Pluram*," 192–93.

19. There is a Western tradition known as negative or apophatic theology in which God is defined by what God is not.

20. See Jean Baudrillard, "The Precession of Simulacra," *Simulations,* trans. Paul Foss, Paul Patton, and Philip Beitchman (New York: Foreign Agents, 1983), 1–79.

21. Kierkegaard, *Either/Or,* 1:37.

22. Kierkegaard, *Either/Or,* 1:291.

23. D. T. Max, *Every Love Story Is a Ghost Story: A Life of David Foster Wallace* (New York: Penguin, 2013), 265, 262.

24. Wallace's comment echoes Roland Barthes's claim that "Boredom is not far from bliss: it is bliss seen from the shores of pleasure." *The Pleasure of the Text,* trans. Richard Miller (New York: Hill and Wang, 1975), 26.

25. Wallace, "The Planet of Trillaphon," 29.

26. Frank Kermode, *The Sense of an Ending: Studies in the Theory of Fiction* (New York: Oxford University Press, 1967), 4.

27. Jonathan Franzen, *Farther Away* (New York: Farrar, Straus and Giroux, 2012), 20, 39–40.

28. Wallace, "Good Old Neon," 178–79.

29. "A Conversation with David Foster Wallace, by Larry McCaffery," http://www .dalkeyarchive.com/a-conversation-with-david-foster-wallace-by-larry -mccaffery/.

30. Quoted in Tim Adams, "Karen Green, 'David Foster Wallace's Suicide Turned Him into a "Celebrity Writer Dude," Which Would Have Made Him Wince,'" *The Guardian,* April 9, 2011, http://www.theguardian.com/books /2011/apr/10/karen-green-david-foster-wallace-interview.

31. McCaffery interview.

32. Quoted in Adams, "Karen Green."

33. In writing the following account of the last months of Wallace's life, I have drawn on D. T. Max's fine biography, *Every Love Story Is a Ghost Story,* chapter 8.

34. Max, *Every Love Story Is a Ghost Story,* 302.

35. Adams, "Karen Green."

36. See Mark C. Taylor, *Kierkegaard's Pseudonymous Authorship: A Study of Time and Self* (Princeton, NJ: Princeton University Press, 1975).

37. Wallace, "Good Old Neon," 163.

38. Wallace, "Good Old Neon," 179.

Chapter 10. Silence

1. Herman Melville, *Pierre; or, The Ambiguities; Israel Potter: His Fifty Years of Exile; The Piazza Tales; The Confidence-Man: His Masquerade; Uncollected Prose; Billy Budd, Sailor: An Inside Narrative* (New York: Library of America, 1983), 3 (hereafter "Melville Collection").

2. Melville, *Pierre,* in Melville Collection, 160, 245. Porphyrogenitus, which literally means "born in the purple," was a title in the Byzantine Empire given to a son and daughter who were born after the father had been crowned the emperor. "Porphyrogennetos," https://en.wikipedia.org/wiki/Porphyrogennetos.

3. Nathaniel Hawthorne, "Ethan Brandt," *The Portable Hawthorne,* ed. Malcolm Cowley (New York: Viking, 1964), 247.

4. See Mark C. Taylor, *Mystic Bones* (Chicago: University of Chicago Press, 2007).

5. The original spelling of the family name was Melvill. His mother added the "e" after her husband's death for reasons that are not clear.

6. Andred Delbanco, *Melville: His World and Work* (New York: Knopf, 2005), 23. I have drawn biographic details primarily from Delbanco's work and Laurie Robertson-Lorant, *Melville: A Biography* (New York: Clarkson Potter, 1996), 23.

7. Herman Melville, *Moby-Dick; or, The Whale* (1851; Berkeley: University of California Press, 1979), 115.

8. Herman Melville, "Hawthorne and His Mosses," http://xroads.virginia.edu/~ma96/atkins/cmmosses.html.

9. "*Essex* (Whaleship)," https://en.wikipedia.org/wiki/Essex_(whaleship). For a vivid account of the voyage of the *Essex,* see Nathaniel Philbrick, *In the Heart of the Sea: The Tragedy of the Whaleship* Essex (New York: Penguin Books, 2007).

10. Melville, "Hawthorne and His Mosses."

11. Quoted in Delbanco, *Melville,* 127.

12. Melville, "Hawthorne and His Mosses."

13. "Herman Melville," https://en.wikipedia.org/wiki/Herman_Melville; Delbanco, *Melville,* 178.

14. Delbanco, *Melville,* 179.

15. Poe, "MS. Found in a Bottle," in *Poe: Poetry and Tales* (New York: Library of America, 1984), 198.

16. Delbanco, *Melville,* 245.

17. Melville got the idea for *The Confidence-Man* from an Albany newspaper article about the exploits of a notorious con man who used various pseudonyms, which was published April 28, 1855, and reprinted in the *Springfield (Mass.) Republican* on May 5.

18. Herman Melville, *The Confidence-Man: His Masquerade,* ed. Hershel Parker (New York: Norton, 1971), p. i. Hereafter, references to this work are given in the text.

19. "Credit," it is important to note, derives from the Latin *credere,* which means to believe.

20. Melville presents a devastating caricature of Poe in which he describes him as "a haggard, inspired-looking man . . . a crazy beggar, asking alms under the form of peddling a rhapsodic tract composed by himself, and setting forth his claims to some rhapsodical apostleship" (167). Though Poe, like Emerson and Thoreau, was influenced by German philosophers like Schelling, Hegel, and Fichte, he was never inclined to any holistic optimism. The darkness of his vision is, in fact, much closer to Melville's own outlook than he ever realized.

21. Edgar Allan Poe, "The Gold-Bug," in *Poetry and Tales* (New York: Library of America, 1984), 653. Hereafter, references to this work are given in the text.

22. Ralph Waldo Emerson, "Nature," *The Selected Writings of Ralph Waldo Emerson,* ed. Brooks Atkinson (New York: The Modern Library, 1950), 6.

23. Herman Melville, "Letter to Nathaniel Hawthorne, June [1?], 1851." http://www.melville.org/letter3.htm.

24. This is the phrase the well-known French biologist Jacques Monod uses to express Darwin's theory of evolution. See *Chance and Necessity: An Essay on the Natural Philosophy of Modern Biology,* trans. Austryn Wainhouse (New York: Knopf, 1971). Darwin did not publish *The Origin of Species* until 1858, two years after *The Confidence-Man* appeared, but Melville was aware of his work from a series of sketches published under the title *The Encantadas,* which appeared in *Putnam's* in 1854.

25. These lines are from Shakespeare's *As You Like It,* Act II, scene vii, 139–42.

26. More of a "punster" than the characters he so describes, Melville plays with almost all the names in his tale in a way that turns them from proper to the improper. "Frank Goodman" suggests both the cosmopolitan's forthrightness and his belief in the fundamental goodness of human nature. But, as John Irwin notes, Melville also indicated that "Goodman" was "the Puritan title of address: as well as "a cant term for a thief . . . and a Scottish title for the Devil" (Irwin, *American Hieroglyphics: The Symbol of the Egyptian Hiero-*

glyphics in the American Renaissance [Baltimore: Johns Hopkins University Press, 1983], 336). The barber's name, William Cream, calls attention to the veneer applied to strip away the masks or to create the disguises people wear. Cream objects to Goodman's confidence in his fellow human beings: "What, sir, to say nothing more, can one be forever dealing in Macassar oil, hair dyes, cosmetics, false moustaches, wigs, and toupees, and still believe that men are wholly what they look to be? What think you, sir, are a thoughtful barber's reflections, when, behind a careful curtain, he shaves the thin, dead stubble off a head, and then dismisses it to the world, radiant in curling auburn?" (199).

27. Marc Shell points out that the figure of the goose can mean ghost or phantom banknotes as well as a person tricked into accepting such notes. In addition to this, the image of the goose appeared on some American banknotes. See Marc Shell, *Money, Language, and Thought: Literary and Philosophical Economies from the Medieval to the Modern Era* (Baltimore: Johns Hopkins University Press, 1993), 21.

28. Irwin, *American Hieroglyphics,* 342.

29. It is instructive to recall that Freud repeatedly associates money with human excrement. For the most suggestive interpretation of the implications of Freud's insight for the economy of faith, see Norman O. Brown's analysis of Luther's scatological texts. *Life Against Death: The Psychoanalytic Meaning of History* (Middletown, CT: Wesleyan University Press, 1975).

30. Melville, *Moby-Dick,* 168.

31. Quoted in Delbanco, *Melville,* 247.

32. Quoted in Watson Branch and Harrison Hayford, "Historical Note," Herman Melville, *The Confidence-Man: His Masquerade* (Evanston, IL: Northwestern University Press, 1984), 318.

33. Herman Melville, *Journals,* ed. Howard Horsford and Lynn Horth (Evanston, IL: Northwestern University Press, 1989), 628.

34. Herman Melville, *Journal of a Visit to Europe and the Levant, October 11, 1856–May 6, 1857,* ed. Howard Horsford (Princeton, NJ: Princeton University Press, 1955), 137.

35. Delbanco, *Melville,* 291.

36. Quoted in Laurie Robertson-Lorant, *Melville: A Biography* (New York: Clarkson Potter, 1996), 559.

37. Melville, *Billy Budd,* in Melville Collection, 1419.

38. Cited in Robertson-Lorant, *Melville,* 539.

39. *Selected Poems of Herman Melville,* ed. Robert Penn Warren (New York: Random House, 1970), 95.

40. Melville, *Moby-Dick,* 197–98.

41. Melville, *Pierre,* in Melville Collection, 368.
42. Herman Melville, "Pontoosuce," *Selected Poems,* 344. The following quotations are all from this poem. When *Weeds and Wildings Chiefly* appeared after Melville's death, "Pontoosuce" was not included.

Chapter 11. Earth

1. Noel A. Taylor and Alfred L. Vandling, *Activity Units in Biology* (New York: Oxford Book Company, 1954), 1. These lines were written by Alfred, Lord Tennyson, in 1863 and are on a plaque at the base of a memorial statue in Lincoln, England.
2. Friedrich Nietzsche, *The Gay Science,* trans. Walter Kaufmann (New York: Random House, 1974), 215.
3. Ralph Waldo Emerson, "Address to the Inhabitants of Concord at the Consecration of Sleepy Hollow," September 29, 1855, http://www.bartleby.com /90/1121.html.
4. Others buried in the Sleepy Hollow Cemetery include William Ellery Channing, Sophia Hawthorne, Daniel Chester French, and Ephraim Wales Bull (the creator of the Concord grape).
5. "Concord, Massachusetts," https://en.wikipedia.org/wiki/Concord,_Massachusetts.
6. Robert D. Richardson, *Henry Thoreau: A Life of the Mind* (Berkeley: University of California Press, 1986), 204–5. Richardson's work is the best intellectual biography of Thoreau. Throughout this section, I have drawn on his study for many of the details of Thoreau's life.
7. Richardson, *Henry Thoreau,* 205.
8. "Ralph Waldo Emerson's Eulogy of May 9th, 1862," *Atlantic Monthly,* 1862, http://thoreau.eserver.org/emerson1.html.
9. Between 1836 and 1840, a group of young thinkers and writers who formed what came to be known as the Transcendental Club met regularly to discuss German philosophy and to criticize what they saw as the shortcomings of American society, culture, and religion. Members included Frederick Henry Hedge, Emerson, Thoreau, Bronson Alcott, Orestes Brownson, William Ellery Channing, James Freeman Clarke, Theodore Parker, Christopher Pearse Cranch, Sylvester Judd, Margaret Fuller, Elizabeth Peabody, Ellen Sturgis Hooper, and Sophia Ripley.
10. Richardson, *Henry Thoreau,* 27.
11. For an analysis of this German tradition, see Mark C. Taylor, *Journeys to Selfhood: Kierkegaard and Hegel* (Berkeley: University of California Press, 1980).

12. Ralph Waldo Emerson, "Nature," *The Selected Writings of Ralph Waldo Emerson,* ed. Brooks Atkinson (New York: The Modern Library, 1950), 14, 35, 6. Some of Emerson's formulations are completely consistent with Poe's appropriation of Schelling's Idealism in *Eureka.* Consider, for example: "So intimate is this Unity, that, it is easily seen, it lies under the undermost garment of Nature, and betrays its source in Universal Spirit. For, it pervades Thought also. Every universal truth which we express in words, implies or supposes every other truth. *Omne veerum vero consonant.* It is like a great circle on a sphere, comprising all possible circles; which, however, may be drawn, and comprise it, in like manner. Every such truth is the absolute *Ens* seen from one side. But it has innumerable sides" (25).

13. Quoted in Richardson, *Henry Thoreau,* 248.

14. "Ralph Waldo Emerson's Eulogy."

15. Hegel was completely informed about the status of the natural sciences in his day. See especially *Philosophy of Nature,* trans. A. V. Miller (New York: Oxford University Press, 1970).

16. Henry David Thoreau, *A Week on the Concord and Merrimack Rivers* (Princeton, NJ: Princeton University Press, 1980), 325–26.

17. Richardson, *Henry Thoreau,* 259.

18. Henry David Thoreau, "Walking," http://www.transcendentalists.com/walking.htm.

19. Quoted in Richardson, *Henry Thoreau,* 120.

20. Thoreau, "Walking," http://www.transcendentalists.com/walking.htm.

21. Thoreau, *A Week,* 181, 187, 189.

22. Richardson, *Henry Thoreau,* 20. I have drawn the details of this episode from Richardson's biography.

23. For the remainder of this section, references to *A Week* are given in the body of the text.

24. See Taylor, *Journeys to Selfhood.*

25. Johann Wolfgang von Goethe, *Italian Journey,* trans. Robert R. Heitner (New York: Suhrkamp, 1989), 299.

26. *Goethe's Botanical Writings,* trans. Bertha Mueller (Honolulu: University of Hawaii Press, 1952), 93–94. Unless otherwise indicated, parenthetical references in the following pages are to this book.

27. Goethe, *Italian Journey,* 299.

28. Thoreau, *A Week,* 331.

29. Thoreau, *Walden* (Princeton, NJ: Princeton University Press, 1989), 304–5, 306. These lines are included in the most important passage of Walden, which directly echoes Goethe's interpretation of the significance of leaves. "Few

phenomena gave me more delight than to observe the forms which thawing sand and clay assume in flowing down the sides of a deep cut on the
railroad through which I passed on my way to the village, a phenomenon
not very common on so large a scale though the number of freshly exposed
banks of the right material must have been greatly multiplied since the
railroads were invented. The material of the sand of every degree of fine-
ness and of various rich colors, commonly mixed with a little clay. When
the frost comes out in the spring, and even in a thawing day in the winter,
the sand begins to flow down the slopes like lava, sometimes bursting out
through the snow and overflowing it where no sand was to be seen before.
Innumerable little streams overlap and interlace one with another, exhib-
iting a sort of hybrid product, which obeys half way the law of currents,
and half way that of vegetation. As it flows it takes forms of sappy leaves or
vines, making heaps of pulpy sprays a foot or more in depth, and resembling, as you look down on them, the laciniated lobed and imbricated
thalluses of some lichens; or you are reminded of coral, of leopards' paws
or birds' feet, of brains or lungs or bowels, and excrements of all kind"
(306).

30. Henry David Thoreau, *Wild Fruits,* ed. Bradley Dean (New York: W. W. Nor-
    ton, 2000), epigram. Throughout this section, references to this work are given
    in the text.
31. Friedrich Nietzsche, *Ecce Homo*, 239–40.
32. In "Walking," Thoreau writes, "The Chivalric and heroic spirit which once
    belong to the Rider seems now to reside in, or perchance to have subsided
    into, the Walker—not the Knight, but Walker Errant." All quotations from
    "Walking" are from http://www.transcendentalists.com/walking.htm. See
    Mark C. Taylor, *Erring: A Postmodern A/Theology* (Chicago: University of
    Chicago Press, 1984).
33. Jean-Jacques Rousseau, *Reveries of the Solitary Walker* (New York: Penguin,
    1980), fifth reverie.
34. W. G. Sebald, *A Place in the Country,* trans. Jo Catling (New York: Random
    House, 2013), 60.
35. Jean-Jacques Rousseau, *Reveries of the Solitary Walker,* trans. Peter France
    (New York: Penguin, 1979), 84.
36. Thoreau, "Walking."
37. Quoted in Bradley P. Dean, "Introduction," in Thoreau, *Wild Fruits,* xi–xii.
38. Dean, "Introduction," x.
39. Thoreau, *Wild Fruits,* 3. In this section, reference to this work are given in
    the text.

40. Quoted in Richardson, *Henry Thoreau*, 271, 381.

41. Quoted in Richardson, *Henry Thoreau*, 238.

42. Dean, "Introduction," xi, xiii.

43. Ephraim Wales Bull, the creator of the Concord grape, lived in Concord and is buried in the Sleepy Hollow Cemetery not far from Thoreau's grave. Thoreau, *Walden*, 200.

44. Thoreau, "Walking."

45. Thoreau, *A Week*, 293.

46. Virginia Woolf, *Mrs. Dalloway* (New York: Harcourt Brace, 1981), 69.

47. Friedrich Nietzsche, *Thus Spoke Zarathustra*, trans. Marianne Cowan (Chicago: Henry Regnery), 335.

48. Lesley Chamberlin, *Nietzsche in Turin*, 167.

49. I have drawn the details about Thoreau's last days from Richardson, *Henry Thoreau*, 385–89.

50. Quoted in Richardson, *Henry Thoreau*, 385.

51. See Mark C. Taylor and Christian Lammerts, *Grave Matters* (London: Reaktion Books, 2002); Mark C. Taylor, *Field Notes from Elsewhere: Reflections on Dying and Living* (New York: Columbia University Press, 2009).

52. Henry David Thoreau, "Autumnal Tints," http://www.theatlantic.com /magazine/archive/1862/10/autumnal-tints/308702/. Three decades later, Melville was buried in Greenwood Cemetery in Brooklyn.

Chapter 12. Works Last

1. Henry David Thoreau, *A Week on the Concord and Merrimack Rivers* (Princeton, NJ: Princeton University Press, 1980), 129.

Credits

Kierkegaard, Hegel, Nietzsche signatures: Phil Laughlin Studio.

Valerio Adami, Study for a drawing after *Glas:* © 2016 Artists Rights Society (ARS), New York/ADAGP, Paris.

1841 Observation Tower: DCR, Mount Greylock State Reservation.

Henry David Thoreau, *Wild Fruits,* pen and ink drawing *Smilacina racemosa:* Abigail Rorer, The Lone Oak Press.

Georges Bataille, excerpts from *Erotism: Death and Sensuality.* Copyright © 1962 by Georges Bataille. Reprinted with the permission of The Permissions Company, Inc., on behalf of City Lights Publishers, www.citylights.com.

Excerpt from *Between the Acts* by Virginia Woolf. Copyright 1941 by Houghton Mifflin Harcourt Publishing Company. Copyright © Renewed 1969 by Leonard Woolf. Reprinted by permission of Houghton Mifflin Harcourt Publishing Company. All rights reserved.

Excerpt from *The Waves* by Virginia Woolf. Copyright 1931 by Houghton Mifflin Harcourt Publishing Company. Copyright © Renewed 1959 by Leonard Woolf. Reprinted by permission of Houghton Mifflin Harcourt Publishing Company. All rights reserved.

Excerpts from *Moments of Being* by Virginia Woolf. Copyright 1976 by Quentin Bell and Angelica Garnett. Reprinted by permission of Houghton Mifflin Harcourt Publishing Company.

Excerpts from *Moments of Being* by Virginia Woolf. Published by Pimlico. Reprinted by permission of The Random House Group Limited.

Excerpts from *Between the Acts*, *The Waves*, and *Moments of Being:* The Society of Authors as the Literary Representative of the Estate of Virginia Woolf.

Excerpts from *For Whom the Bell Tolls* and *The Dangerous Summer* by Ernest Hemingway. Published by Jonathan Cape. Reprinted by permission of The Random House Group Limited.

Excerpts from *For Whom the Bell Tolls* by Ernest Hemingway. Reprinted with the permission of Scribner, a division of Simon & Schuster, Inc. from *For Whom the Bell Tolls* by Ernest Hemingway. Copyright © 1940 by Ernest

Index

Illustrations are denoted by italic page numbers.